INSIDE
PEYTON PLACE

INSIDE PEYTON PLACE

The Life of Grace Metalious

❀ ❀ ❀

EMILY TOTH

DOUBLEDAY & COMPANY, INC.
GARDEN CITY, NEW YORK
1981

Permissions

The author gratefully acknowledges permission from the following:

For permission to quote from letters regarding Grace Metalious: Robert Athearn, Knox Burger, Charles Hegarty, Virginia C. Jones, Bucklin Moon, Al Ramrus, John Rees, Kelly Blakeslee Rogers, Louise Harriman Taylor.

Columbia University Library, for permission to quote from letters in the Paul Reynolds Collection, Butler Library; John Rees, Oliver Swan, and Philip Wittenberg for letters in that collection.

For permission to quote from Grace Metalious' unpublished writings: John Rees.

Library of Congress Cataloging in Publication Data
Toth, Emily.
    Inside Peyton Place.
    Bibliography.
    Includes index.
    1. Metalious, Grace—Biography. 2. Metalious, Grace. Peyton Place. 3. Novelists, American—20th century—Biography. I. Title.
PS3525.E77Z89   813′.54 [B]   AACR2
            ISBN: 0-385-15950-1
Library of Congress Catalog Card Number 80-2880

TO MY PARENTS
Dorothy Ginsberg Fitzgibbons
AND
John Fitzgibbons

Acknowledgments

Any biographer is a detective—pursuing clues, following hunches, attempting to uncover the truth lurking in countless bits and pieces of information. When I began my pursuit of Grace Metalious in August 1977, I knew only that the author of *Peyton Place* had been an eccentric woman who died much too soon. I now know my quarry much better than I used to, thanks to many generous people who shared memories, pictures, letters, and—sometimes—tears. Some preferred not to be mentioned by name, and they appear in my text under pseudonyms.

Besides those listed below and in my bibliography, I owe special thanks to Laurose Wilkens, Grace's closest friend, who spent countless hours with me and her daughter, Joanne Wilkens Pugh, reconstructing Grace's life. I now know why Grace Metalious so enjoyed gossiping in Laurie Wilkens' kitchen—and why she had her most famous pictures taken at Laurie's house.

This book also owes much to George Metalious and his daughters Marsha and Cynthia, who answered my questions patiently, even when it was sometimes painful. Bernard Snierson and John Chandler helped me untangle Grace's legal affairs, and also led me to John Rees, the last man in her life. John Rees has been exceptionally generous with unpublished materials, letters, pictures, and memories.

I owe further special thanks to Grace's niece Suzanne and her father, Roger Roy; to Bertrand Marcotte, Grace's oldest friend; and to Bob and Ruth Athearn, for memories, hospitality, and bits of wisdom. Oliver Swan and Doris Flowers explained the intricacies of publishing, shared letters and documents, and did legwork far beyond the call of duty. Alan "Bud" Brandt and Howard Goodkind reconstructed the *Peyton Place* publicity campaign for me—and Howard Goodkind's mother-in-law, Irene Kraus, located T. J. Martin ("T.J. the D.J."), Grace's second husband and my essential source for the "party years" after *Peyton Place*.

I am very grateful to Robert B. Perreault, who showed me the

Manchester described in *No Adam in Eden,* shared his interviews with Grace Metalious' relatives, and found answers to my endless questions. Bucklin Moon generously shared his recollections as Grace Metalious' last editor; Jack Mertes provided materials from his collection of Metalious clips; Richard Sorrell let me read his unpublished study of Grace Metalious and Jack Kerouac as Franco-American authors; and Elizabeth Strode helped me develop an idea into a book possibility. My mother, Dorothy Ginsberg Fitzgibbons, is the major source for *Peyton Place* mentions—and much of my inspiration.

Barry Lippman, my editor, and Elaine Markson, my agent, deserve particular thanks for hard work, good humor, and patience. Mary Jane Lupton and Janice Delaney, co-authors of my first book *The Curse: a Cultural History of Menstruation,* taught me about writing, and helped me find my own voice.

For aid, support, and inspiration, I am also indebted to Max Van Deusen Badger, Gerard Brault, Cathy N. Davidson, Dennis B. Fitzgibbons, John Fitzgibbons, Patricia Gallagher, Philip Klass, Susan Koppelman, Vickie Leonard, Thomas Magner, Charles Mann, Nancy McCall, Harrison Meserole, Shirley Rader, Larry L. Sullivan, Daniel Walden, Rodelle Weintraub, Stanley Weintraub, and Philip Young.

The Institute for the Arts and Humanistic Studies and the College of Liberal Arts, both at Pennsylvania State University, helped support the research for this book. I am also indebted to the following libraries and librarians:

Association Canado–Américaine, Manchester (Robert B. Perreault); Boston *Herald American* (John Cronin); Paul Reynolds Collection, Butler Library, Columbia University (Bernard Crystal); Gale Memorial Library, Laconia, New Hampshire (Barbara Cotton); Manchester Historic Association (Elizabeth Lessard); Manchester *Union Leader* (Claudette Gammon); Special Collections, Ezekiel Dimond Library, University of New Hampshire (Barbara White); New York Public Library, Lincoln Center branch; Interlibrary Loan, Pattee Library, Pennsylvania State University (Noelene Martin and Ruth Senior); Special Collections, Pattee Library, Pennsylvania State University (Charles Mann and Sandra Stelts).

The manuscript for this book will be deposited in the Pattee Library at Pennsylvania State University, together with other materials useful to future researchers.

Bruce Toth, probably the only American teenager who managed not to read *Peyton Place* in the 1950s, has cheerfully lived with it, Grace Metalious, and me over the last several years. We appreciate his presence.

CONTENTS

INSIDE
PEYTON PLACE

PROLOGUE

"When I told my side of the story to the newspapers, it created a bit of a stir," Grace Metalious said later.

The headlines roared the news.

"WARM" NOVEL RAISES
CAIN IN N.H. TOWN

TEACHER FIRED
FOR WIFE'S BOOK

TOWN FOLK WILL READ
IT—BAN OR NO BAN

By August 28, 1956, Grace's "stir" had become more like a hurricane. Gilmanton, New Hampshire, the tiny settlement where Grace Metalious lived with her ex-schoolteacher husband and their three children, had come under siege.

The thunderstorm began brewing earlier that week when Hal Boyle, syndicated columnist and Pulitzer Prize winner, had huddled with Grace Metalious for a top secret interview in New York. Grace Metalious had had a lot to say about places like Gilmanton —places like the town in her new novel, *Peyton Place*.

"To a tourist these towns look as peaceful as a postcard picture," she told Hal Boyle, her eyes flashing with anger. "But if you go beneath that picture, it's like turning over a rock with your foot —all kinds of strange things crawl out. Everybody who lives in town knows what's going on—there are no secrets—but they don't want outsiders to know."

Grace Metalious had made sure everyone would know. She'd written a novel telling the truth about small-town New England, where she'd lived all her life. "And I feel pretty sure of one thing," she told Boyle. "It'll probably cost my husband his job."

In fact, she said—it already had. Because of *Peyton Place*—which hadn't even been published yet—her husband had been fired.

When Boyle printed the news, under huge headlines, the siege of Gilmanton began.

On Monday, August 27, the phone wires started buzzing. Associated Press reporters wanted quotes from the postmistress, the school board, the owner of the corner store. Reporters began trickling into town, buttonholing anyone they could find, and giving the business to taciturn Bob Zanes, whose neighbors watched in amazement.

"They say there's something about everyone in town in it," Zanes, a retired telephone company employee, had told inquiring reporters. *Peyton Place* didn't worry him, he said, "I just spend my time puttering around. But everyone here sure is talking about the book."

The next day, the storm broke.

Reporters, scenting a story and clutching directions from the publisher's PR people, converged on Gilmanton. The invaders madly snapped pictures, created traffic jams, and accosted astonished townspeople with strange sets of questions.

Up at her farmhouse, Laurose Wilkens had been supervising the gardening and summer pickling and generally minding her own business, when she was horrified to see huge shiny cars zooming into her yard, parking every which way. Doors slammed abruptly; strange men, all sizes and shapes, purposeful gleams in their eyes, leaped out—swarming in every direction.

Children were shrieking, "What's happening? What's happening?" Correspondents lurked around the house for hours, and one straggler was still creeping through the grass, peering through windows, long after the others had gone—to find his car keys, he claimed sheepishly.

At the Gilmanton Corners general store, all was chaos. A crowd besieged the owner, Fred Bucciarelli; no one got in or out without an interrogation. One father of a family, arriving in town in his beach wagon, found himself surrounded by reporters who insisted one of the pretty girls inside *had* to be Grace Metalious.

When a local workman emerged from the store with a big cigar clamped in his teeth and his evening snacks tucked under his arm, reporters pounced on him. He must really be a school committeeman in disguise, they insisted—he had to be part of that infamous cabal that fired George Metalious for his wife's book.

The locals defended themselves as best they could. When reporters periodically leaped into their cars and tore off down the road, townspeople quickly congregated to express their real opinions. But when the reporters returned, the habitual silence descended again.

One clever journalist did get into a house with a ruse: a gray-haired, sweet-faced lady he introduced as his wife. They asked if they could just glance at an advance copy of the controversial book—and when he and his wife came in, a photographer was close behind—"just to look, of course," Laurie Wilkens reported the next day in the Laconia *Evening Citizen*. "And if he quickly got in a picture or two, it was all calm and courteous and strictly for the sake of art."

It wasn't until midnight that the cavalcade of cars and city folks left Gilmanton.

And where was the suddenly notorious author in all the hullaballoo?

During one foray into the Wilkens yard, a gaggle of correspondents had hollered at Laurie Wilkens, "Are you a friend of Mrs. Metalious?"

"No," said Laurie, desperate to escape.

Then a man's voice boomed from the distance, "Get off this property! We'll not be talking about that!"

The reporters departed hastily, not knowing that Grace Metalious herself was cowering in the Wilkens' bathroom—a small, windowless room, cool and dark, where she could neither see nor be seen. It was the perfect sanctuary for an author beginning to wonder what she'd wrought—and what she might become.

Until that day, Grace Metalious had been an obscure schoolteacher's wife—and a closet writer of novels and short stories. Her creative urges had long put her at odds with traditional notions of woman's place—and now the private woman, the mother of three, had become the famous author of *Peyton Place*.

She would never again have a private life.

PART I

❀ ❀ ❀

Dreamer

CHAPTER 1

"What were you like as a child?" a newspaper reporter once asked Grace Metalious.

She'd felt lonely and isolated, Grace said thoughtfully. "The adults around a creative child can be a headache. They have the advantage of age and size."

"But what were you really like?" the reporter persisted.

Grace smiled suddenly. "Actually, I was an awful pain in the ass."

For one thing, she frequently refused to leave her aunt's bathtub.

On visits to her Aunt Georgie's, Grace would slip away with a pencil, a few pieces of paper, and a tiny stool with a flat surface, as a writing desk. She'd hide in the bathroom, soaking in the tub for as long as her aunt would let her. There she'd scribble her poems and stories, her comical descriptions of people she knew.

If her aunt called, Grace would answer, "I'll be out soo-oon"—but she emerged only when she chose to.

Grace knew that her aunt, Georgianna DeRepentigny McConnell, needed the bathtub for her work as a physical therapist—but Grace *had* to write. She had always written. Writing came to her as naturally as breathing, she said—and Aunt Georgie's bathtub gave her the solitude a creative spirit needs. Even as an adult, Grace Metalious liked to take long baths at her aunt's. The bathtub was her first writing studio, and it gave her what she never had until *Peyton Place* made her internationally famous. Aunt Georgie's bathtub was a room of her own.

Grace DeRepentigny could not have her own room at home. She was not born into a life of leisure, nor even middle-class security. Her family had managed to pay for one middle-class amenity: Laurette Royer DeRepentigny had gone to Notre Dame Hospital to have her first child, at a time when most millworkers' daughters gave birth at home.

Still, Notre Dame lay in the heart of the French-Canadian ghetto, on the west side of Manchester, New Hampshire. Until a long and bitter strike in 1922, Manchester had been considered a placid industrial utopia. Afterward, local millworkers were, without knowing it, in rehearsal for the Great Depression. The west side was already a depressed area.

A heat wave in early September 1924 had made everyone irritable—and it was abruptly followed by the coldest September 8 in Manchester history. Even in northern New England, no one expected a 41° reading at 7 A.M. While workers shivered at the mills, and housewives struggled to kindle fires, Marie Grace DeRepentigny was taking her first breaths.

Grace Metalious often claimed she'd been given a grandiose name at birth: Grace Marie Antoinette Jeanne d'Arc de Repentigny. But her birth certificate reads "Marie Grace DeRepentigny," and her baptismal record "Marie Grace de Repentigny." The extra middle names—the warrior saint and the foolish queen—are Grace's first literary creations, the work of a storyteller seeking a heroic destiny, or at least a notorious one.

Unlike most French-Canadians* in Manchester, Grace did not grow up on the west side. From an early age, Grace's mother had been emancipating herself from her working-class roots. Laurette Royer had learned to speak American-accented English; she'd come to despise mills and millworkers though both her parents had worked in the mills. She had been a dental assistant when she

---

* In Grace's youth, "French" and "French-Canadian" were often used interchangeably for both French speakers born in Canada and their American descendants. In recent years "Franco-American" has been used for people who, like Grace DeRepentigny, are born in the United States but whose ancestors emigrated from French Canada, usually Quebec.

married Alfred Albert DeRepentigny, a printer, and their first home was at 104 Ash Street at the corner of Bridge—not too far from the north end, Manchester's wealthiest and most exclusive neighborhood.

The address signified upward mobility for Laurette—and gave the young couple some needed privacy. When Laurette and Al were married on May 12, 1924, it was a scant four months before the birth of their first child—a fact that would not have gone unnoticed in the traditional French Catholic community of the west side. By living in north central Manchester, the DeRepentignys escaped gossip and censure—but also gave up membership in a cohesive ethnic community.

Manchester in 1924 had fairly strict ethnic boundaries. Nearly all the "French," a third of the city's 80,000 people, lived on the west side ("Little Canada"). There were also enclaves for Greeks, Germans, Belgians, Poles, and even Swedes. But the upper classes of Manchester were the "Americans" of the north end: English-speaking by birth, and English or Scottish by ancestry (with an occasional Irish family mixed in). The "Americans," who looked with considerable disdain upon those they considered "Canucks," formed the city's leadership. French-Canadians and Franco-Americans made up most of the working class.

According to Manchester ethnic lore, each national group had its own peculiarities. The WASPs were thought to be cold and austere, and the Irish, pugnacious. Southern Europeans were believed to be pungent-smelling (like their food), and "greasy." The French were considered industrious, stable, devout, and—most of all—docile. They depended heavily on their priests; they raised large, close-knit, even clannish families. They placed little value on higher education; they preserved their French culture, and scorned Americanisms. Typically, their children dropped out of school at fourteen to work in "the Amoskeag."

Though Manchester did have cigar and shoe factories, it was essentially a one-company town. The Amoskeag Corporation was the world's largest textile plant, with thirty major mills and over 17,000 workers—and the Amoskeag had made Manchester a French-Canadian city. At the turn of the century, corporation representatives had fanned out over rural Quebec, wooing workers away from depleted farms, scarce resources, and hopeless poverty. The recruiters made factory work in the United States sound much more attractive—and a direct railroad line from Montreal to Boston made travel easy.

The Royers and the DeRepentignys had taken that route to the United States, and their younger children were born in Manchester: Al DeRepentigny in 1902 and Laurette Royer in 1903. By the time Al and Laurette reached their teens, both their fathers had abandoned the families; both their mothers—Grace's grandmothers—were forced to do the hard, dirty, noisy work of the mills.

Aglae Royer worked as a spinner, and Florence DeRepentigny as a weaver. Both were paid fairly well, at least for women—because the Amoskeag had a very progressive policy: equal pay for equal work, regardless of sex. Thus, though Grace's Grandmother DeRepentigny was a traditional French-Canadian woman at home—strict, religious, hard-working, sewing her seven children's clothes until three in the morning—outside the home, she also had attained an unusually high status as the family breadwinner. She encouraged her children's ambitions as well: Al's, to be a pressman and printer; Georgianna's, to study human anatomy. Grandmother Royer, equally ambitious, supported her daughter Laurette's efforts to escape the mills.

Both Grace's grandmothers were, for their era, very independent women.

Even in conservative New Hampshire in 1924, the rights of women were a subject of great interest. Women had won the right to vote in national elections in 1920; nearly half the students in American colleges and universities were women. (This was not true again until the late 1970s.) Though the American Federation of Labor convention in New Hampshire, held when Grace DeRepentigny was eleven days old, passed a resolution condemning the Equal Rights Amendment,† women were winning battles on many other fronts.

† That amendment, the same as today's Equal Rights Amendment, was the focus of a bitterly fought campaign throughout the 1920s. The amendment then languished in Congress for almost fifty years, until the House finally

"The increasing interest and participation of women in politics," Ann Story wrote in the Manchester *Union Leader* two days before Grace's birth, showed women to be "more efficient and harder workers than their masculine colleagues. When the women have made determined efforts to get out the vote, they have made a splendid showing."

Determined women were also encroaching on what were usually considered masculine prerogatives. On Grace's birthday, a Philadelphia woman died from drinking bootleg whiskey. A woman's illicit drinking was, by then, not uncommon. Partly because Prohibition lent drinking a forbidden glamour, women were becoming social drinkers—for the first time in American history.

Women were also becoming more assertive in crime. When Grace DeRepentigny was five days old, the *Union Leader* reported an unusual escapade: "YOUNG WOMAN HOLDS UP MOTORIST, THEN WITH MAN ESCAPES SHERIFF'S POSSE—Bobbed Hair Bandit and Companion Secure Small Amount of Cash from Vermonters in Salisbury, Refuse Watch." Women were also expected to be crime fighters: on September 16 the Manchester Police Commission heard a recommendation that one or more policewomen be appointed in Manchester with "equal authority and equal pay with the men of the force."

Then, on October 1 the newspaper jubilantly reported "A VICTORY FOR 'MA'"—the story of "Ma" Ferguson's successful fight to be listed on the Democratic ticket for governor of Texas. Her opponents had fought against having a woman on the ballot, but the District Court ruled in her favor (she was later elected governor). "Discrimination against women because of their sex," the *Union Leader* concluded, "is getting to be rather an old-fashioned and reactionary business."

Meanwhile, new ideas coexisted with old fashions and habits. During Grace's early days, ten local department stores were promoting the brand new product, Kotex. (Women had been accustomed to washing and reusing rags each month.) But another,

---

passed it in 1971, and the Senate in 1972—thus sending it to the states to be ratified. As early as 1921, ERA supporters had pledged to continue their struggle "until an amendment of this general nature is adopted, or the leaders of the Woman's Party all die of old age."

more traditional, department store had a sale on women's lingerie of the older style, including "envelope chemises," "women's step-ins and bloomers with knee ruffles," and "women's sleeveless under-vests in built-up shoulders only."

Politics were also in transition. Though Laurette DeRepentigny, eligible to vote for the first time in 1924, had her choice of a record twenty-four women candidates for the state legislature, she also had to pay the "women's poll tax," a New Hampshire requirement, before she could cast her ballot.

Grace, the first grandchild, was born into a changing world, and into a family of fairly emancipated women: supporting themselves without men, living outside traditional French views of woman's place. Nevertheless, Grandmother Royer, who lived with Laurette and Al and their baby, Grace, spoke no English. Grace learned very early to speak French to "Mémère" (pronounced "Me-may"), but always spoke English more fluently. English was the vehicle for upward mobility in Manchester—while Mémère, who adored Grace, still cherished some decidedly old-fashioned ideas.

Mémère retained her strict Catholic beliefs and the French-Canadian emphasis on cleanliness—the style Manchester natives called "nasty-neat Frenchman." Mémère's housekeeping resembled Monique's in Grace's last novel, *No Adam in Eden:* "When she polished her furniture she looked upon each piece as a danger-ous enemy ready to attack her with filth and germs until she had scrubbed and waxed it into sterile submission. It was the same with her floors and woodwork, with the clothes her family wore." Monique—a character created to resemble Grandmother Royer—lacks any other outlet for her fierce energies.

Mémère did all the housework; Grace, considered a "little prin-cess," was not to soil her hands. As a result, Grace never really learned how to clean house—or at least learned to avoid house-work as much as possible. Throughout Grace Metalious' life, neighbors and reporters gasped (or giggled) about her wretched housekeeping, and Grace herself said she needed only five minutes to "turn an ordinary room into a sty."

In some ways, Grace was a very spoiled child. Aunt Georgie made all of Grace's clothes; Grandmother DeRepentigny bought Grace her own little table, with matching chairs—and splurged on strawberries, because Grace loved them. As soon as Grace and her younger sister, Doris May, were big enough, Al bought them bicycles. Georgie took her nieces along when she called on patients, and treated the girls to special excursions to Pine Island Park.

Grace was two years old when her sister, always called "Bunny," was born. By then Laurette and Al had moved to 251 Pearl Street, still in north-central Manchester, a few doors away from the other DeRepentignys: Grandmother, Aunt Georgie, and Uncle Wilfred. Grace frequently trekked down the street for her beloved baths—and sometimes for escape.

After spats with Mémère, the household disciplinarian, Grace would retaliate by "leaving home." Packing her carriage with her doll and toys, she would march to Aunt Georgie's. Later, when Georgie cleaned house, she would put Grace's possessions downstairs, to get them out of the way. At that extra affront, Grace would produce a theatrical tantrum—but afterward, always succumb to the inevitable. She would take her carriage, doll, and toys, and go home.

"You're French, so speak French," Grandmother DeRepentigny had always told her children. "Anybody can learn English," she insisted, "but French is hard." She did not thoroughly approve of the Americanization going on in her son Al's household, and she said so. Most French-Canadians in Manchester had been poor Quebec peasants, but Grandmother DeRepentigny had lived in Montreal—and she was very proud of that. When Uncle Wilfred discovered a book called *Le Chien d'Or* (*The Golden Dog,* by William Kirby), a saga of Old Québec with a hero named de Repentigny, everyone assumed the novel contained their family's history. Moreover, Grandmother's husband, Jean, despite his impecunious ways and ultimate disappearance, had had an even more illustrious past.

Jean DeRepentigny's father or grandfather—the story was not clear—had been Parisian, and had spoken a pure Parisian French, not the Canadian patois. Like many French-Canadians, the DeRepentignys stressed that part of their background that was truly "French, from France." Even Laurette, the daughter-in-law, prided herself on that Parisian heritage, and sometimes claimed to be descended from a count.

The stories of a glorious family past fired Grace's imagination, and helped her escape the more difficult parts of her childhood—for her own picture of growing up was far bleaker than her Aunt Georgie's memories. Though in early years Grace was pampered and indulged, encouraged in childhood scribblings and treated as a little princess, she later described her childhood as something out of a naturalistic novel: poverty, drunkenness, violent fights—and no father.

While Grace was still a baby, her father had gone along on Sunday family promenades, taking pride in his little daughter's prettiness. But Al was also rarely at home: he worked during the day, and by his own admission, "stepped out" at night. Though he lived with the family for her first ten years, "I scarcely remember my father," Grace later claimed, "and never had a conversation with him in my life."

Grace also said little about Grandmother Royer, who actually raised her—told her stories and insisted on good behavior. Later, when Grace talked or wrote about her childhood, she made her mother the central figure—and the villain of the piece.

Laurette had given birth to another child after Grace and Bunny: a baby boy who died (apparently a stillbirth). While her daughters were growing up, Laurette worked in a yarn shop, and as a city hall clerk handling birth records. She was slim, elegant, and well-dressed; in later years she wore her prematurely gray hair in a perfect bun on top of her head. She had also developed a certain disdain for her husband, according to her son-in-law, George Metalious, and frequently bemoaned having married "beneath her."

Al DeRepentigny did work steadily for three newspapers, using English and French—but he was always a printer, in a blue collar trade. Al provided material things, Laurette reportedly said, but little else. She considered him no gentleman, just "an uncouth barbarian who couldn't do anything but make money." According to George Metalious, Al was much misunderstood, "soon grew tired of trying to cope with a household of females," and left.

Al may have had other reasons: in-law troubles, disparate goals —and lack of money. During the early 1930s Al and Laurette moved four times in four years, as the Depression deepened. Though Al still worked as a pressman, Aunt Georgie had had to take a job as a rayon inspector. When the Amoskeag closed its doors in 1936, she lost even that job—as the economy of Manchester died. (Grace records the terrible suffering of Manchester millworkers in *No Adam in Eden,* when her "Northeast Manufacturing Company" closes during the Depression.)

Laurette and Al had passed their eleventh wedding anniversary on May 12, 1935—the same day Grace was confirmed at St. George Church. But on Grace's twelfth birthday, September 8, 1936, Laurette filed for divorce.

Her grounds were Al's "willing absence for two years together without making suitable provision for support and maintenance"— and the court ordered Al to pay Laurette ten dollars a week for child support. The divorce became final on December 1, 1936.

The following year, Al left Manchester, and joined the Merchant Marine.

Laurette, meanwhile, escaped the Depression through her imagination of something better. She used to read stories to her daughters before they could read themselves; she stressed "culture"; and she had Bunny and Grace reading the New York *Times Book Review* by the time Grace was twelve. Laurette had literary ambitions, and dreamed of selling stories to *Harper's;* she enjoyed going to auctions for cheap antiques, which she would claim were "family heirlooms." She dreamed, her daughter Grace said, of "Paris trips, a chauffeured limousine, and a Colonial house with a fanlight over the front door." Grace and Bunny learned about silver, fine table linen, Beethoven, and dressing well—the last a lesson that did not take.

"As a child I was forced to be dressed," Grace told Patricia Carbine for a 1958 *Look* magazine profile. "I said to myself, 'If ever there is a time when I don't have to, I won't.' I hate clothes. I'd go naked if I could."

In later life, Grace was highly critical of Laurette—but always responded when Laurette called. She had gained a certain insight into her mother's frustrations as a woman. "I think there was a time when she wanted everything," Grace wrote in *The American Weekly* in 1958, "but she finally had the desire beaten out of her by the tongues of the people who surrounded her."

The neighbors, Grace reported, had little but contempt for Laurette's ambitions, characterizing them as "champagne ideas on a beer budget." But the daughter could understand the mother's yearnings. "A woman has recently written a book called *All I Want Is Everything*," Grace wrote. "I think it is one hell of a title. All *I* want is everything, and I want it all the time."

Still, all she saw were the brakes put on women's yearnings: her mother's thwarted desires for "culture," her grandmother's use of housework as an outlet for untapped energies. She saw talent and drive forced into uncreative—even destructive—channels. As an adult, Grace was often more critical than loving when she talked about women. With few exceptions, she preferred men as her friends: their problems were not so close to hers. She criticized women—yet saw their lives with a fierce and piercing clarity.

"Now we will be comfortable at last, just the four of us," Mémère said after Laurette and Al were divorced. When Grace quoted Grandmother Royer in *The American Weekly*, she added that Bunny had since married two older men. "With my two-bit psychology I have often wondered if she has been making a vain search for the father she has never found."

But the loss of a father shaped Grace's own life as much as it did Bunny's, and Grace often blamed herself for his departure. His absence reinforced a common pattern in girls' lives: the search for male approval, with the fantasy of the perfect man—strong, virile, all-loving, all-understanding. Though such a fantasy was especially encouraged in the 1950s, when Grace Metalious finally had the money to pursue it, it had lodged in her mind long before that. Al had come to represent her dreams of male companionship: "He was the shining prince and I the only object of his affection." In her earliest writings, Prince Charming played the central role.

Sending Grace and Bunny to parochial school was never considered—though not because success in Manchester meant assimilation: escaping the mills, the west side, and Catholic schooling. Grace and Bunny went to "Protestant school" because St. George School charged tuition, and Laurette and Al could not afford it.

In the public schools, "French" children were often looked down upon: their "Canuck" accents mocked, their names mispronounced. The family pronounced their name "De-re-PEN-ti-nee," or—even more French—"De-ray-PON-tee-nee"—or sometimes "De-re-PEN-tsi-nee," the "ts" characteristic of French-Canadian pronunciation. But school teachers and pupils Anglicized the name as "Der-PEN-ti-nee" or even "Der-PET-i-nee." The name was written as one word, with a capital D, American style. Elementary school taught Grace about ethnicity—but not about ethnic pride.

"Boy, that sure was one hell of a lousy firetrap," Grace said later about Ash Street Grammar School, at the intersection of Bridge, Ash, Pearl, and Maple—across the street from her first home. (Bridge and Ash is also an important setting in *No Adam in Eden.*) Even in the 1930s, Ash Street School—now on the National Register of Historic Places—was an old building. Its tall red towers and ornate outside fire escapes had a certain grandeur in 1876, when the building won its first architectural prize—but the structure was indeed a firetrap, with wooden staircases and strange twists and turns. Still, at Ash Street School Grace DeRepentigny, otherwise an indifferent student, followed her mother's direction, cultivating a habit that sustained her throughout life. She learned to read.

By the time she was eleven, she had read all the Nancy Drew mysteries; she also devoured murder and adventure stories, and historical novels—all the available escape literature. Then she raided Laurette's bookshelf, and learned about adult life from Guy de Maupassant and Charles Dickens. Later her favorite novelists were W. Somerset Maugham and F. Scott Fitzgerald—but she read few, if any, women authors.

When she finished her mother's books, she began going to the public library—where she insisted that she had to take out adult books for her mother. The children's librarian believed her, or pretended to, and Grace remembered the librarian as unusually kind. "You'd have to be, to work in the children's room at a library," Grace remarked—qualifying, as she usually did, her assessments of other women.

Grace read everything she could, as fast as she could; she had no money for library fines, nor for much outside the essentials. But creative writing was free—and as early as fourth grade, Grace was writing stories about an imaginary brother.

Her father, though still legally married to her mother at the time, had been lost to her; Laurette's baby boy, the one who died, became a character in Grace's mind. Grace also decided that Bunny, who inherited their mother's slimness, was beautiful and charming. Grace thought herself—with her father's chunky build—homely, fat, ugly, and stupid. But her fantasy brother loved her in spite of her flaws—and in his eyes, she blossomed and grew beautiful. He gave her the male approval she never had at home.

But reality intruded when she let another person into her fantasy world. She turned in a school composition called "My Brother."

"You know you don't have a brother!" her teacher insisted. "How dare you pretend you do!"

"But—but I thought—it was just a story . . ." Grace, dark eyes filled with tears, hadn't the words to explain what she really meant: that an imaginary brother met her needs, and "What I Did Last Summer" did not. Though the truth was boring and dull, it seemed to be a school requirement. Grace learned to retreat, and to conceal her imaginative flights.

In seventh grade she wrote her first novel, *Murder in the Summer Barn Theater*. The book had a female protagonist: Sherry Wynters, girl sleuth—whose teenage boyfriend was even more WASP: Nyles Carleton Thurston. *The Summer Barn Theater* resembled the world of Nancy Drew: no French-Canadians or other "ethnics" intruded, except as potential villains. A murder was committed—but the "crazy butler" did not do it. Instead, the crime was committed by the actor who *played* the crazy butler.

By the time she was thirteen, Grace had begun a more ambitious project: a long historical novel, "about dukes and duchesses and stuff like that" (according to her account)—but she never sent it, nor anything else she wrote as a teenager, to a publisher. She wrote because she felt driven—and writing came easily to her. It helped her escape the daily life of Depression-era Manchester, and her own troubled home.

Laurette, meanwhile, had a variety of boyfriends, and came home from her dates, George Metalious remarked later, "with an alcoholic flare lighting the way." But George had had conflicts with Laurette DeRepentigny from the start—as he reveals in *The Girl from "Peyton Place,"* his 1965 account of Grace's life (written with June O'Shea).

George reports that Grace had been told, at nine, "Don't play with those awful little people over there"—Laurette's voice implying dire things. Al, Laurette, Bunny, Mémère, and Grace were living at 963 Hanover Street, near the old Boston & Maine railroad tracks—and Grace was not to play with those children across the tracks. "They're foreigners," Laurette said.

Some she called "greasy Greeks"—like George Metalious, who was younger and smaller than Grace, but a year ahead of her in school. George was a first-generation American: his father, Theophanes, had been born in Greece, and his mother, Lena, in Holland. They were twenty-one and nineteen when they eloped to Maine in October 1924—a human-interest item reported in the Manchester *Union Leader,* when Theophanes' father tried, unsuccessfully, to block the wedding. George was born six months later, on April 5, 1925, and by the time he was two, his parents were divorced. Lena (known as Helen) remarried and had a second family, and George grew accustomed to new babies around the house.

Naturally, the facts of life interested George; Grace, meanwhile, enjoyed making up stories and acting them out. Soon they were "playing house" in a little shed behind Grace's house. A bigger child, Bud, played Daddy; Grace was Mommy; and George "baby."

Inevitably, they were caught.

Al, who'd found Grace with her dress up and panties down, hauled her and George before the household tribunal: Laurette and Grandmother Royer. (Bud had run away.) George was spanked and sent home—after Grace, in George's account, blamed everything on him: "He made me do it. I don't know what it was he wanted, but he made me do it."

Laurette and Grandmother Royer lectured Grace on how wicked it was to play with little boys—the kind of lecture Allison and Norman hear in *Peyton Place*. It was both vague and threatening. Grace was told to mend her ways.

A few months later, she tripped and scraped her knee while she and George were playing tag. "George pushed me!" Grace wailed. Laurette sent George, the "foreign brat," back across the tracks—with pinches and threats.

Finally, at an auction several years later, when Grace was fourteen, Grace spotted her childhood friend George. She began to say hello—just as Laurette, looking up from her search for "family heirlooms," saw what might happen.

She poked her daughter—and Grace snubbed George.

Unwittingly, George had intruded upon Laurette's world—as a "foreigner," "greasy Greek," "nasty little boy." However misguided her efforts and threats, Laurette was protecting her daughter: She knew which sex paid the greater price for early sexual experience. Moreover, Laurette wanted her daughter to "get ahead in life"—which meant more than just collecting valuable trinkets, living away from the west side, and escaping the mills. Most of all, it meant marrying someone "suitable."

Laurette's snobbishness placed her distinctly in the American tradition: She had assimilated WASP prejudices against "foreigners." She also believed firmly in an ethnic hierarchy—in which the "Americans" came first, but the more ambitious French-Canadians were catching up. The newest arrivals held the lowest rungs on Manchester's social ladder—and Greeks were among the newest.

George Metalious, meanwhile, thought Laurette both "haughty" and "domineering." She was, he says in *The Girl from "Peyton Place,"* "forever trying to push Grace into a strata of society that was not her own." Though much of Laurette's hatred was directed against him, George does concede that her aristocratic pretensions had value for her daughter: "Perhaps this was where Grace acquired her underlying feelings of needing to achieve the heights."

As a Central High School student, Grace was not yet sure what "heights" she wanted to achieve. In adolescence, she faced the major conflict of women who want to reach heights outside the home: whether she would continue to create herself—through her writing—or conform to traditional notions of woman's "place." The women around her were independent—living without men— and yet not at peace with their lives, each other, or themselves. They all wanted something more than they had.

Writing had given Grace her greatest pleasure as a child. It had helped her escape the quarrels at home and imagine a far more exciting life for herself. But much of her escape also came through creating a Prince Charming, a substitute for her absent father. As she grew into womanhood, Grace DeRepentigny continued dreaming about the perfect man—that prince of a fellow—and also wondered if he might exist in real life.

In high school, she began the serious search for the woman she might become.

CHAPTER 2

Though Grace jauntily called Central High School "the worst hell-hole you ever saw," she might have been even more critical of other institutions: West High School, filled with Franco-Americans from the west side who could not afford the tuition to Catholic high schools; or St. Joseph's Catholic High School for Girls, where there was considerable censorship of the students' reading. "She was enough of an iconoclast not to take kindly to dogmatic teaching," says Louis A. Freedman, who taught her English class junior year.

Louis Freedman had been teaching at Central High for thirteen years when he encountered Grace DeRepentigny in the fall of 1940. A 1920 graduate of Bates College in Maine, he had struggled against anti-Semitism to find a teaching job: hatred of "foreigners" (non-WASPs) was particularly strong in the 1920s. The year Grace was born, the Ku Klux Klan had been holding "pro-American" rallies all over New Hampshire; three years later, Sacco and Vanzetti, the Italian-born anarchists, were executed in Massachusetts.

In New Hampshire, too, Americans were fiercely opposed to "outsiders," and the Central High faculty was dominated by New England WASP women, graduates of Wellesley and Radcliffe with such names as Miss Fairbanks, Miss Dodge, and Miss Eastman. They were high school teachers because, even in the exhilaration following suffrage, few women had strong encouragement to go on to graduate school or careers outside teaching. Female teachers were usually single, for women who married were expected—and sometimes required—to leave their jobs.

Louis Freedman was something of an anomaly, although during the personnel shortage of World War I, a Jewish woman had been hired at Central High to teach bookkeeping. Her presence was still talked about as a novelty. (Later, Franco-American teachers would congregate in the halls and deliberately speak French, excluding others—but not in the 1930s, when jobs of any kind were difficult to find.)

Grace took the standard academic curriculum, including four years of English and courses in ancient, medieval, and American history, science and math, and foreign languages (French or Latin, because German had been eliminated from the curriculum during World War I).

Grace's English curriculum covered grammar, "oral topics" (public speaking, required of all students), and literature—mostly British and Victorian. Students read *David Copperfield, Idylls of the King,* and *Macbeth.* They also read George Eliot's *Silas Marner,* but otherwise encountered very few female writers—only Edna St. Vincent Millay but not her sonnets criticizing masculine eccentricities; Elizabeth Coatsworth, an obscure poet from Cape Cod; and a few short-story writers, among them Mary E. Wilkins Freeman, whose "The Revolt of 'Mother'" might be discussed as comedy—but not as a critique of "Father's" insensitivity. The literary tradition presented to Central High students was mostly masculine, and thoroughly WASP.

In Mr. Freedman's eleventh-grade class, students also wrote one theme a week, developing such topic sentences as "Is honesty the best policy?" and "Is it always wise to tell the truth?" Mr. Freedman disliked such traditional subjects as "What I Did Last Summer," and insisted that students form opinions and support them—but he was also aware of his audience's limits.

With *David Copperfield,* students rarely sympathized with David's troubles, and insisted that "no kid at this high school ever behaved that way." Grace DeRepentigny, in particular, was something of a youthful cynic, the sort to insist, "David is a sissy."

Asked to develop her opinion, she'd say, "No boy today acts the way David did with Dora. That's too artificial." Mr. Freedman could hardly disagree. Like most teachers, he was pleased that a student cared enough to criticize.

Unmoved by Victorian romantic posturings, Grace was insistently "modern," also looking on Tennyson's *Idylls of the King* with a very jaundiced eye. "No modern girl would carry on like that, just because her boyfriend did this or that," Grace would say about Elaine of Astolat's sufferings for love of Sir Lancelot. At least in class discussion, Grace DeRepentigny had little sympathy for women who lived for love.

From among the thirty-five students in junior English, Mr. Freedman still remembers that Grace struck him as good college material: conscientious, outspoken. "She had curiosity," he remembers. "She wasn't a dumb head."

But she was not, in his recollection, anywhere near an outstanding student. She had C's and B's, and "I can't imagine her having much talent," he says today. She showed no particular literary skill, and he still suspects that *Peyton Place* was heavily edited by someone else.

Louis Freedman never saw Grace DeRepentigny after high school, except on television. During one interview, he noticed that the slight figure he remembered had become fat and shapeless. Later, when he heard a particularly intelligent discussion on a Boston radio station, he wrote Grace Metalious a congratulatory letter—and never received an answer. But after her death, he learned that his letter was among the personal effects she saved.

Grace was not active in high school extracurricular activities. She took no part in athletics (which, for female students, consisted of basketball), nor did she perform in the yearly Gilbert and Sullivan productions—although she learned to love the music and the play of wit. She published nothing in *The Oracle*, Central High's literary magazine—yet she was not a late bloomer. She had a highly creative life outside school.

She enjoyed solitary walks to Derryfield Park, at Bridge, Belmont, and Reservoir Avenues ("Deer Park" in *No Adam in Eden*). She liked the Ledge, a rock quarry with a pool bottom, where each year impetuous youths would take 50- and 100-foot dives—and some would get hurt. (During the winter, the Brownies, a physical fitness group whose members included Al DeRepentigny, would cut holes in the ice to show they could swim in February.) Grace admired the violets and mayflowers and reddish sunsets; carried home handfuls of flowers, especially lady's slippers; and enjoyed observing nature's dramas—young birds breaking out of their shells, and ants fighting to the death. She also liked being alone with her imagination.

As she presents herself (Lesley) in *No Adam in Eden,* Grace DeRepentigny was a dreamy child whose nose was always in a book, and who scarcely recognized real life until it hit her in the face. (Lesley meets her lifelong love when she trips on the ice in front of him, while contemplating the trees.) But in real life Grace had an eccentric, comical side that made her the center of an unusual trio of young people.

"The nucleus was Grace," Bob Athearn, an older friend who was something of a mentor to them, wrote in 1980. Around Grace "two young men orbited rather faithfully, with others on the fringes, one of those groups of bright and sharp young people who exist in most high school classes and whose interests and abilities in general outrun the processing the school provides and which too often has the effect of a slower-moving interference blocking a fleet ball carrier in football."

One of the two young men was Grace's neighbor, Francis J. Boivin, who called himself "Jay" (though his mother called him "Tweets"). Jay, who chose his name because it sounded better for the radio career he wanted to pursue (and did), lived on Blodget Street, across the alley from Grace, who lived at 753 Beech Street near Blodget. They became companions and fellow adventurers— and attracted a third pal, Bertrand Marcotte, on an excursion to a play at the Practical Arts Auditorium of Central High. Bert joined them in mocking the performance, a farcical saga by the senior dramatic club: *The Rise and Fall of Cuthbert Gleep.* Grace, Bert, and Jay were convinced they could do better themselves.

First they joined a YMCA drama group, where their ideas were considered too bizarre. "We wrecked the place and waltzed home," Bert Marcotte recalled, perhaps with exaggeration, in 1980. They often waltzed home, in fact—and on one such occasion Grace dislocated her knee and lay writhing on the ground, much as her Lesley does in *No Adam in Eden:* "She landed hard on the concrete, her right leg twisted painfully beneath her."

As Lesley falls, a passing truck driver sees her and rushes to her side. Gino Donati—"big, black, curly headed," with "shoulders like a Mack truck"—carries Lesley to her house. She has "an almost overwhelming desire to sob and rest her head against his shoulder." She does, and within weeks she is in love—with the kind of man who always attracted Grace DeRepentigny: tall, dark, handsome, and massive. Protective, dominating, fatherly.

But when Grace herself dislocated her knee and lay writhing on the ground, she was somewhat plump. Neither Bert (on the slight side) nor Jay (taller, but very thin) could pick her up. They finally half-helped, half-dragged her home, laughing much of the way, feeling far more satirical than romantic. Once Grace was on the mend, they also found for themselves a drama group more conducive to their peculiar notions of humor—and they owed their "find" to World War II.

Even before the Japanese attack on Pearl Harbor in December, 1941, the United States had been preparing for war. Al DeRepentigny by this time was making bullets in Connecticut; young men were mobilizing at Grenier Air Base south of Manchester. It was an era of excitement and fear. But the young enlisted men were often at one base for months at a time, with little to do—and Barbara Roberts, a young wife and mother and Sunday school teacher, wanted to do something to keep them entertained.

She began a little theater group, to put on performances in the Unitarian Church basement. Female co-stars were recruited from the "Y" and from newspaper ads—which enticed Bert Marcotte, Jay Boivin, and Grace DeRepentigny to come to the church, across the street from Central High School.

Their early performances were extemporaneous—some including imitations of regional accents (with Barbara Roberts playing the Vermonter). The group cooked international dinners, though the young men objected to the low tables for authentic Japanese meals. But the group members most wanted to put on plays.

Unfortunately, with the vicissitudes of military service, the male stars were apt to be transferred to another base right after—or even during—the time they learned their lines. Whole chunks of the cast could be lost within a few days. So Barbara decided the casts would be small—and since they had no money to pay for plays, her performers would have to write their own.

Grace DeRepentigny quickly became a playwright and a frequent visitor to the Roberts' home. "You knew she was in the room, because she really had a presence," Barbara Roberts said forty years later. She recalls Grace as round, pleasingly plump, healthy looking—with a kind of sparkle: "bright, scintillating, full of ideas." Grace laughed easily, seemed to have great potential—and appeared to be "looking for something to fill her life."

Grace never talked about styles, fashions, or "girlish" subjects. She was interested in ideas and reading—especially W. Somerset Maugham—and welcomed suggestions. If she wanted to learn to write beautifully, Barbara Roberts said, Grace should read Charlotte Brontë's *Jane Eyre* (whose Rochester resembles the male figure of Grace's life: tall, dark, big—and old enough to be the heroine's father).

At Barbara's home, the young people plotted their plays, assigned roles, revised the plays as a group effort—and "I guess I let them get away with a little," Barbara remembers. But her three stars wanted more than a little.

Before joining the Unitarian group, Grace, Jay, and Bert had already mounted one production of their own: *Speaking of Angels,* an original play by Grace "de Repentigny," as she preferred to write her name. Jay directed, Bert designed sets, and Grace starred in the drama—performed in a garage owned by a German refugee family, who used to listen to suspicious shortwave broadcasts. The German family's son, John, played the leading man, and in real life Grace had a short-lived crush on him.

The play for the Unitarian Church basement audience was far more ambitious: a combination variety show and Gay '90s melodrama. It also turned into Grace's first encounter with censorship.

"You can't put on such a play, with a boy dressed as a girl!" the Unitarian minister objected, on behalf of his congregation's sensitivities. Drag shows were hardly in vogue in New Hampshire in the early 1940s.

"They've worked hard on it, and they're putting it on!" Barbara

Roberts insisted. The show did go on, but the minister stayed home.

In the Unitarian Church basement, the theater group set up tables: For their twenty-five cents, the audience got the play plus refreshments. Though George Metalious later wrote that Laurette spent Grace's high school years pursuing men friends, Laurette did attend the gala performance—even collecting money as part of her contribution to Grace's creative endeavors.

Grace, of course, had written the play, introduced by a narrator. Then the curtain opened to reveal the home of Lulubelle Snapgarter, played by Bert—wearing his mother's green alligator shoes mounted on roller skates. (He had to cut out the backs of the shoes to make them fit his feet.) Lulubelle, holding knitting needles, was "knitting a hot water bottle," Bert recalls. "She" also wore a wig, and balloons for breasts.

As Lulubelle knitted, her daughter Daisy Mae Snapgarter (Grace), an innocent village maiden with golden hair, sang a ditty about going to the dangerous but exciting big city (a comic foreshadowing, Bert thinks, of Allison MacKenzie in *Peyton Place*). Daisy Mae's "mother" listened dutifully, until Daisy Mae's boyfriend hove into sight. Then Bert, as Mrs. Snapgarter, put on his hat, roller skated across the stage, and slammed into a wall. (Some of the play was improvised.)

After this comic interlude, Daisy Mae's suitor, Jay Quizzlewham Gottabottle (played by another student, Eugene Chase) entered the scene.

MRS. SNAPGARTER: What business are you in?
GOTTABOTTLE: I have fresh eggs in my business.
MRS. SNAPGARTER: Are you in poultry?
GOTTABOTTLE: No, I'm a bouncer in a saloon!

Such routines, cheerfully plagiarized from a current joke book, formed most of the play. Jay Boivin played a moustachioed villain, the kind who'd tie a shrieking heroine to the railroad tracks. In the end true love triumphed—while Bert took a hatpin from his wig and popped his balloon "breasts." The audience loved the performance.

The theater group lasted about a year, and it was during that time that Grace, Jay, and Bert made friends with Bob Athearn. Then the Unitarian Church organist, Bob Athearn was some ten years older than Grace and her "satellites," and he was also a questioner of received ideas. He had grown up among reserved WASPs in the north end of Manchester, and had been trained to look down on French-Canadians for their ornate church ceremonies and the warmth and "touchiness" of their relationships.

When he met Grace, Bert, and Jay, Bob Athearn had been emancipating himself. His wife, Luce, was French-Canadian, warm, and physically outgoing—"touchy," and by 1940 they had two young sons. The bright high schoolers immediately began hanging out at the Athearns' on Orange Street.

Grace and her two comrades learned they could drop in, sit on the floor, exchange ideas, and sometimes drink beer or "Jesus juice," their own concoction of grape juice and gin. They talked about their courses and teachers, and Grace never hesitated to call teachers by less than flattering names if she disliked what went on in class. Bert recalls that none of them studied particularly hard in high school, but always got good grades—except for his F in typing.

The Athearns' house was filled with books, and Grace was very well-read—though probably not in the books her teachers told her to read. Bob Athearn also recommended that she read *Jane Eyre*.

Together, Bob, Luce, Grace, Jay, and Bert would read Shakespeare's plays aloud and admire the word play, especially in *Henry IV*. They also favored Eugene O'Neill's *Desire Under the Elms,* with its dark vision of New England sexuality (much like *Peyton Place's*) and its portrait of a young woman marrying a man old enough to be her father.

Grace thought a lot about her father—and felt deeply rejected by him. During her teens she went through a "kick Mother" phase —sharply critical of Laurette—but Laurette's emphasis on culture helped Grace appreciate what Bob Athearn could teach her about classical music. She especially liked one organ piece by Percy Whitlock (on which Bob wrote, "Grace"), and Grace learned to love Bach, an admiration she retained to the end of her life.

Grace's high school crowd also included a few young women: Ethel Grodzin, who later wrote a feminist book; another student named Ruth; and occasionally, Grace's sister, Bunny. At their Aunt Georgie's, Grace and Bunny sometimes disappeared into the back room for a few nips of booze, discreetly hidden in a teapot. Grace also learned to smoke in high school—but did not, apparently, learn to make close friendships with other women. Possibly her home background—including her mother's departure, one entire winter, to vacation with a boyfriend in Florida—made Grace not want to rely on other women. Instead—like so many fatherless girls—she learned to value men more highly.

Jay and Bert were her closest and most uninhibited friends. With them and a few others, Grace used to play strip poker— "Somehow Grace always wound up taking off more clothes than anyone else," Bert recalls. "But she always wore more, too."

The three inseparable friends shared a locker in high school, leaving each other childishly smutty notes and pictures between classes, and contriving fiendish devices to jump out at the next unsuspecting soul who opened the locker. Grace wrote short stories and wanted to be an actress—but Laurette liked to think Grace might marry Jay, who was properly "French." "Marry your own" was the conventional wisdom. But the three-way friendship was strictly pals—which may be why, in their theatrical productions, they always imported an outsider to play Grace's boyfriend.

Grace did have boyfriends—a new one every semester, Bert recalls—and he suspects she was "fast." She dated a Bob Archambault and a George Terwilliger and a fellow named Murray, but her closest friends were Bert and Jay, who encouraged her creativity. With boyfriends she had to play a feminine role—flirtatious, passive, cute, but deferential. With her pals and with Bob Athearn —who, blue-eyed and five feet six to Grace's five-four, was not her physical "type"—Grace could be herself.

As her contemporaries, Bert and Jay saw Grace's fun-loving, eccentric side—but Barbara Roberts, at thirty, and Bob Athearn, at twenty-six, were mature enough to see something else under her sparkling, clever surface. "There was a sadness in her, too," Barbara Roberts recalls. "She couldn't reach out and tell what was way down deep." Instead, she left her older friends with impressions: that her household was full of conflict, that her father had rejected her, that Bunny was not a true friend—and that she defi-

nitely did not want to go home in the afternoons. Neither Bob nor
Barbara ever met Grace's parents, and by the time Grace graduated from high school, Bob and Luce and their sons had moved to
York Village, Maine. Barbara Roberts, who never saw Grace
again after high school, says, "She'll always remain a bright spot
in my life."

Barbara Roberts, Bob Athearn, Louis Freedman, Bert Marcotte, and Jay Boivin have no high school memories of George
Metalious, but George reports being very aware of Grace, though
not of her creative side. He saw her as a woman first.

Until her senior year, George recalls in *The Girl from "Peyton
Place,"* Grace was called "Slats"—a negative tribute to her flat
chest. But toward the end of school, she filled out considerably.
With other high schoolers, she frequented the Puritan ice cream
restaurant (the Pilgrim Ice Cream Parlor in *No Adam in Eden*),
where George's father Theophanes Metaleos* was a baker and
candy maker. Though the boys congregating at the Puritan still
called Grace "Slats," they examined her with much more admiration. One of them was George Metalious.

One day, seated with a crowd of boys, George was watching
Grace DeRepentigny, with her friends at another booth. As
George recounts it, the boys had much to say about Grace: "She
sure has changed"; "A real rare one"; "But you can't date her.
She's always with her two pals."

George broke in. "So she can't be dated, huh?"

"Bet you a half you can't."

"You're on," George said, slapping a half dollar on the table.

"I want a date with you," he announced at Grace's table. "How
about next Friday night? I'll come to your house."

Taken aback, Grace tried to be sophisticated, and haughty—but
she also told him what he needed to know. "I live in the north
end, on Beech Street."

She had not committed herself, but before she could say anything more, George strode back to his own table—and collected his
half dollar.

Grace's friends warned her that Laurette would hardly want her

---

* The spelling of the name varies.

daughter dating a "greasy Greek"—and besides, "He'll be pawing you all night." Grace suspected as much, considered George quite uncouth, and wondered what on earth she would have in common with him.

When George appeared at Grace's (one of six apartments in a large, brown-shingled tenement), he made his way up a narrow, dimly lighted stairway. Inside he met Grandmother Royer, stoking the stove; Bunny, idle, since she and Grace were not expected to do housework; and Laurette, who emerged from a nap and treated him as she always had: "You know, George, living in this part of town gives Grace a chance to meet the better people in town."

George lived in the Greek section, in south Manchester; he and his buddies all wanted to go out with Grace but didn't dare ask because, he recalled later, she didn't pay attention to "boys like us." Laurette pinpointed George's insecurities, and he never forgave her.

Somehow George and Grace managed an hour together—"doing and saying very little," he wrote later—before he left.

But Grace's version made a better story, far more romantic. She had gone to school dances before, she wrote in *The American Weekly* in 1958, "but George was my first solo flight with a boy who had a license to drive a car."

In 1965 George recalled, laconically, that their first real date was the senior reception; Grace wrote in 1958 that "He took me to a movie and, for the first time, I had my hand held by a male. I don't know if I had been too well wrapped in the cocoon manufactured by my mother and grandmother, or if all girls feel the same way on their first date."

George had a distinct advantage over other boys in Grace's eyes, now that she had suddenly stopped being flat-chested: "He was the first boy who ever looked at my mouth when I was talking."

George was also tall, dark, good looking, and big—her ideal physical type. Further, though he was hardly fatherly, he looked much older than sixteen.

The outcome was inevitable. "Before a week was gone we were necking in the car his stepfather loaned him, and I had decided I was in love."

Her tone may be ironic, mocking (seventeen years later) her adolescent vulnerability—or it may reveal the more romantic side of Grace DeRepentigny. Bob Athearn had always suspected that when Grace mocked David Copperfield's idealism, it was really to cover up her own sentimental side. Grace did have a more openly emotional side, investing her dates with a romantic aura—based, possibly, more on her imagination than on what actually happened.

Her description of falling in love may be an attempt to portray herself as classically "feminine": romantic, emotional, vulnerable—without the youthful cynicism that was part of her creativity. George's recollection, meanwhile, fits a stereotypically "masculine" approach: a short, unemotional recounting of facts. While Grace struggled with two possible roles—the creative person and the dependent woman—George had only one pursuit: proving himself as a man.

According to his self-portrait in *The Girl from "Peyton Place,"* George had his own insecurities, including a desperate need to appear strong and masculine. After his parents' divorce, he lived with four older cousins, who sometimes bullied him because he was younger and smaller. As he grew up, he tried to prove himself in sports, although his mother insisted he must not play: "I don't want you getting hurt," she said.

But George felt far more hurt when other boys called him "Sissy," at an age when peer pressure has the most power. He played baseball and football, but since he had skipped a grade in grammar school, he remained younger and smaller than the others—a recipe for failure. He withdrew into long silences, his way of escaping painful confrontations.

He got along better with girls and older people because he had cultivated an air of maturity, an unusual ability to listen, and what he later called a "dubious knack": the ability to sound convincing when he was thoroughly insincere.

George wanted to be looked up to, as a man who was powerful, strong, and silent. Grace wanted a powerful, strong, and understanding man to confer the kind of male approval her friends could not give, and that her father had denied her. It was wartime, and young people clutched at each other for security in an uncertain and frightening world. Both Grace and George came into adulthood thinking—as seventeen-year-olds often do—that another person could fill all their gaps, meet all their needs.

CHAPTER 3

Laurette, as expected, violently opposed Grace's dating George. Why see a Greek when there were nice boys in the north end? she demanded. And besides . . . "She always couched her objections to our going together in the vaguest of terms so that I never knew just what she meant," Grace wrote in 1958.

Grace learned to be secretive. Bert and Jay knew nothing of the dates George reports in his biography: summer days at the Ledge, bicycle trips to Goffstown, hikes up the Uncanoonuc Mountains. Grace, unconsciously, gathered material for future reference: Uncanoonuc, a Native American word for "breasts," suits the rounded curves of the mountains—and also suggests the female imagery that begins *Peyton Place:* "Indian summer is like a woman." At stopping places, Grace and George, overlooking the whole region, talked about their families, and each other. They shared loneliness, a powerful bond between adolescents.

In the evenings, George borrowed the family car and took Grace to Oak Hill at the top of Derryfield Park, near the city reservoir and the Weston Observatory—a stone tower that was a popular spot for "parking." Grace and George chose their own special place: a dead end marked by the sign, "ROAD'S END." They sat for hours, overlooking the city lights of Manchester, thinking they understood everything about one another—and sharing a powerful physical attraction.

George had graduated from Central High in June 1941, and was working as a listing clerk in a shoe shop while Grace finished her senior year. Her Aunt Georgie—deprived of her own higher education by the Depression—wanted Grace to go to college after her graduation in January 1942. Aunt Georgie even offered to contribute toward tuition—but Grace had other interests.

For a while she worked as a typist in Connecticut, earning $50 a week—a considerable sum then for a girl not yet eighteen. She liked to buy books—several cartons' worth by the time she returned to Manchester. But she most enjoyed horseback riding, and George Metalious—who left for the University of New Hampshire in September 1942.

Durham was scarcely an hour away, and George felt lost at college: He couldn't study, or adjust to the college routine. He began coming home as often as he could, and turning to Grace for solace.

Grace, feeling lonely and unloved at home, had written about Prince Charming for years: even in her comic plays, the heroine had yearned for something or someone outside herself. The heroine's escape most often took the only acceptable form for a young woman: a man.

Grace and George saw each other nearly every weekend, either in Manchester or Durham. When Grace visited Durham, she stayed at a small rooming house at the edge of town, where the strict landlady insisted on parlor visits only—and properly chaperoned. Coed dormitories were unheard of at the University of New Hampshire (or almost anywhere else), and female college students had curfew hours. Opposite-sex dorm room visits were rare and strictly supervised; young people had few chances to be alone together.

Grace accepted those rules and proprieties when she had to, but followed her own impulses whenever she could. One weekend she *had* to see George—but could find no bus or train to take her from Manchester to Durham.

She decided to take a taxi.

Unfortunately, she found herself in Durham without enough money to pay the fare—and the university president, Fred Engelhardt, was called in to handle the crisis.

"Well, I had to visit my Gee-Gee," Grace explained, fighting back tears, "and that was the only way I could get here."

The president paid the fifteen-dollar fare.

George, meanwhile, was "the first person in my life who made me feel special," Grace wrote later (in a private paper George quotes in *The Girl from "Peyton Place"*). Bert and Jay loved her humor, her creativity, and her eccentricities—but George said he loved her as a woman, and she felt he saved her from the fate of the women in her family: "I might have wound up a thin-lipped, frigid woman if it hadn't been for him."

Just before Christmas, Grace and George became lovers.

George was very gentle, she said, "and initiated me into the realm of sex with a great deal more wisdom than one might have ever expected from a seventeen-year-old boy." He treated her with passion—but also with a loving tenderness she'd never had from her father, or from any other man.

"That night, he took me in his arms, laid me on the bed and began kissing me gently," she recalled more than fifteen years later. Sex was something "I had craved for a long time. As he kissed me, I, in turn, began kissing him with great affection. It made me feel secure and happy. He kept kissing me very gently, my mouth, my breasts, and I gave in gradually to the pleasures of ecstasy. I felt as though I had found someone to whom I meant something, something to have, something to want, something to hold.

"He was kind, considerate, and thoughtful. Never once did he hurt me. The only thing that puzzled me at the time was the blood. If I wasn't hurt, then why should I bleed?"

In love with Grace and not at all interested in his studies, George decided to drop out of college. Grace made him much happier, and she needed him. They also wanted to get married, but both families objected furiously.

Grace and George had been raised to marry "their own" in language, religion, ethnicity—and they were "foreigners" to each other. They had also been raised to please their mothers—who hated one another. Grace was no better than her mother, Helen insisted to her son George; Laurette DeRepentigny demanded, "What has that black Greek done, got you pregnant?"

Grace and George decided on defiance: They would live together. In early 1943 that was a scandal: outside bohemian circles in big cities, unmarried young people just did not cohabit. Though

Grace and George managed to get a landlord to rent to them, neither family visited throughout January, while they "lived in sin"—until finally both families relented. George, underage, had parental consent to marry.

Still, the relatives wanted the marriage done right, and Grandmother DeRepentigny insisted on a church wedding. Grace was no strong believer—and George was not even Catholic.

To placate the DeRepentignys, he agreed to instruction from a priest. He listened dutifully for a few visits—and then attacked as "unrealistic" virtually everything the priest had said. That was George's last session, but another Catholic priest agreed to marry him and Grace: Father T. J. E. Devoy, an Irish pastor from Quebec who had also married Grace's parents.

After the ceremony at St. George Church on February 27, 1943, Aunt Georgie held the reception at her home on Ash Street, with two long tables and a delicious buffet lunch for thirty guests. According to George's brief account, the parents were "especially cordial" to one another, all things considered—but Grace later gave reporters a much more colorful version, starting with her father's arrival at the wedding with a new lady friend.

Laurette, his first wife, objected to his companion.

Words were exchanged, and finally blows, and Laurette and the lady friend got into a hair-pulling match—the highlight of the day. If it happened—Grace had a tendency to dramatize—it was an inauspicious beginning to a marriage that everyone said could never last. And why were they marrying so young in any case—Grace at eighteen and a half, George two months shy of eighteen?

Everyone assumed Grace was pregnant.

"I said nothing," she told reporters years later, "but when we'd been married nine months I gave the biggest party I ever threw, and I laughed in everybody's face. I was as flat as a pancake."

She was also a mother—for her daughter, Marsha, was born seven months and three weeks after the ceremony. But the big party was one of her favorite stories, and she rarely missed a good tale—a characteristic that infuriated George. He preferred facts, and did not appreciate Grace's demonstrating her creativity. He called her stories lies.

"If George eventually came to the conclusion that I hadn't an honest bone in my body," Grace wrote in 1959, "he was absolutely right." She cited her childhood memories of "total inadequacy," said her happiest youthful moment was the discovery that she could leave home, and blamed her mother's aristocratic pretensions. Laurette would claim that their clothes were bought in the best shops; that family trinkets were heirlooms; that she came from a background of gentility, breeding, and wealth—and so Grace lost, she said, a respect for the truth.

Still, Grace knew the truth was more complicated. She absorbed from her mother both self-hatred—for her appearance, for her relative poverty—and a desire to impress others. She criticized her mother's hypocrisy and pretense—but not the woman's yearnings that stimulated them. She loved literature, art, and music just as Laurette did, and was not thoroughly opposed to her mother's "champagne ideas on a beer budget." After all, Grace herself constantly yearned for something better than she had.

Throughout the first year of their marriage, Grace and George sought to ignore "well-meaning" relatives: "We tried blindly to reassure one another that we were a going concern, that we had something so beautiful that nothing could shatter us." And she wondered, in 1959, "what would have happened in the end if we had concerned ourselves more with strength than with beauty."

But at eighteen, very much in love, Grace and George preferred dreams of beauty—though ugly realities intruded. They lived on very little money from George's work: first as a store clerk, then as a construction worker in defense plants. Neither family gave financial help, nor was Grace very adept as a housewife.

Mémère had always cleaned house, and done all the cooking. Rebelling against "nasty-neatness," Grace never kept a tidy household—but she did want George to think she could cook. After he left for work, Grace would slip out of their apartment, and take a load of groceries to Grandmother Royer (then living with Laurette at 111 Third Street). Mémère would cook dinner, Grace would carry it home—and George would congratulate her on her cooking, until one day when Grace's sister Bunny revealed the truth.

George just looked at Grace—whose hunger for approval had

led her, in the past, to "get around" her mother with little lies. George, too, was more inclined to evade issues than confront them —and Grace did, finally, learn to cook. They laughed together, loved one another, and tried to share everything. When Grace had morning sickness, George waited outside the bathroom for his turn to be sick. They were as close as their personalities and insecurities let them be.

Grace finally let Bert, her pal, know she was married, sending him a picture of herself and George. Bert had gone into the service after graduation, knowing only that Laurette had always hoped her daughter would marry Jay. He was very surprised to learn that Grace had become Mrs. Metalious.

Not long after the wedding, George had also tried to enlist, but the Seabees rejected him for poor eyesight. Then, four months after the wedding and two months after he turned eighteen, George received his "greetings."

He was delighted, but Grace was devastated—and George could not understand her reaction. He insisted, as always, on the facts: "There's a war on. I can't shirk . . ."

But Grace, expecting her first child, felt little sympathy for such abstractions as patriotic duty. George was about to leave her—just as her father had. She conceded that other men might want to leave their wives to fight for their country—"but there must be something wrong with me, that my Gee-Gee wants to leave."

By the time George left for Fort Devens, Massachusetts, in early July 1943, Grace's pregnancy was quite apparent. "Immediate assignment to a basic training unit" turned into months of anticipation—but close enough to see Grace on weekends.

Grace, meanwhile, had moved back with her mother, Bunny, and Mémère on Third Street—the only time Grace ever lived on the west side. Even then, she was outside the French enclave—in a German-Belgian neighborhood called "Squog." Her life, she told George, was much as it had been before marriage: constant bickering, now spiced with lurid tales of deformed babies, hardly encouraging to an expectant mother. It was not the situation Grace had envisioned when she escaped home to be married.

Laurette, at forty, was trim, attractive, and popular, and enjoyed out-of-town excursions. But after one exhausting trip, she called Grace from a nursing home and said she was dying. Grace—thrown into a panic—called George, to come home immediately.

He raced the sixty miles from Fort Devens—then reacted with rage when he found the emergency was Laurette's. Focusing on the fact that Laurette did not seem to be dying, he could not understand Grace's guilt, nor her thwarted desire for her only parent's love and approval. Meanwhile, Grace believed that her mostly silent husband had let her down when she expected him to be strong.

When Grace was in her ninth month of pregnancy, George finally received his orders—to a medical basic-training unit at Camp Barkely, Texas. Eager to prove himself as a man, he did not know that Grace came close to death proving herself as a woman.

Before she gave birth to Marsha Joan on October 22, 1943, Grace was in labor for three days—and took three weeks in the hospital to recover. Her narrow pelvis made childbirth difficult and very dangerous, and John Deitch—the gruff old Manchester doctor who'd also delivered Grace—told her she must never have another child.

If she tried, he told her flatly, she might die.

Grace telegraphed George the news that he had a baby daughter; later she wrote him that Marsha ("Mee-Jee") was gorgeous: big, brown-eyed, with a soft fluff of brown hair. But she did not tell George what she'd gone through to bring Marsha into the world.

Grace had little sympathy from those around her, and she felt unwelcome at her mother's house—and especially so when her allotment checks were late. George, in Texas, could not help her.

As a child, Grace had written of her father as "the charming prince and I the only object of his affection." As a young adult, she invested the absent husband with the same aura of power and strength. George would give her the love and happiness she needed, if she went to him.

She decided to surprise him, in Texas.

Marsha was five weeks old and the winter snowfall had begun when Grace left Manchester. Gee-Gee would be lonely, Grace thought, and she would fill his loneliness, as he would fill hers.

Then they would live happily ever after—but a certain apprehension led her to send him a telegram from St. Louis, just in case: "WILL BE IN ABILENE TOMORROW MORNING WITH OUR NEW FAMILY ADDITION."

But there was no George to meet her. Instead, her welcoming committee was George's Army buddy—who told Grace that George had KP duty and couldn't switch with anyone else.

"You could have been there if you'd wanted to," Grace said when she finally met George.

"Maybe," George conceded. "But you just don't tell the Army what to do."

"But surely . . ." Grace put in.

"And you didn't even tell me you were coming until the last moment. Christ, what did you expect?"

"But I thought . . ."

"It was a foolish thing to do, anyway."

Struggling not to cry, Grace protested: "But, Gee-Gee, you could at least be glad to see us."

"Well, I am. But what are you and the baby going to do here?"

George managed to find Grace and Marsha a two-room shack not far from the base. The neighbors were sympathetic and friendly, but Grace was frightened and lonely for much of the time. In the past, she might have created stories about a charming prince—but the needs of a baby interrupted any reveries she might begin. Instead of freeing her, life in Texas made her feel more dependent, more confined than ever—and more inadequate, especially as a woman.

At a neighbor's party, Marsha began to cry, and Grace ran to warm up her bottle. Meanwhile, an Indian woman who'd just given birth herself began nursing Marsha—until Grace returned, outraged. "She's not feeding my baby!" Grace insisted, and railed against "that Indian" for hours afterward. She had no racial prejudices, Grace insisted: she just wanted to feed her own baby.

But Grace never had enough milk to nurse Marsha herself. *I'm not a real woman,* she told herself—and while George slept peacefully, Grace cried quietly into her pillow.

"If I had felt unwanted at 'home,'" Grace wrote later, "it wasn't a patch on how I felt in Texas."

Grace's needs made George impatient. He had a man's job to do, he said: he couldn't spend time with silly problems. But Grace had no one else, nor the experience to understand what had happened to their lives. George had his man's world, in the Army; in her two-room shack with Marsha, Grace had no part in his world —and no world of her own.

Though George wanted to send Grace and Marsha back to New Hampshire, they followed him to Springfield, Missouri, for medical training. Grace rented a small, shabby room, furnished with double bed and hot plate; George spent weekends, reluctantly, in that room. "It seemed to me that everybody else's husband was so pleased to have his wife with him except mine," Grace wrote later.

"I don't know where I got the idea that marriage could be one long, magnificent love affair," she added, since she'd never seen anything like that at home. Though George insisted that no honeymoon lasted forever, Grace wanted the romantic little touches: love notes, phone calls, gifts. George hated the phone, and thought presents were a waste of money—and Grace felt shunned.

In January 1944, a month after their first Christmas together as a family, Grace decided to take Marsha and go "home"—by way of Memphis, where Laurette and Bunny were living. She got little sympathy from her mother and sister, and found, in Manchester, that Grandmother Royer, then sixty-eight, was trying to take care of the five-room apartment on Third Street with almost no money. Grace, nineteen, went to work: at the Air Transport Command, at Leavitt Company, as a clerk. Mémère raised Marsha, just as she'd raised Grace.

Grace had never seriously worked before, or had anyone depending on her—but hard work and independence had become national ideals for women in 1944. "Rosie the Riveter"—drawn by Norman Rockwell in a construction outfit, with brawny arms—symbolized America's "heroic woman," Rockwell said: she did a "man's job," took her part in the "war effort," and contributed to American strength.

Movies during the 1940s also encouraged independent work for women. In *His Girl Friday* (1940), Rosalind Russell as a fast-talking reporter is clearly the equal of Cary Grant, her editor—and both love their work. In *Woman of the Year* (1942), Katharine Hepburn plays a political journalist who compromises only slightly to make marriage work with Spencer Tracy, a sports reporter. That two of the most popular movies of the forties featured women as writers would not be lost on Grace—nor would she miss the Hollywood message that though it helped to have a man, a woman could also go it alone.

. Though Grace rarely enjoyed her jobs, she did learn to live on her own—something she would not have discovered otherwise. If she wrote during the war years—and she often said that she had been writing all her life—none of it survives, though World War II is mentioned briefly in *Peyton Place* and *No Adam in Eden,* where Lesley de Montigny's beloved father is killed in the Pacific. (Al DeRepentigny was still alive in 1980 and living in Portland, Oregon.)

Grandmother Royer shared the load with Grace: She was the housewife, and Grace the breadwinner, and Grace adored Mémère. But Grace's burden was soon doubled, when Laurette and Bunny returned to Manchester. Grace's earnings supported them, too.

Still, the war years were not entirely grim. Grace kept up old friendships: When Bert Marcotte, who now called himself "Marc," came home on leave, Grace went on picnics with him. She wrote to Bob and Luce Athearn, and in the summer of 1944 visited them in York Village, Maine, with Marsha and a hostess gift: a Red Seal recording of Brahms' "Academic Festival Overture," an Athearn favorite, and the "Haydn Variations."

Grace and "Mee-Jee" stayed for a week, sharing old times and new discoveries. Grace introduced Bob to daiquiris; he played for her Wanda Landowska's new recording of Bach's "Goldberg Variations"—and Grace treasured the record. On one dark, warm night on the beach, Grace and Luce created another memorable moment when they insisted on all-over wading—and Bob found himself on the sand in the dark, unable to see anything except his own arms, outstretched like a scarecrow's and festooned with women's underclothing. On the way home, Grace dangled her underpants out the window, to dry in the breeze. (Later, in more flamboyant days, she insisted publicly that she never wore underwear.)

At home in Manchester, Grace wrote faithfully to George—more frequently than he wrote to her—but she also began to notice the Air Force pilots at the Air Transport Command. They were handsome, well-built, and dashing, and about to risk their lives for their country. They flattered her and took her to the Officers' Club at Grenier Field. At parties in the Hotel Carpenter in Manchester, Grace and Bunny enjoyed being the centers of attention.

For a while, an older man took Grace to dinner and bought gifts for her and Marsha—but she wrote George that there was nothing sexual in the relationship. She said less about her double dates with Bunny and enlisted men—and when George took a quick (unauthorized) trip home from Pennsylvania, his reunion with Grace was "far from successful," he said. He found her just coming home from a very late solo date with an Air Force man.

Other men were giving Grace the male approval she needed, and Mémère's caring for Marsha freed Grace for an active social life. Still, she insisted that she had never been unfaithful to George. "I had dates with only the nicest officers," she said in 1958, "the ones who would take you to dinner and not expect you to pay off afterward."

George returned for spontaneous visits—and finally, unusually exhilarated, announced he was about to go to England. Grace feared abandonment; George assured her he'd send extra money—and his world of facts and hers of emotions remained far apart. As the major breadwinner and often the only worker in her household, Grace also coped with shortages: she bought coal, stood in ration lines, smoked "foul cigarettes," and learned to apply leg makeup in place of stockings.

Grace did manage to send George pictures of Marsha in a baby swing: "You can be swinging on a star, but this is more fun," Grace wrote on the back. George got pictures of Marsha's first steps (marked, "Well, gee, I'm just learning how, Daddy!") and Marsha's trying to escape being photographed ("How these camera hounds annoy me!"). In their own imitation of the military world, Grace and Marsha appear in a picture labeled "Right face!"—both of them facing left.

Then Grace "became really upset," George records in his biography, when he wrote from England that he was applying for combat duty. Her other "upset" came when she learned that he had been in the Battle of the Bulge—in the Ninth Army artillery, bombarded day and night by a new German V-weapon.

Grace refused to read newspapers or listen to the radio, and her co-workers agreed not to tell her about the Ninth—that on January 5 the Ninth Army had gained one mile and beaten off eighteen counter-attacks in twenty-four hours. Nor did Grace know, until it was over, that more than 40,000 Americans had been lost at the Bulge.

"The war was thinking that, of course, George was not going to be killed because that sort of thing only happened to other people," Grace recalled in 1958.

George did survive—as did her pal Marc, who continued to visit Grace in Manchester. Though Marc had realized, in the service, that he preferred men to women, he had always been attracted to Grace, and not just as a friend. He loved her sense of humor and her unconventionality, and questioned why she'd married George. Toward the end of the war, Marc says, they became lovers—but he never considered asking her to leave George.

CHAPTER 4

When the German armies surrendered in May 1945, George Metalious had barely turned twenty. Army combat had let him prove himself: He felt strong and capable and grown up, and in no hurry to return home. He asked to be transferred to the Pacific, where the war continued until August, when the atomic bombs dropped on Hiroshima and Nagasaki opened the nuclear age.

But George was not present: The Army kept him in Europe until six months after V-E Day. Grace, wondering if George would ever come home and whether he even cared about her and Marsha, turned twenty-one in September. George missed her birthday—and much more had happened, he told Grace when he finally returned home.

He had taken to drinking heavily during the last six months, he confessed—and before the Army let him return home, he'd had to "dry out." Grace, who drank very little then, was sympathetic about the stresses of military life.

But there was something else, too. In Germany he'd had an affair—with a German woman, Elfreda, who'd helped relieve the tensions of ten months of combat duty.

Grace tried, at first, to be cosmopolitan. "After all," she said, "I never expected you to sit and look at four walls after months of combat."

Since Grace seemed forgiving, George added, "She reminded me of you."

"But I don't want to remind you of HER!" Grace cried, deeply hurt. "I want to be separate—and special." She had been faithful throughout the war, she said, though at times she'd felt desperate sexual temptations. She'd kissed other men, she conceded, but had never wanted an affair. Once, in a captain's hotel room before a party at the Officers' Club at Grenier, Grace'd had a few drinks—and the captain made a pass. She was sitting on the bed, his hand on her thigh, when she said no, thinking, "Gee-Gee wouldn't like it."

She often reminded George about Elfreda and his drinking. She did not mention staying with Marc.

"I guess a lot of people did their growing up during the years of World War II," Grace said later. "I was not one of them." But she tended to disparage her growth and achievements, perhaps because they contributed neither to the creative role—her writing self, submerged though not abandoned—nor to the romantic image of a woman in love. Instead, she grew up in a practical way, as family breadwinner.

Until Laurette married Charles Kugel, an accountant, Grace had supported her mother while Laurette had a succession of boyfriends. Marc met one of them, a "runt" who was a race track tout on the side. Charlie Kugel was also small and unassuming, and usually kept in his wife's shadow.

During the war Grace had also supported Mémère, who raised Marsha, and Bunny, who worked intermittently as a clerk at Marshall's Drug Store. Grace wrote George that she was faithfully banking the money he sent, and that they could buy their own home when he returned—but she was really using the money for five people to live on. She had become an adult, a provider.

She and George had not seen each other for a year and a half when he returned on New Year's Eve, 1945, just after the heaviest blizzard of the season. They were ecstatic to be together again, and "their welcoming kiss lasted until they had to come up for air," George put in his biography.

New Year's Eve was for romance; New Year's Day, for planning their future in the grown-up manner George now preferred: insurance, mortgages, security. Their bank account could be used, he said, for a down payment on their own home, since government financing made home buying easy for veterans. And then George could use the G. I. Bill as thousands of ex-soldiers had, to get his college education and become a professional.

Taking a deep breath, Grace confessed the truth. She had no money saved. In fact, she owed three weeks' back rent for the apartment on Third Street. She'd had to support everyone, and take care of the house—and she looked to George for sympathy and understanding.

"How could you be so stupid!" George roared. "Everyone in your family is just playing you for a sucker!" He resolved to put a stop to that immediately, over Grace's anguished protests. When she would not—could not—throw her family out or force them to go to work, George did.

Grandmother Royer, then becoming senile, was sent to Laurette in New York, though Grace insisted to George that the Kugels had no room for her. Laurette promptly put Mémère in a nursing home. Grace visited her later, in a hospital, and said the experience was so terrible that she could hardly bear ever going to a hospital again. (In *No Adam in Eden,* Lesley's senile grandmother appears more disgusting than pitiful, as if Grace needed to allay her own guilt by blaming the victim.)

Within a few years, Grandmother Royer had died—"a fact which I still cannot bear to think about on long, cold, dark nights," Grace wrote. Then Laurette and Bunny played on Grace's guilt, too: "She always loved you and Marsha, and she couldn't stand it when you didn't want her around." Grace *had* wanted her around—but George had not.

As for Bunny, she "escaped into a terrible marriage for which I have always felt responsible," Grace wrote. Bunny, nineteen, married Roger Roy of Manchester on January 3, 1946, three days after George Metalious' homecoming. They had two children, Suzanne and Richard, before separating in 1949; for a while in the late 1950s they reconciled, while Bunny was between marriages. Suzy Roy spent much of her childhood with Grace, who by then had resolved not to turn away needy relatives, especially female ones.

Grace never stopped feeling guilty for having sent her family away, and "When I look back," she wrote in 1958, "I wonder if it was then that I began to dislike George." Her commitment to women conflicted with her obligations to a man—and George never understood her fears and hopes for the women in her family. Nor did he like the behavior of the remaining female in the household: Marsha, twenty-seven months old, in the "Terrible Twos" stage of development.

Used to military discipline, George expected Marsha to "shape up"—but like her mother, she'd been coddled and made much of and generally considered queen of the household. She'd learned a favorite technique for getting her way, especially her dessert first: holding her breath. That would stop immediately, George declared —and ignored Mémère, Bunny, and Grace, all terrified that Marsha would choke to death. Marsha did not, and she learned tantrums wouldn't bring her dessert.

George simply asserted authority over Marsha, but Grace knuckled under less easily. Before the war she'd wanted a strong and powerful man she could lean on, a big man to hold and protect her. Afterward, she had some firm ideas of her own.

Like many veterans, George at first floundered, moving from one job to another. For a while he belonged to the Fifty-two Twenty Club, set up for nonworking veterans after the war; he tried, unsuccessfully, a summer stint in school. Grace worked for a while in the payroll department at a textile mill, but became pregnant within a few months—for, according to George's biography, "the only time they seemed completely happy was when they were in bed together." Grace was eager to learn about sex, George writes, and he was eager to teach and to improvise.

During her pregnancy, however, Grace was too ill to work. Desperate, George finally took a job at the Limerick Yarn Mill, doing the mill work Grace had been brought up to despise and fear. He worked the day and night shifts, and sometimes both—but his pay checks could not cover their needs, and they moved in with his family.

After the new baby was born, Grace insisted, they would have a place of their own—for owning one's own home, especially in the suburbs, had become the new American Dream. Behind their white picket fences, women—fired from work when the war ended, so that men could have jobs—would be wives and mothers, happily settling into domesticity (a vision that Betty Friedan later punctured in *The Feminine Mystique*).

In 1946 Grace's relatives had little sympathy for her wishes—such as a season ticket to the civic music concerts. Her bigger dreams, especially the home of their own, got the same reactions Laurette always inspired when she shared her hopes:

"Champagne ideas on a beer pocketbook!"

"Who does she think she is?"

"She always did set herself above the crowd!"

Laurette, in her own way, would have understood, but not Grace's mother-in-law, who said, "She never was good enough for George." "Good enough" seemed to mean "feminine enough": passive, docile, accepting.

Even George was hardly supportive. "Why can't you be like everyone else?"

Not that Grace was "a plaster saint" through all the abuse, she recalled later. "I wasn't. I fought and kicked like a steer at branding time." She hated everyone except Marsha, and to Marsha she whispered her deepest dreams and convictions:

"It's not always going to be like this. Someday everything is going to be beautiful and you're going to have every single thing you've ever wanted." Marsha smiled as if she understood.

Finally, when she was close to giving birth, Grace took a stand. She wouldn't leave the hospital at all after the new baby was born, unless she and George had a place of their own. They took Laurette's and Mémère's furniture out of storage and moved into 19 Twardy Street, in a housing project set aside for veterans and their families. Though the apartments were olive-drab converted barracks, they were at least private homes.

But the new baby decided to be born during the worst blizzard in forty-seven years. When his wife began to have labor pains, after he'd worked all night, George was scarcely sympathetic: "Why the hell can't you do things like everybody else?" He meant the words as affectionate kidding—but Grace interpreted them differently.

"What the hell am I supposed to do?" she yelled back. "Make it stop snowing?"

By the time they reached the hospital—after George trudged

three blocks to fetch his Uncle John, who had a car—Grace felt considerably cowed. She remembered when she gave birth to Marsha: three days of labor, three weeks in the hospital to recover. She recalled that Dr. Deitch had told her never to have another child, that she might die.

Fearing he'd think less of her as a woman, she had never told George about that. But she had read nineteenth-century fiction, in which women frequently died in childbirth. She also knew *Gone with the Wind,* in which Melanie Wilkes—with a narrow pelvis, like Grace Metalious'—dies trying to give birth to Ashley's child. Scarlett O'Hara, seeing Melly die, realizes how much she misses her own mother's love (a theme Grace would not have missed). Then, with Ashley, whom she's always coveted, Scarlett finds herself much stronger than the man she hoped to lean on—another theme Grace had certainly noticed.

In any case, Grace did not need her vivid imagination. In pure terror, she begged George, "Don't leave me. Don't leave me alone."

Thinking it some romantic whim to keep him nearby, George insisted on going home to sleep. "For God's sake, Grace, I've been working all night. You'll probably be here for hours before anything happens."

"Then promise me you'll be here when I wake up."

"I promise."

When Grace awoke at seven for hospital visiting hours, George was not there, and she was devastated. Ten years later, she wrote, "I still remember the terrible feeling of aloneness, of desertion"—evoking all her childhood fears of abandonment by the man in her life.

George had slept until the next morning—then called the hospital, to learn that Grace had given birth to a baby boy the night before. He borrowed his father's car and had an auto accident on the way to the hospital—so it was ten o'clock in the morning (by his account; afternoon by Grace's) before he got to the hospital.

Grace never forgave him.

Meanwhile, she did take pride in having given her husband, the last male in the Metalious line, a son. "I wanted to feel like an empress," she said later, with the mocking tone she so often used to describe her own dreams. "I wanted the bells to peal, but I felt like a cow and the only bell that rang was the one I pressed when I needed a bedpan."

Still, the "empress"—or the cow—had had a much easier time than expected. Christopher George Metalious, born on February 21, 1947, had arrived in an ordinary childbirth. While George's father named the little boy and Grace nicknamed him "Mike" for the "deviltry" in his eyes, she again concealed from George her doctor's warning about more childbearing.

Through the summer of 1947, Grace and George shared child care, saving the price of a sitter. Day-care facilities had been set up during the war for working mothers, but closed right afterward, with the assumption that women would prefer to stay at home—though many women, like Grace, still had to work outside. Luckily for Grace, George had frequently babysat with his three younger stepsisters, felt at ease with children, and enjoyed their company.

George took the day shift at the mill; Grace worked from 7 P.M. to midnight as a cashier at Pine Island Park. Their jobs paid very little, and their social life consisted of evenings at home, with friends coming over for cards and drinks. Grace seldom drank: at most, two screwdrivers. Though her job gave her no great pleasure, she was twenty-three, trim, attractive, and delighted to be in the outside world again. At home, she and George had little time or energy for affection—and she began coming home later and later: after midnight, then one, two, three o'clock.

"I had to work late cashing up," she'd say, or "I stopped off for something to eat"—but did not tell George what he eventually learned from a mutual friend: Grace was having an affair with one of the men at the park.

Grace denied, then admitted it, adding, "Well, after all, honey, I didn't start this sort of thing first."

George conceded that, then—characteristically—withdrew into silence. Grace, too, appeared to forget the incident—but another unspoken animosity remained between them. George, recalling the occasion much later, felt that Grace's lover was distinctly inferior to her—as if she'd chosen a man who, unlike George, would be no challenge. She seemed to be seeking excitement and independence

—but most creative outlets were blocked. An affair was an easy way to register a protest and get the male approval she missed at home—but it was not a way to change her life.

For the rest of 1947, George changed jobs continuously, hoping to find something he would enjoy—but still thinking about the G. I. Bill and returning to college. According to George's recollection, Grace finally made the decision in January 1948. He would go back to the University of New Hampshire, she said. She would work, and though it would be hard financially, they'd manage.

According to Grace, however, George made the decision—perhaps because she still liked seeing him in a dominant role. In her account, George came home from work one morning, and announced he'd had enough of factory work. He would go to college and become a teacher.

Mired in a dead-end job herself, Grace liked the challenge, and the thought set her dreaming: They'd all move to Durham, she'd get a job, George would get a degree "and, at last, everything was going to be all right."

"All right"—the happily-ever-after dream Grace still nourished —proved to be, instead, months of confusion and trouble. The influx of veterans had more than doubled the university enrollment; Durham became so crowded that the Metaliouses could not even find housing together. Grace worked as an IBM operator at Westinghouse Electric Supply Company and lived in a furnished room at 372 East High, where the landlady did not allow children. Marsha and Mike, at ages five and one, had to be boarded out during the week.

On weekends the Metaliouses all lived together—but with George's mother. As usual, Grace and Helen did not get along —perhaps because Grace insisted on being an individual first, and then a wife and mother. After one argument during what Grace called "that ugly time," Grace packed up Marsha and Mike and took them to her High Street room. Luckily, her landlady was away for the weekend.

George accompanied them, reluctantly and mostly silently. At six that Friday evening he left, saying he was going back to college at Durham. Though he planned to look for family housing, he did not say so—and Grace concluded that he had no feelings.

Grace, Mike, and Marsha cuddled together in her one bed, making an adventure of necessity. When they trekked to Bunny's two-room apartment on Bowman Street the next morning, Grace had to heat Mike's bottle under the hot-water tap—and she never forgot her anger and desperation. She had no idea where George was; she felt sure he "didn't give a damn about me or the kids"; and she "tried all night to tell myself that I hated him." Around the same time she also planned to leave George—for she knew she could support the children herself: she'd done so all winter, and supported five people during the war. She was no dependent housewife.

But when George wrote her, the following week, that he'd found an apartment at Wentworth Acres in Portsmouth, a short drive from Durham, they became a family again. Grace continued working at Westinghouse, but for the first time they were part of campus life, living in a housing project occupied mostly by students.

They played bridge with their next-door neighbors, the husband a student, the wife a U.N.H. graduate who seemed to think her degree gave her the right to put on airs. Grace, irritated (and always feeling somewhat inadequate because she had no college background), waited for her chance—which came the night the wife discoursed on psychology. She particularly admired "those two fellows, Krafft and Ebing," the wife said—while Grace and George looked slyly at one another.

Finally Grace said, her voice sweetly modulated: "Don't you know that Krafft-Ebing is one person, not two?"

The wife was much abashed; Grace, quite pleased with herself. She was self-taught, and well read. She had always preferred reading to cleaning house. She also had verbal skills sufficient for any battle.

Like most returning veterans, George now found college work easy and enjoyable, but Grace felt overburdened as both housewife and breadwinner. She did all the child care, and held a series of "ghastly jobs in offices full of malevolent looking machines," she told Sidney Fields in 1958.

Since neither her checks nor George's G. I. payment ($110 a month) nor his occasional jobs "slinging hash" added up to enough, Grace also used her verbal skills to wheedle creditors—something she wanted George to do, in his role as protector. Since he would not play that strong man role, she considered him a failure, and kept telling herself, "It's not always going to be like this." She retreated into dreams and books and reading everything she could—including the student newspaper, *The New Hampshire*. Its picture of student life—student hijinks, sorority and fraternity rituals, jokes, sports, and trivia—must have seemed to Grace like news from another world.

While Grace and George struggled to find housing together, a *New Hampshire* editorial was devoting fierce criticism to the flying of paper airplanes in the freshmen dining halls. In January 1949, while Grace battled her mother-in-law, the *New Hampshire* began printing 4 x 5 pictures of different "Kampus Kittens"—with height, weight, hair and eye color, organizations, and relationship status ("going steady" or not). Occasionally the "Kitten," always a conventionally pretty student, listed her major as well, but not always —for women students were assumed to be pursuing a B.A. to get an "M.R.S." (Mrs.), or sometimes a "P.H.T." ("Putting Hubby Through").

Grace, a P.H.T. herself, hated that life—so different from her independent status during the war. The postwar women's image promoted in the media and in education had much more to do with the Kampus Kitten than with Rosie the Riveter, Katharine Hepburn, Rosalind Russell, or the suffragists of the 1920s. The image of the strong, achieving woman was being quickly, and forcefully, replaced by a domestic one: the loving sweetheart and devoted wife who lived only for (and through) others. When the rights of women were discussed at all, they were apt to be satirized.

Even women who remembered the days of "fighting feminism" supported domesticity after the war. The U.N.H. dean of women, for instance, had obviously come of age during the suffrage struggle. Miss Ruth J. Woodruff, whom *The New Hampshire* called "a trim little woman with a keen sense of humor," had degrees from Bryn Mawr and Radcliffe; she had been a U.N.H. administrator for eighteen years; and she was also an associate professor of economics. Yet "Miss Woodruff"—Dr. Woodruff, as a man with her credentials would normally be called—did not encourage U.N.H. women students to lead independent lives, as she had done.

Rather, they should live primarily to serve others, not to enlarge or enrich themselves, she told new women students in *The New Hampshire* of September 22, 1949. "After college," she wrote, "your reasonable expectation includes a period of employment, marriage, coping with meals and a budget, and at the same time serving as a motivating force in your community whose horizons today embrace the world." All women, it seemed, should follow this one pattern. There was no mention of the eccentric, ambitious individual who might consider domesticity and volunteer work too small a world.

Even women students themselves chose to limit their own horizons. In the fall of 1949 the Association of Women Students considered a curfew change for freshmen women from 8 o'clock on week nights to 8:30, so they could see the complete first feature at the Franklin Theatre and not have to leave in the middle of the picture.

After much debate, the Association of Women Students refused to change the rule.

The curfew, implying that women needed to be locked up and protected, encouraged early marriage—but so did virtually all the messages young women received. "Fulfillment as a woman had only one definition for American women after 1949—the housewife-mother" Betty Friedan points out in *The Feminine Mystique*.

By 1950 the median marriage age in the United States was twenty for women and twenty-two for men—the youngest in the history of the United States, and one of the youngest in the Western world. By the mid-1950s, 60 percent of American young women dropped out of college to marry. In the post-war baby boom, the American birth rate began to approach India's. Feminist ideas—careers rather than jobs, a variety of roles besides motherhood—withered.

The message appeared in all the media, especially in the 1950s. Movie stars appeared only in relation to men—Marilyn Monroe as sex symbol, Debbie Reynolds as the girl every boy wanted to take home to Mother. Newspaper articles about famous women mentioned their accomplishments as singers, writers, or actresses—but always showed them at home, amid husbands and babies and pots and pans, demonstrating their credentials as women. Women's magazines, once full of stories about intrepid heroines, world peace, and current issues, ran articles only about marriage, home, and family. The male editors of women's magazines—who had replaced the female editors of the 1930s and 1940s—told Betty Friedan: "Women can't take an idea, an issue, pure. It has to be translated in terms they can understand as women."

Men were to have the choice of careers; women had one career to choose. In his education courses, George Metalious learned about "functionalism"—the sociological theory that such institutions as marriage and the family survive as they do because they serve a needed function: Whatever is, is right. George learned that social science supported the feminine mystique: the man's place in the world; the woman's place in the home. Men were fulfilled through work; women, through husbands and children—and if women were not, Freudian theory assured everyone, they suffered from "penis envy." Anatomy was destiny.

Inequalities often seem muted on college campuses—where students take the same courses, share the same scholastic problems. But young women at U.N.H. had few role models for independence, though slightly older women—like Grace Metalious—were around as G.I. wives. The wives, generally, lived the feminine mystique, and expected other women to do the same—as Grace learned when she and George moved during the middle of his college career.

The housing project on College Road in Durham consisted of wooden barracks shipped from Fort Devens, where George had begun his military career. The barracks were drab buildings, each on a pile of sand, with eight small apartments on each side. Hordes of children played in the sand, and were constantly dirty. Indoors, the only heat came from kitchen stoves, with pipes all over the walls. The walls were thin enough to inspire a local joke: If a man in one apartment pounded his fist against the wall, he might find himself shaking hands with the couple next door.

The Metaliouses lived in Apartment E-6; Apartment E-11 was

occupied by Frederick Jervis, a young professor of psychology at the university, and his wife, Jan Williams, also a psychologist. Fred Jervis, who is blind, recalls vividly what other people said about Grace: She could not focus on the children or the house; she always seemed distracted; she had little sense of commitment to the children or the community. She did not fit the feminine mystique in attitude, or style. The neighbors criticized her for being unkempt, although the clothing that later became her trademark—rolled-up blue jeans, plaid flannel shirt—was the uniform everyone wore in the winter.

Grace and George were both loners, the neighbors felt, but Grace got much more condemnation for being "unfriendly" and "snobbish." She was "rough around the edges, and didn't dissimulate," Jan Williams recalls. "She didn't have time to stand under the clothesline, chatting." She had more important things to do.

She did sometimes share cigarettes and food with the neighbors. Toward the end of the month the Metaliouses were frequently reduced to spaghetti, low-budget casseroles, and soups concocted out of whatever Grace could find in the almost-bare cupboards. She never enjoyed cooking, and the food she most savored was out of her reach: Greek food and seafood. The children considered George a better cook.

Everyone on College Road was aware of the Metalious children, since everyone took care of them. Marsha and Mike would appear on other people's porches, their noses running with the cold, because Grace had locked them out. The neighbors watched them, and condemned Grace as a bad mother—but Jan Williams says now that Grace had a "singular purpose," to do something that was to her far more important.

Locked in the apartment, Grace was writing.

CHAPTER 5

"I am trapped, I screamed silently," Grace said later about the years at U.N.H. She had no silence except what she could make for herself, no privacy to let her mind grow. "I am trapped in a cage of poverty and mediocrity," she thought, "and if I don't get out, I'll die." Like the little girl who scribbled for hours in Aunt Georgie's bathtub, Grace Metalious at twenty-six turned with a kind of compulsion to her writing, as an escape.

What she was writing, no one knew—though years later, when *Peyton Place* appeared, people who scarcely knew the Metaliouses on College Road said, "So *that's* who lived in E-6." People who knew Grace slightly better were convinced that parts of *Peyton Place* were about themselves. At least a dozen College Road people thought they found themselves in the book. Some were flattered; more were angry.

Still, at the time Grace did have some companionship. Carl Siprelle, who later went to the University of Georgia's psychology department, was Grace and George's closest friend. Grace also shared confidences with Joy Reynolds, her next-door neighbor and closest companion, and when Betty Menge, another neighbor and the wife of a professor of education, needed an obstetrician, Joy and Grace both recommended Dr. Jesse Galt of Dover.

Grace knew about Dr. Galt, because during the second year at U.N.H., she had become pregnant again. In the fifties, the Pill and the I.U.D. were not yet available, abortion was thoroughly illegal, and big families were part of the American Dream. After wartime separations, G.I.s and their wives generally wanted to create the homes they had lost. The postwar baby boom hit even college campuses, where married student apartment buildings were frequently dubbed "Fertile Valley."

Though Grace knew childbirth could be dangerous for her, she disliked using a diaphragm; condoms were the only other reliable contraceptive. Their use of birth control was, George admits, "intermittent."

On July 11, 1950, Grace gave birth to another daughter, Cynthia Jean, by breech birth. Grace thought Cindy was a beautiful child, "all pink and white, with a pale blond fuzz of hair" and enormous eyes. Cindy was also the only Metalious child born without instrument marks on her face or head. But Grace had entered Wentworth Hospital in Dover on Sunday morning, and Cindy was not born until Tuesday afternoon—and in the interim, Grace nearly died. Years later, she told her friend Laurose Wilkens that she'd seen a tunnel and lights—she'd gone into death and come back to life.

Still unaware of Grace's struggle to give birth to Marsha, George took her to the hospital, then insisted on going home. He'd take care of Mike and Marsha, he said—and what good could he do Grace at the hospital?

When Grace awoke from the anesthetic, it was just as it had been with Mike: George wasn't there. "He doesn't really care enough," she thought. "I almost died having one of his children, and he doesn't really care." And George lacked the words to tell her how he felt.

When Grace returned to College Road with Cindy, she was too weak to keep house. George studied, went to classes, did the housework, took care of his wife and three children—and finally learned what Grace had concealed: that she'd almost died when Marsha was born, too.

When Cindy was four months old, Dr. Galt told Grace she must not have any more children. Grace laughed at first. She'd been told that before, she said, and she'd survived. But then Dr. Galt turned even more severe. "If you try to have another baby, you will rupture internally and be dead in a matter of six hours."

Grace stopped laughing, but it wasn't until the spring of 1951 that she agreed to have her tubes tied. She considered herself a failure as a woman.

"What are you squawking about?" Dr. Galt said in his gruff way. "You already have three children. Some women can't have any."

George assured her that if she'd been sterilized after Marsha, he would not have felt differently. "It was you that I loved and not the fact that you're a woman who can bear my children. I want you alive, not dead."

Grace agreed to the operation and went into the hospital—but George could visit her only a few times because of his work schedule. When George did visit, he was not as loving as Grace wanted him to be.

"So what!" he said when she mourned her loss of "womanhood." "As it is, I'll have to break my back for the rest of my life to take care of three kids. Thank God there aren't going to be any more."

To Grace his honesty seemed brutal, and seven years later she wrote that she had been screaming inside: "What about me? What about me?" She was full of self-pity: "Every single time you see a pregnant woman you wonder. And all the time you don't feel like a woman at all.

"You are sterile. Barren. Even an alley cat can reproduce her own kind, but you can't.

"You begin to look for a substitute. Somehow you are going to create something. And then one day you look at your typewriter."

As Grace described it, she began writing as a replacement for the fourth child she could never have. But on another occasion, she said that between 1938, when she was fourteen, and the time she published *Peyton Place* in 1956, she'd written some three hundred short stories. She'd always had the "singular purpose" Jan Williams noticed—but for a woman to have such a purpose in the early 1950s was very odd, if not un-American, subversive, or even Communist.

Just as they did after World War I, Americans in the second postwar era drew inward, suspicious of anything "foreign" or unusual. President Harry S Truman waged the Cold War, mostly with propaganda, against the Soviet Union and its satellites "behind the

Iron Curtain." Senators Joseph McCarthy of Wisconsin and Richard Nixon of California, among others, vigorously pursued evidence of the "Communist threat," denouncing anyone with suspicious ideas or associations.

In February 1950, while the student wives on College Road were struggling to survive on the G. I. Bill, McCarthy showed the Wheeling Women's Republican Club a list he said contained "205 known Communists" in the State Department. It was the first of many such dramatic announcements, and though McCarthy was eventually censured by the Senate in December 1954, his scare tactics had taught an effective lesson.

Meanwhile, Richard Nixon had made his name on the House Un-American Activities Committee, where he produced the Alger Hiss-Whittaker Chambers conspiracy case in 1948, sending Hiss to prison on evidence hidden in a pumpkin. In 1950 Nixon defeated his California opponent Helen Gahagan Douglas—one of very few women remaining in American politics—by circulating a "Pink Sheet" that claimed she had voted the same way as a "notorious communist-line congressman" from New York. Nixon called his opponent "The Pink Lady"; after he won the election, a small Southern California paper, the *Independent Review,* began to use the name "Tricky Dick."

The search for hidden "Communist" influences had touched the University of New Hampshire by 1949, George Metalious' second year, when the university's president, Arthur Stanton Adams, assured a state committee there was no evidence of "subversive" activity on his campus. Yet G. Harris Daggett, an assistant professor of English, was apparently denied promotion to the next rank because of his membership in the Progressive Party—or so *The New Hampshire* reported in May 1949. Daggett's fight for his academic reputation continued for several years (and a meeting room at the U.N.H. Library is now named after him).

Communists and "fellow travelers"—such as members of Leftwing political parties—were believed to threaten the "American way of life," a rarely defined system of beliefs that included, for women, the feminine mystique. Pictures of "unfeminine" Soviet women—large, overweight by American standards, unfashionably dressed, and working at difficult jobs—appeared in American news media to show the dangers of "creeping socialism." Soviet women's place was not solely in the home. Though encouraged to have children, they were also expected to contribute to the world outside. By American standards, they lacked "femininity": Neither passive nor vulnerable, they did not devote all their lives to pleasing and serving others.

The feminine mystique for women and McCarthyism for men (and some women) proved to be, like the Soviet values they were supposed to fight, powerful tools for thought control. Both enforced the major American value for the Silent Generation of the 1950s: conformity.

Grace Metalious, however, did not conform. When she wrote self-pityingly about not being able to have more children, she did say what "feminine" women were expected to say—since the secret of "feminine fulfillment" was to consist in having children. But not contributing to the birth rate and not conforming to feminine behavior patterns gave Grace an opportunity, which she recognized and used by spending hours at her typewriter, creating herself as a writer, choosing her own destiny.

George recalls that Grace, always the dreamer, could be an entertaining storyteller for children. But her stories for adults tended to be too juvenile, their plots all the same feminine wish-fulfillments: A poor little heroine meets a strong handsome hero who sets everything right. Still, such stories were staples in American magazines, since they expressed the conventional view of women's destiny. By the end of 1949, as Betty Friedan shows, only one out of three heroines in women's magazines had a career (and by 1958–59, only one out of a hundred).

In finding Grace's early stories uninteresting, George reveals the gulf separating the masculine and feminine worlds of the 1950s—identity through work for men, and fulfillment through husband, home, and children for women. If she is not to have a career, a woman needs the perfect man, to define her life for her. After Cindy's birth, however, Grace began more and more to define her own life—and her fiction became less conventional, and more interesting to both sexes.

Her first short story in the new vein involved a little boy, Norman Page. Delicate and timid, Norman was overprotected by his mother, who—like George's mother—feared his associating with other children and getting hurt. Norman's mother let him play with girls, but not with tough, rough boys. So Norman became an observer rather than a participant in life, and he liked to watch Hester Goodale, the old spinster who lived in the house across the street, alone except for her big black cat. The town children considered her a witch (not an uncommon fantasy about a nonconforming woman who lives by herself).

In Grace's original story, Norman and his girlfriend undergo several "scary" experiences, before they solve a mystery about Miss Goodale's cat. Later, with very adult, gothic additions—voyeurism, kinky mother-love, cat strangulation, and Miss Hester's death while watching an act of cunnilingus—Norman Page's story became part of *Peyton Place*.

At U.N.H. Grace also drew inspiration from a real-life story. A local music teacher, said to be homosexual, committed suicide—fearing discovery, everyone assumed. Grace's story describes David Strong, a music teacher who considers himself different from others, more sensitive. Grace knew about music from Bob Athearn, and about the oppression of homosexuals from her pal Marc. Eventually her David Strong admits his homosexuality—and then commits suicide.

The David Strong story ultimately formed part of Grace's own favorite novel, *The Tight White Collar*.

Writing about little boys and male homosexuals, Grace extended her range, though she continued to identify with the outsider, the character dependent on others for approval. Neither David Strong nor Norman Page fits the standard male role—the breadwinner, the positive, rational, and invulnerable man—who was the masculine counterpart to the feminine mystique. Like most writers, Grace found androgynous characters who depart from conventional sex roles more interesting—and as she gained the ability to see the world through other people's eyes, she gained power as a writer.

At the same time, during the fall of 1950, Grace wrote a story set in a small New England town, with a mill the only important industry—much like the locale for *The Tight White Collar*. Her town's thorough dependence on the mill echoed the relationship between Manchester and the Amoskeag. Grace could draw on George's experiences at the Limerick Yarn Mill, as well as her grandmothers' at the Amoskeag, and later she described the terrible side of mill work in *No Adam in Eden*.

Her last 1950 story centered on a doctor, one of many in her fiction, mostly the same type: gruff, profane, and blustery—but tender-hearted underneath. Grace's interest in medicine came earliest from her Aunt Georgie, the physical therapist, intrigued by the workings of the human body. Aunt Georgie, born in the suffrage generation, had wanted further medical training, but the Depression had made that impossible—and had probably produced her strong and unfulfilled wish to send Grace to college.

Grace's fictional doctors, in any case, are all male, and George believes that Dr. Deitch, who delivered both Grace and Marsha, was the ultimate real-life model for Grace's medical men. But U.N.H. people cite Dr. George McGregor, an unconventional character known to everyone around Durham.

Doc McGregor, whom local residents recall as a "jewel in the rough," rarely minced words: With new patients, Doc McGregor gave his common greeting, "What the hell do you want?" Doc reportedly smoked a cigar while operating, and was oblivious to ashes dropping in incisions. Still, he was greatly admired: a medical building in Durham is now named after him, and for a while his portrait hung in a local bank.

In Grace's story, a generous and humanitarian doctor resembling Dr. Swain in *Peyton Place* and Dr. Southworth in *No Adam in Eden* delivers a Mongoloid (Down's syndrome) baby. The story eventually became another part of *The Tight White Collar,* with the major doctor's name "Jess Cameron," a possible echo of Grace's obstetrician Jesse Galt. But the story's situation closely resembles what Grace observed in 1950—for Doc McGregor and his wife had a Down's syndrome child named Robin.

Dr. McGregor's wife devoted herself to Robin until the girl's adolescence, when she was sent away to school. In *The Tight White Collar,* a young wife guiltily insists on caring for her Down's syndrome daughter by herself, though the task of being a loving mother—fitting the feminine image—almost destroys her marriage and herself. Probably to keep Robin McGregor firmly in mind, Grace called her own fictitious child "Robin"—but her practice of not changing characters' names eventually caused enormous trouble (and a libel suit) with *Peyton Place*.

When Grace decided to write a novel in the winter of 1950–51 while George was finishing his junior year, she included three of her four short stories in a novel about a college town. She invented two working titles for her unpublished works, "The Tree and the Blossom" and "The Quiet Place," and shifted stories between the two. She also thought about publication, but sent nothing to magazines or publishers. She was not yet ready to attempt the leap from amateur to professional. (A fear of that commitment, Betty Friedan says in *The Feminine Mystique,* makes so many housewives "fool themselves about the writer or actress they might have been.")

Grace needed another push—which came after the Metaliouses left the relatively protected college community and Grace was plunged fully into a role she detested: "Mrs. Schoolteacher."

By the time George finished his practice teaching, the Metaliouses owed the University $300 for tuition. He could not have his degree until the bill was paid, and without his degree he could not teach—so Grace, grumbling but resourceful, borrowed $300 from a friend of Laurette's. At George's baccalaureate, Dr. Abram L. Sachar, president of Brandeis University, spoke; George's commencement speaker was the University president—but Grace never got to see George graduate.

He had been hired to teach social studies in the high school at Belmont, New Hampshire, a village of several hundred souls, seven miles south of Laconia, in the Lakes Region of north central New Hampshire. George would earn $2,500 a year, with another $100 for coaching basketball—making $92 twice a month for the family's net income. The basketball money usually went for babysitters, since the girl cheerleaders had to have a chaperone for out-of-town games. Grace, as coach's wife, was elected.

Through the winter of 1952–53, Grace despised being a schoolteacher's wife. Except for Durham, which as a college community was full of transients, she had never lived in a really small town. Manchester is New Hampshire's largest city, with big-city anonymity and relative tolerance. Like many urban wives in the fifties who rushed to suburbia because it "was better for the kids," Grace found that physical space did not give mental space. In fact, it seemed to do the opposite, for constant scrutiny meant a narrower code of behavior, less margin for eccentricity—especially for the mother of three children and the wife of a schoolteacher.

Lack of money distressed Grace, but she was used to that. She could also cope with George's immersion in work and long absences from the family: Like many wives, she had grown used to living in a separate world. What disturbed her most was the role she had to play: "I did not like belonging to Friendly Clubs and Bridge Clubs. I did not like being regarded as a freak because I spent time in front of a typewriter instead of a sink. And George did not like my not liking the things I was supposed to like."

One picture from that era, later printed in *Cosmopolitan,* shows the Metaliouses playing their roles at a school function. George converses happily with three young women students, all standing over a buffet table. Grace, her hair in her characteristic ponytail and dressed in a proper white blouse and dark skirt, wears a tentative smile but stands slightly behind George—as if hiding.

By this time, much of her psychic life went into her writing. She felt she and George had little in common besides the children, and they had trouble communicating. "I have always thought, and still do," she wrote about that time in 1958, "that the degeneration of a relationship between two people is the most horrible sight in the world to watch, let alone live through."

To escape either watching or living it, she avoided arguments and "ran to my work more and more. I tried to escape from reality by writing oceans of words."

Meanwhile, at twenty-eight, Grace was reaching one of the critical stages in adult life—what Gail Sheehy in *Passages* terms "the Catch-30 phase." That passage, most commonly spanning the years between twenty-eight and thirty-two, often involves turmoil, change, crisis—"and the urge to break out." One common reaction to this urge, Sheehy notes, is to tear up the life put together during one's twenties by embarking on a new direction, a new marriage, or both—all in an opening-up process that often does not end until the early forties (a serene phase Grace Metalious did not live to see).

For men, Catch-30 often means the final choice of vocation. For women authors, it often means making a serious commitment to writing. Edith Wharton published her first adult story, "Mrs. Manstey's View," when she was thirty; Dorothy Parker's first volume of poems, *Enough Rope,* appeared when she was thirty-three; Erica Jong changed direction, from poetry to *Fear of Flying,* at thirty-one. But Wharton, Parker, and Jong all lived in New York, were comfortably middle class, knew the publishing world—and had no children.

For a woman confined to the feminine sphere but finished with childbearing, the Catch-30 question is typically, "What do I do next?" As Friedan notes, many women during the era of the feminine mystique turned to affairs, alcoholism, and suicide—all of which Grace Metalious tried, later on.

But first she tried the more positive path, committing herself to an unusual degree. Sheehy shows that the willingness to risk is usually based on "a history of accomplishments"—which Wharton, Parker, and Jong all had as writers. But apart from the high school plays she produced before marriage, war, and motherhood intervened, Grace had no such history, and no connections.

What she had was an extraordinary will to emancipate herself— and it impelled her to try to sell her novel.

She had moderate encouragement from George when she sent a ninety-seven-page manuscript, *The Forbidden Fruit,* to Simon and Schuster publishers. She mailed the manuscript, containing some of her U.N.H. stories, on May 25, 1953—and it immediately landed in the "slush pile," the collection of unsolicited manuscripts that a few underpaid publishers' readers plow through, trying to find something publishable. (The chances of getting such an "over-the-transom" submission published have been estimated at one in 20,000.)

When Grace heard nothing within a month, she came to New York—"in a swivet," recalls Oliver Swan, the agent whose office she visited on June 30. Somehow she had learned that authors need agents to sell their work—to open doors to editors, to keep abreast of what publishers are buying. Seeing an agent marked another step in committing herself to professional writing.

Grace Metalious seemed very young to Ollie Swan—like "a

freckle-faced kid of seventeen," he recalled later. She seemed naïve, sincere, and likable, with a definite vulnerability. She was also very oddly dressed for New York, in her blue jeans.

She was worried about her manuscript and wanted it back from Simon and Schuster, she said. Swan called the publishers for her, and learned that a reader had found the manuscript unsuitable. It was returned by messenger, and Swan himself did not read it.

Meanwhile, Grace Metalious had written her name on a card, to make sure Swan had the correct spelling. Later she sent a few short pieces which did not impress him, and he returned them, unsold. When he next heard of her, she and George had made the headlines: "TEACHER FIRED FOR WIFE'S BOOK"—in the Boston newspapers he read while on vacation in Boothbay Harbor, Maine. Grace was the notorious author of *Peyton Place*—and someone else's client.

While Grace was seeing her first literary ambitions blocked, George had found another job. After a summer as a delivery man for a Laconia dairy, he began teaching at Coe-Brown Academy, a private school in Northwood, New Hampshire, about twenty miles southeast of Belmont, on the road to Durham.

During the summer Grace had taken the children—now three, six, and nine—for picnics and swimming, and they enjoyed such excursions. Meanwhile, she had her writing as an escape, but George had nothing, and the tensions between them increased. George talked—idly, Grace thought—of dropping everything and going to California (not an uncommon impulse during the Catch-30 phase).

But after George had been teaching at Coe-Brown for three weeks, Grace suddenly realized he had not just been speculating. He announced that he was fed up with teaching. He wanted to go to Florida.

That sounded like a good idea to Grace, who had always had a hankering for escape.

One Sunday morning they quickly packed the car, telling nobody, and took off for the South. Sleeping in the car most of the time and living on hamburgers, they saw Miami, the Gulf of Mexico, the bayou country of Louisiana (where they slept on the beach, near the shrimp boats), and Texas. While the leaves were changing color and falling in New England, the Metaliouses reveled in the Sunbelt, though some of them enjoyed it more than others.

"The kids thought it was one long picnic," Grace recalled later, "a sort of glorified camping out, but by the time we left Florida and headed West the novelty had worn off for George and me." She still liked the idea—"the only crazy, impulsive thing that George and I ever did together"—but criticized George's lack of humor. "Things that had the kids and me in hysterics would leave George absolutely cold, so our trip was mostly made in strained silence."

Marsha, the only one old enough to remember much, especially enjoyed living on a boat near Seattle. Then, after three weeks in an apartment, the parents decided, according to Grace, that "New Hampshire was the only place for us after all." She wired a friend in the East for money to come home—but then tried one more alternative.

Grace's old friend and musical mentor from Manchester, Bob Athearn, had moved out West after the war. He and Luce had been divorced; Luce joined various Left-wing causes in the East. In Butte, Montana, Bob and his second wife, Dora, and their two sons lived in a tall, turreted house at the top of a mountain. One day Bob got a mysterious phone call: "Is this the residence of Bob Athearn?" the operator asked. Bob said yes, and the party at the other end hung up.

The next day Bob was teaching music in their home studio when he saw a car come slowly up the street, bearing New Hampshire plates. A round female figure dashed from the car, and when Bob opened the front door, Grace threw her arms around him—and asked if they could stay with the Athearns until she got money from home. Amused, Bob agreed, and he and Dora dragged out mattresses for all five kids to stay upstairs.

Grace and George had completely run out of money in Spokane, they explained—hence the mysterious phone call. They stayed for a week or two, admiring the West, and Bob took George to visit the Montana School of Mines and the superintendent of schools. George learned that he could have a teaching position, if he wanted it.

Grace, who seemed to Bob as bright and sharp as ever, chattered happily (and now insisted that she never wore underpants). Still rebellious, she left much of the child care to George, and both were permissive parents by fifties standards. One time Marsha, thoroughly naked, came downstairs from the kids' lair to ask a question. Grace and George answered without, apparently, noticing her attire, and Marsha scampered back upstairs.

Though George wanted to stay in Butte, Grace finally insisted she had to get back to New Hampshire to finish her novel because she could write it nowhere else. She also told Bob a great deal about the novel, and he said it sounded too idealistic to him—and when *Peyton Place* came out, with much more sex and violence, he wondered if his comments had influenced the course of the book. (But Grace's friend Marc thinks the untitled book that Grace discussed with Bob Athearn became *No Adam in Eden*—a book full of bitter disillusionment, the other side of idealism.)

In the West, the Metaliouses also saw the Hoover Dam, gambled at Las Vegas, and admired the Painted Desert and the Grand Canyon. But Marsha remembers most that the kids didn't have to go to bed any special time, and could choose what they wanted to do.

"We want to go to the movies!" they demanded at one stop.

"We don't have much money," Grace told them, "so you have a choice. You can go to the movies or you can eat."

"We want to go to the movies!"

They sat through the movie several times: *Latin Lovers,* a romance with Ricardo Montalban and Lana Turner (whose acting career was later resurrected with *Peyton Place*). Their stomachs growled more and more through each showing, but they had to have their money's worth.

They drove back through the Dakotas, skirted Chicago, took the newly constructed Pennsylvania Turnpike, and traveled on into New York City, where Grace stopped off, ostensibly to try to find a job. She stayed with Marc, who had gone to New York as a designer. Jay had become a radio announcer—and only Grace had not achieved her high school ambition, to be an actress. She told Marc she was thinking of leaving George—and a job would mean independence.

Meanwhile, the children and George went to Manchester, where —Marsha remembers—they lived with a false name on the mailbox. Mysterious men would come to the door and ask for Marsha's parents, and wonder why she was not in school.

Later she learned that the mysterious men were seeking Grace. Before the Metaliouses left on their jaunt, Grace had passed a bad check, and now George told police he had no idea where his wife had gone.

Meanwhile, Grace said later, she waited to hear from George, who had promised to write as soon as he got to his mother's. After ten days of silence, Grace felt sure something terrible had happened, and called. His mother did not want to let Grace speak to him, and when George finally came to the phone, Grace recalled later, "He told me that I shouldn't have been so dumb as to call, that if anything had been wrong he would have called me."

Grace had wanted reassurance: George focused on facts. Grace began to cry and insist, "But, darling, I love you."

"Ditto," George said—his usual answer when Grace said, "I love you." It saved time, he said.

But his first response—that she shouldn't have called—was a crushing blow. "I have been slapped a few times in my lifetime," Grace said later, "but never to equal this verbal punch in the mouth."

Eventually Grace did go home and Bernard Snierson, a Laconia lawyer she called, extricated her from the bad-check charge. She had postdated a check—not a criminal offense. (Later, in an apparent burst of bravado, Grace told Sidney Fields that she had been jailed, and he published that in a syndicated series.)

"I cannot bear to go through the time after I came home," Grace wrote later. George worked as a cab driver and short-order cook; Grace worked as a clerk. With help from Grandmother DeRepentigny and Aunt Georgie, Grace managed to find a small apartment and rescue her furniture from Northwood. Grace called it their "time to pay the piper" for their jaunt across the country —but more penance remained.

In April 1954 George took a teaching job at the State School for the mentally retarded in Laconia, and the Metaliouses returned to Belmont, renting a small four-room upstairs apartment in an oversized white wooden house on Church Street.

There Grace ran into the weight of small-town disapproval for being "different," for having run away from responsibilities. "If you think that going back to a small New England town is easy after you have done something unconventional, I'd advise you for your own sake not to try it," Grace said later. From Mrs. Schoolteacher, she became Mrs. Crazy—if not Mrs. Public Enemy.

What happened, she said, resembled what Quakers call "shunning," or the British "being sent to Coventry": social ostracism. In particular, Grace—already considered a poor housekeeper and bad mother—was blamed, and neighbors agreed it must have been "Grace's crazy idea," to go running off across the country, because "good old rocklike George" could never have thought of such a thing. George had violated his job responsibilities, but Grace—in fifties' terms—had violated her femininity. Women, perhaps threatened themselves by the presence of someone who did not think woman's place was in the home, were especially critical. Though George told her to ignore the gossip, Grace—always sensitive to criticism—could not.

Soon their Belmont landlord became anxious about renting to people who were so "unreliable." Besides, he said, the noise of Grace's typewriter disturbed him and his wife at night. Grace, George, Marsha, Mike, and Cindy were told to find another place to live.

By that time, news that Grace Metalious was writing a novel had gotten around Belmont and the neighboring communities. It was whispered that she was writing about local people, and that she was negotiating with a publisher. Scenting a story, Laurose Wilkens, a reporter for the Laconia *Evening Citizen,* went to interview the notorious Grace Metalious.

It was Grace's first encounter with the media.

CHAPTER 6

"It did not take long," Laurie Wilkens wrote in the Laconia *Evening Citizen,* "to realize that Grace Metalious was an extraordinary woman of brilliant intellect."

Laurie first visited Grace when it was rumored that a New York publisher wanted a novel Grace had written. "And the assignment turned out to be a pleasure," Laurie wrote. "The slender young girl with the flashing brown eyes asked us in. We were given a cup of coffee and the hospitality of the house."

As for the novel Grace was writing: "It took only a short perusal of the script freely presented for our appraisal to know that here was a real novel, written by a gifted person." That particular novel, then called *The Quiet Place,* was never published—but in the meantime Laurie Wilkens became Grace's closest friend, companion, and sounding board. Laurie was also Grace's guide to the ways of Gilmanton, the tiny village six miles southeast of Laconia that had been the Wilkenses' home for the previous seven years.

The only child of a wealthy New York family, Laurie had traveled to Europe and grown up with servants. She had attended Sweet Briar College, graduated from Barnard, thought about a career in journalism—and then turned her back on the upper-class New York world. After she married Bill Wilkens, they bought a 200-year-old farmhouse in New Hampshire, on a large plot of land that Laurie, wondering if they'd ever succeed in farming, dubbed "Shaky Acres." There they settled down to raise four children, later adopting a fifth.

Among people whose ancestors had always lived in the area, the Wilkenses were outsiders—like the Metaliouses. Laurie, who had golden hair, bright blue eyes, and an infectious enthusiasm for anything different, was eleven years older than Grace—but they shared interests in music, theater, and literature. For the first time in her small-town life, Grace Metalious could talk about the books she loved.

A compulsive reader who would read cereal boxes if she had nothing else, Grace especially admired F. Scott Fitzgerald's writing (and echoes his style in parts of *No Adam in Eden*). She loved W. Somerset Maugham's writings, so different and so English—and found Sadie Thompson, the incorrigible shady lady in his story *Rain,* a fascinating character. She admired Maugham's Rosie, in *Cakes and Ale:* lively, sensual, generous, a thorough mystery to the male narrator—who muses about the writer as "the only free man." Rosie inspires—but men create.

Rosie, Sadie, and Fitzgerald's heroines all appear through men's eyes, as images with a mysterious attraction. They appear mainly in relation to men, not as independent individuals, and the reader does not get the women's own point of view. Nor did Grace read enough women authors to see a woman writer's point of view, though she did read women's life stories—notably Diana Barrymore's *Too Much Too Soon,* a story of the actress' alcoholism and self-destruction. Grace enjoyed murder mysteries and magazines and the New York *Times*—and loved Ben Hecht's autobiography, *A Child of the Century,* with his speculations about God, writing, anti-Semitism, Hollywood, and sex, the last a rather taboo subject in the fifties.

Grace and Laurie also talked about *Kings Row,* Henry Bellamann's popular 1940 novel about scandalous secrets in a small town. In *Kings Row* an adolescent girl has an incestuous relationship with her father; a malicious doctor unnecessarily amputates a young playboy's legs. (Ronald Reagan played the playboy Drake McHugh in the movie version, still Reagan's favorite role. The title of Reagan's autobiography comes from Drake's first words when he wakes up legless: *Where's the Rest of Me?*)

In *Kings Row,* shack dwellers show more nobility than the most prosperous people in town, including a corrupt businessman who has a clandestine affair with a mulatto schoolteacher. The teacher is Melissa St. George—the maiden name of the heroine (Lisa Pappas) in Grace's third novel, *The Tight White Collar.* The businessman is named Peyton.

While Grace talked about *Kings Row* and Maugham and Fitzgerald, everyone else in Belmont, Gilmanton, and Laconia seemed to be talking about Grace's novel-in-progress, which she continued typing. When the Belmont landlord decided to evict the Metaliouses, Grace's reaction was the usual: "George, *do* something!" —but it was Laurie who found them a new place to live.

The Metaliouses stayed, briefly, in a 150-year-old house at Gilmanton Corners, the intersection of routes 107 and 140 across from the village store—and then they moved to Laurie's "find."

The new place resembled a Hansel and Gretel house: sharply pitched roof, miniature rooms added on at odd angles because a Mrs. Stickney, who had built the house, wanted more space for her many foster children. She had also planted flowers everywhere and installed four bird houses—all of them knocked down by Mike, a mischievous child, within a few days after the Metaliouses moved in. There was a stone well and a pine grove in back, and the house was neatly tucked away on a dirt road in Gilmanton, three miles from the blacktop.

It was also little more than a shack. Doors swayed on the hinges; windows fell out of their frames. The windows opened in winter and refused to close; in summer, they refused to open at all. Nor did the asbestos siding provide much insulation. Still, the house had a rustic charm, it rented for $35 a month, and in front of it stood a sign, "It'll Do."

"It'll Do" belonged to Curtis McClary, a local farmer whose brother Bertrude had lived in the house before the Metaliouses moved in. Would they mind if Bert continued to stay in one room? No, he was welcome.

They moved to "It'll Do" in the fall of 1954, a particularly beautiful autumn—much like Grace's descriptions of Indian summer in *The Tree and the Blossom,* the working title for her novel-in-progress (similar descriptions appear in *Peyton Place*). Grace considered the elm tree in front of "It'll Do" the most beautiful tree she'd ever seen, and called it "the only magic thing" about the house.

Despite its obvious failings, the children loved "It'll Do." Cindy, a chubby, blonde four-year-old at the time, feels they had the most fun as a family then: hiding coins in baked potatoes, and eluding the bees that seemed to consider Marsha and Cindy's upstairs room their home. For adults, though, the house was less pleasant—especially when the well went dry, as it often did in the summer.

George, meanwhile, had his contract renewed for a second year at the State Training School, and made a new friend. Tom Makris, a big, handsome fellow teacher recently graduated from Ithaca College, became George's hunting companion. Makris gathered that George was unhappy with life at "It'll Do"—and perhaps with Grace as well—and talked it over with a friend, Louise Riegel.

On a good-will errand, Louise Riegel went to see the famed would-be authoress and notoriously poor housekeeper Grace Metalious—and was shocked at what she saw.

"It was a little shanty house," she recalled in 1979, "with dirty dishes everywhere." Everything was covered with grime and dirt—except one spotless corner, where Grace kept her typewriter.

"Grace, you must be out of your mind!" Louise cried.

"Let's not talk about it now," Grace replied, friendly and matter-of-fact, and began to make coffee.

But Louise refused to touch anything in the house. According to local gossip, George rarely brought friends home because the house was so dirty and Grace was always in her sloppy blue jeans. Louise now believed what she'd heard (but had no inkling that Grace might prefer being alone with her typewriter, and that George might support her choice).

Over the next months, Louise tried to befriend Grace—and change her. Grace's singular purpose as a writer left Louise unmoved. What did a clean typewriter corner matter, Louise demanded, if the rest of the house was filthy? Why couldn't Grace just settle down to being a good wife and mother, like everyone else?

Louise also invited Grace for dinner, hoping to inspire her with visions of gracious living. Louise carefully left out her silver tea set, "to show Grace what a nice life was like."

Grace acquired no new yearnings for gentility.

She remained friendly and affectionate toward Louise, "but her hands were always dirty," Louise recalls. One time Louise even asked, "Grace, don't you believe in grooming?"

"Louise, I'm not you," Grace said.

Nor was she much like anyone else—although Laurie Wilkens did seem to complement her creative side and her eccentric sense of humor. When they weren't going barefoot, men's shirts hanging out over their blue jeans, they wore slave sandals, laced halfway up their legs. They laughed at their "beatnik" appearance, and egged each other on. Grace and Laurie rarely disagreed, and Laurie recalls only one piece of advice Grace ever gave her, after a trying barnyard bout: "Get rid of those chickens!"

Grace also began spending more and more time at the Wilkens' farmhouse, where Laurie had a long, big, comfortable country kitchen, and they could sit in rocking chairs in front of the fireplace.

"There was always excitement about her," Laurie remembers. "Everything was a lark." Sometimes they spent whole days and evenings together, sharing a bag of potato chips, a tin of chive cheese, and one quart of beer, since neither drank very much. Occasionally, George and Bill Wilkens would come, too, and watch television in the kitchen while the women talked.

Grace and Laurie took their children on excursions to concerts and picnics whenever they could. Joanne Wilkens, thirteen in 1954, remembers Grace's infectious enthusiasm: "Will you come?" she'd say, leaning forward, warmth in her dark eyes. "We'll have fun."

On winter nights at Laurie's, she and Grace played games, especially when the McClary brothers, Bert and Curt, came to visit. One favorite was a marathon, night-after-night song contest, in which the winner had to come up with a song none of the others had ever heard. Grace particularly enjoyed the game, since she knew peculiar ditties few other people knew, but on one occasion Curt vanquished them all with the "Prune Song," which reduced Grace to helpless laughter.

No matter how young a prune may be,
He's always full of wrinkles. . . .
Some folks wear them on their face;
Prunes wear them everyplace. . . .

Another game was to name "the most gross ornament" the players had ever seen—such as a self-satisfied Venus with a clock embedded in her belly. They spent hours describing greater and greater degrees of tackiness. There were contests to select "the most asinine song," and one strong candidate was "the itsy-bitsy spider climbed up the water spout," the kiddie song they all loathed.

Grace and Laurie read together, and sometimes Grace would become excited and enthusiastic. "You've *got* to see this!" she'd exclaim, grabbing Laurie's arm, shaking her finger in Laurie's face.

At other times, they worked together. As they sat, Laurie would read aloud what Grace had written—to get a feel for the weight, the sentence rhythms, the sound of the prose. Grace loved to hear her words in Laurie's voice—and much later, local gossip had it that Laurie and/or George had actually written *Peyton Place* (possibly because they had more formal education than Grace did).

For a while, George contributed to the confusion, for he says (in *The Girl from "Peyton Place"*) that *Peyton Place* began as his and Grace's collaboration, but that Grace also discussed her work with a friend—and "did not, as was planned, tell anyone that George was helping her and collaborating with her. It seemed judicious to George for Grace to garner the full glory and therefore 'find herself.'"

But Grace told interviewers about the sessions in Laurie's kitchen; fragments of the manuscript are in Grace's handwriting; and Grace had typed the pages Laurie read aloud in her kitchen. Grace would live her characters, think out entire chapters, recite them aloud—and then write them down. About *Peyton Place* she said later, "I thought twenty-four hours a day for a year. I wrote ten hours a day for two and a half months."

Asked in 1978 about his role, George Metalious said, "Let's

just say Grace wrote *Peyton Place*. That's the easiest way to say it."

In any case, George contributed what most wives do for author-husbands: he did the cooking, whatever cleaning got done, and housework—while Grace composed, her battered manual type-writer on her lap, because she had no desk. George collaborated by making his wife's work possible—in a way that was far from usual for men in the fifties. Grace recognized his contribution when, later, she dedicated the first editions of *Peyton Place* to George, "For All The Reasons he knows so well."

Laurie knew a great deal about the Laconia-Gilmanton-Belmont area, and she shared local lore with Grace as they rocked by the fire. Grace listened, fascinated, and one story particularly caught her attention.

When Laurie had just begun the farming business at "Shaky Acres" in the spring of 1947, she mentioned to a neighbor that she wanted to buy sheep. The neighbor sent Laurie to see a family in Gilmanton Iron Works, a village six miles down the road. The Glenns lived slightly off the main road, with what looked like a sheep pen rather distant from the house.

When Laurie went to inquire, a beautiful brown-eyed girl with long dark hair said they had no sheep for sale—"Nothing for sale," she insisted. She wore a pretty purple dress, which Laurie noticed because it seemed so incongruous.

"She gave me a creepy feeling," Laurie told her neighbor—and within a few months she found out why.

Jane Glenn, the odd and beautiful girl who answered the door, ran the Glenn household and worked in a mill near Laconia. Her older sister and two brothers had grown up and moved away; her mother, whom neighbors remembered fondly, had died some ten years before, and Jane was raising her younger brother Orly—staying at home because "I can't leave Orly to face things alone," she once told the town police chief, Frank Dowst.

Their father, Martin Glenn, had been something of a fixture around the post office, where he sat on the steps and entertained his neighbors with tall tales about seafaring adventures. Neighbors remembered him as slight, mild-mannered, and inordinately fond of his ten-gallon hat.

Since he was often away with the Merchant Marine for months at a time, his long absence was not particularly noted—until his two older sons came home for a visit and wondered why he had not written them for some time. Eventually they learned the reason from their sister Jane, and in September 1947 the Laconia *Evening Citizen* ran an enormous headline: "Gilmanton Girl Confesses Shooting Father Last Christmas."

Jane was charged with shooting her father and burying his body underneath the sheep pen in the family barn. Though it had been two days before Christmas, the warmth of the sheep kept that ground from freezing. Her brother Orly, sixteen, helped her. In her confession Jane told the county solicitor, William W. Keller, that she shot her father because he "threatened her with harm" when she failed to meet him at the railroad station on his return from a voyage. Earlier she had told Police Chief Dowst about "intolerable conditions" during her father's visits home.

The story became an immediate sensation in the local press: "Jane, Quiet Black-Clad Girl of 20, Tells Where She Dragged Dad's Body"; "Jane Hunted Chief Night She Killed Dad"; and even "Jane's Fan Mail Heavy." Then the legal processes followed: "Jane Reported Sane by Tests"; "Brother and Sister Indicted for Second-Degree Murder"; "Family Behind Jane and Orly to Limit, Says Brother." Jane seemed more concerned for Orly than for herself, reporters noticed.

Early in December, Jane and her defense lawyer, F. A. Normandin of Laconia, made their way to the courthouse for the trial. Arlene Rowe, then an eighteen-year-old secretary newly hired by the firm and also dark-haired and dark-eyed, was mistaken for Jane and besieged by reporters demanding pictures and quotes.

But no trial ever took place, for Jane pleaded guilty to first-degree manslaughter, receiving a minimum prison sentence. Orly, also pleading guilty, was put on probation and sent to an institution. "Family pride," the Laconia *Evening Citizen* reported, motivated Jane to plead guilty and "avoid taking the stand to reveal the sordid details of an unhappy childhood and young womanhood"—and to spare her brothers and sister similar ordeals.

The truth soon became known: Martin Glenn had been sexually molesting his daughter since she was thirteen—and had reportedly also abused his older daughter and threatened violence to his sons. Jane Glenn had killed her father in self-defense—and few people in the area condemned her for it.

After her prison sentence, Jane married and moved away—but the story of "the sheep pen murders" remained in the local lore that Grace Metalious heard in Laurie Wilkens' kitchen.

Certain details etched themselves in Grace's mind: the beautiful girl, the evil father, the sheep pen, the frightened brother protected by his sister—and rape as seen through the eyes of the victim. The Jane Glenn story made its way into *The Tree and the Blossom,* and then into *Peyton Place* as the story of Selena Cross —but it also reminded Grace of a story in Bellamann's *Kings Row,* of another beautiful girl who becomes her father's victim.

Like many exposés of small town life, *Kings Row* had shocked its first readers and been immensely popular. By the time Grace's friend Marc read the book in 1943, it had gone through eighteen printings. Carolyn Rhodes, later an English professor at Old Dominion University, recalls that it was considered a "wicked" book —like Sherwood Anderson's *Winesburg, Ohio* in 1919. Anderson and Bellamann, like Sinclair Lewis, attacked bourgeois hypocrisies and showed the sordid motives—sex, money, power—dominating people's actions. All three novelists contributed to American writers' "revolt from the village." But until *Peyton Place,* the dissectors of village personalities and mores were virtually all men. Though interested in women characters, the male novelists in revolt rarely portrayed women from the inside, nor made them their central figures.

Kings Row's central figure, Parris Mitchell (played by Robert Cummings in the 1942 film version) is a philosophical child who, like Grace's Norman Page, seems destined to be an observer more than a participant in life. He studies medicine with Dr. Alexander Q. Tower (Claude Rains), who apparently has no patients, and seems to conduct mysterious experiments. The doctor's daughter, Cassandra (Betty Field), attracts Parris with her beauty: her "amazingly white" skin and vivid red mouth, her full breasts, her long green eyes, and brilliant copper-colored hair. When Parris kisses Cassie during a storm, she suddenly flings off her clothes— and insists that he make love to her.

Afterwards Parris has several rendezvous with Cassie, who seems to him violent and fascinating—with an excitement he almost dreads and a mystery he does not understand. During one meeting, Cassie suddenly demands that Parris run away with her—but refuses to tell him why. The next morning she is found dead of poison, administered by her father—who then committed suicide. Afterward, going through Dr. Tower's papers, Parris discovers the truth: the doctor had been having sexual relations with his daughter from childhood on—and Cassie, in a kind of dazed compulsion, could not escape him.

Grace immediately spotted the similarities with Jane Glenn's true story: the powerful but mysterious father; the beautiful, long-haired, vulnerable daughter; the two of them in an isolated household—and death as the result. (The movie substituted insanity for incest, but the result was the same.)

Cassie Tower, however, does not fight back. Rather, she throws herself at another man. She does not seek independence. Moreover, Cassie's feelings never appear, except through Parris Mitchell's limited understanding.

Jane Glenn, on the other hand, had refused to be passive. Instead of submitting or dying, she acted in her own defense. Jane Glenn's story, the young woman's fighting back against her father, eventually made a deeper impression on Grace's imagination—and shaped more fully the character of Selena Cross.

The sexually demanding side of Cassie became part of Grace's Betty Anderson, instead—the millworker's daughter who ripens early and uses her sexuality for power over men. While Grace wrote the more shocking and sexual scenes in her book, George noticed the effect on their lives: "She seemed able to express words which before had been sacred to the couple who embraced sex in such an uninhibited manner. George and Grace were certainly well mated by now. First she whispered, yes; then, yes, I like it; then, yes, do it to me, baby."

In the spring of 1955 Grace's "fourth baby"—*The Tree and the Blossom,* later *Peyton Place*—was finished, toward the end of George's school year. Also that spring, George—dissatisfied with the frustrating and slow work of teaching retarded children—welcomed another job offer: to be teaching principal at the Gilmanton Corners School. He was hired and signed a contract—and then a town faction thought they might not want him after all.

Olive Besse, a school-board member and an Irishwoman from Boston, led the vendetta against George—or partly against him, and as much against Grace (who referred to her privately as "Messy Besse," and created a damning portrait of someone like her in Doris Delaney Palmer in *The Tight White Collar*).

Later George imagined the behind-closed-doors talk about himself: "a foreigner, a Greek . . . not a responsible person . . . nervous breakdowns . . . Communistic tendencies . . ." And then: ". . . that wife of his . . . writing that dirty book . . . They say the whole book is about Gilmanton. How will that look if it's published and he's teaching here?" George and Grace did not "look" right: They did not conform to the image of Mr. and Mrs. Principal.

Amid rumors, threats, and promises, a town meeting was called. Grace was frantic, defensive, fearful. George, she told friends, "does nothing but wait and see what will happen in that maddening way of his." As usual, Grace focused on her emotions; George insisted on facts—the fact that he had a contract in hand.

During the hearing, George stayed home with the children, seemingly unconcerned—while Grace made her way to Laurie's. She announced she was giving up. "If it didn't matter to my husband," she recalled later, "why should it matter to me? It seemed as though I had tried as hard as I knew how to help him, but things were no different from what they ever had been. He didn't even seem to care."

Meanwhile, Bernard Snierson, a respected lawyer in Laconia and a friend of Grace's, had brought a tape recorder to the meeting. When those who objected to George were asked to speak, no one would, with the tape recorder running. The threat passed—for that year, as George had a one-year contract.

Early that spring, 1955, Grace took another step toward being published. In the library she'd found a directory of literary agents, and selected one, she said, for his French name: Jacques Chambrun.

That evening, she told Maurice Zolotow much later, she wrote

Jacques Chambrun an "anguished five-page letter"—with her dreams and hopes, including her determination to become a published writer someday. "I just picked your name cold out of a book," she told Chambrun. "It is the same system I use in playing horses, and I often win." She said she'd written a novel which Vanguard and Bobbs-Merrill had rejected; she asked if Chambrun would read the novel and represent her.

Jacques Chambrun's answer was tactful but not enthusiastic: "I shall be glad to read your novel and to handle it for you if it seems to be salable. It is only fair to tell you, however, that there is at present a slump in the market for first novels."

There was also a slump in the market for Jacques Chambrun, but—having no contacts in publishing—Grace could not know her French-named agent's terrible reputation. He told her that he represented W. Somerset Maugham, long one of her favorite authors; he did not tell her that Maugham had fired him in 1948, after discovering that Chambrun had pocketed a considerable portion of Maugham's earnings. Nor did Chambrun tell Grace—even after she enriched him enormously, with *Peyton Place*—that his percentage from her earnings was paying his debts to other authors whose profits he had diverted, notably Jack Schaefer (author of *Shane*), and the estate of Fulton Oursler (author of *The Greatest Story Ever Told*).

Taking his letter as encouragement, Grace sent Jacques a 312-page manuscript, *The Quiet Place*, about a young married couple and their struggles while the husband attends college on the G. I. Bill. *The Quiet Place* was rejected by Houghton Mifflin, Crown, Longmans Green, Julian Messner, David McKay, and Alfred A. Knopf—but while it made its rounds, Grace had been completing *The Tree and the Blossom*, a 619-page novel which arrived at Jacques's office in April 1955.

The Tree and the Blossom went to Lippincott on May 2 and was returned on July 13. It was mailed to Little, Brown and Company on July 14, and came back on July 25. Sometime along the way it was also turned down by Houghton Mifflin in Boston. Perhaps at Grace's urging, Chambrun had tried Boston publishers first—though their Boston staidness made them exactly the wrong places.

Nevertheless, Leona Nevler, a free-lance manuscript reader who used to work for Little, Brown, happened to read *The Tree and the Blossom* for Lippincott. Nevler, now vice-president and group publisher at Fawcett and known for her eye for popular fiction, was then in her twenties, with only a few years in publishing—but she recognized something winning about *The Tree and the Blossom*.

It was "fun to read," she remembers, and it reminded her of other successful novels, such as *Kings Row*. But for Lippincott, *The Tree and the Blossom* was definitely too racy.

That summer Nevler happened to be job-hunting, and had an interview with Kathryn G. Messner, the president and editor-in-chief of Julian Messner, Inc. Since Messner, Inc. needed a promotion/publicity person, while Nevler wanted an editorial job, they came to no agreement—but Leona did tell Kitty Messner about the promising manuscript she'd read for Lippincott: *The Tree and the Blossom*.

Kitty Messner got the manuscript from Jacques Chambrun by private messenger, and broke a dinner engagement to stay home and read the novel.

The next day, one of the hottest in August 1955, changed Grace Metalious' life forever.

PART II

❀ ❀ ❀

Pandora in Blue Jeans

CHAPTER 7

By August, much of what makes 1955 memorable had already happened. On January 1 American aid to South Vietnam began; on April 12 scientists concluded that the Salk vaccine was definitely effective in preventing polio; in June the major world leaders held their Geneva summit conference. But more dramatic events were still to come: On August 28 Emmett Till, a fourteen-year-old black youth, was lynched in Mississippi for whistling at a white woman; on September 30 James Dean, the *Rebel Without a Cause* actor, died in a car crash and became a cult figure; and on December 1 Rosa Parks refused to give up her bus seat to a white man in Montgomery, Alabama—beginning the civil rights movement.

But in August 1955 summer doldrums predominated, though "Rock Around the Clock" by Bill Haley and the Comets was the number one song—and rock 'n' roll, a special derivative of black rhythm and blues, was capturing the audience of white teenagers, starved for something to set them apart from their elders. Chuck Berry, Bo Diddley, and Fats Domino were also on the charts—along with the adult-approved Frank Sinatra, Nat King Cole, and Les Paul and Mary Ford.

In August the New York Yankees and Brooklyn Dodgers led in baseball, and the Postmaster General, Arthur Summerfield, wanted to raise the price of stamps to four cents. Top movies included Walt Disney's *The Lady and the Tramp* (a love story featuring dogs); *Summertime,* in which Katharine Hepburn succumbs to the charms of Latin lover Rossano Brazzi; and *Land of the Pharaohs,* an Egyptian costume epic about a wicked queen (Joan Collins) who gets her way by seducing and manipulating men. *Land of the Pharaohs'* director was Howard Hawks, noted for orchestrating Rosalind Russell's portrayal of the independent woman in *His Girl Friday*—but Hawks' pictures now conformed to the fifties' world view, showing women almost solely in relationship to men.

On August 17, 1955, two live television dramas featured women, but both women were defined by their connections with men. "The U. S. Steel Hour's" *The Bride Cried,* showed "a girl who waited—and found you can wait too long"; *The Failure* on the "Kraft Television Theatre" featured "a woman married to a man who is a failure in business, but a success in her eyes."

The real-life heroine of the day was Gloria Lockerman, a black twelve-year-old from Baltimore. She had just won $8,000 for spelling "antidisestablishmentarianism" on television's "$64,000 Question" quiz show. But the only real-life drama on August 17 came from the "Red scare." Paul Robeson, the black actor and singer, was denied a passport because of his "pro-Communist" leanings: citing the U. S. Constitution, Robeson had refused to sign a "non-Communist affidavit" to get a passport. Though Robeson lost, the power of the House Un-American Activities Committee, investigating "the Communist influence in show business," was obviously waning. Of twenty-three witnesses called during New York hearings, only one cooperated and "named names"; the others took the Fifth Amendment and protected their friends.

Still, the pressures to conform were extremely strong, especially for women, black people, and anyone not leading a bland, middle-of-the-road life—anyone not ordinary, brave, clean, reverent.

"There was a certain ripe smell about all of us," Grace later wrote about August 17, 1955. They all desperately needed baths since the well had been dry for nine weeks. Grace awoke spouting unprintable words, followed by, "Damn it all! I hate you, world."

No water meant not washing her face in the morning, nor the children's, though they all looked "sticky." It meant a two-mile trip to the spring, with empty milk cans; no milk, because they were out of the real stuff and had nothing to mix with powdered milk; and lettuce and tomato sandwiches for lunch. "AGAIN?" the children wailed.

Desperately, Grace took them with her to the supermarket. They were eleven, eight, and five—all hot, tired, dusty, and whining. Grace spent $18.27 for food, saving a dollar for gas—and then took them all to Opeechee Park for a swim. "Believe me, we all needed it."

By the time they reached home, Grace felt hot and hateful: angry with the kids, furious with George (then working for a dollar an hour at the State Highway Department to provide their only income), and generally in a rage against the world. The mail contained the usual unpaid bills—and a telegram.

"Please call me at your earliest convenience. Regards Chambrun."

"Gee-Gee, come quick, hurry!" Grace shrieked. "He's sold it!" —as George, setting the table, dropped knives and forks and spoons all over the floor.

"Don't be silly," George said—but waited tensely while Grace put through the call to her agent in New York.

Jacques had believed in her novel, and now . . . "I've sold the book to Julian Messner, the publishers," he said, in the come-wiz-me-to-ze-Casbah accent that both charmed and amused Grace. "Come to New York in two days, to sign the contract."

"Thank you! Thank you!" Grace said, helplessly laughing. "Are you sure? They can't change their minds, can they?"

"Non, non," Jacques said, laughing too.

Still half-laughing, and now half-sobbing, Grace called Laurie Wilkens—who, as soon as she heard Grace's voice, *knew*. "He sold it!" she screamed.

A few minutes later, George asked, "For how much?"

Grace realized she'd forgotten to ask.

Two days later Grace was on her way to New York, telling herself that at last she'd be right: "It isn't always going to be like this."

New York both thrilled and frightened her—as did Kitty Messner, Julian Messner's widow, who owned and ran the publishing house. After she read the manuscript, Kitty had called Leona Nevler and said, "I know this is a big book." She'd called Jacques Chambrun and said, "I have to have it."

Kitty Messner was dashing, worldly, smart, and sophisticated—and Grace Metalious, in her girlish dirndl skirt with a matching pale blue linen blouse, had "never been so frightened of anyone in my life." Not only was Kitty Messner tall, towering over Grace's five feet four, but "she has the most beautiful square shoulders in the world, which didn't help matters at all because, if there was only one thing I could change about myself it would be my shoulders. They slope."

At her first meeting with her new author, Kitty wore beige slacks with a matching jacket. (No one recalls ever seeing her in a dress.) She used a cigarette holder, and sported a white carnation in her lapel.

"She looked as if she had never had a hot uncomfortable moment in her life," Grace remembered, and again felt inferior. "As for me, my armpits itched. I stuck to the chair and my hair had gone all limp."

"I didn't expect you to be so young," Kitty said.

With her delicate features, lack of makeup, and hair pulled back, Grace hardly looked like a woman who'd soon turn thirty-one.

And then Kitty Messner said what Grace considered "the most beautiful words she has ever said to me."

"Sweetie, I've read your book. I love it."

Grace nearly wept.

When the contract was produced, Grace had to be shown where to sign for her $1,500 advance. Everyone shook hands—including Leona Nevler, who wore dark glasses "so that I couldn't see her eyes," Grace wrote later. (Nevler had a sty on her eye that day—but thinks Grace intended a sinister implication.)

Despite the glasses, Leona Nevler could easily see Jacques Chambrun hovering over Grace. Because of his bad reputation for pocketing authors' money, there were those who would not deal with him—but Grace, unaware, enjoyed his French manners, and admired him enormously.

Jacques Chambrun dressed with formal elegance: very stiff collar, pin-stripe suit, shirt with cufflinks, a flower in his buttonhole. He appeared sophisticated and suave, but had dark black hair that looked dyed, and possibly even marcelled. He kept a chauffeured car and a Fifth Avenue office across from the Plaza, one of the grandest hotels of New York, and he said he was related to the counts de Chambrun in France. Grace, entranced with the New York publishing world, found him thoroughly delightful.

Oliver Swan had treated Grace as a professional writer; Jacques Chambrun catered to her as a *woman,* with the practiced graces of a professional charmer. Jacques played to her need for male approval, and for years she remained under his spell.

After she signed the book contract, Jacques took Grace for her first celebration drink, at "21"—which, she had learned from Ben Hecht's *A Child of the Century,* was Hecht's "favorite New York saloon." Grace later called it "the fanciest saloon in New York."

The head waiter greeted Jacques by name and discussed the weather with him—in French. (Though Jacques's detractors suspected he was not truly French and might even be from the Bronx, his French did pass muster.) Grace ordered a daiquiri, "all pale green and so cold it hurt my teeth," and "Monsieur Chambrun" told her to call him by his first name. He received phone calls while they were at the table, and was treated with enormous deference. With a snap of his fingers, he could get tickets to Broadway shows that were standing-room-only to everyone else. Grace felt overcome: "I was an author with a contract which said so. I had a French agent and a lady publisher. I was in '21.' I had arrived."

Laurie Wilkens soon announced Grace's arrival in the Laconia *Evening Citizen:* "New York Publishing House Signs Gilmanton Mother for Three Novels." In an accompanying picture, Grace and George smile at one another, and the article—as pieces on successful women always did in the fifties—assured readers that the successful author was also a splendid wife and mother.

Grace had "found her staunchest admirer, her most constructive critic, and her best proof reader in the young teacher who never doubted her talent," Laurie wrote. Asked to come to New York, George's wife found that "like all mothers of families . . . 'getting away' from the youngsters even for a short time is a most difficult task." But friends and family pitched in, to free Grace to meet Kitty Messner and sign her contract.

During the winter, Grace's children Marsha and Mike would attend the Gilmanton Corners School, the article said, while Grace worked on another book, also set in New England. "But if fame does come her way, home in Gilmanton still holds for her the very best in happiness and security."

Grace's image in the Laconia *Evening Citizen* conformed to what was expected in 1955. Laurie Wilkens could hardly have written anything else. But she knew and admired Grace's unconventional side—and the singular purpose that made her an author. Laurie also learned—with Grace—that publishing meant much more than just writing a book.

"The title's too poetic," Aaron Sussman, head of the advertising agency handling *The Tree and the Blossom,* told Kitty Messner. "It won't sell."

"Then come up with a better one," Kitty challenged him.

"Call it *Peyton Place*."

"Fine."

Leona Nevler had thought *The Tree and the Blossom* a reasonable title—symbolizing the book's parents and children, with the blossom falling not far from the tree. The title also suits the young heroine Allison's discussions with Dr. Matthew Swain about nature, time, and the seasons. Doc quotes Allison a line of poetry she never forgets: "I saw the starry tree Eternity, put forth the blossom Time."

But *Peyton Place* was a title more like *Kings Row*, still fondly remembered in publishing circles, and Aaron Sussman knew his business. Meanwhile, Kitty Messner wanted Leona Nevler to work for her, editing the manuscript—a process that soon became very painful.

"When I think of the thirteen months that elapsed between the time the book was bought and the day it was published," Grace wrote three years later, "I wonder if I'd have the stamina it took to go through it again."

When she began editing Grace's manuscript, Leona Nevler was doing a great deal of other free-lance work. Working fast, she made what proved to be a tactical error: she wrote her revision suggestions directly on the manuscript. "The comments were not that demanding," Nevler recalls, and the manuscript shows that most were deletions or questions. Miss Kramer, a "lacquer-haired, red-nailed receptionist" whose haughty ways drive Allison to a different literary agent, was marked "cut"—her scene contributed little to the book's forward momentum, and she never appeared after that scene. Similarly, a retelling of Allison's prize-winning story, "Lisa's Cat," was marked "delete."

Nevler also had some larger suggestions. In Grace's original manuscript, Selena's killing her father takes seven sentences. She keeps striking him with the fire tongs, for fear he's still alive, and the fire tongs strike "not with the crashing, breaking sound that they had made at first, but with a mushy, soft sound."

The final printed version takes three sentences, without the sound, because of Leona Nevler's penciled suggestion: "Selena should be fighting for her life here—Lucas might try to kill her when she resists his advances. She should not go on striking him in such a bloody way."

But other Nevler suggestions troubled Grace more. Next to a description of Allison's would-be lover, David Noyes, "a hollow cheeked burning eyed" young man, Nevler had penciled, "this is a cliché of a young writer." In the final printed version, the description no longer appears.

Nevler also wanted to delete four paragraphs of Allison's conversation with her roommate Stephanie ("Steve") Wallace and David Noyes. Steve decides that David is "a desperate young man, pining away with unrequited love" for Allison—who scoffs, "Don't be ridiculous. He is much too enamored of his own prose to waste any love on anything or anyone else." Three of Grace's paragraphs were cut, but a sentence in the fourth remains in the printed edition: David tells Steve, "I wish that Allison would look at me just once, the way she looks at Brad Holmes all the time," followed by a sentence about Allison's love and worship.

Nevler marked that whole paragraph "stilted"—but she was most critical of Allison's one love scene, her first sexual experience with her agent, Bradley Holmes. Nevler eliminated one sentence: "Years later, when Allison was very old, she once said that it was a good thing for a young girl to have an older man as her first lover, for Bradley Holmes had none of the fumbling awkwardnesss which is too often conducive to contemptuous laughter than to excitement." Later on Nevler also eliminated Bradley's philosophy of lovemaking: "Shame is the cause of frigidity and withholding, while pride is generous and passion making."

"This whole scene, in which Brad schools Allison to love making is somehow unreal + a little embarrassing," Leona Nevler wrote in the margin—and that comment troubled Grace the most. Though the comments overall were not particularly demanding, first-time authors tend to have fragile egos. Hence, editors generally avoid writing comments on the manuscripts of authors they do not know well—to prevent wounded feelings.

Grace's feelings were definitely wounded, she recalled later. On her manuscript, she said, Leona Nevler had penciled "various and sundry comments," together with a letter and "a long list of things with which she disagreed in the book." Grace went through it all, "my rage and hurt getting worse every minute." Finally she called Laurie Wilkens for support.

"Come down and take a look at this!" she roared over the phone. "You'll never believe this!"

Laurie, too, was outraged, and they asked each other, "Why did they buy the damned thing if there was this much wrong with it?"

Grace wrote Jacques Chambrun an indignant letter, "calling Miss Nevler every name under the sun." She sent the manuscript back with only a few changes, the ones she agreed to—and then, angry and tearful, she left her children with Laurie and headed for New York.

Leona Nevler had, in the meantime, taken a job with Fawcett Publications, but she offered to take Grace to lunch at the Absinthe House. Their conversation was pleasant enough—though Leona noticed that Grace drank three strong martinis and toyed with her shrimp salad, without eating it.

Since Leona had a holiday the next day, Columbus Day, she invited Grace to her apartment, and cooked lunch for her—although she remembers that Grace ate little, preferring to drink beer. They exchanged "girlish chit-chat" and did virtually no work on the manuscript. Nevler considered taking Grace out for dinner —but with Grace in blue jeans, there were very few places they could go in New York, in 1955. They parted very amiably, Nevler thought.

But Grace interpreted their conversation differently. She spent one afternoon at Nevler's apartment, she wrote later, "during which she tore *Peyton Place* to bits." By the time Grace left the apartment, Jacques had left his office, so "there was no one I could turn to."

Alone in New York, Grace began walking all over the city, "hugging my precious manuscript to my heaving bosom"—a melodramatic expression she probably meant ironically. Like so many other writers, she found her way to Greenwich Village, located a bar, and "drank myself cockeyed."

Grace also read her book over again, from beginning to end, and decided, "She's wrong! I'll never change a damned word. Let her write her own books."

After the bar closed, Grace walked some more, drank enough coffee to make her shaky, and by nine the next morning was waiting for Jacques outside his office. He arrived, dapper as always—and Grace threw her manuscript at him.

"Take it!" she screamed. "I don't want to sell somebody else's book. If it can't be mine, I don't want any part of it!"

Accustomed to authors' wounded feelings, Jacques took off Grace's coat, lit her cigarette, and said soothingly, "Oh, come now, chérie, you're tired. Leave everything to me."

And so Grace started to depend heavily on Jacques and his approval. She also agreed to work directly with Kitty Messner as her editor, and Kitty told Leona Nevler a few days later that Grace "needs a mama's hand. She's going to do it all for me."

Though Kitty Messner later sent Leona Nevler some $1,100 in bonuses for her role in finding *Peyton Place,* Leona never really shared in the book's success—and she learned that Grace had made hostile comments about her in letters to Kitty. Nevler, a rather shy person herself, found Grace's about-face after their day together "a shattering experience." Though Leona Nevler did gain a certain fame as the discoverer of *Peyton Place,* she never saw Grace Metalious again.

Revisions of *Peyton Place* and publicity arrangements took nearly a year. Grace took several trips to New York; "great gobs" of manuscript flew back and forth between Gilmanton and the big city. When she began working directly with Kitty Messner, Grace had doubts: "I wondered if I hadn't jumped from the frying pan into the fire." But Kitty Messner, who had said, "She needs a mama's hand," became the most influential woman in Grace's life at that time.

Kitty was exactly Laurette's age—fifty-two—but much more restrained, even maternal in her treatment of her new author. "To describe Kitty Messner's voice is impossible," Grace wrote. "It is deep but still beautifully feminine. She never goes squeaky with excitement or harsh with anger." When they disagreed, Kitty was calm, healing—the way Grace had always wanted Laurette to be.

"Kitty understood Grace," says Howard Goodkind, a Messner editor who arranged the publicity for *Peyton Place*. "It was impossible for Grace to get Kitty angry, no matter what she did. Kitty was always interested in her problems and listened to her by the hour." Though Doris Flowers, then sales manager at Messner's and later executive vice-president, doubts that Kitty was a "surrogate mother-figure" for Grace, Kitty nurtured Grace in a way that could be called maternal. With her French agent hovering around her, taking away her burdens as a father would, and her "lady publisher," with her mama's touch, Grace had a haven in the publishing world.

Further, Kitty Messner was the total career woman, a type Grace Metalious had never met before. Except for Helen Meyer, who directed Dell, Kitty Messner was the only woman running a major publishing house on her own. But Kitty Messner had always led a life unhobbled by preconceived ideas—thoroughly unlike Grace's.

Born Kathryn Grossman in Chicago (on November 25, 1902), Kitty attended the University of Chicago, then headed East to make her fortune. After a detour—a short-lived marriage—she opened the Kathryn Karn Bookshop, at 16 East 50th Street, in 1928. The next year the shop, prospering, moved to 642 Madison Avenue, where Kitty operated it until January 1930, while doing editorial work on the side for Liveright publishers. In 1929 she had married Julian Messner, a Liveright editor sixteen years her senior (and the man who had given an aspiring playwright named Lillian Hellman her first editorial job).

In the depths of the Depression, the fall of 1933—while Grace DeRepentigny was scribbling stories in Aunt Georgie's bathtub—Kitty and Julian Messner took the plunge and started their own publishing company.

They rented office space at 8 West Fortieth Street, where they remained as Julian Messner, Inc. They wanted to publish books that most interested them, including juvenile books; their adult list would be small, so they could give each book individual attention. They already had one major author: Frances Parkinson Keyes, the historical novelist, who stayed with Messner's for the rest of the firm's life. Keyes' *Senator Marlowe's Daughter* made Messner's 1933 book list, one of four books published that first year. Another novel on that list was *Prescription for Marriage* by John Anders (really Kitty Messner).

For the first few years Kitty and Julian did everything. He was president and in charge of sales; she was secretary, treasurer and all-around clerk, doing typing, filing, bookkeeping, and manufacturing. Both did editorial work, and except for the advertising—handled by Aaron Sussman from the start—Kitty could do any job in the publishing firm.

Then, in 1944, Kitty and Julian Messner were divorced, a fact not widely known in publishing circles, or easily forgotten—because they continued working together as always. Kitty defined herself by her work, not by her relationship to a man—and she would hardly give up her self-definition.

When Julian Messner died in 1948, Kitty was his logical successor as company president—but the Messner's board of directors had doubts about giving a woman such a post. Hence, they appointed a vice-president—Philip Wittenberg, a noted publishing lawyer—to be in charge of the president. But it soon became apparent, Wittenberg said later, that no such office was needed. Kitty could handle everything on her own—with a staff that consisted almost entirely of women.

Doris Flowers, hired in 1950, was virtually the only woman sales director in publishing; Carolyn Weiss served ably as secretary and general assistant; Lora Orrmont took the publicity job for which Leona Nevler had been interviewed. When Kitty hired Arthur Ceppos in 1951 to head a new Messner line, his gender was considered noteworthy enough for mention in *Writer's Digest* —together with an implication, not uncommon in the 1950s, that a man might not be comfortable working for and with women. "Ceppos, a handsome, enthusiastic man," Pauline Bloom assured *Writer's Digest* readers, "is unruffled by the femininity around him."

In 1952, three years before she met Grace Metalious, Kitty Messner had married again—to James J. Finn of New York, a graphic arts consultant. But the marriage lasted a very short time. Kitty's only long-term marriage had been built on working and sharing together; she would not settle for less.

"She had class, and style, and a swing as she walked through the office," Howard Goodkind recalls—and it was the Kitty Messner style, as much as her accomplishments, that made her talked-about in publishing.

With dresses and skirts so universally expected that Grace Metalious' jeans were considered shocking in New York, Kitty Messner wore trousers. Her jacket and pantsuits were expensive gabardines, and tailor-made for her, but definitely modeled after men's suits. Perhaps, as Leona Nevler suggested much later, Kitty lacked some confidence about being a woman in a "man's job"—and her trouser suits, made in various shades of brown, were her way of dressing for success.

Kitty Messner was a tall, striking woman with a commanding appearance—an air that struck many people, in the conservative 1950s, as distinctly "mannish." Naturally there were speculations that Kitty was a lesbian—but Kitty ignored what other people said, and did whatever she chose. When Grace Metalious became a Messner's author, Kitty would take her for lunch and drinks at the 440 Club, in the Messner building on Fortieth Street. Kitty always sat at the same table, and ate the same lunch: steak with horse-radish sauce. Every year Kitty vacationed at the same spot, in the Dominican Republic: generous to her friends, she might pay their way to join her. Her life was precise, methodical—the life of a woman devoted to achievement—and she disliked coverage that pigeonholed her by standards of femininity. Editing Messner's twenty-fifth anniversary article in *Book News,* Kitty crossed out a line describing herself: "Very feminine, she nevertheless is usually attired in one of her collection of several dozen slack outfits." Kitty substituted a sentence about Messner's editorial policy. Unlike Grace, Kitty was sure of her goals—and sure that she wanted to be judged as a creative person first, apart from being a woman.

Kitty Messner was also a meticulous editorial disciplinarian, with an excellent reputation as a line-by-line editor. Publishers always assume that manuscripts can be improved; authors always feel, as Bennett Cerf of Random House once said, that every word set down on paper "automatically becomes a priceless gem." The slightest suggestion that an author change anything is "an unforgivable insult."

Grace Metalious took her place among women writers with many self-doubts—and fears for her manuscript. But Kitty understood Grace's fears. Some of the changes Leona Nevler had suggested were not made, to avoid hurting Grace's feelings. Though rumors always persisted that Kitty had turned a shapeless mass of lurid material into a novel, Kitty actually made few changes—and in an interview three months after *Peyton Place* was published, Kitty called Grace's work a "product of genius" whose success made her "feel good all over." Through Grace found the editing painful, the book remained her own, the product of her thinking about women and men, sex and violence, power and powerlessness.

CHAPTER 8

Under Kitty Messner's direction, Grace Metalious made many small stylistic changes in *Peyton Place:* cutting extra words, trimming repetition. Long philosophical passages about nature, reminiscent of *Kings Row,* were deleted, including Allison's fear of winter winds that made her "feel inadequate and helpless"—one of many instances where Allison clearly represents Grace DeRepentigny.

Together Grace and Kitty cut unnecessary foreshadowings, such as, "Years later, Allison would recall . . ." Occasional satirical comments were dropped, such as a reference to "old-time confession magazines in which Wayward Girls were always and forever being forced to leave their happy homes to go to live with Maiden Aunts (pronounced Ants) in Vermont as Payment for the Wages of Sin."

Grace—or Kitty—also eliminated a long anecdote showing how Marion Partridge, the town snob, came to detest Dr. Swain—for his satirical jibes at a cocktail party. In Grace's manuscript, Swain deliberately provokes Marion's sister-in-law with predictions of war with Japan, and "one of those little yellow bellies staring at your skirts with lustful eyes." Then, told that the sister-in-law was born in Japan, the Doc trumpets: "I'll bet she's got Made in Japan stamped all over her ass!"

In the published version of *Peyton Place,* however, Marion Partridge detests the doctor for a simpler reason: He tells her that her "delicate stomach" symptoms are menopause, and that he knows she's lying about her age. The new version of Marion Partridge's hatred is more female-centered, though less original than the "Made in Japan" episode.

Little Norman Page, Allison's sensitive childhood friend, also underwent some changes before his story saw print. In *Peyton Place,* Norman's overprotective mother gives him enemas; he has wet dreams; town gossip claims that his mother "tit-fed" him until age four; and his mother still resents his friendship with Allison and insists he not see Allison again.

But the manuscript includes another paragraph apparently too kinky for 1956. Norman agrees not to see Allison, and "It had seemed to be the thing to do at the time, though, he thought, with his mother standing over him with a leather belt in her hand and him lying naked on the bed, not minding at all when she hit him. He had finally promised, and his mother had put salve on the welts that were all over him, and she had kissed him and slept all night in a chair next to his bed."

Early in the editing, Grace agreed to drop one character, a minister who went insane, because "everybody thought this was just too much" (although remnants of such a story exist in Reverend Fitzgerald in *Peyton Place*). And then one big part of Grace's novel had to be revised: the story of Selena Cross.

Originally Selena, like Jane Glenn, had been raped by her father. Selena resembles Jane—long dark hair, uncommon beauty—and even wears the purple dress that Laurie Wilkens remembered. Unlike Cassie in *Kings Row,* Selena is presented from the inside, for sympathy and insight. Grace also added a further plot twist: Selena becomes pregnant by her father.

The gruff but tenderhearted town physician, Dr. Matthew Swain, performs an illegal abortion—then confronts Selena's father Lucas, knowing Lucas (in the manuscript) "was guilty of the crime of incest, a crime worse than child abuse between homosexuals, in the doctor's mind."

Kitty said that incest/rape could not be published, not in 1956.

Heartbroken, Grace made the change. Lucas Cross would be Selena's stepfather, and Grace wrote a new scene and lines here and there to explain his marriage to Nellie, Selena's mother. "But she felt her book was destroyed," Laurie Wilkens recalls.

Grace thought Selena's situation was no longer a tragedy. No doctor would perform an abortion if the rapist were just a stepfather, Grace reasoned—after all, the doctor could not justify the abortion for medical or genetic reasons. In her eyes, the change made the book "trashy" rather than tragic.

Grace did not see that the story's impact was not lessened, since its power came from the point of view. The rape appears through the eyes of the violated child, her innocence contrasted with her stepfather's rage and power. The doctor gives her an abortion for humanitarian reasons, not medical ones, and Dr. Swain becomes far more of a hero, a man who recognizes not only medical facts, but women's emotions. Rather than showing rape as a male rite of passage—in an era when Caryl Chessman, the convicted Red Light rapist of California, had enormous liberal support to avoid the electric chair—Grace showed rape as it appeared to a woman: ugly, violent, a destruction of innocence.

Grace made other changes at Kitty's request. Kitty—and, Leona Nevler recalls, the Sussman ad agency—wanted another love scene between Tomas Makris, a big, handsome school principal, and Constance MacKenzie, Allison's blonde, sexually repressed mother.* In the new scene, Connie confesses her hidden past to Tom. Then she undresses before him for the first time, and demands that he make love to her. "I love this fire in you," he says, "I love it when you have to move." And then: "Your nipples are as hard as diamonds," and then: "Your legs are absolutely wanton, do you know it?" while Connie murmurs, "Yes, yes, yes, yes" and "Don't stop" and "Again, darling. Again."

Grace pounded out that scene on a typewriter in Kitty's office, while furiously puffing on a cigarette. Then she growled, "Take your goddamn love scene!" as she handed it over.

Tom Makris was clearly the romantic hero: strong, brave, sensual—but his appeal had to be slightly dampened. The words of the Pittsburgh secretary who'd been his last fling had to be cut: "I knew that you'd leave me," she said in the manuscript, and then, "You were too goddamned good in bed to be true." Also elimi-

---

* Following a libel suit by George's friend Tom Makris, the name was changed to "Michael Rossi" in paperback, movie, and television versions of *Peyton Place*.

nated was Grace's description of Tom Makris as he walked up Depot Street: "swinging his huge arms restlessly, he looked as out of place as a phallus in a toy shop window." That was too strong for 1956.

Kitty's editing dampened some of the most shocking material, strengthened the impact of people's choices in defining their lives, and generally avoided sentiment. Kitty cut Selena Cross' avowal to her childhood sweetheart, Ted Carter, about to betray her: "You are my sun and my moon and stars, and my centrifugal force, if people have such a thing." But in avoiding sentiment, Kitty became most ruthless in editing the book's last section—where Allison MacKenzie goes to New York to seek her fortune as a writer.

Though only Selena Cross' story was based on a true episode, Grace knew people with similarities to most of her other characters: town drunks, high school principals, rough-speaking but kindhearted doctors, dreamy adolescents. She knew their thoughts and had watched them in action. But only her childhood friend Marc had ever gone to New York to seek his fortune—and in the manuscript version of Allison's story, numerous items, small and large, reveal Grace's unfamiliarity with the New York world. She writes that Allison has published in a "smooth paper magazine" (changed to "slick" in editing). Almost immediately, Allison finds an agent who also edits her manuscripts and sells enough stories to make her a living as a writer—a virtually impossible feat for an unknown. But Grace had the most difficulty with dialogue—with the way up-and-coming New Yorkers talk.

Grace had a good ear for speech. Her New Englanders sound true to life, even to regional pronunciations: Norman, for instance, renders Pillsbury as "Pillsbree." Grace also uses classic New England understatements: asked why he didn't tell a newcomer that the train station would be closed all night, one local explains, "He didn't ask me."

With Laurie helping her, Grace captured the speech rhythms of "shellback Yankees" (her term in *Peyton Place*), "ax mouths" (her term in real life), and the kind, generous, and heroic villagers. But her New Yorkers speak a strangely stilted half-colloquial, half-bookish dialect.

Steve Wallace, for instance, once suggests to her roommate,

Allison, that Norman Page is "queer" (her typical way of speaking)—but then suddenly intellectualizes him as the victim of "a Silver Cord Complex." Steve's assessment of Allison's home town sounds more like writing than speaking: Peyton Place is "a state of mind . . . full of back-biting and stinking of morality." Grace, it appears, could not decide whether a New York career girl's speech should be girlish or literary—and Kitty finally deleted most of Steve's part, although Steve remains a loyal friend to Allison.

Even more troublesome were Grace's male characters—for the romantic literary male was not a type common to Manchester or Gilmanton. When Allison's agent, Bradley Holmes, is about to take her to bed for the first time, he begins by lecturing her about the "normal feminine fear" that he will think badly of her afterwards. "Most women need excuses of one kind or another," he says, and suggests possibilities: "Some women proclaim that they are in love, while others say that some man got them drunk and took advantage of them, and still others go so far as to claim out and out rape."

About that last sentence, Kitty wrote in the margin, "Is this a little too talky for preliminaries?"—and it was cut from the final printed version.

Allison's would-be lover, David Noyes, sounds equally stilted. Grace was at home with describing Allison's hair as "fine, limp, and plain brown"—exactly like her own—but David's description of Allison's "lovely hair" seems otherworldly: "It is of that delightful shade which the French call 'blonde cendree.' To me, your other physical attributes pale when compared with the loveliness of your hair." Kitty cut that speech.

Treated as a romantic heroine, Allison is no longer herself—and Kitty's cuts generally restored the Allison of the earlier pages: romantic and idealistic, but also tough-minded, ambitious, and self-centered in a positive way. To focus the last part on Allison's development, Kitty removed other characters' thoughts and unnecessary information: in print, Allison discovers that Brad is married, but not (as in the manuscript) that his wife and children live in Scarsdale. Allison's desperately unhappy face after that revelation was enough, Kitty thought, and deleted a friend's extra comment that Allison looked "like she had just been slapped across the face with a dead fish."

Overall, Kitty made the most changes for Allison-in-New-York, and many of them cut Allison's role as a writer: her thoughts about short stories versus novels; her plans to put Norman Page in a book (with "something dramatic, to turn him against all women but his mother for all time"). In the manuscript, Allison frequently compares literature with life: her seduction scene with Brad reminds her of "bad novels" and "heavily-censored movies" —with the "deserted farm house, the glowing fire, the wine, the older man, and the young virgin." In *Peyton Place,* Allison has no such thoughts.

Moreover, Allison's own writing is more significant in the manuscript than in the printed version. In manuscript, her sin weekend with Brad includes reading her newly completed novel; in *Peyton Place* Brad tells her to leave the manuscript home, and they spend their weekend in bed. In the manuscript, Brad sells her novel, *Samuel's Castle;* in *Peyton Place* Allison's novel is not good enough to sell, because she lacks experience with life.

Essentially, Allison in manuscript is more introspective, more aware of herself as a writer. Allison in *Peyton Place* is less literary —more sexy—more commercial.

Since Allison most closely represents Grace Metalious, cutting Allison's role as a writer diminished Grace's role—and later she told many people, including Bob Athearn, that *Peyton Place* wasn't the book she had wanted to write. He agreed that the book she'd told him about had sounded less sexy, less commercial, and more idealistic than the finished product. He also knew the theory that "Everyone has one book to write," a cliché among writers and critics—the assumption being that everyone can be autobiographical, once. But Kitty Messner's editing limited *Peyton Place* as autobiography, and Grace later returned to unfinished autobiographical business in *No Adam in Eden,* her last novel and the only one Kitty Messner did not publish.

Grace finished the final changes on *Peyton Place* in New York and Gilmanton, where she, George, and the children were still making do at "It'll Do." Then Grace sank into the deep post-book depression common to writers. With *Peyton Place* done and on its way to publication, her old emotions surfaced: "I couldn't have a baby; I couldn't start another book."

George spent many evenings away, coaching basketball. Laurette was in New York, living in a Central Park West apartment that, Marc said, was strewn with magazines—for she never gave up her interest in reading. Bunny, divorced from Roger Roy, had married Charlie Farrell in Manchester; he was said to have a drinking problem.

Grace occasionally visited Aunt Georgie and Grandmother DeRepentigny in Manchester, and used to ask her grandmother to make buttonholes for her, but she asked in broken French, and her grandmother would become highly annoyed at Grace's not knowing the language well. "I have no women friends," Grace used to say—to which Laurie would respond, "What about me?" But Laurie was the only one. Grace felt desperately lonely, and abandoned—and in need of male approval.

Over the phone she began a mild flirtation with Jim Bonnette, a disc jockey at radio station WFEA in Manchester. George's silences had always irritated Grace; disc jockeys have a superficial gift of gab—and Jim Bonnette appealed particularly to housewives. He would begin commercials with the less happy side of the feminine mystique: "Are you tired of being chained to the house? Enslaved in the kitchen? Buried in diapers?" Aware that housewives spent eighty-seven cents of every dollar, he made a point of slanting his commercials toward them—but not only to get them to buy products.

Considering himself quite a bit smarter than his bosses and his listeners ("There's not a whole lot of intelligence in media," he said in 1980), Jim Bonnette specialized in sexual innuendo for the discerning listener. Grace Metalious, a housewife who called him up one day, seemed to him "a perfect delight." She caught every level of innuendo, including horrendous puns; they got along beautifully; and he discovered "she had one hell of a sense of humor."

He remembers having long conversations with her, but says he never really knew her. She seemed a "montage of personalities," as if practicing different roles. Her stories varied from day to day, especially about her extramarital sexual adventures. She seemed, he thought, to be looking for something to appeal to him—as if seeking his approval. He called her "Arachne," the spider—and she laughed, thinking he meant she was weaving a web around him. But he also thought of the female spider who enjoys sex and then devours the male after the act.

Her husband was a schoolteacher, Grace told Jim Bonnette, making it clear that she was very unhappy with poverty, and with her circumstances in general. Then one day she told him she was coming to Manchester for shopping, and would like to meet him.

They met at a Manchester store which Bonnette says he won in a Boston poker game: Fletcher's Paint, on Elm Street. Grace came in wearing a housedress and very little makeup, and looking very plain—hardly dressed for an assignation, if she intended one. She told Jim she wanted to talk with him privately, and they withdrew to a private corner of the store.

"I really don't know how to begin," he recalls her saying, but her exact words after that are less clear in his memory. She seemed to be offering to live with him, and promising, "I'll be anything you want me to be"—though she also told him, "I have some work that I need to do." (Much later he realized "some work" was her writing—and that she had already written *Peyton Place*.)

"I already have a roommate," he told her—and says that "made her madder than hell," and she stormed out, angry and tearful.

The next day, he says, she called and apologized, and later visited and called again—but she was never again the cheerful, humorous, sparkling woman he had originally known on the phone.

Every disc jockey has a following of admiring women, most of them discontented housewives, and Jim Bonnette says he has met many unhappy women, "but none as unhappy as Grace"—or perhaps none with the dramatic storytelling quality she had. He rated her 8 on his 1 to 10 scale; how she rated him is unknown. But clearly he served as a kind of rehearsal for another disc jockey, a few years later, who would turn her life upside down.

Meanwhile, "I couldn't make my husband happy," Grace recalled after she became famous. "In fact, he seemed happier away from me than at home. Everyone told me how wonderful he was at school, how happy he was." Wendy Wilkens, who learned how to write a research paper from George Metalious, thought him one of the best teachers she ever had. But Grace "gave up completely. I started drinking like a fish and was soon embroiled in a very stupid love affair."

Because George was so often away coaching basketball, Grace saw less and less of him—and began paying more attention to her neighbor, Carl Newman. She still needed male approval, and Carl, the physical type she always admired—big, broad-shouldered—was available.

Carl Newman, a tall, granite-faced New Englander, was an itinerant farmhand whose major pastime was, reportedly, drinking. He was also ten or fifteen years older than Grace, then thirty-one.

How the attraction began and grew, no one knows—nor who began it. To one observer, Carl was gentle, unassuming, and Grace "steamrollered him."

In any case, Grace was soon seen drinking regularly with Carl at the Rod and Gun Club, a blue-collar hangout on Beacon Street. She was a good listener who looked deeply into men's eyes as they spoke, and she easily attracted male companions. She was also gathering material—buying older men drinks so they'd tell her their stories—but in visiting bars with a man not her husband, she sinned against the rule that woman's place is at home, with her spouse. She was meeting her own needs, rather than the needs of others—and local people considered her conduct with Carl "flagrant."

The disapproval of the "ax mouths" made Grace even more defiant, and she declared to all and sundry her belief in honesty: "Whatever you're going to do, do it on Broadway and Forty-second Street at high noon."

Her sentiments gained her a reputation for "coarseness, crudeness, loudness," Louise Harriman Taylor, a New Hampshire native who never met Grace Metalious, recalled in 1980. Further, outlandish rumors circulated: Grace had disappeared for a three-month binge in the woods with another man; or, Grace had gone to the door nude to meet the milkman.

Nor did the affair with Carl make Grace happy, at least in retrospect. Since he admired her despite her self-doubts, she wondered about his discernment. "The man was a farmhand with no education and I didn't even have to try to measure up to him," she wrote later. "He thought I was spectacular. He told me I was beautiful, smart, and wonderful. It was nice to hear and stupid to listen to."

Why did she listen? "I had finished *Peyton Place* and it seemed to me that I faced a terrible vacuum." Carl filled the vacuum, and so did heavy drinking. For the first time, Grace began to use alcohol for an escape from her doubts and fears.

CHAPTER 9

For a while George seemed unaware of Grace's affair with Carl, but Marsha, then in seventh grade, noticed that "Mr. Carl" spent considerable time with Grace in her bedroom. Marsha threatened to tell her father, and somehow George found out.

"That awful winter of 1955 to 56," George called it later—the winter Grace waited for her book to be copy edited, set in type, proofread, bound, printed, published, and George waited for her to give up Carl. Grace and George had violent fights, and Grace retaliated by staying out until early morning with Carl, and drinking more and more.

She did have some simpler, happier moments that winter. Once during a blizzard she trudged to Laurie's house and found herself stranded for several days—along with Laurie's children, who loved the lively stories she told, and Richard Stinson, then a ninth-grader and one of many young people who used to visit at Laurie's because there were always people to see and things to do.

Stinson, who lived in Laconia, was a tall, blond youth, two years ahead of Marsha Metalious in school, a year ahead of Wendy Wilkens, a year behind Joanne Wilkens. "Stins," as Grace called him, admired Grace's uninhibited way of expressing herself. He recalled her comic desperation when she ran out of cigarettes and began scrounging for butts in the fireplace. She preferred Parliaments, but what could one do in a blizzard? Stinson became a protégé of Grace's, and she always joked about "the butts."

Since he enjoyed Grace's company, Stinson tried to ignore the town gossip about her. He admired her generosity: her first purchases with her $1,500 advance for *Peyton Place* were bathing suits for Marsha and Cindy and Laurie's daughters, Joanne and Wendy.

Grace also knew exactly what she wanted to do with the rest of her money.

For a long time she had been coveting a house: a small Cape Codder known locally as "the Mudgett homestead." In the months it was for sale, Grace and Laurie often drove past it. They had picnics on the grass behind the house; sometimes, giggling wickedly, they jimmied open a window and sat in the living room.

The house, some 180 years old, sat on fourteen acres, partly wooded. It was painted white, with what New Englanders call "Indian shutters"—shutters to defend the windows against real or imagined Indian raids. The center door had two shuttered windows on each side; the downstairs living room, where Grace and Laurie liked to sit, had a hand-hewn beamed ceiling, and adjoined a kitchen and woodshed. The central hallway led to a master bedroom, another small bedroom, and bath. Two additional bedrooms were in the small upstairs.

Grace thought the house would be perfect for the children, and she loved its reputation: Its most notorious occupant had been H. H. Mudgett, a gangster who, during a sojourn in Chicago, reportedly killed thirty-six people. When she learned that Mrs. Mudgett was said to haunt the house, Grace became even more eager to buy it, despite its remote location on Meadow Pond Road, accessible only through the twists and turns of a tiny dirt road.

In early summer 1956, Grace decided to try to buy "her" house. She went to Byron Parker, president of the Laconia National Bank, and asked to borrow $1,500 for a down payment on the Mudgett house.

What collateral was she offering? he asked.

"I have a book contract," she said—though she had no money beyond the first advance, which mostly went for living expenses. But she knew the book would earn enough to pay back her loan, she told Byron Parker.

No, the book could not serve as collateral, the banker said.

Could she sell the book to the bank? Grace asked desperately.

No, that wouldn't do, either.

Eventually, though, Byron Parker arranged a loan for her on a personal note, to be paid back monthly. And so Grace bought her house: in George's words, "her little dream house on the hill . . . out in the sticks of an even stickier township."

She adored the house, Grace said, and would never change it. During the third week in August, she and George, Marsha, Mike, and Cindy moved in, taking only personal possessions and books, since the Mudgett homestead was already furnished. Within a few years, "It'll Do" had burned down—but Grace, for the first time in her life, had a house she could call home.

Meanwhile, as expected, George's contract as teaching principal at the Gilmanton Corners School was not renewed. The local opposition had won the war, and George accepted another teaching job in Stow, Massachusetts. Grace would stay with the children in Gilmanton.

Later, both were aware, they could get a divorce, and end the marriage that seemed to both of them a disaster. Grace and George had separated for two weeks early in August. When they came back together, she told him her affair with Carl Newman was over. She had been a "stupid girl," he wrote later, "and from then on, things were going to be different." But they were already different, as the publicity campaign for *Peyton Place* got underway.

Grace liked to visit the Laconia *Evening Citizen* office with Laurie, one of the paper's star reporters. Grace would sit on a desk, Indian-style, and chat with Larry Smith, the *Citizen* photographer. When the New York publishers wanted pictures of their new author, Laurie asked Larry Smith to take them—and so he came to the Wilkens' farmhouse with his old Burkin-James press camera.

He took many pictures, including one that made Grace look like Whistler's Mother; later the New York publicists took many more glamorous photos—but they preferred one of Larry's: the picture that became known as "Pandora in Blue Jeans."

At first Grace considered the whole idea foolish. Laurie wanted a colonial atmosphere; Grace thought it was "icky"—but went along. In the picture, Grace is sitting in one of Laurie's Early

American chairs, looking pensively at her typewriter, the battered Remington on which she wrote *Peyton Place*. Her hands are clasped in front of her mouth, and she wears her characteristic checked flannel shirt, blue jeans, and sneakers. With her hair pulled back and her thoughtful expression, she looks very young, innocent, vulnerable—not at all like the lady whose scandalous novel was being readied to shock America.

The picture became the public's first image of Grace Metalious: It filled the back book jacket of *Peyton Place*. When Laurie went to New York a few months later, she saw the "Pandora in Blue Jeans" picture everywhere—and came to the *Citizen* office in tears, because Larry Smith was not getting credit for the picture.

Finally he did get a credit line for the portrait, the most famous picture he ever took. He sold his collection of other Grace Metalious pictures over and over for years afterward, to people as far away as South Africa (where *Peyton Place* was banned until 1978). But he never profited from the "Pandora in Blue Jeans" shot—he'd sold it to Messner's for fifteen dollars.

Who actually named the picture "Pandora in Blue Jeans" is uncertain. Howard Goodkind thinks he might have dreamed it up; Aaron Sussman has claimed it; but Doris Flowers attributes the title to Carolyn Weiss, Kitty Messner's secretary, who said that *Peyton Place* "opened things up like a Pandora's box."

But Howard Goodkind opened up the possibilities for Grace Metalious, through decisions that were to transform her life irrevocably. That spring Grace had visited New York for a meeting at Messner's. In her blue jeans and ponytail, she looked young and out of place, and still awed by the New York publishing world. Goodkind, a tall, thin, up-and-coming editor just Grace's age, spotted her unique potential.

Messner's had not expected an enormous profit from *Peyton Place,* a book very different from the inspirational best sellers of the day, such as *The Nun's Story* and *The Power of Positive Thinking. Peyton Place* might sell 3,000 copies, a decent sale for a first novel, and then earn an extra $3,000 on the paperback sale (from which Grace would get $1,500 and Messner's $1,500). But when Howard Goodkind met Grace Metalious, he recalled in 1980, "something clicked."

He found her nice, talkative, friendly, and interesting—and in many ways not so different from other frustrated housewives, casualties of the feminine mystique. "All over the United States there were women with children saying they could write"—needing to make the commitment Betty Friedan says is necessary to growth— "but Grace Metalious had gone ahead and done it," Goodkind recalls. Surely those housewives would want to read what Grace Metalious had done—and he asked Kitty Messner to gamble $5,000, get a good press agent, and really promote Grace Metalious and her book.

Kitty, a gambler with a flair for betting on horses, agreed to bet on Grace and *Peyton Place*. She staked Goodkind to his $5,000, and he immediately called CBS, asking them to recommend a publicist who'd never done a book before.

They gave him one name: Alan "Bud" Brandt, an ambitious PR man who, still in his thirties, owned his own company, and had promoted "Howdy Doody," Harry Belafonte, Mike Wallace, and "The $64,000 Question."

"Can books be sold like TV shows?" Goodkind asked Brandt.

"Why not?" Brandt said, and asked to see part of *Peyton Place*.

He read the galley proofs with a publicist's eye, and said, with more than a little pleasure, "It's a *very* dirty book. They're doing and saying *very naughty things*."

Howard Goodkind agreed. When he'd read the book, he'd been especially struck by the back-seat grappling scene between Betty Anderson, the millworker's daughter, and Rodney Harrington, the owner's son.

> *"Is it up, Rod?"* she panted, undulating her body under his. *"Is it up good and hard?"*
>
> *"Oh, yes,"* he whispered, almost unable to speak. *"Oh, yes."*
>
> (Betty pushes him away, jumps out of the car, and screams): *"Now go shove it into Allison MacKenzie!"*

"Wow!" Brandt and Goodkind agreed. Brandt also felt that this Grace Metalious was a fine storyteller: her book had "a ring of truth, even the 'naughty' parts." *Peyton Place* was also highly unusual for its time: not only in the "naughtiness," but in Allison's going out on her own to become an independent woman.

Bud Brandt and Howard Goodkind went out on their own to promote *Peyton Place*. Both were native New Yorkers, and Goodkind confesses that he once believed the Norman Rockwell image of small towns: fishing poles, patriotism, apple pie, the Fourth of July. *Peyton Place* proved a revelation to him—and so did the July trip he and Bud Brandt took to Gilmanton, to "do" Grace Metalious.

"This can't be the place," Bud said as they arrived at "It'll Do," the shack where Grace lived. To enter the house, they had to step over a pile of garbage at the door. Inside, it seemed that nothing put down was ever put away. Dirty dishes lay everywhere. Flies swarmed around an open jar of marshmallows, and when the children said they were hungry, Grace told them, "Make yourself a peanut butter and marshmallow sandwich"—and handed them a goo-covered knife. On another occasion, she picked up what she thought was a Brillo pad—and found a dead mouse.

The children themselves were sloppily dressed—though Marsha, at twelve, seemed to have a "certain dignity," the publicity men remember. George was also there, but mostly silent.

Grace escorted the two New Yorkers to a Grange supper—the first in their lives—and sat between them, sometimes giving a running commentary. "See that man?" she said once, indicating one of the local people. "*His* wife and *her* husband"—gesturing toward someone else—"were out on the ice together in a car and left the engine running. The ice melted, and they drowned." She told the story with obvious relish.

Feeling a bit like a traveling circus, Brandt and Goodkind took pictures of everything: the Metaliouses' fat black puppy, Ernie; the Gilmanton Corners School; the corner store; the little Keytones, busily learning a square dance in the auditorium.

As they drove past one house, Grace told another favorite story. "See that house? A girl who lived in there had panties for every day of the week. And then," Grace said, with the expectant hush of the skilled storyteller, "she lost 'Tuesday.' And her father *really* beat the shit out of her!"

Toward the end of their stay, Grace mentioned that her husband's contract was up at the local school. He'd be losing his job, and they didn't know what they'd do.

No one is quite sure what was said next, but Bud Brandt suspects he said something like, "It's a shame it's not because of the book."

Grace looked thoughtful and said something like, "Well, in a way it is . . ."

And Brandt said, "Well, it's certainly a good story . . ."

He wanted to think it was true, because her husband's being fired for her book made such superb publicity. At the same time Grace, seeking male approval, wanted to please Bud Brandt. Her husband's firing also fit so well with Grace's image: the unconventional character, the town revolutionary. Neither Brandt nor Goodkind chose to investigate further.

Returning to New York, they carried a strange memento from Grace: a turtle egg embedded in sand. They also had a possible key to their publicity campaign in George's job troubles—but only if Grace followed it up.

Meanwhile, Grace was finding the publicity side of writing a book very strange, and Laurie Wilkens recorded her friend's thoughts in the Laconia *Evening Citizen*. "She had written the book the very best she could, and she had believed that it would stand or fall on its worth as literature, or its value as a true picture of a part of America not yet touched by writers. But she was assured that this was just a beginning. There would be lots more indeed."

In July Grace also got her advance copies of *Peyton Place*. She gave Laurie the number one copy, and later wrote, "I don't imagine that I'll ever feel again about any book I may write as I did about the first one. To me, it was the most beautiful sight in the world to see my name on the spine of a hard cover. I kept one copy of the book for myself and gave the others away, perhaps not as discreetly as I should have done."

But Grace had always insisted on being indiscreet. Now she had a partner: The publicity campaign Bud Brandt was running—through little gossip column items, to get the public ready for *Peyton Place*. Readers of Dorothy Kilgallen's syndicated column on August 7, 1956, for instance, learned that "Publishing circles are gabbing about a forthcoming novel titled *Peyton Place*—a shocker about life in a small New England town. The author, mother of three, is the wife of a school principal in New Hampshire."

The item gave, in essence, what publishing people call a book's "handle"—the way it will be marketed. The appeal of *Peyton Place* would be the contrast between the respectable author—who, as small-town mother and schoolteacher's wife, fit perfectly the image of fifties' conformity—and the shocking contents of her book.

The publicity campaign did have Grace worried.

One day that summer, Bernard Snierson's secretary told him a "very agitated" woman was in the outer office, wanting to see him.

Grace Metalious came in, her hair in a ponytail, her hands gesturing nervously. "I've written a book, and when it's published, I'll have to move out of Gilmanton," she told Snierson.

"Then don't publish the book," he said, somewhat amused.

"But I have to!"

He shrugged, figuring she'd do as she chose. But he became Grace's trusted legal advisor—and later, when she called him to negotiate the movie rights for her book, he began to take the whole business much more seriously.

He also tried to give Grace advice about publicity, but she was her own best PR woman. The Messner publicists had stressed the small-town angle, and hinted the book would be shocking—but Grace made sure it would be a best seller, once and for all.

"I feel pretty sure of one thing," Grace told Hal Boyle, the big, gruff, cigar-smoking Associated Press columnist. Bud Brandt had set up the interview, and Grace delivered the word on *Peyton Place:* "It'll probably cost my husband his job."

The Boston *Traveler* of August 29 bore a two-inch headline:

TEACHER FIRED
FOR WIFE'S BOOK
Gossipy, Spicy
Story Costs
Him His Job

Grace Metalious' story pushed everything else out of the headlines: the jury selection for the Brink's robbery case; the recovery of Jacqueline Kennedy, wife of Massachusetts Senator John F. Kennedy, from a miscarriage; and even the story of a New Haven nurse accused of shaking three infants to death—a cheerful woman "acutely embarrassed by her inordinate size, a lonely woman who seemed to have no life of her own and tried to enjoy vicariously the lives of her temporary employers."

Grace Metalious was enabling everyone, especially housewives, to live vicariously, to read about—and deplore—the "schoolteacher's wife" who had produced a "literary sensation."

"Three people have already cut me dead on the street," Grace told Hal Boyle, "and the book isn't even out yet." Bud Brandt remembers how Grace's eyes flashed with anger and tears as she told Boyle: "I'm afraid the school board won't want to keep as principal a man married to a woman who wrote about the things I did."

She left "the things" unspecified, but Boyle filled in enough: Grace Metalious had set out to "lift the lid off a small New England town," and "wound up by pulling it off its hinges." As for the book's contents: "With Freudian frankness she unveils high-level brutality and low-level squalor, hidden vices and illicit romances, petty meannesses and quiet heroism." She also includes "a few love scenes that might raise Ernest Hemingway's eyebrows or cause Kathleen Winsor to blush."

Indeed, said Boyle, using the handle Bud Brandt had given him for *Peyton Place,* "It's an odd book to come from the typewriter of a plump, 32-year-old mother of three children. But Mrs. Metalious is no ordinary housewife."

Grace had gone to New York several times to huddle with the publicity people. She hated to drive and hated the bustle of New York, and usually took someone with her: Laurie, Laurie's daughters Joanne and Wendy, her own daughter Marsha. On one trip, she realized she had "nothing to wear" to see the publicists—and gave Joanne Wilkens, fourteen, $25 and sent her out to buy a dress. Joanne, delighted, came back with a very teenagey ensemble: a pink angora sweater, a black wool skirt—but Grace was grateful and enthusiastic, "Oh, they're beautiful!"

Grace looked like a little girl, "off to see the lions," Laurie thought. Often Laurie went with her on publicity interviews—for the adventure, and occasionally to curb what Grace said. What Grace considered honesty, others sometimes considered brutal frankness, and one day when Laurie wasn't along, Grace made the comment that gave her trouble for years afterward.

What about New England? Hal Boyle had asked. "To a tourist these towns look as peaceful as a postcard picture," Grace said. "But if you go beneath that picture, it's like turning over a rock with your foot—all kinds of strange things crawl out. Everybody who lives in town knows what's going on—there are no secrets—but they don't want outsiders to know."

Gilmantonians never forgave her for that remark.

Still, Grace reiterated to Hal Boyle, she had no intention of leaving Gilmanton for the pressure-filled life of New York or Boston. "Why, I wouldn't want to live anywhere else." In a small town, she said, "there is time for everything. The 'ax mouths' may talk about you, but if you want to be let alone, they'll let you alone—utterly and finally alone. No matter what crime you commit, you can always go on living in a small town; that is, unless you are caught stealing.

"A parent in a small New England town would rather it be known his teenage daughter was having an illicit romance than that she had been caught taking a nickel candy bar from a store."

Grace's reflections did not endear her to Gilmanton—nor did the Associated Press story by Joseph Kamin, giving the "facts" of the case: that a young grammar school principal whose wife had written "an earthy novel about life in a small New England town" had been fired from his $3,000 a year job.

"They told me it was because of my wife," George Metalious had said. "They don't like her book."

And Grace added that her husband's firing "is an example of small-town intolerance. You live in a town, and there are patterns.

"The minute you deviate from the pattern," she continued, "you're a freak. I wrote a book, and that makes me a freak. They don't like that."

The book was not a portrayal of Gilmanton, Grace insisted. "It's a composite picture of life in a small New Hampshire town, but it's not Gilmanton. As a matter of fact, the book was three-fourths written before I moved here."

But she had still more to say about Gilmantonians: "To a majority of people who live here," she said, her eyes flashing, "it's a dirty book. Word has got around that it's a shocking book. People suddenly decided that George is not the type to teach their sweet innocent children."

Under such headlines as "TEACHER'S WIFE DEFIES TOWN OVER HER NEW BOOK," and "FUROR OVER WIFE'S NOVEL GETS PRINCIPAL SACKED" and "EARTHY NOVEL MAY MAKE LITERARY HISTORY," newspapers all over the U.S. included pictures of the Metaliouses as an all-American family. In one picture Grace, Marsha, and Mike do a jigsaw puzzle together, laughing, while George hugs little Cindy on his lap. In another, Grace and George eat breakfast and read the newspaper together, smiling.

In the most popular photo, the one on the front of the Laconia *Evening Citizen,* Grace and George sit together on a sofa, George holding his pipe and reading from a book on his lap (presumably *Peyton Place*). Grace, her finger to her mouth, leans toward him, her elbow resting on his shoulder: she looks both affectionate and provocative. There are few pictures of Grace alone. She almost always appears in the bosom of her family, as a happily domestic housewife and mother.

Meanwhile, school-board members in Gilmanton (population 800, 448 of them voters) disagreed vigorously with Grace and George's version of events, according to the Associated Press.

"We just thought a change might do George good," said William Dunn, chairman of the three-member Gilmanton school board. "His wife's book had absolutely nothing to do with it. It was a personal matter.

"I like George," Dunn added. "I always did like him, and I wish him lots of luck in his new job. He started to do a beautiful job here, but other things entered into it.

"The book was the last thing in the board's mind—we didn't have any idea what was in it. All I can say is, we have our own reasons."

He had talked with people who said they'd read parts of *Peyton Place,* Dunn reported. "It sounded to me, from what I was told, that she is opening up some old wounds in Gilmanton, and I'm afraid there will be some trouble."

"As far as I'm concerned, it was strictly a matter of Mr. Metalious' qualifications," insisted Olive Besse, a school-board member further identified by her husband, Harry's, position: town moderator and president of the Boston Stock Exchange. Mrs. Besse was candid about George: "I was against him from the start, but I was outvoted, and I'd be against him again." But her opposition, she said, had nothing to do with *Peyton Place*: "I haven't seen the book. I don't know what it's about. It was just a simple matter of doing the right thing for the pupils in our school."

The third school-board member, Bill Wilkens—Laurie's husband—was not quoted. As Grace often pointed out, no public reason was ever given for George's dismissal.

On August 30 the media invaded Gilmanton: buzzing through town in big, shiny cars; accosting local people and posing peculiar questions; lurking around Laurie Wilkens' farmhouse, disrupting summer pickling; and taking innumerable photographs of the town Americans everywhere assumed was "the real Peyton Place"—despite Grace's denials.

Early in the day, Gilmantonians had been confused—but as the madness continued, they turned silent. And then angry, when they learned what Hal Boyle had said about *Peyton Place:* It "brings *Tobacco Road* up North and gives it a Yankee accent." Townspeople were more than miffed when they realized reporters actually considered Gilmanton a northern Tobacco Road. As Laurie Wilkens pointed out in the Laconia *Evening Citizen,* it took a white-haired lady, Mrs. Maude Schultz, to defuse the tension. (Years later, Mrs. Schultz's niece, Ruth Chandler, married Grace's friend Bob Athearn.)

Maude Schultz lived at "Frisky Hill," a gracious 200-year-old house nestled among guardian maples. The view from Frisky Hill was magnificent; the home, Laurie wrote, "is the epitome of all that is beautiful and beloved in New England living."

Tucked away in her ultra-dignified setting, Mrs. Schultz contrived a sign in big red letters, and stuck it under the guardian maples, at the edge of her well-swept drive.

The sign read: "TOBACCO ROAD."

As word got around, the incongruity of the sign moved local people to helpless and relieved laughter: "For in one great and humorous gesture," Laurie wrote, "Mrs. Schultz reduced the whole furor about our town into a ridiculous heap. . . . And thus valiantly did this proud white-haired lady vanquish the tabloids, and restore laughter to Gilmanton."

Grace was not laughing, however. The media invasion terrified her. Then the news that her sister Bunny's husband Charlie had been killed in an accident—news Grace got in the newspaper, not from Bunny—threw her into a state of depression and loneliness. But no one knew, for as Laurie wrote, "the machinery of publicity was grinding well, and had no room for personal sorrow."

CHAPTER 10

Peyton Place would not be published until September 24, but the furor continued, as newspeople pursued the story to George Metalious' new job—interspersing their coverage with daily bulletins from Gilmanton. According to a United Press International report reprinted in the Laconia *Evening Citizen,* school officials in Stow, Massachusetts (population 1,700) had no doubts about George's fitness for his new job.

The Stow School Superintendent, Edward J. Harriman, said George had been thoroughly investigated, and found acceptable in all respects. Durwood R. Frost, the school-committee clerk, added that unless *Peyton Place* "contains something detrimental to the community or the country, I can't see why he, Metalious, should be jeopardized for something his wife has written."

Meanwhile, the tone in Gilmanton was "more varied," the wire services reported.

"I don't know what's in the book," Police Chief Roland Hawkins said, "but I am to make sure that no book written to corrupt our morals is offered for sale here."

Some people, who refused to be named, felt the book contained thinly veiled Gilmanton characters. But Art McClary, a farmer who had read an advance copy, said, "It is dirty, but I couldn't tie it to any people living here."

Fred Bucciarelli, who ran the Gilmanton Corners general store, had grudgingly given the Metaliouses credit when they couldn't pay for groceries, and he had decided views about *Peyton Place*. "From what I heard, it's going to hurt a lot of people."

He himself had not read the book, he conceded, but announced that he would not stock it. "Not with a ten-foot pole will I touch it. I'm darned if I'm going to take sides on a story that has split the town in half."

Mrs. Nellie Clifford, who had been running the town's two-room library for the previous eighteen years, agreed that "This is awful for the town's reputation. I doubt if this library will carry the book. Our annual budget is only one hundred dollars."

But Mrs. John Gard dared to express the most common sentiment: "I'm dying to read it."

Meanwhile, the Boston *Post* reported from Stow, "This staid little town in the Nashoba apple-growing belt seethed with excitement tonight after it was learned that the wife of a newly appointed high school teacher has authored a lusty Tobacco Road type of book about New England small town life."

"That book by the new teacher's wife" was the only topic of conversation all over Stow: in the police station, the fire house, the library, the fraternal organizations, the ice cream parlors, and candy stores. Everyone wondered what the new teacher would be like—and most important, "Where can I get a copy?"

The Stow school authorities remained on the defensive. Durwood R. Frost, "heaving a big sigh" as he answered questions in his apple orchard, told reporters that "this is definitely a staid New England town," and the book "certainly has gotten things started here. It is a great way to sell a book with all this fanfare."

Frost insisted on the town's interests: "If the reflection of this notoriety affects Mr. Metalious' teaching ability or in any way is harmful to the boys and girls in the high school, I think we might have to revoke his appointment. But if his wife's novel is a big success, he probably won't need a teaching job.

"We have always been conservative in this town. In fact, when we were looking for a picture theme for our high school, where Mr. Metalious is scheduled to teach, we had a hard time.

"Finally we settled on a painting showing a man plowing and a woman spinning. A typical New England scene of yesteryear."

And that was much of the problem for Stow: Grace Metalious

and her book—which was still three weeks from publication—did not appear to fit the image of New England, at least as the natives wanted to see it.

Nevertheless, it was an unusually interesting time, according to one Stow official: "There hasn't been so much excitement here since the battle at nearby Lexington and Concord."

Meanwhile back in Laconia, Grace gave her first radio interview, on station WLNH. Esther Peters, who'd called Grace as soon as the "scandal" broke about George's job, was then the only female broadcaster at the Laconia station. Though a Manchester station had hired one woman, and Mary Margaret McBride did national radio programs, women in the mass media were extremely rare.

"You have a good radio voice," Arthur "Roxy" Rothafel, owner of WLNH, had told Esther Peters at a party. She paid little attention to his remark until the day Roxy's lone woman broadcaster broke her leg skiing. Roxy called Esther and said: "You take her place."

Esther, who'd never done anything in broadcasting, began by demanding equal rights. What salary did she want? she was asked, and answered, "I'll take the same as the men are getting." She knew that women in broadcasting generally were paid less, but she got equal pay—and soon opened bank and charge accounts in her own name, a radical step for a married woman in the fifties. As Roxy's representative, she joined the Chamber of Commerce, as its only woman member, and in the meantime, raised Roxy's consciousness about what the station could do for women.

WLNH had the standard format: music, news, and sports—which, Esther said, did not meet women's needs. Women at home during the day should hear more about their communities, she argued: they'd be better-informed and make better conversationalists if they knew Who and What and When. When Roxy agreed, Esther began her own show, "Around Town": two segments, 90 minutes in all, of interviews and service pieces.

When Grace Metalious came to WLNH in early September 1956, she wore moccasins without socks, her hair in a ponytail, a checked cotton shirt (she had cotton ones for the summer, wool for the winter), and what Esther remembers as "her famous dungarees." She made her way nervously to the studio, then on the second floor of the Masonic Temple next door to the Laconia Tavern. It would be her first radio interview ever—but she and Esther immediately took to each other, recognizing kindred, independent spirits.

Grace told Esther and the "Around Town" radio audience about *Peyton Place,* her unpublished novel—a story written from several characters' points of view, she said. A book club—maybe the Book of the Month Club, she thought—had considered *Peyton Place* as a selection, but with a catch: they wanted Grace to delete some passages and change some episodes.

"Will you?" Esther asked.

"Oh, no," Grace said firmly. "I'm not going to do that. That's my work, and I'm not going to change it for anybody."

"Good for you," said Esther.

Since the book had not yet been published, Esther Peters had no idea what a stir it would cause, particularly among those who knew the Glenn family and the "sheep pen murder." When the book did appear, neighbors were shocked that Esther let her children—then sixteen, fourteen, and eleven—read the notorious best seller. But Esther always liked Grace and respected her right to be herself, to write and do what she chose.

A week before publication date, *Peyton Place* was already fourth on the best-seller lists, and Twentieth Century-Fox was bidding for the film option.

The day before publication, Messner's took a full-page ad in the New York *Times Book Review:* a paste-up of newspaper headlines Doris Flowers (of Messner's) and Mel Fauer (of the Sussman Advertising Agency) had put together over Labor Day weekend. They had gotten the keys to the office, contrived the ad very quickly, and delivered it by hand to *Publishers Weekly* and the *Times.*

Under the banner, "This is the explosive book that was headlined all over the country!" they superimposed over a picture of *Peyton Place* eleven of the choicest headlines—among them, "BOOK HAS N.H. TOWN AGOG," "CRITICIZE TOBACCO ROAD SLANT TO N. H. NOVEL," and "TOWN FOLK WILL READ IT—BAN OR NO BAN."

On September 24, 1956, *Peyton Place* finally appeared on bookstands. It stayed on the best-seller list for twenty-six weeks; within a month after publication, 104,000 copies had been sold. (The average first novel in the United States sells no more than 3,000.) Even in Laconia, one bookseller told Grace he was selling a hundred copies a day in the middle of an "I-hate-Grace campaign."

Meanwhile, the campaign took its toll. In the wee morning hours, Grace got anonymous phone calls: "Get out of town or else." Threatening obscene letters came through the mail—along with odd appreciations: "I'm sure you're writing about my town. I live in Peyton Place," or "If you think Peyton Place is bad, you should live in my town."

When Jane Glenn's brother Orly sent Grace a threatening letter for using their family story, Grace tried to joke about it to Bernard Snierson: "Do you think he'll bury my body in a sheep pen?"

Snierson, not amused, called the F.B.I.

Letters to the editor debated the book's merits; libraries worried whether to purchase it—and local people wondered if their children should be in school with the Metalious youngsters. Marsha, twelve, was most aware of hostility—the withdrawal, the name-calling; Joanne Wilkens was one of few friends who stayed loyal. Marsha found herself crying a lot. "People were so mean that I didn't want to go to school," she recalled years later. In January 1958 she left for Stow, to live with her father and go to high school there.

Peyton Place was banned in Fort Wayne, Indiana, where Allen County Prosecutor Glenn Beams termed it "lewd and indecent," and in Rhode Island, where it had been found "objectionable for sale, distribution, or display for youths under eighteen years of age." It was the first novel to appear on the Rhode Island Commission's blacklist.

Though the Laconia public library did buy three copies of *Peyton Place,* other libraries adamantly refused. Anne LeCroy, later an English professor at East Tennessee State University, remembers a large sign in front of her public library in Beverly, Massachusetts: "THIS LIBRARY DOES NOT CARRY 'PEYTON PLACE.' IF YOU WANT IT, GO TO SALEM." Since Salem was then regarded as a Skid Row area where Beverly people went to wallow in vice, the sign amounted to saying, "Go to Sodom."

Prospective readers could not go to Canada, where the importation of *Peyton Place* had been banned. Canadian Revenue Minister J. J. McCann ruled that the book fell within the scope of Tariff Provision 1201, which prohibited importing books "of an indecent or immoral character." Several other departmental reviewers, the Associated Press reported, also read the novel before the decision was reached.

Each banning increased sales enormously, and led to more letters to the editor, especially in the Gilmanton/Laconia area.

"Perhaps there is some virtue in living in a small town for half a century," Dorothy S. Rollins, a Republican town chairman, newspaper reporter, and mother of three, wrote to the Laconia *Evening Citizen*. (When she turned ninety in 1980, Rollins, also author of a poetry collection called "Rimes of a Rural Riter," was featured in the Manchester *Union Leader*. Publisher William Loeb credited her with showing Ronald Reagan the way to the White House, by teaching him to "campaign New Hampshire style.")

Small-town living teaches basic goodness, Rollins said in her letter to the editor—as opposed to what "the cigarette butts of the gutter" teach in a place like New York. She was referring to a book she did not mention by name: "the latest best seller, which in certain wide quarters has been called the filthiest, most vile book (?) ever penned in this state." (The question mark is Rollins'.)

"One could pardon the rottenness and profanity (that the book reeks of in almost every sentence) if it had been localized in that same section of the eight million teeming inhabitants, but can the stigma of such a piece of attempted literature built around any small town be forgotten or eradicated?"

Such trash had nothing to recommend it but obscenity, Rollins insisted, but "There is just one merit in this current salacious hodgepodge of reading. It will never be placed on the book shelves of any library for posterity to refer to and revere, but it will be thrown into the garbage barrel where it belongs!"

Rollins' was not an isolated sentiment, especially in New Hampshire. William Loeb, the arch-conservative publisher, devoted an editorial to *Peyton Place,* under the headline "The Filth They Live By." He did not mention the name of "a particularly filthy book" alleged to depict life in a New Hampshire community, but said the book would have great appeal to "certain people for whom the sordid has a morbid fascination." He added, in large capitals: "THERE ALWAYS ARE PEOPLE WHO ARE MORE PREOCCUPIED WITH THE BARNYARD ASPECTS OF EXISTENCE THAN WITH THE BRIGHT LIGHT THAT SHINES FROM ABOVE AND DISTINGUISHES MAN FROM THE BEAST."

He concluded that when such a book could become a best seller, then "This sad situation reveals a complete debasement of taste and a fascination with the filthy, rotten side of life that are the earmarks of the collapse of a civilization."

Grace did not take criticisms silently. Even before *Peyton Place* was published, a fruit stand owner named Gene DePontbriand had written a critical letter to the Nashua, New Hampshire, *Telegraph.* Grace fired off a quick reply, which the editors duly printed, "after slightly editing her copy which is really kind of abusive from the typewriter of a young married woman, any way you look at it."

"I am writing this letter against the advice of my agent, my publishers, my attorney, and my husband," Grace said in the published version of her letter. She had learned, she said, that it was good public relations to reply to letters of praise and good reviews, but useless to defend oneself against attacks. Nevertheless, she had some things to say about Gene DePontbriand.

"For someone who would like to sound highly allergic to sex, this DePontbriand certainly seems fairly familiar with the works of the late Dr. Kinsey and has apparently gone to a great deal of trouble to ferret out any and all sexual passages in 'Peyton Place.' Methinks DePontbriand doth protest too much."

And then Grace pinpointed the focus of countless attacks on her and her work: DePontbriand "goes along with the popular notion that because a woman happens to be a teacher's wife, she must automatically give up seeing, hearing, and thinking." Moreover, DePontbriand had suggested sending the book to the Soviet Union, but Grace suggested sending *him*—"he would make a fine ambassador" and could "really spread his ideas of freedom around like crazy."

She was also amused, she said, at DePontbriand's use of the word "filthy," as she'd been hearing the word a lot lately, and "apparently the shoe pinches just as badly in Nashua as it does in some of our smaller communities. I, too, would welcome an 'open-minded' discussion of the book with anyone of intelligence, but unfortunately it won't be with DePontbriand," whose reading, she imagined, "has been limited to the easy beginning, middle, ending single plot of the whodunits or the confessions."

She concluded that evil is in the eye of the beholder, "and poor DePontbriand must have an evil eye indeed." She offered to refund the $3.95 he'd spent to buy her book, since he seemed so worried about its juvenile delinquency and depravity. With the money he could "go out to buy comic books or make a down payment on a picture tube for the television set which, of course, never includes juvenile delinquency or depravity. Sincerely, Grace Metalious."

When the editor gave DePontbriand the last word, the fruit stand owner listed the great writers and books in his home library: Steinbeck, Fitzgerald, "Hemmingway," *Power of Bishop Sheen, Profiles in Courage, Iron Curtain Over America.* He said he recognized what Grace Metalious was writing: a compilation from such scandal sheets as *Confidential, Expose, Hush-Hush, Top Secret,* and their like "into one novel. This anyone can accomplish and really make a dollar in this day and age." And so, her book would never adorn a place in his home, he said, nor did he think it should be in a public library where it might be read by growing youngsters.

"Your reckless and irresponsible attack upon me has only justified you, the author Grace Metalious . . . I sincerely thank you once again, Mrs. Metalious, for 'Flipping Your Lid.' You are entitled to just that here in free America. My stand still remains unchanged about your book, and your attack upon me has been welcomed."

If in the future, trends in novels changed, DePontbriand concluded, he would be happy to have a clean novel by Grace Metalious in his home.

In an afterword, the editors of the Nashua *Telegraph* reported that the book had already sold five hundred copies in Nashua, in only two weeks. Moreover, the Nashua public library would carry the book, though not in the juvenile section.

During the first ten days it was out, the book had sold over 60,000 copies—despite some rather negative responses by literary people. Sterling North, the critic, expressed shock that a young mother should publish a book "with such uninhibited language." And in Paris, novelist Pierre Fisson, winner of the Prix Ranaudot, said in a newspaper review that if Paris ever banned any book, it ought to ban *Peyton Place*.

Small-town reviewers were more hostile; big-city ones often saw some virtues in the book, or at least some promise. "The writing is good of its kind, but has a lush over-ripeness that matches the tone and pace of the tale. That pace is swift, for Mrs. Metalious has great narrative skill," Edmund Fuller wrote in the Chicago Sunday *Tribune*.

"When Authoress Metalious is not all flustered by sex, she captures a real sense of the temper, texture, and tensions in the social anatomy of a small town," the *Time* reviewer wrote.

"She has humor, heart, vigor, a feeling for irony (as well as unblushing candor and a relentless flow of profanity)," Phyllis Hogan said in the San Francisco *Chronicle*.

The book was reviewed everywhere, including the Sunday New York *Times Book Review,* whose reviews have the greatest influence on book sales. There the critic was a noted academic, Professor Carlos Baker of the Princeton English Department, who pointed out that Grace Metalious was writing in the tradition of great American authors who exposed the underside of small town life: Sherwood Anderson, Edmund Wilson, John O'Hara. "Sinclair Lewis would no doubt have hailed Grace Metalious as a sister-in-arms against the false fronts and bourgeois pretensions of allegedly respectable communities."

What Grace Metalious did was perhaps a little "riper," a little more "hotly passionate" than the others' writings—"and, perhaps, a little more widely inclusive."

"Mrs. Metalious," Baker said, "is a pretty fair writer for a first novelist . . . with the Indian Summer air of an emancipated modern authoress who knows the earthy words and rarely stints to use them." Baker recalled some of the novel's more sordid adventures, but concluded on a positive note: "If Mrs. Metalious can turn her emancipated talents to less lurid purposes, her future as a novelist is a good bet."

Her future as a celebrity and notorious public figure seemed even more certain, especially with negative reviews like that in the *Catholic World:* "This novel is one of the cheapest, most blatant attempts in years to present the most noxiously commonplace in ideas and behavior in the loose and ill-worn guise of realistic art."

While Grace both reveled in her fame and feared it, readers all over the country sampled the notorious book. Publicists can make a book sell at first, but after that word-of-mouth takes over. For a book to sell continuously, it must meet readers' needs—and *Peyton Place* met all kinds of appetites.

CHAPTER 11

"I didn't find out about masturbation until I was eighteen and going to Finch College," rock singer Grace Slick told Karl Fleming and Anne Taylor Fleming, editors of *The First Time.* "I was lying down on the bed, reading a book called *Peyton Place,* and it was a horny book. It was resting on my crotch and I was reading along and all of a sudden it got me off. I had gotten off with boys before, either dry-fucking or actually doing it, but I'd never done that before. I didn't know about it. For the next two weeks I went bananas with it."

Grace Slick managed to read *Peyton Place* openly, as adults everywhere did. At Fort Chaffee, Arkansas, Michael True remembers, he could walk down the center aisle of any barracks and see forty men lying on their bunks, all still in army boots, reading the paperback version of *Peyton Place.* Everyone was reading it: college graduates (like True himself, fresh from a Master's program at the University of Minnesota); high school dropouts; even "Ozark Mountain boys" who rarely read at all. All were waiting, he suspects, for Indian summer as Grace Metalious describes it on the first page of *Peyton Place:* "Ripe, hotly passionate, fickle."

The book was so popular that Doris Flowers at Messner's had to ration the printings, to make sure at least some hardback copies —never enough to keep up with demand—would get to every part of the country. Once the Dell paperback came out, younger readers could also buy the book at their local drugstores—although a Rhode Island bookseller was fined for selling the book to minors. Teenagers knew they weren't supposed to be reading *Peyton Place*. They also knew they *had* to read it.

High schoolers hid *Peyton Place* behind physics books, between yearbooks and record albums, under blankets, in attics, inside lunch boxes, under the debris in school lockers. They passed the book around in study hall; they read it aloud at pajama parties; they kept it under their bedcovers, with a flashlight handy. Honor students, allowed access to the "suppressed shelf" in libraries, passed over the bare-breasted natives in the *National Geographic* —and took up *Peyton Place*.

Baby-sitters combed their employers' shelves for the book and read it quickly—praying the children wouldn't wake up and catch them with the forbidden book. Then the baby-sitters begged to sit again for the same people—so they could finish the book.

Peyton Place gave suburban teenagers "the real world"—or so most of them thought at the time. (More than fifty people eagerly described to me their first encounters with *Peyton Place,* and they spoke with the kind of relish usually reserved for sexual initiation. Some still did not want their names mentioned.)

Nearly a quarter-century later, first readers can still recite the breast references: "nipples hard as diamonds"; "the breasts of a virgin . . . the sexy sag of maturity." Teenage readers remember the rape of Selena Cross, Selena's killing her father in self-defense, and the dramatic moment when gruff Dr. Swain confesses that he gave Selena an abortion—to save her future. Early readers recall the squirming love scene between Betty Anderson and Rodney Harrington on the beach, and Betty's question to Rodney in the back seat of a parked car: "Is it up, Rod? Is it up good and hard?" The adolescents of 1956 still revel most in the midnight swim Constance MacKenzie takes with the massive, virile, high school principal, Tom Makris (Mike Rossi).

> *"Untie the top of your bathing suit," he said harshly. "I want to feel your breasts against me when I kiss you."*

Readers now in their late thirties and mid-forties still cite that scene as the quintessence of romance—showing an adolescent urgency about sex that appeared in nothing else teenagers could read. That *Peyton Place* was forbidden made it a necessity, and when one very liberal Los Angeles parent bought her daughter a copy, the teenage daughter was enraged: "I wanted to buy it myself, so I could rebel!"

To teenagers in 1956, *Peyton Place* represented lust and rebellion—against boredom, conformity, the double standard. Teenage girls noticed that when Allison MacKenzie goes to the big city, she has sex outside marriage, with a man she doesn't love—and is not punished for it, contrary to advice given in such books as Evelyn Mills Duvall's *Facts of Life and Love for Teenagers*. Allison's adventures—like Elvis Presley's performances—suggested that adults might not have all the answers.

In 1955 the top teenage singing idol had been Pat Boone, whose white bucks, short hair, religious orientation, and clean-cut looks made him the perfect boy to bring home. His songs about teenage love were equally clean-cut: meetings at the corner drugstore; walking home together on Saturday afternoons. But in January 1956, Elvis Presley made his national TV debut.

Elvis had long hair and sideburns, a lazy sensual smile, and a deep, growling voice on "Heartbreak Hotel" and "Blue Suede Shoes" and "Baby, Let's Play House." His movements below the waist earned him the nickname "Elvis the Pelvis"—and on Ed Sullivan's show he was photographed from the waist up, only. From the studio audience's screams, TV watchers could tell something else was happening—the forbidden fruit which *Peyton Place* also delivered: intimations of sex. The week *Peyton Place* was published, the number one song was Elvis Presley's "Don't Be Cruel." It was also the number one song of the year—as *Peyton Place* was the number one book.

Elvis Presley and Grace Metalious both proclaimed that young people had more choices than suburbia and gray flannel suits (although Sloan Wilson's *The Man in the Gray Flannel Suit* was still an adult best seller). Elvis and Grace suggested that women could be sexual—and under the right conditions, ought to be. But not all adults appreciated their messages.

"I readily confess that I never read *Peyton Place,* just skimmed thru it, even tho it was 'guaranteed' to employ often throughout the book all of the 7 basic four-letter words," Louise Harriman Taylor wrote in 1980. "Being a native of New Hampshire and proud of my state, it may rightfully be presumed Metalious' book annoyed the aitch out of me. Metalious won a reputation for a finely honed nose for dirt and well-developed meanness of spirit." As for *Peyton Place:* "The book, I am sure, is a compilation of truths, half-truths, distortions of the truth and once upon a time might have had the distinction of being called a 'pot-boiler' or 'hack writing.'"*

"The book hurt a lot of innocent people," claimed a University of New Hampshire professor in 1980 (and insisted that his name not be used). Asked who had been hurt, and how, he refused to elaborate. Asked his own opinions, he said, "I never read the book. There's enough sordid in this world."

Finding sordidness in *Peyton Place* is not difficult—although characters guilty of sordid behavior are usually punished. Finding the "7 basic four-letter words" is impossible, since *Peyton Place* contains only three of the seven traditionally banned from the air-waves: shit, piss, and tits. "Frig" and "friggin" represent the common four-letter word for which Ben Hecht, in *A Child of the Century,* substituted "futter" (as in the adventures of one reporter who "futtered" twenty-five women in one night).

Nevertheless, readers of—or about—*Peyton Place* generally found what they were looking for. The "good parts" were well-known—and most copies opened to them. But those who read the entire book found a great deal more: an attack on small-town hypocrisy and conformity, on violence against the powerless, and on restricted lives for women—all the traps Grace Metalious hoped to escape by writing a book.

"Indian summer is like a woman," *Peyton Place* begins, in a lush opening reminiscent of *Kings Row*—but Henry Bellamann's descriptions are general, not particularly female. "Ripe, hotly passionate, but fickle," Grace Metalious continues, "she comes and goes as she pleases so that one is never sure whether she will come

---

* No actual New Hampshire town corresponds to Peyton Place in both population (3,675) and location (on the Connecticut River, north of Manchester, above White River). The closest geographical candidate is Hanover, site of Dartmouth, population 6,147—but when Grace was considering a third *Peyton Place* book in 1961, she insisted that Peyton Place had never been a college town.

at all, nor for how long she will stay. In northern New England, Indian summer puts up a scarlet-tipped hand to hold winter back for a little while."

Like *Kings Row, Peyton Place* begins with an aerial view of the town, and then introduces village characters: old men lounging at the courthouse, commenting on town events; a tipsy handyman whose profane comments amuse the schoolchildren; a spinster schoolteacher who is a perceptive and devoted molder of young minds.

Readers meet the children as she sees them: a full-lipped budding playboy; a sensitive boy the others think is "queer"; an early-blooming girl, with intense and secretive eyes; an other-side-of-the-tracks girl who is pretty, coarse, and shrewd; and a dreamy, thoughtful, "different" young person who doesn't fit in with the others—and is the teacher's special pet.

The first four characters—*Peyton Place's* Rodney Harrington, Norman Page, Selena Cross, and Betty Anderson—strongly resemble their *Kings Row* counterparts. But for the fifth, the sensitive adolescent who becomes the center of the story, Grace changed the sex. Bellamann's Parris Mitchell becomes Grace's Allison MacKenzie, who—like Parris—loves nature, leaves her small town to make her way in a larger world, but returns home deciding it is the only place for her after all.

"Not since *Kings Row,*" the *Peyton Place* jacket proclaims, "has there appeared such a penetrating study of human nature, such a frank, uninhibited story of violent emotions." *Kings Row* showed Grace Metalious the kind of book she wanted to write: an anatomy of small-town virtues and vices, with sordidness and nobility, seriousness, and humor.

"Reading *Kings Row* helped Grace realize that she had a story to tell, too," says Helen Meyer, president of Dell Publishing when Dell did the *Peyton Place* paperback. But Grace Metalious' book is shorter, faster-paced, and less philosophical than *Kings Row*— and far more interested in what women can do with their lives.

As editor, Kitty Messner had cut several long descriptions of nature, and eliminated some graphic passages about the sexual kinks of Norman Page and the virility of Tomas Makris. But she left untouched the tight, interlocking plots of *Peyton Place:* Allison MacKenzie's becoming a writer; Constance MacKenzie's recognizing her own sexuality; Selena Cross's victory over her rapacious stepfather; Dr. Matthew Swain's nobility in protecting Selena's future; the local hands' comical and disgusting winterlong drinking binge; and Rodney Harrington's sudden death, a punishment for his own selfishness and his father's exploitation of the poor and the weak in Peyton Place.

Peyton Place retains the vivid descriptions of New England life: changing seasons, forest fires, village carnivals, town meetings. Kitty also kept the book's satirical side, including the town drunk, Kenny Stearns, whose inebriated murmurings are taken for "the unknown tongue" by the worshippers in the Peyton Place Pentecostal Full Gospel Church—better known as "That Bunch of Holy Rollers Down on Mill Street." Hearing his babblings, believers immediately baptize Kenny Stearns and ordain him a minister of their sect.

Allison's early writings also come in for satire: "Lisa's Cat," her prize-winning story, is a parody of Somerset Maugham—about an English Foreign Service gentleman who, when he hears a black cat's cries, finds his faithless wife Lisa in her lover's arms. Allison's gentleman then travels "up country," catches the plague, and dies—and both Connie and Tom wonder how such a story ever won a prize.

Grace was undoubtedly poking fun at her own youthful writings —and *Peyton Place* also includes two characters she created years before, at U.N.H.: Hester Goodale and Norman Page. Moreover, "Anyone who writes draws from his experience," Grace said more than once, "and anyone who says he doesn't is a liar. I write what I've heard and seen and even what I've lived through. I have to write what I know"—and *Peyton Place* includes a great deal of Grace Metalious' past, together with her dreams for the future.

Ash Street Grammar School, where Grace DeRepentigny first learned to read, inspires the Peyton Place elementary school: "Victorian architecture at its worst, made even more hideous by the iron fire escapes which zigzagged down both sides of the building, and by the pointed, open belfry which topped the structure." Peyton Place's street names are Manchester's—with Elm as the main street. Allison even lives on Beech Street, where Grace DeRepentigny lived during her high school years.

Allison has a lot of Grace DeRepentigny: her reading tastes (fairy tales, mysteries, de Maupassant, Maugham); her love for solitary walks in the woods; her literary ambitions. Physically, Allison resembles Grace DeRepentigny: fine, limp, brown hair in a ponytail; a round face that seems too round to her; a body that seems too plump in some places and too flat in others.

"As a child I had Allison's feelings of loneliness and isolation," Grace once told Olivia Skinner in a St. Louis interview. "I was an awful little stinker, but now that I think of it, she was too. Part of the trouble was that the adults around a creative child can be a headache." But Grace had also been troubled, as Allison is, by the lack of a father. Allison, like her creator, thinks her absent father must be "handsome as a prince" and "the kindest, most considerate gentleman in the world." Though she knows he's dead, Allison prays for her father's return—and seeks a father-figure in her agent.

Unlike Grace, however, Allison finds a father, for in *Peyton Place* Grace sometimes rewrites the script of her own life. Unlike Grace, Allison is solidly middle class, thanks to her mother's career as a dress shop owner—and Constance MacKenzie also marries, in Tom Makris, the perfect father for Allison (and Grace DeRepentigny). Tom is strong, kind, honest, and loving—and helps bring about a reconciliation between Allison and her mother. He does, in fiction, what no one could do for Grace—and Laurette—in real life.

Peyton Place is about several pairs of mothers and daughters and about wife-beating, rape, abortion, independence—the "women's issues" of the 1970s and '80s. The perceptions in *Peyton Place* are unusual for 1956: that wife-beating is not inevitable; that rape is an act of violence, not sexual pleasure; that abortion can mean saving a life—the mother's. Women who depend too heavily on men—for sex, money, or a sense of self—lose out in *Peyton Place*.

The winners are independent women like Allison, who pursues her writing, putting an unhappy love affair behind her; Connie, who acknowledges her sexuality—and keeps her career; and

Selena, who transcends desertion, rape, and murder and relies on herself—and her female friends. Allison and Selena both find women's friendships the most enduring relationships in Peyton Place. Unlike Grace Metalious in real life, women who succeed in *Peyton Place* depend less on men, more on a community of women, and most on themselves.

Nevertheless, *Peyton Place* does bear the marks of the fifties—notably the mass media's obsession with breasts. Marilyn Monroe, Jane Russell, and Jayne Mansfield filled movie screens in the mid-fifties, and virtually every female character in *Peyton Place* is defined by breast size, shape, or condition. Betty Anderson's nipples are "always rigid and exciting and the full, firm flesh around them always hot and throbbing"; Connie's nipples are "hard as diamonds" and "all pointed and tip tilted." But Connie and Betty also have thoughts and ambitions, and men who see women only as sex objects are punished in *Peyton Place*—as if Grace deliberately criticizes a one-dimensional view of women. Lucas Cross praises Selena for "the prettiest tits I ever seen"—and she kills him; Rodney Harrington reaches for his date's breasts—and is run over by a truck. In effect, "Slats" has her revenge.

Peyton Place is also Grace Metalious' revenge against the hypocritical and the powerful. Small-town morality condones (or ignores) Lucas Cross' depredations, because he pays his bills and minds his own business. Connie MacKenzie cannot be a happy, mature woman until she frees herself from her paralyzing, small-town fear of being talked about. Connie learns to be honest with others, and herself, just as Grace Metalious always proclaimed her honesty—but was often punished for it.

Meanwhile, the townspeople of Peyton Place, controlled by hypocritical mores, are also dominated by Leslie Harrington. An all-powerfull mill owner, Harrington thinks he can buy his way out of any difficulty: an inconvenient pregnancy his son has caused; a young woman's arm lost in carnival machinery because of his negligence. Like Harrington, the owners of the Amoskeag in Manchester, when Grace DeRepentigny was a child, never lost what the workers lost in the Depression. But Grace Metalious' created world is a just one: Leslie Harrington has his "comeuppance"—and it is a singularly satisfying sight for most readers.

Though *Peyton Place* sold as a notorious book about sex and violence, it had a great many positive messages—about honesty, integrity, and justice as well as sexual freedom and self-defense. *Peyton Place* mocks romantic and sexual pretenses—but supports women's friendships, women's anger, and creativity. At least intuitively, readers recognized the feminist messages in *Peyton Place* (though neither they nor Grace Metalious were apt to use the word "feminist" in 1956—since the struggle for suffrage was mostly forgotten).

But in print, no reviewers recognized *Peyton Place* as an attack on the feminine mystique—against the view that women should have only one destiny in life. Critics did see *Peyton Place* as an attack on bourgeois conformity; some recognized that Grace Metalious was breaking new ground for women writers—and they savaged her for it. In the New York *World Telegram,* Sterling North compared *Peyton Place* with the works of "masculine writers who have refused to use euphemisms where four letter words will do." Hemingway, James Jones, and Nelson Algren he found praiseworthy—"But never before in my memory has a young mother published a book in language approximately that of longshoremen on a bellicose binge." To him, Grace was a mother first—then a writer.

Margaret Latrobe, in her syndicated column, "Fairly Spoken," was even more negative toward *Peyton Place's* "outhouse verbs," "moral filth"—and female author. Some male writers, she said, sprinkle books with dirty words to "remind us that they are 'all boy,'" and "down-to-the-sod linguists. Somebody might think writers were effeminate! Gad!" As for Grace Metalious, she "apparently wants to prove that women writers aren't effeminate, either; that at least one can be just as ugly-spoken as any man writing."

North nevertheless conceded that Grace Metalious had "vigorous talent"—but Latrobe, one of the first women reviewers to attack Grace's gender as well as her book, made no such concessions. She had not one good word for *Peyton Place,* because Grace Metalious had sinned not only against canons of taste for books—but also against canons of taste for women.

Nevertheless, as Allison's story, *Peyton Place* stands as a portrait of the artist as a young woman—virtually the only one from the 1950s. As Connie's story, *Peyton Place* shows a woman who "has it all": blondeness and beauty; a loving, close relationship with her child; a successful career; and the perfect man (the fantasy figure Grace Metalious longed for: tall, dark, and handsome— but also honest, kind, and intuitive). Though Grace puts much of her past into Allison, it is Connie, a year older than Grace when *Peyton Place* opens, who represents Grace's dreams for the future. Moreover, Connie "has it all" without pretense, being fully herself—something Grace Metalious never felt herself allowed to do.

Neither money nor fame could emancipate Grace Metalious from her self-doubts, nor from the limits on women in the fifties —although, for a while, she thought she could break free.

When Grace went to New York in October 1956 to sign her movie contract, she felt she was "living on a pink cloud." On other visits she'd stayed at the Gladstone Hotel on East Fifty-second Street and Park Avenue, where Kitty Messner lived during the week. Now she went, instead, to the hotel famous for writers: the Algonquin, on West Forty-fourth Street off Sixth Avenue.

From there the New England housewife whose explosive best seller had reportedly cost her husband his teaching job surprised New Yorkers with her quiet ways. She wore no makeup except lipstick, kept her hair in a ponytail tied with a blue rubber band, did not swear at all, and drank, at most, an occasional bloody mary.

For the movie signing, George also came to New York, as did Bernard Snierson, though Kitty Messner had offered to provide a New York lawyer for Grace. Grace, George, Snierson, Jacques Chambrun, a movie company representative, and numerous other attorneys and publicists gathered for the great moment in Jacques's Fifth Avenue office.

Jerry Wald, the large, shrewd, ambitious producer who had just moved from a $3,000-a-week job at Columbia Pictures to an even better deal at Twentieth Century-Fox, wanted all the *Peyton Place* rights: movie, TV, and even rights to the name "Peyton Place." George hesitated over some of the clauses, and Grace also had her doubts—though she did not know that selling rights out-right was very unusual. Most contracts provide for residuals for the author, in case the book is an enormous success.

Jacques Chambrun advised her to take the offer: $250,000 with $75,000 on the spot.

"But it's my baby," Grace cried—and then finally, "Take it!" (Later she told T. J. Martin, a Laconia disc jockey who became more than that in her life, that she had rejected a percentage deal —because she didn't want continual reminders that she'd sold her "baby" to the ogres of Hollywood.)

Afterward at the Algonquin, George, Grace, and Bernard Snier-son set up a financial arrangement: a yearly income for Grace and trust funds for the children. A mother should provide for her chil-dren, the men said.

"How much do you need to live on?" Bernie Snierson asked Grace.

"Eighteen thousand a year, maybe," she said uncertainly. "But does this mean I won't control my own money?"

"Of course you won't control it," said Bernie, exasperated. "That's what this arrangement is for."

"I don't know, then . . ."

Still, George and Bernie thought they'd convinced her that the plan made good sense. Grace agreed that once Snierson put to-gether the proper legal papers in Laconia, she would sign them.

On the way back, Grace and George stopped in Boston to dis-cuss trust funds with a bank. Then George returned to teaching in Stow, while Grace went back to Laconia, where Byron Parker, president of the local bank, also urged her to set up trust funds. Bernie Snierson drew up the necessary papers.

Grace never signed them.

In Gilmanton, many debts awaited her. John O'Shea, owner of O'Shea's Department Store in Laconia, had always given her credit when she needed it. Other local creditors had not been so char-itable.

Ever since the Metaliouses had moved to Belmont in 1952, their family physician had been Dr. Leonard Slovack, a gruff ex-Marine whom Grace liked because he never minced words. Slovack, who called himself "charming as a snake," also came from a working-class Manchester background. His being Jewish interested Grace, and she was delighted to attend his son's bar mitzvah. She had also once shown him part of *Peyton Place* in manuscript, and he'd leafed through it, his cigar dangling from his mouth, and growled, "It'll never get off the ground."

Dr. Slovack usually gave the Metaliouses credit in a rather offhand way, but not long before *Peyton Place* appeared in print, his secretary had sent Grace a dunning letter. Grace owed four dollars.

As soon as she returned from New York, Grace drove to Dr. Slovack's office. She said she wanted to pay her bill with a check.

"Very well," said the nurse on duty. Grace handed the check over, and the nurse screamed for Dr. Slovack to come immediately.

"Cash that goddamn thing!" he roared back, keeping his teeth clamped about his cigar.

"I can't!" the nurse wailed, and pointed to the check.

It was Grace's movie check, for $75,000.

Grace was also in debt to Fred Bucciarelli, owner of the Gilmanton Corners general store, where she bought milk, meat, and other staples. "Butch" kept a complicated system of chits on the wall for "non-paying" customers like the Metaliouses. He had never liked Grace Metalious, and her sudden fame incensed him.

On one occasion, he overheard a tourist speaking breathlessly on the phone: "Joan, guess where I am! I'm in Peyton Place!"

Butch broke in abruptly. "No, ma'am, you're in Gilmanton."

Bucciarelli was glad, nevertheless, when Grace Metalious stopped at the corner store one day and said she wanted to pay her bill. "But can you take a check?"

"Of course."

"Can you cash a personal check made out to me?" A sly look came into her eye.

"Of course," Butch said impatiently.

"It's a rather large check."

"I can handle it," Butch insisted, more and more annoyed.

Grace handed him the movie check, for $75,000.

News of Butch's squelching spread all over town, and Grace reportedly played the same trick on other creditors. With her new earnings, she did pay off her bills, and bought a newer car, a 1951 Cadillac.

She had also managed to make herself even more unpopular—though at least one other local resident enjoyed the notoriety.

When tourists stopped at a shop belonging to Clint Brown, he sometimes told them he'd been the model for one of the characters in *Peyton Place*.

Looking at Brown, a cherubic-faced, fragile man who appeared to be in his late seventies, tourists always asked, "But who?"

"Rodney Harrington, of course!"

"The function of a novel is to entertain, but you can grind an ax at the same time," Grace told the Laconia Chamber of Commerce at their weekly luncheon in October. Peter Karagianis, a local merchant whom the news media persisted in calling Grace's uncle (because of his Greek name), issued the invitation—and got his share of hostile phone calls for doing so. But the luncheon itself attracted one of the largest crowds in Chamber history.

Grace arrived "dressed up," in a skirt with blouse and jacket—and she surprised her audience with a warm, winning, and gracious manner. She answered questions about her writing background (no formal training); her choice of Peyton Place as a name ("a two-word name with balance" and not the name of any real American town"); and her style of writing ("I just try to tell my story as clearly as I can").

Her story could happen anywhere, she said, and not only in small towns—but people in Gilmanton "are even less fond of me" since *Peyton Place* appeared.

But what about the claim that she'd described—and slandered—people in Gilmanton and Belmont?

"I hope I have more imagination than that," she answered, but did not deny the power of the pen. In any case, she said, she'd never intended to publish *Peyton Place*—but when she read it to her husband, he'd said, "You ought to sell it. We can use a few bucks."

Over the next months, Grace gave many reasons for writing
Peyton Place, but usually ended with, "And besides, we needed
the money"—as if to deny her need for creative self-expression,
and her commitment to her work. Citing George as the one who
wanted to market her work, she presented a more acceptable
image to those who believed that husbands should define wives'
destinies. In fact, however, Grace made independent choices—and
took the consequences, she told the Chamber of Commerce. In the
face of local criticism, she said, she was becoming thick-skinned—
developing an instinct for self-preservation.

Meanwhile, *Peyton Place* was sold to Frederick Muller, Ltd.,
one of England's most conservative and prestigious publishers, for
a British edition. Sidney Skolsky's movie gossip column called
Peyton Place the most exciting thing to hit the Coast in years. In
New York, Messner's wined and dined their best-selling author—
as did Dell, the sales and distribution arm for Western Printing
publishers, who'd bought the paperback rights before publication.

Allan Barnard, Western Printing's managing editor, had read
Peyton Place in galley proofs and recognized a "very commercial" book: sexy, reminiscent of *Kings Row*. He also doubted that
his boss, Frank Taylor, would like the book.

"I want you to buy *Peyton Place,* but don't read it," Barnard
told Taylor, then Dell editor-in-chief.

"Why shouldn't I read it?" Taylor asked, intrigued.

"Because if you read it, you probably won't want to publish it."

Trusting Barnard's "impeccable judgment," Frank Taylor did
not read the book—but authorized Barnard to outbid Fawcett for
Peyton Place. Fawcett had offered $10,000 for the paperback
rights; Dell offered $11,000 plus a $4,000 bonus if a movie were
made.

Though Dell went through many struggles over how to market
the book—the art department wanted a black cover with a railroad
station, but the sales force said it would never sell—*Peyton Place*
quickly became one of Dell's all-time best sellers with more than
12 million copies in print.

Helen Meyer, then president of Dell, considered *Peyton Place* a
"wonderfully written book"; Don Fine, then managing editor at
Dell first editions, still considers *Peyton Place* "the best novel of

its kind ever written" and "the premiere novel of its genre": small town, multiple viewpoints, what goes on behind the façade. Fine, now head of Arbor House publishing, thinks *Peyton Place* far superior to *Kings Row* in warmth, credibility, and honesty.

But Helen Meyer, Don Fine, and others also wondered about Grace Metalious, who struck them as very vulnerable and unable to cope with sudden success and attention. ("This book business is some evil form of insanity," Grace had written to Bob and Dora Athearn on November 6, 1956.)

Like Grace's neighbors at the University of New Hampshire, people in publishing became very aware of the Metalious children —because editors, agents, and salespeople often took care of them. On Grace's first visit to New York with her children, Doris Flowers took Marsha to her hairdresser; on another occasion, at the Plaza, Doris brought a game for the children, who had nothing to do. Helen Meyer once found herself baby-sitting while Grace met with movie and publicity people: the children struck her as well-behaved, and fun to be with.

On still another occasion, Knox Burger, a Western Printing editor, found Grace Metalious crying at his desk about, he recalls, "a kid she'd stashed in a hotel with a doubtful baby-sitter." Grace seemed to be having something of a breakdown, and Burger thinks Jacques Chambrun went back to the hotel to see that the child was all right. Already knowing Chambrun's reputation for fleecing authors and distrusting Chambrun in general, Knox Burger remembers thinking to himself, "What wretched casting!" Grace, Knox thought, had beautiful eyes—and he felt very sorry for her.

Still, Grace enjoyed some of the prerogatives of fame. At her request, she had lunch at the Algonquin with James Jones, whose *From Here to Eternity* she had long admired. Gloria Jones recalls that her husband had a good time at that lunch and liked Grace, but Howard Goodkind, who was there, remembers only one very uninteresting discussion about subsidiary rights.

Other writers and celebrities were not uniformly gracious. When Grace spotted Orson Welles in a restaurant, she sent a note that she'd like to meet him. He read the note, crumpled it up, and threw it away. But Hermione Gingold, on a similar occasion, flew to Grace's table and embraced her.

"Since *Peyton Place*," Grace told one reporter, "I haven't gotten up one single morning until noon, and I never expect to again." Still, as the only celebrity in Gilmanton, Grace quickly attracted hangers-on who would appear at her house, with or without bottles, at all hours of the night. She loved to be hospitable, and she thought her dream had been realized: "From now on everything was going to be wonderful forever. Life was going to be all beer and skittles and nothing unpleasant was ever going to happen to me again."

But a major problem still remained for the author usually described as mother of three and wife of a New England schoolteacher: her marriage.

George, living in a single room in Stow, would come home on weekends and disapprove of the goings-on in Grace's house. He called her new friends "commandos," Johnny-come-latelies, and exploiters. Grace called him antisocial, and said, "If you don't like my friends, then get the hell out."

Their quarrels followed the pattern from more than thirteen years together: George insisted on facts (the guests drank Grace's liquor) while Grace focused on emotions (the guests made her happy). George retreated to other parts of the house.

That fall Grace met another "commando" who soon became much more than a friend.

PART III

❀ ❀ ❀

The Party Years

CHAPTER 12

"I don't want them to miss Mama on the radio," Grace said when she called T. J. Martin, the afternoon disc jockey at WLNH, Laconia. She was going to New York the next day to be interviewed by Jinx Falkenburg and Tex McCrary, and she wanted to know if any Laconia stations carried "The Tink and Jex Show" for her children to hear.

"It's only on in New York," T. J. Martin said, but offered her a tape to record the show, and promised to play it over the air for Marsha, Mike, and Cindy when she returned.

"I wonder if anyone else in the world has ever begun to fall in love over a spool of magnetic tape," Grace wrote later.

The Tex and Jinx interview never was recorded, because of a union dispute, and Grace never got around to returning the blank tape. But she did get to meet Thomas James Martin, "T.J. the D.J."—who had the radio announcer's gift of gab, and much more.

"I have never learned to speak in public with any equanimity," Grace wrote a year and a half later. "To get up in a room full of people has always frightened me and still does. On this particular day I spoke to the Laconia Chamber of Commerce at the Tavern Hotel"—and right after the talk, T.J. was waiting, as if he understood.

"Come into the lounge," he said gently. "I'm going to buy you the biggest drink in the house."

He did—then and for many days afterwards. T.J. the D.J. was a smooth talker, whose voice reminded Grace of "maple syrup poured over vanilla ice cream. He was the only disc jockey who could make love to one woman over the air all day."

They had clicked from the first moment, over the phone. When T.J. had first moved to Laconia that September, after radio stints in California and Texas, he was told that "Nothing ever happens in Laconia, New Hampshire." That soon became a standing joke, for Arthur "Roxy" Rothafel, the WLNH owner, also told him that "a girl's written a dirty book about this area."

When Grace called T.J. the first time, she was typically self-deprecating: "Well, I've written this book, and the people in New York seem to want to talk to me."

But their conversation quickly turned spicier than she revealed in writing. "I'll provide you with a tape recorder," he said, and then, lower, "The tape will be our special gift."

"Oh, would you do that?"

Her voice had gone soft and purring, and "she sounded beautiful," he recalled in 1980. "We were outsexing each other over the phone, from the first moment."

He took the tape to Grace's house—and the first night they stayed up until 4 A.M., talking.

The second night, he stayed over.

T.J. had been doing the "Around Town" show with Esther Peters—but alone, as the afternoon D.J., he began making love to Grace Metalious over the air. He dedicated songs to her, especially "My Funny Valentine." He sang, hummed, and whistled along. He directed in-jokes toward her.

Grace, meanwhile, found him handsome, her "type": six feet two, dark-haired, big, with deep blue eyes. Despite a gap between his front teeth, he resembled a "chubby Robert Goulet," observers said. Once in New York several tourists, mistaking T.J. for Goulet, congratulated him on his performance.

Though T.J. was not the Princeton graduate he sometimes claimed to be, Grace found him charming, with a smooth, self-confident manner she admired. He was twenty-eight (born November 20, 1927—though Grace liked to say he was exactly her age, 31). He was also available: since his divorce in August

1955, the month Grace signed her *Peyton Place* contract, T.J. had left his wife and two children in Trenton, New Jersey.

Unlike George, who'd lived with Grace during struggle and poverty, T.J. symbolized glamour and wealth, male approval, and protection she'd never had before. He had graceful manners, and knew how to comport himself, Esther Peters recalls. He could "squire a woman, and make her feel like a princess."

Grace, who had written and thought about Prince Charming since childhood, discovered that once she had money and success, she could also find—as Connie MacKenzie had—her perfect romance. She seemed to believe the myth of the perfect man: that he exists, and that a woman who plays her cards right will have him—even in real life.

In Indian summer, Grace's favorite season, she fell in love.

"The world is full of cynics who will tell you that love cannot happen to people the way it did to T.J. and me," she told readers of the *American Weekly* in 1958, "and I think that in the beginning both of us were a little apprehensive. Magic is not supposed to be made of stainless steel, and excitement is usually as fleeting as yesterday's carousel ride."

But when T.J. came into her life, she wrote, her marriage had already "gone to pieces, by mutual consent." She felt lost, and "If a drowning man is morally to blame for saving himself by grabbing hold of somebody's neck, instead of waiting for a proper life preserver, then I guess I was to blame for grabbing hold of T.J."

Her marriage had made her feel neglected, she wrote. "There comes a time when you look at someone and you begin to think of all the things you've never had, and of the person you've never been. You think of all the places you haven't seen, the fun you haven't had, the laughs you haven't laughed, the warmth and joy of love which somehow has always been just out of your reach."

But at that critical time, "if you are unbelievably lucky, you find the one person who can make you whole. T.J. has done this for me."

By late fall, T.J. had become Grace's acknowledged lover, and she made no effort to hide their relationship—which cynical town gossips said represented a rise in status. With Carl Newman she'd gone to the Rod and Gun Club, a rugged hangout for farmhands and outdoorsmen; with T.J., she began frequenting the Laconia Tavern, gathering place for businessmen and civic leaders. The Tavern had been the first place in Laconia to serve hors d'oeuvres with drinks, and the Stafford family who ran it were delighted with the new patronage they attracted because of Martin, Metalious, and their entourage.

Grace also made T.J. her manager. She could not cope with calls from *Time, Newsweek,* radio, television—and his job was to keep them away, or comfort her when they were around.

T.J. frequently stayed overnight with Grace, who was having her dream house remodeled. When the children's Christmas vacation began, the living room floor—much of it a yawning hole because it had collapsed—was covered with planks and workmen's tools. The front door stayed open.

One evening T.J. and Grace had been drinking beer, had made love, and gone to sleep. They did not see the headlights shining up the driveway at 2 A.M.—nor did they hear someone slipping upstairs to her bedroom.

But they did awaken when the flash bulbs went off: one after the other, six pictures in a row of Grace and T.J., together in bed.

"What nerve!" Grace screamed, leaping out of bed to attack George—who'd stayed away for three weeks, developing his plan and readying a camera with flash attachment, to catch Grace and T.J. in the act.

"Martin, his eyes bulging, looked ridiculous in shocked disbelief, but said nothing," George wrote later. At his insistence, Grace and T.J. put on some covering—shorts for T.J., a blanket for Grace—and went downstairs to discuss the situation.

Originally, though, Grace had shouted to T.J. to *do something* with George. Remembering the convenient drop in the living room floor, she demanded, "Throw him in the hole! Throw him in the basement!"

Downstairs, Grace and George argued with increasing ferocity, while T.J.—who'd now met George for the first time—said very little. "You're not leaving!" George had told him—and threatened to call the police. Adultery was a serious crime in New Hampshire, and George had the proof.

"Now I've got you. You're going to jail, Martin," George said.

"I'm not trying to leave," said T.J.

"And you," George said to Grace, "you're going to be back in the house, be my wife."

As George describes it in his biography, he ached to fight with T.J. and "I kept needling him hoping he would explode—but how can one detonate a charge if there is no power in it to begin with?"

T.J. made no effort to defend himself, but Grace "fought like a tigress with her cub, and I called 'that man' everything that my vocabulary could handle." Had anyone spoken to George that way, he wrote, "I'm positive that we would have 'gone around a little,' regardless of the outcome."

Instead, Grace insisted on divorce, and consulted Bernie Snierson the next day about a financial settlement. "I could demand half of *Peyton Place*," George pointed out—but said he'd take just enough to get his master's degree. George and Grace signed an agreement; George turned over the incriminating film, and drove back to his room in Stow. T.J. spent Christmas with Grace, Marsha, Mike, and Cindy.

"Almost as soon as T.J. had come into my life, he and I began to function as a family unit," Grace wrote in 1958. "My children fell in love with him almost as quickly as I had done, and he with them."

Grace somewhat overstated the case—perhaps to present herself as fulfilling the feminine mystique, as the happy homemaker in the bosom of her contented family. Mike, nine, and Cindy, six, did sometimes call T.J. "Daddy"—which Marsha, at thirteen, found intensely painful. But more often, they all called him "Teej."

T.J. tried to include the children in his activities with Grace—and they liked that—but they resented his making them eat Brussels sprouts. He considered Cindy his pet—"my little blonde butterball," he called her—but she suspected there was something phony about him. Once when Esther Peters was visiting, T.J. patted Cindy on the head. Cindy turned around and bit him.

T.J. continued to amuse radio listeners, especially with his commercials. Very near-sighted, he disliked wearing glasses—except dark ones to hide the ravages of the night before. Esther Peters used to marvel at his handling of ad copy he couldn't read. "To hell with that!" he'd shout, throwing the text over his shoulder, gleefully ad libbing. When he liked a business, he might invent a five-minute commercial on the spot—which got him into a little trouble with higher-ups.

Sometimes his radio tricks included calls to Dr. Leonard Slovack, who treated him for the laryngitis his smoking aggravated. (T.J. admitted his heavy smoking was bad for his voice, but insisted he owed it to his advertisers—among them L & M cigarettes—not to stop.) During one celebrity interview on the radio, T.J. suddenly became concerned about his guest's ear wax. He phoned Slovack for advice.

Not knowing T.J. had him on the air, Slovack roared into the phone: "Tell the damn fool to put peroxide in his ear!"

T.J. could drink anyone under the table, Slovack recalls. He, Esther Peters, and others used to see T.J. and Grace in the Tavern Hotel lounge, drinking and sampling the hors d'oeuvres. T.J. would hold forth from 4 P.M. on into the night, with new jokes and stories. Grace, seated with him, said very little and let him be the entertainment. T.J., Esther recalls, seemed "larger than life."

He also made Grace feel good, as she told Bernard Snierson: "He's the only man who makes me feel like a woman." He made her feel pretty, and unconcerned about the future, as she wrote in 1958: "I cannot imagine growing old with anyone else and, because he is by my side, growing old is not the bogeyman it used to be."

With T.J., Grace behaved differently—and not everyone appreciated him. Laurette considered him charming, and called him "Thom-AHS," accenting the last syllable. But T.J. and Grace's old friend Marc took an instant dislike to one another and argued over Marc's friendship with Harry Belafonte. T.J.'s presence also affected Grace's own manner.

Bud Brandt, the publicist who promoted *Peyton Place,* respected Grace Metalious at the start. She was "dirty, untidy, dishonest, difficult, and irresponsible"—but was also a tough-minded woman "hacking her way out of a shack to something she wanted: money and fame."

With T.J., Grace had a certain earthy humor, Brandt recalls. She loved to make sexual references such as, " 'I'm on cloud nine,' and she wasn't talking about his intellect." But with T.J. she also seemed to be playing out a fantasy of herself as feminine and dependent—"Scarlett O'Hara, her lip quivering"—always asking T.J.'s advice, as if to say, "Help me—what shall I do?—only T.J. knows the answer."

Her appearance with Mike Wallace especially brought out that side of her. Wallace's "Night Beat" had just started on WABD-TV in New York—though Wallace, then 39, had already been doing radio and TV interviews for some sixteen years.

On "Night Beat," Wallace told *Look* magazine later, his experience, the late night time slot (10–11 P.M.), and the climate of the times all came together for particular success. Wallace soon became known for hard-hitting, penetrating interrogation, in an adversary style. Interviewing Jack Douglas, author of *My Brother Was an Only Child,* Wallace asked, "Just what do you mean, you're a writer?" He asked famous actresses if they were really as sexy as they pretended to be; he encouraged gambler Mickey Cohen to denounce Los Angeles police officials—who promptly sued for slander. With Mr. John, Wallace asked the question no one else dared ask in the fifties: "What's it like to be a homosexual designer?" And he even got broadcaster-columnist Mary Margaret McBride, a symbol of motherly propriety, to confess on the air that she was a virgin and never felt she'd missed anything.

Like *Peyton Place,* "Night Beat" was denounced for poor taste and excessive emphasis on sex. Wallace himself calls that charge "asinine. We might have done one piece in twenty that had anything to do with sex." The real objection to "Night Beat" was the same one leveled at *Peyton Place:* too much realism.

Grace Metalious and Mike Wallace were both seeking unvarnished truths about private individuals. "Possibly *Peyton Place* and 'Night Beat' were spiritual cousins," says Al Ramrus, then a writer for the Wallace show. They shared a refusal to accept fifties blandness, puffery, and happy talk. They insisted on honesty, and Wallace's audience loved to watch famous people squirm.

Grace Metalious had not been the easiest celebrity to handle, Doris Flowers remembers. Grace drank to fortify herself for public appearances; when asked questions, she tended to go off on tangents, rambling until talk-show hosts pulled her back to the subject. On the "Dave Garroway Show," Bernard Snierson remembers, Grace sat twirling her ponytail, and "exuding venom."

Nor did she particularly look forward to being in the public eye. On the way to New York for one TV appearance, she spent most of the time sobbing, her head in Howard Goodkind's lap, telling him she was frightened and couldn't face doing the show.

"What am I going to do?" she wailed to Bud Brandt at the WABD studio. "I can't handle this show."

Brandt reassured her. "You can handle anything," he said.

She waited tensely through the first bits of "Night Beat": news headlines, a teaser ad, commercials, introduction—and finally, Grace Metalious. For the hour-long show, Mike Wallace always had two guests on hand—figuring that if the first session went badly, he could cut it off quickly and go to the second guest.

Grace Metalious was his lead interview, and she sat gingerly in the guest's chair, the standing mike beside her. Produced by Wallace's partner Ted Yates (later killed in the first day of the Six-Day War in Israel), "Night Beat" was the first show to use "open pore shots" regularly: entirely talking heads, closely photographed against a black curtain, for a very stark effect.

Wallace smoked throughout the interview, and the smoke would curl up in front of the guest, making a frame. Sometimes the close-up camera seemed cruel, with nervous or unhappy guests who could not escape its scrutiny, but the audience got to see Mike Wallace's guests well, warts and all. When he asked tough questions, Wallace particularly liked the camera to photograph the guest's eyes "as the reaction hit."

"I expected her to be a seductress—a dish," recalls Burton Bernstein, now with the *New Yorker* but then the writer who did the "Night Beat" pre-interview with Grace. He thought she'd be someone who'd "gone through the events in *Peyton Place*"— though he wasn't thoroughly sure what was in the book. He'd been given the assignment on very short notice, and had read what he could of *Peyton Place* and clippings about Grace Metalious in about an hour.

He met her in mid-afternoon at the Hampshire House—and did a double-take when he saw her. She was "chubby—plain—like a New Hampshire farm lady." Since he'd gone to Dartmouth, they discussed New Hampshire. But Grace was disappointingly vague on meaty subjects—such as which *Peyton Place* characters were based on real people, and how her husband reacted to the book.

Grace seemed vulnerable, even unsteady—and to put her at ease, Bernstein told her Mike Wallace's real name: Myron Wallach. Wallace hated to be called "Myron," Bernstein added. Grace stored up that information.

When Grace and T.J. arrived at the studio, by limousine, Al Ramrus was also disappointed in the famous author. "One might have expected a very flamboyant, outspoken, colorful woman—but she could just as easily have been sitting behind a drugstore counter," he recalled in 1980. She seemed to him sad, overweight, and colorless.

As production coordinator for "Night Beat," Marlene Sanders greeted Grace and ferried her to the makeup room. Grace, who looked both plain and pale (and generally eschewed cosmetics), sat down at the makeup table. She stuck out her head rather belligerently, and said, "Make me beautiful!"

Makeup did what they could, and just before going on the air, Grace met Ted Yates, Mike Wallace's co-producer. Yates assured Grace there'd be no discussion of her "tender point" about *Peyton Place:* whether it was her autobiography. T.J. remembers that Yates had a "soft, gentle, parish-priest manner," and Grace had said, "I like that man."

Grace did not meet Mike Wallace until the show itself. Wallace preferred a spontaneous, first-meeting exchange on the air—especially since the show was live, untaped, and unedited. Grace, clearly nervous, vowed she could not go on without T.J.'s support —and he situated himself under her legs, handing her cigarettes out of range of the camera, as she talked. After the preliminaries, Wallace turned to Grace. "Grace, tell me," he began. "Is *Peyton Place* your autobiography?"

Put on the defensive, Grace could barely answer—and Wallace continued with that line of questioning.

"What gives you the right to pry, and hold your neighbors up to ridicule?" he asked—a question that made Grace's eyes big and tearful. To another Wallace comment, "I thought your book was basic and carnal," Grace responded, "You did, huh?"

They talked for a while about Potter's Place, New Hampshire, where Wallace had gone to camp as a child. There he'd gotten the second of two childhood nicknames he liked. His favorite was "Chinky," because of his eyes; the Potter's Place name was "Q.L.", for "Quivering Lips," bestowed by a girl who liked the way his lips quivered when he kissed her.

Grace constantly played with her hair, upstaging her own words —and Mike Wallace's main memory of the interview is Grace's playing with a long braid.

But at one point she sat up straight, looked Wallace in the eye— and called him "Myron."

Then the war was on. T.J. remembers her asking Wallace how many times he'd been married (three—a sensitive point with him). She asked other questions, and all in all, T.J. says, "She seemed to do quite a job on Mike."

Afterward Wallace shook hands with Grace warmly and affectionately and told T.J.: "You've got a hell of a woman there."

"I'm surprised she's so dowdy," Burton Bernstein said later, as the "Night Beat" staff sat over coffee and drinks.

"I find her very attractive," Mike Wallace said, and twenty-four years later he described her as "ample, not unattractive"—and very much in charge of herself, despite her protestations.

"How did I do?" Grace asked T.J. right after the show.

"You killed them," he assured her.

But later Grace claimed that Wallace had "massacred" her. Knox Burger thought Wallace had been exceptionally rough. Donald Murray, a Pulitzer Prize-winning editor from Boston, remembers that after a while Grace seemed almost "paranoid," as if sure people—probably including Wallace—were out to get her. She was "laid psychologically bare, as she revealed her anger at her neighbors," Murray remembers.

But Bud Brandt thinks Grace loved every minute of it: the chance to be angry, to snarl. Mike Wallace says she enjoyed playing the innocent, toying with her hair. Both believe she enjoyed the confrontation, and Wallace remembers her as both articulate and interesting, clearly "bent on benefiting as much as she could from the publicity generated by her book. She knew she was a phenomenon of sorts, and she intended to capitalize on it—and I saw nothing whatsoever wrong with that."

But expressing anger (arguing publicly with a man and standing up for her rights), and showing ambition (wanting to use the show for self-promotion) both worked against the standards of femininity: softness, self-abasement, passivity. To confess ambition might mean, in the fifties, being labeled "masculine"—so, rather than risk being "unnatural," Grace housed "masculine" purposes under a suitably "feminine" manner: playing with her hair, allowing her eyes to fill with tears. Hers was a clever performance—but also torn with conflict.

After the Wallace show, Grace and T.J. returned to Gilmanton, where he worked as Grace's "manager." He signed checks for her; screened media requests for interviews; told her whom to trust; insisted she get an answering service for her phone; and tried to keep her from sending money to every bizarre cause or person who contacted her through the mail.

She still wrote sympathetic letters to such people, including a man who was about to be hanged in Texas, but she did not send a check. She kept few records of her spending, and once even began to give the contractor renovating her house a sheaf of signed blank checks, so he could finish the work without her. T.J. insisted she be more sensible about money.

Because he knew media people and their quirks, T.J. protected Grace in ways George could not. At the same time, she told virtually everyone, T.J. gave her what she wanted—and she called him her "stud" and her "stallion."

Bernard Snierson, whom she called her "good gentle friend," felt sure town gossip about Grace and T.J. would hurt. He begged her to underplay her affair. But she refused to be hypocritical. Wherever she went, T.J. followed.

CHAPTER 13

"Peyton Place had nothing to do with our misunderstandings," George Metalious told the Associated Press, according to their stories of January 23, 1957. Grace, en route to Hollywood with her children (and T.J. Martin, whose name did not appear in reports), announced through Bernard Snierson that she and George had indeed separated, but "no divorce proceedings are pending and there are none contemplated." George said, "divorce seems to be the solution," though he and his wife had not discussed the future.

Grace and George rarely saw each other; T.J. had become the man in her life, showing her how to live on a grand scale. "She had the money," Esther Peters recalls, "but he could teach her how to do things"—how to live like a rich person, something she had never seen before.

During a January blizzard, Grace, T.J., Marsha, Mike, and Cindy set off for Hollywood, the children and Grace replaying their cross-country adventure of three and a half years before. But in the fall of 1953 they'd been fleeing George's job, poverty, and despair; in early 1957 they were celebrating success, money, and fame—with T.J. Martin.

On their way south they stayed with the Peyton family of Capron, Virginia, for Mr. Peyton had written an admiring letter about Grace's use of "his" name. Grace called that visit one of her most enjoyable, observing that "One evening of kindness and affection makes up for a lot of wretchedness. When you begin to wonder if the world is mostly populated with monsters, you remember people like the Peytons and your faith in mankind is restored."

T.J. drove Grace's new white convertible on the trip, and "we thought this was a real ball," Marsha remembered later. "Our lives were so different"—without the penny-pinching squabbles of the trip before. They stayed in hotels, ate all they wanted, and spent extravagantly on whatever they chose.

However, much of the second trip also turned sour. But this time the fights happened on a grand scale: Once Grace had had too much to drink as they drove across the desert, and she and T.J. had an enormous quarrel. "Let me off!" she demanded. "I'll stay in the desert!" He refused.

Their reconciliations also came on an epic scale: during one, he bought very expensive matching rings—Grace's engraved, "So much," and his, "Forever."

By the time they arrived at the Beverly Hilton in Beverly Hills, the new white car had become a very dirty beige—as had its occupants. At Las Cruces, New Mexico, they'd all treated themselves to Western outfits, Mike's with a ten-gallon hat besides, and a five-foot bow with a complete set of arrows. They wore their Western gear for two days during the drive—and when they arrived at the Beverly Hilton, their clothing looked distinctly lived-in.

Grace had learned the bourgeois view: "The only place to stay in Beverly Hills, if you have any class at all, is at the Beverly Hills Hotel." She chose the Beverly Hilton instead out of family loyalty —because it belonged to the same people who ran the Plaza in New York, her favorite hotel ("I have not words of praise enough to tell what a wonderful haven it has always been to me," she once said of the Plaza).

"If that doorman at the Beverly Hilton is still alive," T.J. Martin said in 1980, "I know he still remembers us." The Metaliouses and T.J. pulled into the Beverly Hilton at nine o'clock Saturday night—among limousines jostling for choice spots in front of the office, and gigantic, ultra-formal parties going on in every ballroom.

The doorman, who seemed to Grace almost seven feet tall, moved "as if he were starched," she thought. Among the black ties and evening gowns, she felt grateful she had reservations—for her brood of cowboys looked mighty peculiar among the socialites. Nevertheless, she wrote, "There was nothing to do but wear a look of insouciance and try to carry the whole thing off as gracefully as possible."

Mike enjoyed his role: stern-faced and unflinching, he greeted the bell captain. "Hi. Where can I shoot my bow and arrow around here?"

Grace heard whisperings: "Texas oil millionaires"—and reveled in the instant respect. At their suite, four bellboys hovering, she gave in to temptation. Strolling into the elaborate, mirrored bathroom, she shouted in her most hickish tones: "Hey! They put the gol-durned thing right inside up here!"

The bellboys never wavered, but Grace wondered gleefully what they said among themselves on the way down.

Officially, Grace came to Hollywood to approve the *Peyton Place* script—but in fact, she had been invited to Twentieth Century-Fox for the same reason most novelists are brought to film studios: to lend publicity to the film. She had very little to do—and the children, even less.

Studio people did ask if the Metaliouses wanted to meet any movie stars. Mike, nine, chose Marilyn Monroe—and was crushed to learn that she worked for another studio. Cindy, six, chose Trigger—and got to say hello to her favorite horse. Marsha, thirteen, met several celebrities: Pat Boone, whom she thought brusque when he wouldn't sign autographs; Rick Jason, a newcomer whose career as "beefcake hero" never took off; and Elvis Presley, her idol and first choice—who struck her as shy, thoroughly charming, and gorgeous.

Still, several weeks in the Beverly Hilton meant mostly boredom for the Metalious children, with Grace and T.J. otherwise occupied. It rained most of the time; no one could accompany them on excursions, nor was Marsha allowed to take Cindy and Mike out. They all stayed in the hotel, picking fights with hangers, ordering room-service sodas. Mike rode the service elevator down to the bottom, and then up to the rooftop, where he shot his arrows. Still, the children considered the trip "a blast": no school for seven weeks in all, and virtually no restrictions.

Grace, meanwhile, had the royal treatment in some respects: limousines, lavish meals, a private screening of any film she wanted (she chose *On the Waterfront*). She especially enjoyed peering at the Hollywood stars: Jayne Mansfield, the famous sex symbol, who chewed gum incessantly; and Jack Webb, star of the *Dragnet* television show, who had an unusual greeting that Grace learned to imitate—he formed a pistol with thumb and forefinger, then clicked his tongue to sound like a Ping-Pong ball hitting a paddle.

At a Screen Writers' Guild dinner, Grace saw Elizabeth Taylor from afar, and wrote that "She is so beautiful that you find yourself holding your breath, for you feel that someone so gorgeous cannot truly be alive."

At the studio she had one of her biggest thrills: Cary Grant had suddenly appeared, putting on his cufflinks, and recognized her. "Hello, Grace! How are you!" he said—and T.J. had to keep Grace from fainting. She had herself photographed with her idol, and wrote that "Next to T.J., Cary Grant is the handsomest man in the world. He looks like a graying college boy."

She lunched with Frank Sinatra, an interesting talker who proved to be one of the few Hollywood people she liked—for he, at least, responded to her. Jerry Wald, the *Peyton Place* producer, had other uses for her: as a celebrity, but not as a writer.

Grace had never met anyone like Jerry Wald—nor had most people in Hollywood.

Like Grace Metalious, Jerry Wald had clawed his way up from working-class origins—but in a very different style. Where Grace was dreamy, Wald was hardheaded. She sought ideals, while he sought opportunities. At twenty-nine, Grace had been trying to sell a novel, and failing. Jerry was already—apparently—the subject of one: Budd Schulberg's *What Makes Sammy Run?* (1941), a satiric but chilling portrait of an up-and-coming Hollywood producer who has endless drive and no conscience whatever.

Schulberg's Sammy Glick is pragmatic, determined, and primitive—adjectives Hollywood people often applied to Jerry Wald, known as "the fastest and smoothest talker ever born in the borough of Brooklyn." A movie producer while still in his early twenties (he was born in 1912), Jerry Wald specialized in "women's pictures": stories about human relationships, with meaty roles for actresses, whom he prided himself on discovering—though he also took credit for spotting James Dean and Marlon Brando.

When he moved from Warner Brothers to Columbia in 1952 —while Grace Metalious was flubbing the role of "Mrs. School-teacher" in Belmont, New Hampshire—Jerry Wald met his match in Harry Cohn, who took pleasure in blocking Wald's biggest film plans. Cohn, the one-man boss at Columbia, supported Wald's more unusual projects—such as a 3-D musical version of Somerset Maugham's *Rain,* starring Rita Hayworth under the title *Miss Sadie Thompson.* But Wald could get nothing for his classier projects—such as buying film rights to *Andersonville,* MacKinlay Kantor's Pulitzer Prize-winning novel. Deciding he'd had enough from Cohn, who often said the movie business consisted of "cunt and horses," Wald moved to Twentieth Century-Fox in 1956.

When Harry Cohn died two years later, Wald attended the funeral, which attracted enormous crowds, prompting Red Skelton to remark: "It proves what they always say. Give the public what they want to see, and they'll come out for it."

Knowing that Jerry Wald considered Cohn a "sleazy Hollywood hood," reporters asked why he'd come. Wald answered: "I want to make sure the bastard is dead."

Twentieth Century-Fox not only rescued Jerry Wald from Harry Cohn, but enabled him to buy "properties" he liked—such as *Peyton Place.* Wald Productions made the movies; Fox gave Wald a steady salary, equipment, and distribution. With Fox he made *Sons and Lovers,* the D. H. Lawrence novel he'd been itching to film for twenty-five years—and it won an Academy Award. He made many successful "women's pictures," among them *An Affair to Remember* and *Beloved Infidel.* But Wald's most famous and successful picture was *Peyton Place,* which he said had all the ingredients of a great story: pleasure, pain, fear, hope, love, and hate.

Wald had an intuitive feel for books, a desire for "artistic achievements," and no great respect for the cultural level of those around him—especially film stars. He'd conned one famous actor into believing Wald would give him the starring role in a musical version of *The Robe,* the biblical epic. The actor did not catch on even when Wald told the actor the major song: "Get Me to the Cross on Time."

Wald did have somewhat more respect for writers, and repeatedly said, "There are no washed-up stars, just washed-up stories." *Peyton Place,* he said, had the "hard core of moral truth" essential for a popular film. Moreover, it presented the kind of challenge he liked. His critics, whom he called "knockers and needlers and shin-kickers," had said he couldn't make "a decent picture out of a dirty book."

He said he'd show them.

Grace Metalious came to Hollywood knowing little about Jerry Wald, except that he'd been terribly eager to buy her book. (He also bought it very cheaply, considering the enormous profits he made—a sharp deal he bragged about for years.) He talked fast, wore loud Hawaiian shirts, had more ideas than he could use, and clearly had no intention of letting Grace write the film script. Though he talked about his respect for authors, he seemed, in practice, to agree with Irving Thalberg, studio chief in the early Hollywood days: "The writer is a necessary evil."

Grace had expected an office, a desk, and a typewriter; instead, Wald hustled up a photographer for publicity photos. In the pictures Grace does sit at a desk, as if working on a manuscript—but the background is a studio curtain, rather than an office wall. Grace is wearing a clean white blouse, tweed jacket and skirt, with her hair pulled back in a ponytail. She looks young, small, and desperately eager to please. Wald, a huge man whom *Time* called "moon-faced, jowly, barrel-shaped," looms behind Grace—standing up, like the big bad wolf. As the pictures progress, Grace looks more and more ready to burst into tears.

"You treat them like they're cattle," she protested as she watched Jerry Wald casting actresses: "Walk—turn around—lift your skirt—don't call us—we'll call you." Grace found the "flesh market" unbearable, and stalked out, T.J. following. "I never saw anything so disgusting," Grace said. While Hollywood columnists criticized her as "unglamorous," she later wrote caustically about what she'd seen: "All the women are blondes, brunettes, or red-heads. In all my time there, I didn't see one single woman with plain brown hair. Neither did I see one who could be presumed to wear a size 32-A brassiere."

Though she was bothered by Wald, Grace also found Holly-wood more staid than she'd expected. It had "much less scandal than some small New England towns in which I've lived," she said. But Wald's overbearing manner, his handling of actresses, and her treatment as a celebrity, not a writer, all disillusioned and depressed her terribly—to the point, she said, of contemplating suicide.

"It must be terrible to be dead in any way," she told columnist Hal Boyle when he asked her opinion of Hollywood, "but it must be worst of all to be dead in the head." What deadened Holly-wood people? "There is only one word to describe Hollywood—fear. I have never seen so much fear in so many people so much of the time—the fear of losing their jobs. I don't see how they can work in such a dreadful atmosphere."

She wavered between amusement and disgust at what passed for conversation at sophisticated Hollywood parties, she told Boyle, and supplied an example:

"The Beverly Hilton is just a glorified motel," one guest said—to which the other replied, "But aren't we all?"

"This I couldn't understand at all," Grace said. "I never felt like being called Mountain View Lodge or Bide-a-Wee-on-the-Highway."

Though she was called "script consultant" for *Peyton Place,* Grace never did get to see the script. She did sit in on "what was supposed to be a story conference"—and it amazed her.

"I thought they were kidding when they suggested casting Red Skelton in the role of Kenny Stearns [the town drunk] and Pat Boone as 'the good boy in the book.' Then someone yelled, 'Pat's a singer.' Another said, 'We could work up a song for him.' I thought I would get into the conversation and suggested Pat could sing the 'Peyton Place Blues.'"

But when she realized they really meant what they said, "That was enough for me and I took off for home."

Another incident was actually the last straw, as T.J. remembers it. At Romanoff's restaurant, Jerry Wald introduced Grace to John Michael Hayes, scheduled to be the *Peyton Place* screen-writer. Hayes greeted her warmly—then asked the question Grace hated.

Was *Peyton Place* her autobiography?

"I beg your pardon," Grace said in her haughtiest manner.

Hayes repeated his question, and Grace threw her bloody mary in his face.

She stalked off to the bar, leaving T.J. with Hayes and Wald, who fussed and insisted everything was fine, no problem. "And here the guy's going out with a bloody mary eating holes in his shirt," T.J. recalled in 1980, still marveling.

A year later, Grace had become more philosophical about the movies: "The whole trouble with Hollywood and me was that we did not know each other's language. This was no one's fault, but it was unfortunate. I regarded the men who made *Peyton Place* as workers in a gigantic flesh factory, and they looked upon me as a nut who should go back to the farm."

She'd learned something else, too, she told Bernie Snierson when she got back to New Hampshire. Hollywood would be mak-ing her story into something "saccharine," she called it: clean, wholesome, inoffensive to fifties morality. They would be doing exactly what she'd fought against in writing *Peyton Place*—and they even contemplated doing it on her own turf.

A covey of film makers flew East to check out Gilmanton as a possible *Peyton Place* setting. "But it turned out that local senti-ment didn't favor further identification with the book," Walter Lowe wrote tactfully in the New York *Herald Tribune*. Moreover, the film makers found the town "too ugly" to be the prototypical New England town.

During their visit, director Mark Robson and art director Jack Martin Smith did spend some time with Grace at her hangout, the Tavern Hotel lounge. From the hotel they could glance across the street to the Laconia public library, a red-and-gray stone structure with intricate windows and turrets in the style of a miniature cas-tle. A rather forbidding portrait of the castle's donor, Napoleon Gale, still hangs in the Gale Memorial Library.

As Grace, Robson, and Smith sipped cocktails in the Tavern,

Grace looked at them slyly, then pointed to the Gale Memorial Library. "When you look at that building, what do you see?"

The Fox men murmured something noncommittal.

"I'll tell you what *I* see," Grace announced in her most grandiose tones. "I see an architectural monstrosity that a man named Napoleon foisted on this community!"

The film makers dissolved in laughter—but when they told Grace that Gilmanton and Belmont were simply "not New England enough," she (in T.J.'s recollection) "raised the roof." He had to talk to the film makers from then on. Grace no longer would.

The film was moved to Woodstock, Vermont, where the city fathers also vociferously objected. Finally, it was made in Camden, Maine, a pretty coastal village founded in the mid-eighteenth century as a harbor home for Yankee traders. It had elm-lined streets, clean white buildings, green woods and hills, picturesque islets off the shore—and numerous extras eager to be in *Peyton Place*. Over the summer of 1957, as filming continued, Twentieth Century-Fox publicists announced that from a population of 3,000 in Camden, fully 1,700 signed up to be extras in the film.

That April 1957, Grace, T.J., and the children had returned to New Hampshire from California—and Grace had another legal problem.

"That goddamn Makris won't get a cent of my money," she'd growled to a friend before they left New Hampshire—but Tom Makris, who'd worked with George Metalious at the State School, reportedly intended to get quite a lot of Grace's money, in a libel suit over *Peyton Place's* "Tomas Makris." Both Makrises are schoolteachers. The real-life Thomas Makris, whom Grace met a few times, was, by all accounts, also tall, dark, and handsome.

At first the real-life Thomas Makris had been amused at the coincidence. When Grace told him, "Why, you're in my book!" he merely laughed. But on March 14, 1957, while Grace was in Hollywood, Thomas Makris and his wife, Geraldine Gale Makris, filed suit for $250,000 against Grace Metalious and Julian Messner, Inc. They charged that *Peyton Place* caused them to be "brought into public hatred, contempt, ridicule, slander, and disgrace."

Though the Makris case was not particularly strong, Bernard Snierson, who represented Grace, was very concerned. Grace had been living openly with T.J. for nearly half a year; her life and her writings were both Lakes Region scandals. Given town attitudes toward Grace—as a nonconforming and immoral woman—Snierson felt she had little chance of winning a jury trial.

Snierson also called Jerry Wald and suggested that the *Peyton Place* hero's name be changed for the movie version. No other Greek name seemed safe enough, so Tomas Makris became "Michael Rossi"—a Greek with an (unexplained) Italian name. He appears as Rossi in most later editions of *Peyton Place,* and in movie and television versions.

His story remained intact, and Grace remained resentful. In an interview with Maurice Zolotow for *Cosmopolitan,* Grace pointed out that "Makris" is a common Greek name—and that she'd chosen it because of the Makris Diner on U.S. Route 5 outside Hartford, Connecticut.

Nevertheless, Snierson and Philip Wittenberg, the Messner's lawyer, decided to settle out of court, on December 1, 1958. Wittenberg recalls that some $60,000 was paid out to the Makrises and for legal fees. Grace grumbled for years afterward.

Despite missed schoolwork, Marsha graduated from the eighth grade in June 1957, after the Hollywood adventure. Grace bought a pony for Cindy, who always loved horses—and since their house was still unfinished, the Metaliouses and T.J. spent much of the summer at Rye Beach on the New Hampshire coast.

Charles Hegarty, a high school student, worked as a bellhop, gardener, dishwasher, and general handyman at the Ocean Wave Hotel in Rye Beach that summer, and remembers a visit from the Metaliouses. Grace, attired in baggy trousers and a man's shirt, shepherded several undisciplined dogs; the man with her—presumably T.J.—withdrew to the bar.

Grace complimented Charlie on his ability to make a fire, asked him to walk her dogs, and touched his face—all of which he, admittedly "infused with those horny hormones of the early teens," liked to interpret as a sexual overture. Of course, his fantasies came to nothing. ("She wasn't that kind of lady," T.J. says.)

In September Martin returned to being "T.J. the D.J.," but Grace could not settle down to her next book—despite her contract with Messner for two more novels. She rarely talked about her writing, although she considered the workroom ("studio") off her bedroom a kind of haven. She told Hal Boyle that she had in progress a new book called *The Tight White Collar,* a study of "man's inhumanity to man"—but she had been working on that book, sporadically, since long before *Peyton Place* appeared.

Parts she had written in Durham, while George was at the University of New Hampshire; other parts drew on Belmont experiences. Then in June 1956, just before Howard Goodkind and Bud Brandt visited Gilmanton to plan the *Peyton Place* publicity, Grace had consulted Solon Colby, an archeologist and Indian expert, about New Hampshire place names she wanted to use for local color. Colby, an authority on Algonquin Indians, praised the native Americans' imagination in naming parts of New England: *Winnipesaukee,* the lake near Laconia, meant "The Beautiful Water in the High Place"; *Uncanoonuc,* the mountains visible from Derryfield Park in Manchester, meant "Twin Breasts." (In a draft of *The Tight White Collar* Grace described the mountains' "swelling softly to blunt tips.")

Colby, a collector of arrowheads, gave Grace a book of old woodcuts, Indian poems, prayers, and legends. She incorporated the place name information into early drafts of *The Tight White Collar,* but did little more with it.

She had turned her energies toward the man in her life—leaving her creative imagination behind.

CHAPTER 14

T.J.'s living with Grace scandalized the "ax mouths," whose opinions Grace generally professed to ignore. But with T.J. around, she found it hard to write. He enjoyed extravagant parties and purchases (on Grace's open accounts), and during what George called the "party years," T.J. hosted a perpetual open house, and bar.

At times Grace felt grateful for the distraction. Concerned with *Peyton Place* reviews, but excited about the huge sales figures, she became more and more afraid she could not duplicate her success. She remembered a proverb from Grandmother Royer: "Beware of what you desire because some day it may be achieved."

She told Bernie Snierson that she saw her typewriter as a snake.

T.J. orchestrated the renovation of her house, which eventually bore little resemblance to the small, dignified colonial Cape Cod Grace had bought for $5,000. First Grace bought up land around the house, for privacy—and then went to work on the house.

The entire structure was jacked up; bulldozers and graders made a spacious lawn out of the natural terrain. Several tons of fill were brought in, so that the tiny cottage that originally nestled into a hill became a palatial estate sprawled over an enormous bubble of earth.

Workmen added a long gravel driveway, wide enough for two cars and a three-car garage. Above the garage was the large loft area Grace called "the hateful room"—where she hid all the junk she loathed. A solid rock wall, stones put up by hand, was added in front of the house, and in memory of the days without water at "It'll Do," Grace insisted on an artesian well.

Inside, the improvements included a luxurious flagstone patio, a massive fireplace, brick shelving, and a wall of windows. It kept a summery atmosphere all year round, its humidity perfect for plants and flowers—but after a while, because of a poor roofing job, the patio was reduced to a storage area for junk, spreading tomato plants, and a pet crocodile belonging to Suzy Roy, Grace's niece.

Other additions to the house included a pine-panelled dining room, wall-to-wall carpeting, four new fireplaces (brick or quarried granite), a built-in kitchen, a barbecue and bar, laundry room, and huge playroom on the first floor. Upstairs, an enormous master bedroom (20 x 14) was added, with a fireplace and two sliding glass windows looking out over a wooded area. The bedroom adjoined Grace's writing "studio," with her electric typewriter and a tiny built-in desk with many cubbies. The desk was clearly oriented for work: It faced a blank wall.

It was her new dream house—but Grace insisted that the oak-beamed ceiling in the older part of the house be retained, incongruously connected with the newer additions. When the contractor said it would be cheaper to replace the beams with new ones, Grace refused. "I don't care what it costs," she said. "I'll know they're not the same." She liked best the living room, with its six-pane picture window, and always touched the hearth when she came home—to assure herself she really was home.

Renovations to her $5,000 house eventually cost at least $100,000. (When the house was for sale in 1979, it was advertised in the *Wall Street Journal* with an asking price of $215,000.)

Meanwhile, Grace continued to enjoy T.J.'s company—except for their violent fights. George Metalious calls Grace's time with Martin "The tinsel years. She had fallen in love with a voice, a sense of humor, and a gift of gab that the world had not heard the likes of since the days of P. T. Barnum. He made her feel desirable."

They bought matching sweaters, shirts, and shorts, in several colors, when his-and-hers clothes were quite avant garde. They kept a pilot, Donald Vaughan, on call so they could charter a private plane on impulse—for a flight to New York, or Baltimore to see Bunny, or anywhere else they had a yen to visit.

At the Plaza they entertained lavishly, renting entire suites, sometimes spending three thousand dollars a week. Friends and acquaintances came to Gilmanton, at Grace's expense, to stay as long as they chose. Henry Klinger, the Twentieth Century-Fox story consultant, often came with his wife, and brought jars of a certain kind of herring Grace loved. Jacques Chambrun appeared, flattering Grace in his super-suave way—while Marsha wondered what he used to dye his hair so black. Even Kitty Messner appeared—and one of the dogs chewed her shoes.

Kitty was still "everything Grace would have liked to have been," Bernie Snierson recalls. "Tall, gracious . . ." and with a cosmopolitan air that Grace never could pull off. She imitated Kitty's habit of calling everyone "sweetie," but Grace never mastered the air of a *grande dame* or of a socially secure woman.

Kitty used to take her friends around the world, paying their way; Grace did the same with people she brought to the Plaza, but many of them were hangers-on and fortune-hunters, and she seemed unable to distinguish true and false friends. Kitty profited enormously from *Peyton Place* and celebrated mainly by buying an air conditioner for the office and naming one of her New Jersey guest cottages "Peyton Place"—but Kitty had no need to overspend to feel better about herself.

Kitty had always had money, from the time her father gave her a $200-a-month allowance when she left Chicago for New York in 1924. Nor did she need to spend to please any man in her life. Kitty genuinely transcended others' opinions. Grace spent generously, recklessly, wanting to make everyone happy, especially T.J. Yet she also worried about what others thought, even when she made her greatest efforts to shock.

She did remain loyal to old friends. During spring vacation in 1957, Marsha wanted to go to New York with Grace and T.J., and Grace decided to invite Wendy and Joanne Wilkens, too. When Joanne, torn and tearful, said she'd already promised to spend the week with her friend Linda Evans, Grace cried, "Then bring Linda, too!"

The four girls—Marsha, Joanne, Wendy, and Linda—trooped to the Plaza for one of the most exciting vacations of their lives.

Marsha had kept Joanne informed about her newly glamorous life from the time it began. In September, just before *Peyton Place* appeared in the stores, Marsha wrote Joanne excited letters from the Gladstone Hotel in New York: Kitty Messner had turned out to be everything Grace had said she was, and more; Doris Flowers had taken Marsha for a new hairdo. Grace took Marsha to lunch with Jacques Chambrun, and dinner with Bud Brandt and a companion Marsha called "Fish-eye Wheeler." (No one remembers such a person, and Brandt suspects Grace made up the name.) Marsha, not quite thirteen, learned to drink "horse's necks" (nonalcoholic cocktails) on the rocks, and she loved New York.

In January 1957, Marsha wrote Joanne from the Plaza that she'd been to see singer Lillian Roth, whose autograph she got—and Mike, who danced with Lillian, had declared himself madly in love.

Grace, meanwhile, had fallen madly in love with the Plaza—which T.J. had said was classier than the Algonquin, more appropriate to her new status as a woman of wealth and leisure. The Plaza, a truly grand hotel, had an opulence rare even for New York—and represented a world of wealth and privilege that Grace found alien but fascinating.

Grace's grandmother had barely arrived, poverty-stricken, from Canada when the Plaza opened its doors in 1907 to its first customer, Alfred Gwynne Vanderbilt, son of the richest man in America. The hotel, overlooking Central Park at Fifth Avenue and Fifty-ninth Street, had always catered to the ultra-rich—including Zelda and Scott Fitzgerald, who used to romp in the Pulitzer Fountain just outside the hotel, near the hansom cabs.

When Conrad Hilton bought the Plaza in 1943, its aristocratic clientele thought the hotel was doomed, but Hilton preserved its golden elegance, its stately, high-ceilinged Palm Court, and its your-wish-is-my-command service, never cheap. The Boston industrialist A. M. Sonnabend, who bought the hotel in 1953 while publishers were turning down Grace's *Forbidden Fruit,* continued its tradition of excellence—and by 1955, when *Peyton Place* was accepted, the Plaza had a new tradition.

Kay Thompson's *Eloise,* the story of an incorrigible six-year-old who lives at the Plaza, had become a favorite of young girls all over America. A pesky but unbearably cute child, Eloise performs such pranks as summoning room service for a raisin and seven spoons. Once she became celebrated, her portrait adorned the Plaza lobby, where Marsha, Joanne, Wendy, and Linda performed a ritual of greeting each day of their stay. One day when they were gossiping and giggling as they entered the Persian Room, a stern, white-haired man greeted them as "four little Eloises."

They were supposed to stay for only a week, their Easter vacation. By the third week Laurie became concerned. She would call Grace and plead, "Put them on the train"—and Grace would laugh.

The girls flirted with the hotel waiters (and lost their chance to meet the teenage actor Sal Mineo when they went rowing with the waiters instead). They visited Hassan the fortune teller; left their lip-prints for posterity over the walls of the famous "Kiss Room"; instructed entertainer Lynn Richards how to sing "You May Not Be an Angel" at her club; and played the role of eccentrically rich Eloises, ordering a single orange from room service at 3 A.M. Grace shared their delight when it arrived, cunningly bedecked with green leaves and silver foil.

As they grew more at home in the Plaza, the girls became more intrepid. Marsha and Joanne passed themselves off as eighteen-year-olds and had a long siege of drinking beverages considerably more stimulating than "horse's necks." Marsha passed out at 5 A.M., but Joanne continued retching violently.

T.J., gentle and rather amused, held Joanne's head as she emptied her stomach into five different wastebaskets all over the room. When she finally finished, Grace took all the wastebaskets and put them on five different floors of the Plaza, "so no one'll know."

The even younger generation, Cindy and Mike, also had their Plaza adventures. After Cindy broke her leg ice-skating in Rockefeller Center (and Grace rescued her, running out on the ice in three-inch spike heels), Mike delighted in racing Cindy's wheelchair down the corridors of the Plaza. At least one astonished maid fell into the laundry to escape them.

Mike and Cindy explored the upper apartments where they

weren't supposed to go, wheedled pastries from the maids, waged grape fights in bed, and constantly watched TV horror movies—since they really had little to do.

In happier moments, Grace and T.J. loved to hold hands and gaze into one another's eyes. Unlike George, T.J. enjoyed public displays of affection as much as Grace did. For a while, at least, he seemed attuned to her emotional needs.

They loved eating and drinking together, on a grand scale. She grew to 150 pounds—which the columnist Sidney Fields called "weight she took on as a defense when fame forced her exposure to the world." T.J.'s weight shot up to 265. Fat and jolly, they enjoyed laughing together, and abetted each other in jokes and scenarios.

Once in New York they went to a nightclub where Sammy Davis, Jr., was performing. Several hecklers began disrupting the performance, while Davis told a joke about a foreign woman who kept crying, "Get me a doctair!"

The joke was moderately funny, but one heckler suddenly crashed down into his seat, grabbed onto the tablecloth to save himself, and sent food, glassware, silver, drinks, and everything else cascading to the floor with a frightful din—above which Grace Metalious could be heard half-laughing, half-roaring: "Get me a doctair!"

Afterward, Sammy Davis sent Grace a free drink with his compliments, and T.J. frequently told the story to illustrate Grace's cleverness, while she beamed over her cocktail.

T.J. also liked to enact stories, especially his latest money-making scheme. Standing over an imaginary turnstile, he announced that he would soon be exhibiting Grace Metalious, the famous author, for all her loyal admirers—who should step right up, and buy their tickets while tickets could still be had.

They were selling fast, especially for the highlight of the performance: "At eleven o'clock Mrs. Metalious will arise and be fed!" His audience, Grace included, would be convulsed with laughter.

T.J. liked to share his happiness with others. Over the radio (before he found he could not combine working and partying), T.J. held a contest to name his and Grace's St. Bernard. The winning entry, he announced, was "Hennessy," and the winner got an appropriate prize. Hennessy, meanwhile, added to the chaos of the Metalious household: he rudely devoured a friend's pet duck; he left large, warm mementoes of his presence in the bathroom—and T.J. stepped in one pile in his stocking feet, during a large house party.

T.J. took away the burden of making decisions. He handled the money; he named dogs, bought food and drink, planned trips—with a flair that delighted Grace. One February they sat, snowed in, and someone mentioned the Caribbean.

"How wonderful it would be to go there," Grace said wistfully. "The sea, the sand, the palms . . ."

That evening after Grace had gone to sleep, T.J. got on the phone and made all the arrangements: tickets, hotel rooms, even clothes. The following morning he handed Grace a suitcase and said, "We're going."

That night they were in the Caribbean.

When they returned from trips, Grace liked to share her adventures. In Laurie's kitchen she would tell Laurie, the Wilkens youngsters, and other guests about her escapades. Wendy Wilkens remembers especially Grace's tales of her visit to Haiti with T.J.

Grace began the story as a comedy: the Haitian cab following a tortuous, painful (for the passengers) route through the mountains, to reach a secret club. Then a "primitive feeling" took over —darkness and smoke and voodoo ritual, enacted with chickens. "She made you live it," Wendy remembers, "through the eyes of someone who saw the drama and the beauty."

But Grace was using her time and energies in storytelling and excursions, not in writing. She hated to drive, so car trips usually involved an entourage. Laurie drove with her to Auburn, New York, on one venture, and Grace was surprised and amused that a restaurant employee refused to serve her drinks, claiming she was obviously underage. Joanne Wilkens, outraged, insisted Grace must be over twenty-one—"she's my godmother"—but the man remained unconvinced, though obviously attracted to Grace.

Even not knowing she had written *Peyton Place,* many men were attracted to Grace. She had a sensual, exciting aura, and often—with men—a "help me" attitude they found appealing (although others, like Bud Brandt, considered it contrived). With women she often adopted a brash manner that concealed her shyness—and while her fame attracted women, she made few new friends.

In moments of crisis, Grace would phone Laurie long distance— 1 A.M. calls from the Plaza, crying, "You *have* to come down." Fearing something terrible, Laurie would rush to New York and find Grace in the lobby, huddled inside her coat for security, looking desperately dejected. But the next day she might be as jolly as ever.

Despite her doubts about women—most of whom were less tolerant than Laurie, and condemned her for sundry sins—Grace could be unfailingly kind. On one occasion she drove Wendy, Marsha, and Joanne to Bar Harbor, Maine, taking an elderly lady to visit a friend. The elderly lady was incontinent, urinating everywhere, all over the back seat of the car, and the girls, with the intolerance of youth, laughed about it for months afterward.

But Grace never complained about the elderly lady's difficulties, nor about car troubles—even when the brakes gave out momentarily as the car rattled down a steep hill. She was genuinely kind, sweet, and loyal—everything she'd always wished the women of her family would be to her.

Grace rarely saw her mother, Patricia Carbine reported in a *Look* magazine profile published in March 1958. "Grace says she finds it hard to get along with her," Carbine reported, her even tone masking the tensions Grace freely discussed.

When *Peyton Place* became a best seller, Laurette occasionally claimed that she'd dictated the book to Grace, or even written it herself—but her first reaction was much like other people's: "You never learned about those things at home."

But Grace had learned at home both the anger and compassion animating *Peyton Place,* and fame did little to change her troubled relations with her mother and sister. They used to visit together in New York, where Laurette lived, or Baltimore, where Bunny lived, or Gilmanton—but Grace always paid. Though she never refused loans or help when she could give it, the three of them fought constantly—calling each other terrible names, taking after one another with knives and cleavers. Laurie Wilkens, observing the quarrels, learned to "just sit there and smoke."

Not that Grace's mother always exempted Laurie from criticism. When the Wilkenses adopted a five-year-old child, Laurette warned direly: "She looks like an Indian, with that black hair and those high cheekbones. I can easily see it. Watch out—she'll probably tomahawk you." Grace, whose head had been filled with her mother's grotesque stories while she was pregnant, took such prophecies in stride. Laurie felt more than a little resentful.

When the quarrels with Bunny and Laurette grew fierce, Grace would call for help in the middle of the night: to Bernie Snierson, to referee a fight; when he couldn't come, to his partner John Chandler; when they weren't available, to Dr. Leonard Slovack, to administer sedatives for all. (She also summoned Slovack on one occasion when she had a bout of flu in New York. She wanted him to come on her privately chartered plane—but he gave her the name of a New York doctor.)

The Grace-Laurette-Bunny hostility took place in New York, too, where Laurette lived with her husband, Charles Kugel, on Central Park West. She prided herself on their address, although rumors circulated that he was merely the superintendent in the building.

During one taxi ride, when Laurie Wilkens and Charlie Kugel were along, Laurette and Grace began quarreling and shouting insults at one another—starting with "bitch" and "whore." As the squabble escalated, their language became so vile and so obscene that the New York taxi driver pulled up to a curb, stopped his cab, and ordered them out. With a look of pity toward mild, inoffensive Charlie Kugel, the tough New York cabbie said even he couldn't stand to hear it.

The next day, as usual, they acted as if nothing had happened.

Grace's relations with Bunny were much the same. After her second husband Charles Farrell's death, just before *Peyton Place* appeared, Bunny had remarried in Baltimore—to Joe Brouillette, by whom she had a son, "Little Joe." Her daughter by Roger Roy, Suzanne, lived with Grace in Gilmanton for five years; Roger also frequently stayed at Grace's during the party years—while Bunny appeared and disappeared.

T.J. considers Bunny "a hippie before her time," who showed up when she needed money. He remembers her asking for four thousand dollars to fix her teeth, which were crooked and decayed. Grace readily gave her the money, Bunny disappeared with it—and returned several months later, penniless, teeth in the same condition.

"Give the money to the dentist!" T.J. told Grace.

Grace's eyes filled with tears. "But how can I say that to my sister?"

She still felt too guilty to refuse her family, a guilt neither T.J. nor George could understand. Though Grace liked to think herself beyond social expectations, she was still controlled by a vision of what family life should be: harmonious, tender, generous—much like Allison and Connie's relationship at the end of *Peyton Place*.

"Grace was so compassionate that it killed her," T.J. thought in 1980—but in some respects she merely fulfilled the requirements for a "feminine" woman: self-abasement, other-direction, constant and unremitting care. As Erica Jong's Isadora Wing, also suffering the stresses of fame, remarks in *Fear of Flying:* "Show me a woman who doesn't feel guilty and I'll show you a man."

During the party years, which lasted until 1960, Grace and her entourage found it easy to lose track of time. Richard Stinson, Grace's protégé, remembers mentioning on one visit that Hawaii had become a state—several months before. The laughing and drinking partygoers seemed highly amused that they'd missed it.

Grace rarely appeared without a glass in her hand—and sometimes held it up to the middle of her forehead, as if trying to cool her brow, or freshen her thoughts.

When she looked into the glass, she often grew morose—and would call Bernie Snierson in the middle of the night, crying, "I saw my face in the bottom of the glass."

And still, she was not writing.

CHAPTER 15

Peyton Place was coming—or so publicity teasers told Americans during the summer of 1957. Somehow, the smoldering best seller would be filmed.

Each important casting decision got play in the newspapers, especially the choice of Lana Turner to play Constance MacKenzie. Then, after more than three hundred auditions, Jerry Wald and Mark Robson, the director, chose Diane Varsi, a newcomer, to play Allison. Wald called Varsi a "scared, pimply little bunny. Exactly right."

Camden, Maine, was photographed for the New York *Times,* with extras milling about for the Labor Day picnic, created for the movie. In the fall Robson went on a world tour to promote *Peyton Place*—visiting London, Paris, Rome, Athens, Istanbul, New Delhi, Bangkok, Taipei, Hong Kong, and Tokyo, before returning to the United States for the world premiere in December—in Camden, Maine.

The Laconia Chamber of Commerce had suggested the premiere be held in Laconia, and they even cabled Grace while she was at Twentieth Century-Fox:

> IF GILMANTON CAN'T HAVE IT, LACONIA SHOULD BE
> THE NEXT CHOICE. LETTERS STILL APPEAR IN LOCAL
> PAPER. INTEREST HIGH. MAIN STREETERS WANT PEYTON
> PLACE. CHAMBER WILL COOPERATE. DO WHAT YOU CAN.

But the studio publicists alienated townspeople, and the premiere went to Camden, where most of the outdoor shots had been done. Bette Davis, who lived near Camden, lent herself for publicity.

Grace claimed she was not even invited, but T.J. says she was. In fact, Bette Davis herself telephoned, but Grace refused to take the call.

For the New York opening, December 12, 1957, a dozen people from the Laconia/Gilmanton/Belmont area attended, at the studio's expense. At the Laconia Tavern, studio publicists made the arrangements with Olive Hartford, who then shepherded the others to New York, where Twentieth Century-Fox paid for the Hotel Piccadilly, food, tips, and, of course, movie tickets.

The New Hampshire visitors admired the Christmas decorations, but found that a subway strike was on. Ed Eveleth, who insisted (as Grace did) on wearing in New York what he wore in New Hampshire—old jeans, boots, and a flannel shirt with a safety pin holding it together—complained later that, because of the strike, he had had to wear his boots all the time. He said he missed his horse.

Roxy Rothafel, of WLNH and the Radio City Rothafels, escorted the Hartford-Eveleth group to the premiere; Grace and T.J. escorted each other to the last show at the Roxy. They paid $2.75 each for two tickets, and entered the theater just in time to see Grace's name among the screen credits.

According to Patricia Carbine of *Look,* Grace sighed afterward: "Well, *Peyton Place* now has nowhere else to go. It's all over." But Grace gave a more dramatic version in the *American Weekly:* "When the picture was finished I could do nothing but weep." She threw herself into T.J.'s arms, she said, and cried, "It's over. It's all over."

But T.J., the protective man she'd dreamed of, reassured her: "No, darling, everything is just beginning."

T.J. meant their relationship; Grace meant her career—and the film, which Jerry Wald called "no work of art, but a good movie and a hell of a money-maker," served mainly to discredit her as a writer. In order to make a film palatable to an audience and an industry limited by fifties morality and studio timidity, Wald had taken most of the guts out of Grace Metalious' book.

Any screenplay has to condense the book: compressing time,

eliminating unnecessary characters, expressing through pictures what a novel says in words. Screenwriter John Michael Hayes kept most of the essential characters: Allison, Connie, Selena, Mike Rossi (the former Tomas Makris), Rodney Harrington, and Betty Anderson. But he eliminated Kathy Ellsworth's losing her arm in carnival machinery. Selena's abortion became a "miscarriage"; Allison did not have an affair with her New York agent; and Mike Rossi had no midnight swim with Connie MacKenzie.

Hayes, unlike Grace Metalious, had to work within the rules set up by the "Hays Office," organized in 1922 by the Motion Picture Producers and Distributors of America and still powerful in 1957. Faced with constant criticism for sex and violence, the film industry itself had set up the office, headed by Will H. Hays, a Presbyterian elder, chairman of the Republican National Committee, and Postmaster General in the Harding Administration. The rules Hays promulgated, in consultation with the Catholic Church's Legion of Decency, still controlled movies well into the 1960s. (And then, in the late 1960s, the film industry—against similar threats of censorship—devised the G, PG, R, and X rating systems.)

The Production Code, as the Hays rules were called, supported marriage, family, morality, and purity, and decreed what could not be shown on the screen. There could be no perversion; no miscegenation; no sexual parts, including breasts; no swear words; no gory depictions of crimes; no couples in bed together (twin beds only, even for the married); and—most important—no evil without compensating good.

In the Hays Office theory of "compensating values," evil could in fact be shown on the screen—as long as vice eventually was punished, and virtue eventually rewarded. The result was inevitable: reel after reel of sin, vice, crime, and decadence, but good characters rewarded in the last reel, and evil ones either punished or, best of all, converted. "Regeneration" was a Hollywood specialty—especially in films produced by Jerry Wald.

The Production Code did benefit women's roles—for as the film critic Molly Haskell has pointed out, women could not be portrayed solely as sexual objects or as idle rich. To the Hays Office, those were immoral roles. Under Hays Office rules, characters played by such actresses as Katharine Hepburn, Rosalind Russell, and Joan Crawford—whose comeback in *Mildred Pierce* (1945) Jerry Wald orchestrated—had careers as well as men in their lives.

But the Hays rules also led to the creation of stock characters: the hero, who wins out in the end, was always clean-profiled, clear-eyed. The heroine, always blonde and virginal. The other woman: dark, exotic, sensual. The uneducated and lower class: slovenly clothes and Southern accents—even in the *Peyton Place* film. Though the Crosses are clearly New Englanders, all of them except Selena have Southern accents. The Crosses, except Selena, are set up to be losers—but other characters, thanks to John Michael Hayes and the Hays Office, improve their chances in the *Peyton Place* film.

Kenny Stearns, the town drunk in the book, has at most a mild alcoholic buzz in the film—as he's shown winning the beer-drinking contest at Peyton Place's annual Labor Day picnic. The picnic provides opportunities for other wholesome pursuits: Camden extras eating hot dogs and cakes, drinking sodas, playing tug-of-war, singing barbershop harmonies—and definitely not losing any arms to carnival machinery.

Little Norman Page, a loser in Grace's *Peyton Place,* becomes something of a winner in the film. In Grace's original manuscript, he enjoys being nude as his mother whips him; does not mind her giving him enemas; and cooperates with her in pretending to be an injured war hero—though he's really been discharged as a "psychoneurotic." In the published *Peyton Place,* he still has his false limp, his neuroses, and his enemas, but loses his nude whipping. In the film version, he loses his enemas, his neuroses, his false limp—and even his littleness. As played by Russ Tamblyn, Norman joins the paratroopers and is obviously going to be something of a hero.

Rodney Harrington, the thoughtless playboy (Barry Coe), and sexy Betty Anderson (Terry Moore) are also cleansed. Instead of Grace's back-seat scene in which Betty demands, "Is it up, Rod? Is it up good and hard? . . . Now go shove it into Allison MacKenzie," the filmed Rodney and Betty have a short necking session. They share one cheek kiss and one brush of the lips; they slide down on the seat—and then she hits him with her purse and jumps out of the car.

Though they do have a nude swim together (conveyed by a shot of his bare feet, and his pants on the ground), Betty does not become pregnant, nor demand money. Nor is Rodney hit by a truck while reaching for another woman's breasts.

Rather, Betty and Rodney elope; his wealthy father (Leon Ames) wants to disinherit Rodney; and then father and son are reconciled when Rodney is drafted. (In the book his father keeps Rodney out of the draft—but that would be rewarding evil in the film.) Soon Rodney is honorably "killed in action"—a form of compensating values, for his misspent youth.

In Selena's case, too, virtue is more clearly rewarded and vice punished. In Grace's *Peyton Place,* Selena even at thirteen has a "dark, gypsyish beauty" and "eyes as old as time"—but in American movies in 1957, dark and sultry and sensual meant Other Woman.

So Selena had to be played by a blonde: Hope Lange, fresh from a successful role in *Bus Stop*. Moreover, Selena in the film becomes more dependent—thus, presumably, more feminine. After their parents are gone, her brother Paul (William Lundmark), not Selena, runs the household. Selena's mother, Nellie, is played by Betty Field (who played Cassie, Selena's counterpart, in *Kings Row*).

Lucas Cross (Arthur Kennedy) still rapes his stepdaughter Selena—as shown by her terrified face, her hands clutching the bedstead, and her hands torn from the bedstead as a train streaks by on the sound track. The Hays Office would not allow abortion, but Dr. Swain (Lloyd Nolan) does get a rape confession from Lucas—who gets a new speech blaming society for his own viciousness. Nevertheless, after Doc leaves, an unrepentant Lucas chases Selena and tries to rape her again. She falls down a hill and begins to have an apparent miscarriage—which Doc Swain handles for her and keeps secret (thus emphasizing secrecy more than abortion or miscarriage).

In the book, Dr. Swain's revelations of rape and abortion take the place of a trial for Selena; in the movie, Selena actually goes on trial—with all the barbed testimony, twisting of statements, and ridicule that form the stuff of Hollywood courtroom dramas. But Doc Swain's speech does free her, and her childhood sweetheart

Ted Carter (David Nelson), who deserts her in the book, stays with her in the movie. Virtue again triumphs.

Virtue triumphs with Allison, too, as the film omits her affair—but virtually eliminates her career as a writer as well. Though Allison does go to New York, she seems to leave Peyton Place because of anger against her mother instead of literary ambition. Her life in New York—the weakest part of the book, but essential to her becoming an author—does not even appear in the film. Allison's idealism remains—as Diane Varsi dances in the woods, talks to trees, and exchanges chaste kisses with Norman Page—but not Allison's growing toughness, her becoming an independent adult.

Even the adult relationship, Connie MacKenzie's and Mike Rossi's, is made less "adult." Connie and Mike (Lana Turner and Lee Philips) have their first date at a Labor Day picnic. When he visits her house, he invites her to chaperone a high school dance—not to go for an intimate midnight swim. They talk more about love than sex, and Mike Rossi is far less sexy.

As played by Lana Turner, Connie remains blonde and glamorous, as in the book. But Mike, in the original manuscript a "phallus in a toy shop window" and even in print dark, massive, and handsome "in an obviously sexual way," becomes Lee Philips: tall, thin, no longer uncommonly handsome. "No man he to rip off a lady's bathing suit," Paige Knickerbocker wrote in the San Francisco *Chronicle,* "and his voice at times approaches a squeak." He becomes the stock Production Code hero: clear-eyed, clean-profiled—and no more the sensual Greek.

Grace Metalious, along with almost everyone else, thought Philips' performance was "terrible." She expected to dislike the movie, though she knew what Somerset Maugham had said about film versions of his books: "If your characters are well-conceived, they can withstand anything—even Hollywood." The movie of *Peyton Place* actually left Grace "pleasantly surprised, but I thought it was sugar-coated."

Lloyd Nolan was "great" in the role of Doc Swain, Grace thought, and the rape scene was "tremendous." Diane Varsi, who played Allison in her first screen role, "came through fine," and Hope Lange, in Grace's opinion, "did a good job, but didn't *look* like Selena." As for the top-billed star, Lana Turner, Grace considered her performance "good."

Turner, the only real "name" in the picture, had most disappointed the eager extras in Camden, Maine: her part was shot entirely on the West Coast. At thirty-seven, she had considered herself too young to play anyone's mother. Jerry Wald claimed it took him and Mark Robson five hours to convince her to play Constance MacKenzie. They won when they pointed out that playing the mother in *Mildred Pierce* had saved Joan Crawford's career.

Before *Peyton Place* Turner had had nearly a dozen "flops," among them *Latin Lovers,* the movie the Metalious children had insisted on seeing during their first cross-country jaunt in 1953. Marsha, ten, Mike, six, and Cindy, three, thought it was great, but adult audiences found it silly and dull, except for Lana Turner's presence. Her co-star, Ricardo Montalban, could do little with the "turkey of a script"—and even he himself had been an afterthought.

None of the Metaliouses knew the real story, the kind hidden from fifties audiences. Fernando Lamas, originally scheduled for the Latin lover role, was also having a passionate off-screen romance with Lana Turner. But when he saw her dancing with actor Lex Barker at a party, Lamas had made a jealous scene—which included ungallant remarks about Lana's performance in bed.

A week before *Latin Lovers* was to begin filming, Metro-Goldwyn-Mayer replaced Lamas with Montalban—and soon Lamas was gone from MGM. He had broken a major taboo, for 1953: he had announced publicly that he and a woman were sleeping together, outside of marriage.

That escapade, quickly covered up, did no harm to Lana Turner's career, but the string of movie failures did. By the time Jerry Wald was casting *Peyton Place,* Lana Turner and Lex Barker, who had become her fourth husband, were divorcing. Twentieth Century-Fox fought Wald about Lana Turner, and suggested Jane Wyman or Olivia De Havilland for Allison's mother. But Wald convinced the studio that Lana Turner had to be in his picture.

In publicity releases Lana Turner talked about playing Allison

MacKenzie's mother: a mother needn't be "matronly," and "If I'd had my own daughter younger (she's fourteen now) she'd be eighteen too." That daughter, Cheryl Crane, four months older than Marsha Metalious, was part of Lana Turner's necessary image as a concerned mother. But mother and daughter rarely saw one another, as the public learned several months after the *Peyton Place* film was released.

Cheryl was only thirteen when her mother became involved with Johnny Stompanato, a minor gangster and handsome gigolo who took Lana's money and was fiercely jealous. Then, during a quarrel on April 4, 1958, Stompanato threatened to cut Lana's face. Cheryl, fearing for her mother's life, grabbed an eight-inch butcher knife and plunged it into Johnny Stompanato's stomach—killing him instantly.

Cheryl's case—later portrayed, thinly-disguised, in a Harold Robbins novel, *Where Love Has Gone* (1962)—ended in a verdict of justifiable homicide. The scandal naturally intensified interest in the *Peyton Place* film, in which Lana Turner's family is clean, loving, and wholesome, and she and her daughter reconcile in the end.

The *Peyton Place* movie had generally favorable reviews, for—unlike the book or Lana Turner's life—it suited the temper of the times. Turner's many love affairs never appeared in the media: press agents were paid to keep them out and preserve her public reputation. Ingrid Bergman, who had borne a baby out of wedlock in 1950, had been ostracized from American films (even though she later married the father, Roberto Rossellini). Hollywood contracts had morality clauses requiring stars to conduct their lives discreetly, and when Lana Turner became inconveniently pregnant during the 1940s, Louis B. Mayer of MGM quietly arranged an abortion for her. She also had several hospitalizations for "exhaustion" and one "emergency appendectomy"—both common euphemisms for illegal, but safe and hospital-performed, abortions.

Peyton Place, film version, removed Dr. Swain's giving Selena Cross what he called an "emergency appendectomy" (to cover up an abortion)—and the rest of the film's surgery on the book was generally approved. Ronald Johnson, in the Toronto *Globe and*

Mail, liked the film's emphasis on love, a sign of Jerry Wald's imprint; the Chicago Association of Women's Clubs named *Peyton Place* its top film of 1957; the Chicago *Sun Times* called it "one of the best motion pictures ever made." Reviewers knocked actor Lee Philips, but praised Lana Turner, Diane Varsi, Hope Lange, Russ Tamblyn, and Lloyd Nolan.

Virtually all reviewers agreed on one other point: they seized the chance to take gratuitous swipes at Grace Metalious and her novel. The *Peyton Place* script, Jack Edmund Nolan wrote in *Films in Review,* "transformed a worthless, and dirty, book into a good film." John Michael Hayes had created "a clean story out of the literary mess he had to begin with, and Miss Metalious owes him a debt," said *Cue.* Director Robson had rescued the film from "Grace Metalious' immature cynicisms and conscienceless pandering," Elspeth Hart wrote in *Films in Review,* and the Chicago *Sun Times* noted that though Grace's "sordid situations" remained, "the screenplay is always in good taste."

Only two major reviewers, Paige Knickerbocker in the San Francisco *Chronicle* and Bosley Crowther in the New York *Times,* recognized that the film had sacrificed the vitality of the book. Knickerbocker called the film far more "sentimental," omitting Grace's attack on two-faced people: "the shocking impact of despicable qualities concealed by superficial respectability." Crowther said the first part of the movie reminded him of Carvel, Andy Hardy's all-American home town, and the film makers, Crowther said, ignored the core of Grace's story: "the quality of hypocrisy that corrupts a New England community. There is no sense of massive corruption here."

Most critics, however, preferred the movie.

Despite their obvious opposition, the book and movie were both spectacular successes—perhaps because they met different needs. The book, as Mike Wallace had said, was "basic and carnal"; the film was pure, wholesome, and acceptable to polite society. Interested readers, then, could devour the book behind closed doors, in the privacy of their own homes, and enjoy the "good parts" denied them in films. At the same time, they could see the *Peyton Place* movie publicly, without moral qualms, because the film had an A rating from the National Legion of Decency.

It was even nominated for nine Academy Awards: best picture; best screenplay; best direction; best photography (by William Mellor); and best acting by Lana Turner (her only nomination), Hope Lange, Diane Varsi, Arthur Kennedy, and Russ Tamblyn. But *The Bridge on the River Kwai* swept most of the awards that year; best actress was Joanne Woodward, in *Three Faces of Eve.*

During January 1958, while *Peyton Place* was breaking attendance records everywhere, Grace and T.J. had an enormous fight. She loved being with him; he "adored" her—but at times their living together seemed impossible. "I am sure that everyone who has ever been in love has had a fight with the one he loves," Grace wrote later in the *American Weekly.* "A few months ago, T.J. and I had one which might be termed a gasser. For a few dreadful days it really seemed as if the only way either one of us was to survive was to be apart."

Grace never wanted to be without a man in her life—and so, when she and T.J. fought, she sometimes phoned George, still her husband, for comfort. During the "gasser" with T.J., she called George at 2 A.M., pleading with him to come to Laconia (from Stow, where he still had his single room). Reluctantly George went—and found Grace at the Laconia Tavern Hotel, in tears, declaring she had finished with T.J. for good.

But the next night Grace, George, and the children went to Bernard Snierson's house to discuss a picture spread *Life* magazine had planned for her. Grace had a phone call, which she took in another room. Then, after they'd finished the picture plans, Grace sent George home with the children, saying she'd be along soon.

Grace never came home that night.

The next day George learned that she had chartered a plane and flown to T.J. He packed up kids and clothes and went to Stow, where he found a three-room cottage for the rest of the year.

That was in late January—while the newspapers were reporting a reconciliation between Grace and George. "The tabloids must have been hard up for news at the time, because they had a field day with me and with T.J.," Grace wrote in May—and then, without mentioning her sudden flight, she explained that, "No one bothered to say that he was saving my life. Without him I am nothing."

She did give credit, too, to Bernard Snierson, "who made himself available for the picking up of broken pieces." Bernie also worried the most about Grace's financial and romantic indiscretions. He continued begging her to set up trust funds; he pleaded with her to keep her affair out of the newspapers—but she ignored him.

She did hold a news conference February 4, in a plush two-room suite at the Plaza where, the United Press reported, "plump Mrs. Metalious, 33, snuggled with T. J. Martin, also plump and 33, on a sofa." (T.J. was actually thirty—and plump—but her being older embarrassed Grace.)

Grace told reporters that her marriage to George Metalious was finally at an end—and that she was en route to Mexico City to divorce George and marry T.J. But she seemed unwilling to go to Mexico and finish the deed—and the following week she did even more to rumple her own reputation.

"He makes me feel intensely female," she told Sidney Fields about T.J.—and Fields printed her comments in a three-part syndicated series, published February 9–11. What else attracted her about T.J.? "Humor, good looks; he's 6-feet-2 with a crew cut. One of the things that makes him so attractive is that, coupled with all this charm, is a lack of responsibility. I can't imagine anyone not liking him."

But when Fields met Martin, he was less than convinced. "There was something incongruous about his corpulence and his crew haircut, like a man trying to prove his youth." Nor was Fields impressed by Grace's protestations: "She's 33," he wrote, but "Emotionally she's about 13." Still, Fields liked Grace Metalious—and probed further than most reporters into her relationship with T.J.

As Grace's manager and PR representative, T.J. could do things she couldn't, Grace said. T.J. could ask for money due, and say no to people without offending. He could handle all her business affairs—if she'd let him. "He never profited from our relationship," Grace said, obviously sensitive to the charge. "We called it our money, and you know the bit: 'Let's spend it together.' But it never works out that way when the woman has the money. He could never quite forget it."

Had the roles been reversed, of course—a rich male writer totally supporting a female companion—no one would have thought anything of it. But Grace did not make that observation, at least publicly. In that era of conformity, she could not forget what a woman should and should not do. Still, she valued the independence that success gave her.

"For a good number of years if George wasn't home I felt I wouldn't be able to survive," she told Fields. "I didn't know how to do anything. But after *Peyton Place* that was no longer true. There was something I could do." Then she added thoughtfully: "We were married young. He's so kind, and so damned patient."

T.J. meant an escape from lonely memories, Fields reported, but Grace's writing was suffering. As of February 1958, two and a half years after *Peyton Place* had been sold, Grace had completed only one or two chapters of *The Tight White Collar* (with Fields she was deliberately vague, and may have had nothing but scraps).

She blamed her unsettled personal life: "Marrying Martin will settle me enough to get it done," she said. "A portable typewriter is going with us to Mexico. It will be done by April first. That's my deadline. If I make a deal with myself I usually keep it."

Still, she had doubts: "There are always those long, dark, cold nights. I'm damned worried about this next book. What if I don't do well enough? I suppose I'll always live with that fear."

Since she planned to be married for the second time, Fields asked her to list the do's and don'ts of love and marriage, and how she would plead: guilty or not guilty. Grace obliged.

"Don't get married when you're too young to know what you want. Guilty.

"Don't get married for sex alone. Guilty with an explanation. You may not go into marriage with that idea alone, but often that's how it winds up. Having children makes it worthwhile.

"Don't get married if it's going to be difficult financially. Oh, boy! How guilty! We starved for 14 years.

"Don't, unless you're sure it's someone who's going to wear well for a long time. Guilty. But I never gave that much thought.

"Don't, if you think it's going to be a great big bonfire for the rest of your life. Guilty. What puzzles me is when you find out the flame gets less bright.

"Don't get married if you expect the man to be a combination of lover and father.

"Don't do it if you're selfish and self-centered to any great degree. Marriage requires so much giving that if you're not equipped for it, it will come as a shock. Very guilty."

Fields admired her honest postscript: "I bitched up one marriage and almost messed up this second hope for another. How dumb can I be? Look, I'm really the last one in the world qualified to talk about love and marriage."

She also talked very candidly about another subject. "There was a lot of talk around here because Martin was staying at my house," she told Fields. "The worst of this is what you do to other people with your own love affair. The kids, my husband."

Bernie Snierson blanched when he read that—for Grace Metalious had violated a taboo even Lana Turner respected. Grace had said, *in print,* that she was living with a man not her husband, and that they were having "a love affair." She might very well have destroyed her career, he thought.

"We've got to get her divorced and married to Martin," declared Snierson, then at the Plaza with Grace, T.J., and their entourage. Charles Rothenberg, a New York lawyer and friend of Grace's agent, Jacques Chambrun, was deputed to make the arrangements, along with Philip Wittenberg, Kitty Messner's attorney.

Grace told no one—not even her children—what she was up to.

She flew to Phenix City, Alabama, known as "sin city" because it had no residence requirements for divorce. She divorced George on February 25, 1958, two days before their fifteenth anniversary, and gave reporters her characteristic depiction of T.J.: "He is the only man in my world who makes me feel intensely female. A stallion type."

In Elkton, Maryland, where there were no residence requirements for marriage, Grace married T.J. on February 28. T.J. listed his occupation as "Radio Announcer," though he worked as Grace's manager; Grace's occupation is listed as "None"—as if she did not take her writing seriously. Following their habit, they dressed similarly: T.J. in a gray worsted suit; Grace in a gray suit coat and gray veiled hat—and a silver-tone mink stole T.J. had bought for her.

She had said she'd never wear mink—and the night before the wedding, she'd tried to throw the stole out their hotel window during an explosive argument. Grace accused T.J. of marrying her for her money. T.J. shouted, "I don't even want to marry you!" But they reconciled—and Grace adored her mink stole.

The wedding party included Philip Wittenberg, Charles Rothenberg, Kitty Messner, Jacques Chambrun, and a herd of reporters and photographers. Because the media people were restless, Grace decided to hold the reception before the ceremony—so they'd get their pictures and go. Wedding pictures show her cutting the cake, T.J. guiding her hand, and their feeding each other cake.

Even with reporters gone, the minister—a retired nonsectarian named Walter H. Shaeffer, later described by George as "a fat little businessman"—gave the wedding a carnival air, as T.J. recalls it: "We are gathered here—step right up—to join this man and this woman—there's more room down here—now where was I?—in holy matrimony—you little French fellow, you stand right there . . ."

Afterward, Mr. and Mrs. Martin returned to the Plaza, where everyone had always assumed they were married. Grace glanced at the newspapers—and saw their wedding prominently displayed. Mortified, she hid in the bathroom closet when room service came —and it was two days before T.J. could cajole her into showing herself publicly again.

Their wedding had been a happy and festive occasion. It was also, Grace said later, the beginning of the end of their love affair.

CHAPTER 16

Grace and T.J.'s marriage did not appear in Patricia Carbine's article, "Peyton Place," in the March 18 *Look*—because of *Look*'s long deadline time. Carbine also quoted Grace about her "love affair"—but by then Bernie Snierson could relax.

Carbine was the only woman reporter to do a national magazine piece on the author of *Peyton Place*. The assignment was a unique opportunity, and "It appealed to my editor's sense of the paradoxical," Carbine recalls. Daniel D. Mich, the *Look* editor, had extraordinary hiring practices for his era. Most magazines used women as researchers and fact checkers in the office, and men as reporters and writers—but Mich did not discriminate. He hired and promoted Carbine, and challenged her—especially when he dispatched her to interview Grace Metalious in Gilmanton.

Carbine, twenty-six and "naïve as they come," was a singular contrast to the author of *Peyton Place*. The only practicing Catholic on the *Look* staff, Pat Carbine had been taught by nuns for sixteen years. Around the *Look* offices she was jokingly called "Sister Felicita," and everyone wondered how Sister Felicita would get along with "Mrs. Outrageous." (The term "Ms." had not yet been invented; later Carbine helped found *Ms.* magazine.)

Carbine and *Look* photographer Bob Sandberg arrived during a troubled period in Grace's life. Her lawyer, Bernard Snierson ("She keeps me busy twenty-four hours a day," he told Carbine), and her lover, T. J. Martin, seemed her only supports. Otherwise, "she was thoroughly on her own"—apparently without a network of women friends to call on. In the week Carbine spent following Grace around, Grace decided not to remain alone: she would marry T.J., she said. But it was a week full of upheavals.

Carbine and Sandberg arrived in the New Hampshire snow. They stayed at the Laconia Hotel, where Grace advised them to order a "Peyton Place cocktail" (Canadian Club and 7-Up) and declared, "It's going to be very popular." But Pat and Bob spent most of their time with Grace, at the Gilmanton house.

Sandberg snapped pictures of Grace frolicking with the St. Bernard, Hennessy, and Mike swiping cherries to nibble on. He captured Grace laughing with T.J., over their wine glasses, while Carbine quoted her: "I've never had so much fun with anyone." Carbine accompanied Grace on a clothes-shopping expedition to O'Shea's in Laconia, and then the whole group—Grace, T.J., the children, Carbine, and Sandberg—took a private plane Grace chartered, to the Plaza.

They were "an incongruous-looking gaggle of souls," Carbine says, and Sandberg photographed Marsha, Mike, and Grace waiting in the Plaza lobby, Mike twiddling his thumbs in front of the ornate scrollwork on the elevator. The Metalious party were not the typical Plaza clientele—assured, old-moneyed—and Grace seemed uncomfortable with details that come easily to the securely rich, such as the mechanics of checking into a hotel. Pat Carbine, who liked Grace's vulnerability and her outspokenness, finally took charge of registration.

In the week before, Carbine had had ample opportunity to observe Grace's strengths and insecurities. Through saturation reporting—following the subject around, trying to get her to condense several weeks of living into one week, for the camera—"Sister Felicita" encouraged "Mrs. Outrageous" to talk about her life. Grace seemed warm, open, not at all reticent.

"I utterly despise sneaky people," she told Carbine, and there was nothing sneaky about her break-up with George: "the marriage was over before the book came out." *Peyton Place* simply "made a separation financially possible."

Why did she write the book? "I thought about it a good long time . . . and frankly, I needed the money."

For *Look,* a family magazine, Carbine reported only part of

Grace's frankness about sex. "To me, *Peyton Place* isn't sexy at all," Grace declared. "I don't know what all the screaming is about. Sex is something everybody lives with—why make such a big deal about it?" She was never repulsed by sex, she reported: "There are very few things which repel me—such as seeing the kids get a cut finger or pulling out their teeth. Far worse to me than any sex act is unattractive food, and I'm no gourmet."

Was she pleased with *Peyton Place,* which by then had been bought by one out of every twenty-nine Americans? No, Grace admitted. "I don't think it's a good book. God, how I hope the next one is better!" But quarrels with T.J., traveling, and emotional ups and downs were keeping her from her next book, *The Tight White Collar.* Briefly, she split from T.J., giving Pat Carbine still another version of their "gasser" of a fight: "The thing got to be too heavy a burden. We were partying most of the time, and I couldn't work. Nothing is worth this." She turned to George; and then back to T.J., a genial "huggy bear" who abetted her extravagances—but also tried to change her.

Grace still wore her blue jeans and men's shirts, Carbine noticed, though T.J. wanted her to dress more like a rich celebrity. Grace resisted "feminine" clothes, at least for the moment. Whether Grace wanted to shock others or was genuinely indifferent to appearances, Pat Carbine could not tell. Grace did seem uncomfortable with her body: short and broad-shouldered, she did not fit a feminine beauty ideal.

Grace was greatly concerned about clothes for the children, who were apparently being shuttled between Gilmanton and Stow. She wanted them to look good in New York, but doubted her own taste. Shopping at O'Shea's, she constantly asked Pat Carbine's advice: "What do you think? What should they have?" It was partly Grace's "help me" manner, and partly genuine insecurity—but she seemed very pleased to have someone else make decisions for her.

That was the role T.J. played, too: "Before T.J. I never knew the fun of being taken care of," Grace said. "It seems I was always taking care of people."

Her fights with T.J. devastated her. During one trip to the Plaza, alone because they'd fought, Grace attempted suicide. It was a clumsy attempt, obviously a cry for help—and the manager called T.J., who flew to be with her, and they were reconciled for a while.

T.J. obviously enjoyed being with Grace, and told Pat Carbine that he had found "the one woman for me. I have never really loved anyone before . . . Grace and I have tried to make it be over before. It hasn't begun to be over."

Grace, equally passionate, said she had discovered with T.J. that "love doesn't wear out like an automobile tire. The more you use love, the more love you get. The queerest thing is, I cannot imagine its being any other way. I cannot now think about being with anyone but T.J."

But she also had her children—and Carbine reported Grace's views on Marsha's dating, at fourteen: "All her friends are going out. I don't want her to feel like an odd-ball. I refuse to let her go out alone with a boy who drives a car. When she goes to dances at the teen center, T.J. and I take her and pick her up. If she dates, it is with another couple, and she *must* be in by 12 o'clock. Another thing Marsha is not allowed to do is go to the movies by herself."

Because she was fond of Grace Metalious, Pat Carbine presented her as a concerned mother, and labored to make generous comments about Grace's appearance—"nicely shaped legs," she wrote, knowing that Grace would be found wanting according to most standards of dress. But Carbine also printed T.J.'s odd self-defense: "People think I'm a gigolo and a gold digger," he said. "Actually, the services I perform for Grace would cost her a pretty piece of change." And Carbine recorded T.J.'s comment about the wedding plans: "Even if we're not speaking to one another, we're getting married anyway."

Grace seemed to have few friends to invite to the ceremony, and she asked Pat Carbine to come to Elkton for the wedding. "Will you come?" she asked, her eyes wide with generous intensity. Carbine could not come—and T.J. thinks Kitty Messner was the only woman who did.

For a while, divorce and remarriage seemed good for Grace. Divorce can be a necessary rite of passage, Gail Sheehy says in *Passages,* "before anyone, above all herself, will take a woman's need for expansion seriously." After divorce, Sheehy says, one often sees the Changed Woman: more dynamic, losing weight, improving her appearance . . . and for about a year, Grace did play the Changed Woman.

She and T.J. gave up drinking, became slim and tanned—especially after a trip to Florida—and looked healthy and fit. But T.J. thought she could improve her appearance even more—and she resisted.

Though she agreed to have Bergdorf Goodman's bring clothes to her suite at the Plaza, she had little interest in expensive clothes. In part, she still believed herself an ugly duckling—although she claimed not to worry about her appearance.

"I'm just fat and happy," she told Maurice Zolotow, who recorded that her shoes were kicked off on the floor, and "her torso confined in an unstylish tweed skirt and a man's striped shirt."

"I think diets are stupid," she told him. "I don't wear nylon stockings or girdles. I don't waste any time shopping when I'm in New York. These Fifth Avenue stores are strictly for jerks. I get all the clothes I need at O'Shea's in Laconia."

John O'Shea had given her credit when she was desperately poor; out of loyalty she always bought at O'Shea's. When Wendy Wilkens graduated from high school, Wendy's greatest wish was a cashmere sweater, so Grace went to O'Shea's and bought six of them, in six different colors.

For herself, however, she resisted T.J.'s efforts to turn her from wool to cashmere. "I have two suits and a lot of khaki pants and dungarees," she told reporters. "I only wear a dress if I absolutely have to—and even then I don't wear a dress."

She knew that money "is good for the nerves, but I'd rather spend money on my freedom and independence than throw it away on clothes."

T.J. disagreed. "He wants me to be chic," Grace complained to Esther Peters. "He's trying to make me over." He seemed to regard her as Cinderella in need of a transformation—and took her to Saks Fifth Avenue, where the salespeople showed her sophisticated, sexy black dresses.

"Of course you'll need a good foundation garment," they said—but Grace rebelled against that. She also rebelled against T.J.—

who, like virtually everyone else, wanted her to conform to a feminine image.

Her money remained a source of conflict. Bernie and Muriel Snierson would sit up nights with her, trying to convince her to save herself taxes, make herself into a corporation and appoint T.J. as a salaried officer.

"I don't want to pay him," Grace said stubbornly. "He's my husband. He can have anything he wants."

Bernie warned T.J.: "Look out."

Grace had stopped her destructive drinking—as many as eighteen screwdrivers in one night, Zolotow reported—but even T.J. suspected her quitting was temporary. "Grace grew up on a six-pack," he recalls—and her favorite drink, Canadian Club and 7-Up, gave her much comfort.

Her romance with T.J. estranged her from her children—though not at first. Marsha felt harassed during the party years—and T.J. remembers her running around the house, in her bathrobe, acting the "little mother," telling everyone to "Stop talking—shut up—leave me alone!" Marsha was thrilled when T.J. took her backstage to meet Frankie Avalon, one of her singing idols—but she pulled away from accepting a substitute father.

At first, Mike enjoyed "Teej." One Christmas Mike even announced, "You're going to be my dad"—and T.J. was very touched. But that relationship rapidly soured, and Mike was sent away to Emerson, a pre-prep boarding school.

As if to compensate, Grace sometimes became overprotective with Cindy. When Cindy broke her leg skating at Rockefeller Center, Grace hovered hysterically—and when she overheard hospital black humor, a discussion of cutting off someone's leg, she immediately hustled Cindy out of that hospital and took her to the most expensive clinic she could find.

While they stayed with Grace, the youngsters often did not go to school because no one was up and around to take them. At other times—when classmates taunted them with their mother's notoriety—they preferred not to go. Cindy sometimes climbed into Grace's bed when she could not face going to school, and she especially liked to hide next to the wall.

During the party years Cindy and Mike were apt to be petted

and indulged by the strangers always gathered in the house—and on at least one occasion Cindy's pony, lodged in the garage, strolled into the living room in the middle of a lively party.

One guest vowed he'd stop drinking immediately.

Marsha, however, was old enough to attract problems. Older men made passes, and she fled to a friend's house.

Though Cindy recalls that the children were "spoiled obnoxious brats," most adults remember them as nice, well-mannered, and very self-sufficient. Grace's frequent absences taught the children independence. Mike and Cindy could cook by the time they were seven; Grace taught Cindy how to bake bread. Marsha never felt her parents limited her because she was a girl—though Grace gave her advice: "If a guy bothers you, kick 'im right in the nuts!" George was the one who told Marsha about menstruation—but when the time came, Grace showed her about sanitary napkins. Marsha told Cindy.

Moving to Stow made life easier for the children—at least for a while. They escaped the disorganized atmosphere at home—while Grace gave a different, more graceful interpretation to the media. Since the *Peyton Place* publicity had upset her children's school lives, Grace told Pat Carbine, Grace and T.J. decided to take the children out of school—and "talked of having them tutored," Carbine wrote.

"A tutor would be worth every nickel," Grace said. "The kids—especially Marsha—were so unhappy. I always said that when the book begins to touch the children, we'll move. This seems like a better solution. We could try it for a year anyway. And if Marsha wants to go away to school next year, of course, she may."

The children never had a tutor, Carbine reported. Instead, Grace "delivered the children to the care of George. She hoped that, with George's help, the children could make up the work missed while they were out of school for several months."

By that January of 1958, *Peyton Place* had sold more copies than *Gone with the Wind,* and by April it was gaining on Erskine Caldwell's *God's Little Acre*—which it soon surpassed. Grace's earnings were unaffected by a major recession that spring, which had caused the highest unemployment rate of the 1950s: 7.5 percent.

The public had an insatiable appetite for *Peyton Place*—and for news about Grace Metalious, who decided to tell her own story in the *American Weekly,* a syndicated Sunday supplement.

"It makes me so mad when I hear, or read about, people who try to tell you what a chore it is to be rich and famous," Grace wrote to begin her four-part series, "All About Me and *Peyton Place*" (May 18, May 25, June 1, June 8). "While it is true that being wealthy and well known will not solve all your problems," Grace continued, having money "will cause a great many more people to care about your troubles." Given a choice, she said, she'd rather be rich.

The biggest drawback to fame, Grace thought, had been "the misquotes, misconceptions, and downright lies printed about my book, my family, and my life." These articles would be her turn, she said, to give her own version once and for all, "as unvarnished and true as possible."

She described the terrible summer of 1955 at "It'll Do," the poverty, drought, and suffering—all transformed with the magical news that Jacques Chambrun had sold *Peyton Place*. She described meeting Chambrun, Kitty Messner, and Leona Nevler—then flashed back to her childhood writings.

Why did she write? Because "somewhere in my head there is always a story. Perhaps this makes me sound like a candidate for the couch or the funny farm, but it is the only answer I can give which I feel to be the true one."

While she was writing *Peyton Place,* she said, the characters seemed far more real than "the humans who surrounded me"—and she certainly knew the residents of Peyton Place much better. "I knew what every single one of them ate for breakfast and what color pajamas they wore to bed, and by the time the book was finished I was so damned sick and tired of all of them that I never wanted to hear them mentioned again."

But she did want to straighten the factual record about herself. Contrary to articles calling her a "rock-bound New Englander," she'd learned French from her grandmother before she spoke English—and Grandmother Royer "went to her grave thinking that all Americans were uncivilized. If there was ever a New Hampshire household that was un-Yankee, it was ours."

She wrote about her parents' divorce, and her mother's wanting "everything." She described her mother's dreams sympathetically, as if she shared them. Then there were her first dates with George; falling in love; getting married. Though she flaunted her affair with T.J., Grace never admitted in print that she and George had "played house" before their marriage. Instead, she claimed they were married in 1942—making Marsha, born in October 1943, unquestionably "legitimate." For the *American Weekly,* Grace said she and George married when they were both seventeen, and "For a year we played house and then I was pregnant and George was drafted."

She went through what the war meant for her: rationing, dating nice officers, using leg makeup, "smoking foul cigarettes," and worrying about George. Afterward, George had matured, and "had left me far behind." Still, she reported, they stayed together through unpaid bills, misunderstandings, her near fatal childbirth experience—and her first novel, while George studied at U.N.H.

Playing "Mrs. Schoolteacher" had not suited her. She liked it better, she wrote, when she and George and the kids just took off from Belmont: "the only crazy, impulsive thing that George and I ever did together." George lost his teaching job because of *Peyton Place,* she said—but by then they knew the marriage was over. After the publicity had died down, "I'd institute proceedings for a divorce."

And then, T.J. appeared. "It is true that we have fought as if we hated each other at times, but we have loved harder than we have argued and our few days of sadness have indeed been a small price to pay for our months of almost unbearable happiness"—which she said she lacked the words to describe (and perhaps the nerve, for a family audience).

"I only know that T.J. is the bulwark that stands between me and the harshness of the world"—the protector she'd always sought in a man. "His is the hand that comforts me, the voice that soothes me. All I wanted out of life was everything—and I got it. Now we are married and the people who are fond of us have smiled and said, 'It's about time.' We think so, too."

She was also at work on her new book, *The Tight White Collar,* she wrote. "I know that there is never going to be another *Peyton*

Place with all its excitement," but "My life has assumed a pattern now. It is time to go back to work, to return to normalcy"—for the storm had ended. "At last I have found my way safely home."

The picture Grace gave in the *American Weekly* did conform safely: the mother who wanted only the best for her children, the wife who loved and depended upon her man. In outline at least, she followed the feminine mystique, supporting husband, home, and family.

The details that made Grace a unique character—her blue jeans, her earthy language, her willingness to tell everyone that T.J. was her "stallion"—did not appear. "All About Me and *Peyton Place*" has more than a touch of the hypocrisy Grace disdained in others, but it also gained her more respect, something she'd sorely missed.

Unfortunately, the route to respect meant presenting herself primarily as a dependent woman—instead of as an individual, a writer carving out her own identity in a hostile world.

Within a few weeks after the *American Weekly* pieces, Marsha, Mike, and Cindy came back to live with Grace and T.J. ("Grace's children fell in love with T.J., too," read a caption in the *American Weekly*). George went to take summer courses at the University of New Hampshire, where, because of his name, he was much talked about.

Though George smoked a pipe and said very little in class, Robert Geib, a fellow student, recalls the comment that George "lived in Peyton Place." Barbara Taylor, a high school student working in the U.N.H. cafeteria, remembers George's going through the food line and being pointed out as a sort of local celebrity who, as Grace's husband, "had achieved some notoriety, if not distinction."

That summer George took a course called "Case Studies," taught by Fred Jervis—the psychology professor who'd been Grace and George's neighbor on College Road in 1950. For his major project, George did a self-analysis, several hundred pages long, most of them about his relationship with Grace.

Grace wrote a twenty- to twenty-five-page answer, and the two papers, Jervis says, form an extraordinary autopsy of a marriage. But there was no way for George and Grace to reconcile their two sets of perceptions. (In his *The Girl from "Peyton Place,"* George quotes extensively from both papers.)

After summer school George returned to Gilmanton for the children—but found only Marsha. Unwilling to send the youngsters back with him, Grace had taken Mike and Cindy with her and T.J. to a secluded cottage in Rye Beach. Marsha sided with her father's right to custody—and eventually George tracked the others down, and returned to Stow.

Grace, meanwhile, took to drinking heavily, worrying a great deal, and writing very little—though she knew what she wanted her next book to be about. The central figures would be the ruling family in the town of Cooper Station. Their lives would be disrupted, if not destroyed, by the birth of a Mongoloid child. Would the book be another *Peyton Place?* "I don't see how it can be," Grace told Pat Carbine. "This time I'm neither frightened nor hungry nor angry."

She had learned to avoid the publicity appearances that frightened her—but when a chance came to appear on Ben Hecht's television show, she jumped at it. She had loved his autobiography, *A Child of the Century*—and, in her poorer days, had even made off with the Laconia public library copy. "You *have to see* this!" she'd exclaim to Laurie Wilkens, pointing at her favorite lines.

She savored Hecht's youthful "God aversions," and thoroughly agreed that "a man who in his youth embraces God is likely to be a sickly fellow with no more than a trickle of sex in him; or a creature full of low impulses that need concealing." Hecht supported Grace's pugnacious atheism; she thought him brilliant.

A Child of the Century also fed her imagination—since Hecht's story covers a world she (like most women) had never seen. Hecht had been a newspaper reporter in Chicago and Germany; a screenwriter in Hollywood; and an agitator everywhere for the creation of Israel (for which he was denounced by name in the House of Commons—an event that made him proud). His reported adventures include several affairs more farcical than romantic; numerous promotional stunts; and bizarre newspaper features—such as the fornicating dentist whose escapades wound up in headlines: DENTIST FILLS WRONG CAVITY.

Grace Metalious admired Ben Hecht's nerve; she shared his

hatred for conformity and hypocrisy. "I sought to remove the mask from the world," Hecht says, "to look behind it, to disprove loudly the virtues it proclaimed. . . . I dedicated myself to attacking prudes, piety-mongers, and all apostles of virtue"—the sort of people who attacked *Peyton Place* and its author.

Moreover, Hecht reports matter-of-factly that he and his second wife, Rose Caylor, lived together unmarried for some time before his first wife agreed to a divorce. Nor was Hecht a stranger to book bannings, such as *Peyton Place's.* He reports that only H. L. Mencken would publicly defend Hecht's *Fantazius Mallare,* a book attacked as lewd and lascivious because it used the word "pissing."

At sixty-five, Hecht was still earthy, and his television show, "Ben Hecht Is On the Air" specialized in promoting his iconoclastic views, five nights a week. Ted Yates, Mike Wallace's partner in Newsmaker Productions, produced the show and suggested questions for Hecht to ask a variety of guests: Jimmy Durante; Dorothy Parker; several tipsy authors; sundry missile experts (a year after the Soviets had sent up Sputnik, the first space satellite); and a set of Bowery bums whose scheduled appearance was abruptly canceled just before air time.

The Hecht show, which premiered on September 11, 1958, had already established an offbeat format by the time Grace appeared on October 28. Hecht's female helper, a combination sidekick and weather-girl known only as "Missy," introduced him and posed questions to get him to attack politicians, churches, judges, and conventional morality—with, the writer Al Ramrus remembers, "great relish and devastating effect." Missy kept track of the minutes, announced when interview time was up, and brought Ben back after the last commercial for a "bedtime story"—a humorous, sometimes pointless anecdote that he also recounted with relish.

When Grace Metalious appeared, after dinner with Hecht, Missy announced that Ben would "discuss the modern woman and modern man and his love life, with Grace Metalious, the authoress who wrote the best-selling novel, *Peyton Place,* which today leads all previous American novel sales with six million copies sold." Then, sounding like Ed McMahon, Missy proclaimed, "Now, here's Ben Hecht!"

"I love all women," Hecht told Missy, when she asked about "the woman of today." Nevertheless, he admitted he liked sex better in the old days, when it was more hidden—when to find out about women, "you had to steal a copy of the Sears Roebuck catalogue, hide in the attic and then find the breathless section devoted to women's underpants and study it." Now, he bemoaned, you could find 10,000 pictures of women swooning, cooking, "prancing around nude"—with gadgets to "beautify the bosom and the crotch and all of the feminine areas of loveliness."

What effect did this have on men? Missy asked dutifully.

Together with militarism, Ben said, "It helps make great flocks of pansies." He said he'd like a youth pill for himself. Missy broke for a commercial—and then Grace Metalious was sitting opposite Ben Hecht.

"The most enviable novel writer in our country," Ben said. "I bow"—and he broke into spontaneous applause.

Grace looked rather overwhelmed, Al Ramrus recalls, but managed to respond, "Thanks. That's a great compliment."

Then they launched into a discussion of women's and men's roles—an exchange in which neither of them shone. Ramrus, already disappointed with Mike Wallace's show when Grace proved not to be "an outspoken sexy woman with outrageous, challenging opinions and Rabelaisian attitudes," was again frustrated and baffled. Grace seemed strangely inarticulate, with virtually nothing to say.

But the transcript reveals what Al Ramrus also remembers: Ben Hecht was hardly a skillful host. Though he could be entertaining and "savagely witty" in conversation, he was a stumbling interviewer who plodded ahead with prepared questions, apparently neither listening to the answers nor seeking interesting openings. He did most of the talking, and only forceful personalities who damned the questions and forged ahead could fare well on the show. At most a handful of guests, all male, managed to do that.

Ben dutifully followed his script; Grace dutifully followed him—through repetition and clichés. Women were becoming more and more masculine, he lamented. Men had made such a mess of the world that women had to take over, she responded: "Somebody had to get things done."

She said chivalry was dead. He blamed the mothers of America, and she agreed (referring always to mothers as "they," never as "we"). American women, Grace claimed, would love to be "clinging vines"—if they had a man "to do something once in a while." Instead, she said, men seemed to pursue other goals: liquor, their mothers, jobs—and each other.

"Do you think that males marry mostly their mothers?" Hecht asked. "Do you think that's the reason that the rage for big bosoms has come into the movie industry?"

"What else?" Grace said. "The return to the nursery."

There Ben Hecht listened and responded—but usually he blindly followed his script. "I have another question here," he said a little later. "This is very involved. Ted Yates gave it to me. I can't quite get the question"—which seemed to be about "the Christian habit of worshipping a man who never made love to a woman."

"When was this?" Grace asked, surprised.

Ben tried to explain about the worship of Christ, but then decided, "This is very deep, too deep for me. Let's skip it." Instead, he wondered aloud: Could the schools restore women's glamour? "I don't mean falsies or anything"—but training women to be mysterious again.

"Who are you going to get to teach courses like this?" asked Grace, whose practical responses begin to read more and more like put-ons.

When they talked about "good women," the kind who never go out after dark and never let men touch them in any significant place, Grace said, "I haven't seen a woman like that for . . . I think perhaps my grandmother was one." Then she did get off one line appropriate for the scandalous author of *Peyton Place:* "I only know what I hear around, and I hear that virginity is terribly unchic."

She called Hollywood a "wasteland" with "dreadful, dreadful people"—a "junk heap" that she hated. But she perked up when they discussed writers and writing, and listed some favorite books she had read two, three, or more times: Maugham's *The Moon and Sixpence, Of Human Bondage,* and *Cakes and Ale;* Dickens'

A Tale of Two Cities, Hecht's *A Child of the Century* (about which Hecht did not respond), and *The White Tower,* by James Ramsey Ullman. "Marvelous book," she said. "Everybody with a problem climbing a mountain for their own reasons."

She also liked Christopher Morley's *Kitty Foyle,* she said. "An adorable story."

Hecht: "Why did you like that? That was a business girl out to make her way in the world."

Grace: "Oh, but it was so beautifully done. And I couldn't get over the fact that this was a man writing it."

Hecht: "He had a long beard, though . . ."

In his haste to make a brilliant *non sequitur,* Hecht apparently forgot that the last part of *Peyton Place,* Allison's stay in New York, is very reminiscent of *Kitty Foyle*—but he did remember to ask Grace about her future writing plans. She had her second book "almost finished," she said, and after December 1, when it was done, she'd take a month's vacation and then begin her third in January.

And what was book number two about?

"Oh, Heaven help us!" Grace replied. "It's called *Return to Peyton Place*"—same characters, new troubles, some new characters—"I hope real, true, live, breathing people."

She had only a few more words about Hollywood when Missy broke in for a commercial, followed by Ben's "bedtime story": an involved yarn about his roving eye and his aggressive wife—who, he reported cheerfully, would punch out any woman he was tempted to fool with.

Another woman besides Missy worked on "Ben Hecht Is On the Air": an obscure actress who did live commercials for Shiffly Embroidery—and Ramrus remembers her as Grace's physical opposite: "slender, immaculately groomed, husky-voiced, with a suggestive, knowing look in her eye. Surface sex in a very self-conscious way." She seemed to relish pitching commercials—as, a few years later, she relished pitching her own books on talk shows.

The actress was Jacqueline Susann—whose *Valley of the Dolls* made the headlines when it finally outsold *Peyton Place.*

By 1957 Mike Wallace's interview show had been promoted from a local New York station to the network. Ben Hecht's show, more goofy than penetrating, died after twenty weeks, though its schedule called for twenty-six. Officially, low advertiser interest and low audience ratings caused the show's demise—but it died, in fact, for the Hecht qualities Grace Metalious liked most.

Ben Hecht had a tendency to be "a trifle profane" on the air, according to Mike Wallace—and since he appeared live, he could not be bleeped. Finally he was warned by the station bosses: one more time, and you're out!

Hecht felt fairly confident the night his guest was Salvador Dali, the surrealist painter. They got into a discussion of platonic love, and "We figured, what harm can that be?" Mike Wallace recalls. As Dali continued espousing his philosophy, Hecht contentedly rolled his cigar.

"Well, you're in this platonic love between man and woman," Dali said calmly. "Your eyes lock. Your minds lock. You do not touch—but nevertheless, ORGASM!"

"Ben was like a deflated balloon," says Wallace, who calls it the "Orgasm and Out!" show. "You could see his life pass in front of him, because he knew that was it. That was the end of the Ben Hecht show."

Grace would have sympathized—but her strongest memory of her appearance on Hecht's show does not appear in the transcript: the moment her girdle suddenly went WHANG! in the middle of her stint.

"You know how those stretchy things are," she said later. "When they start to go, they dissolve into shreds. I wouldn't even have been wearing the darn thing"—here the reporter undoubtedly cleaned up her language—"if my daughter hadn't gone out and bought it and insisted I wear it." As for the problem: "Have you ever tried getting up out of a chair with a shredded girdle? I clutched my stomach and waddled off to the nearest ladies' room" —apparently during Missy's commercial break.

By the time Ben Hecht's show died, on February 21, 1959, Grace's *Return to Peyton Place* was in the throes of editing—but the book gave her little of the creative excitement she'd felt in producing *Peyton Place*.

In fact, she had not wanted to produce *Return* at all.

CHAPTER 17

Once she left Hollywood, Grace vowed never to speak to Jerry Wald again. Though she loved Hollywood movies, Wald's treatment of actresses disgusted her; though she liked the *Peyton Place* movie, she did not regret pitching her bloody mary at the screenwriter, John Michael Hayes. She still felt she'd been pressured into selling Wald her "baby"—and when he phoned her in Gilmanton, T.J. had to talk with him, in the kitchen.

"We just want a ten-page outline," Wald said, "of what would happen to all the people of Peyton Place if they were still living, if the book went on. For another movie. Of course, we'll pay for all the time involved."

"Frankly, Jerry, I don't think Grace is going to be interested at all," said T.J. (who rather enjoyed telling the famous Jerry Wald: "Look, Jerry, I've got to run—talk to you later").

Undaunted, Wald sweetened the offer: "How about a thousand dollars a page? That'll break a record. Just her thoughts. Ten pages."

No, no, no, no, no, Grace said.

Wald called again. "How about $25,000 for twenty-five pages?" he suggested to T.J.

Then Jacques Chambrun stepped in to cajole Grace, telling her how easy it would be, and so profitable. Kitty Messner, who'd been sending Grace advances on a second book and not seeing anything, thought it an excellent idea. T.J. encouraged her—and pointed out how much she needed money for home repairs. ("That house was her life," he says.)

In the next call, T.J. told Jerry Wald that Grace would do *Return to Peyton Place*.

"How soon?" asked Wald, already planning the movie.

"Two to three weeks."

Return to Peyton Place formed part of Jerry Wald's strategy for recapturing movie audiences lost to television. "We've got to make more movies for women—love stories with big name feminine stars," he told United Press International on August 18, 1958. "What's wrong with having one of the characters say, 'I love you'? I'm for it—and so are feminine moviegoers. If a producer makes a great woman's story, it can't miss being a hit."

But to make that kind of story out of the *Peyton Place* characters, Jerry Wald needed Grace Metalious—for whom he also engineered the paperback rights sale (Dell paid a $165,000 advance) and the hardcover arrangement with Messner's, both editions to come out before his filmed *Return*. Then he announced his plan to the media—but what Grace had actually agreed to do seemed unclear.

"Arrangement calls for authoress to pen original screenplay. Yarn also will later be published in book form," *Variety* reported October 15 under the headline: "GRACE METALIOUS' DEALS: Sells 2d Novel Plus 'Peyton' Sequel to 20th-Fox." At the same time, Fox bought screen rights to *The Tight White Collar*, which *Variety* said was one-third completed.

Time had a different version of Grace's agreement. "Wald has dictated a 95-page outline for Grace Metalious, from which she promises to produce a sequel to *Peyton Place*," the magazine reported on October 6, then added a potshot—more and more the media's way of covering Grace Metalious' writing. "Maybe only Grace will think the result a masterpiece, but if Jerry Wald likes it, it will make a movie—and money."

Grace began *Return* cynically, figuring she would write ten to twelve pages of whatever she felt like writing. T.J. assured her that Jerry Wald would take whatever she wrote. But once she sat down in her writing studio, she could not stop writing.

Somehow she regained the spirit of the original *Peyton Place*.

Inspiration flowed. Sometimes T.J. would not see her for three or four days, as she sat pounding away at her typewriter. She said she couldn't write a synopsis or short story after all. "I have to tell it the way it was, the way I feel it."

Sometimes after a long writing stint, Grace got T.J. to read her words back to her. With the parts she liked, she recaptured the creative delight she'd felt with *Peyton Place*. With parts she did not consider her best, she became upset and angry. But she told herself to forge ahead and get it over with, that the book was just for Jerry Wald.

Peyton Place had taken more than a year's writing, and a lifetime's thinking; *Return to Peyton Place* took Grace just thirty days. "Before anyone knew what had happened," T.J. says, "Grace had written a book"—but the book pleased no one.

The Tight White Collar had been delayed by Grace's self-doubts. Grace felt she owed it to *Peyton Place* readers to do even better—and became paralyzed with fear that she could not.

The thought that "I'm not writing a novel—I'm just doing a little ditty for Jerry Wald" made writing easier, less risky, less an exposure of self. But at other times, when she worried about her literary reputation, Grace would begin making drinks. Parts of the manuscript were fine; others, once she turned to alcohol, were virtually incoherent.

"Grace turned in something so terrible that it wasn't publishable," recalls Helen Meyer, then head of Dell.

T.J. estimates that almost half of *Return to Peyton Place* needed rewriting. It appeared to be by two different people: the Grace who was drinking, and the Grace who was not.

A third person was called in to fix the book.

Warren Miller, thirty-eight in 1959, worked as an agent for Push Pin Studios, whose artists did layouts and graphic designs for book publishers, including Dell/Western Printing, and magazines. Miller had published several books, including the novel *The Way We Live Now,* and was married to another writer, Jimmy Miller (later author of *The Big Win*).

Frank Taylor approached Warren Miller for Western: would Miller "ghost" *Return to Peyton Place?* "He thought it was a hoot to do it," Taylor remembers.

Allan Barnard of Dell/Western agreed that Miller was a logical choice. They needed to continue the *Peyton Place* momentum—and ghosting is hardly uncommon in publishing. (In 1957 editors chuckled when the Pulitzer Prize went to Massachusetts Senator John F. Kennedy, for *Profiles in Courage*—generally known to be written by his aide Ted Sorensen.)

Warren and Jimmy Miller were both surprised at the amount Warren was offered: between $2,000 and $3,000, as she remembers it. But Warren liked the thought of making $1,000 a week once in his life, he told Jimmy—and he did make it, for the time he spent reworking *Return to Peyton Place* from a 98-page manuscript said to be Grace Metalious'.

Before he died of lung cancer on April 20, 1966, Warren Miller had published ten books under his own name—including *Ninety Miles from Home,* a sympathetic account of Cuba right after the revolution; *The Siege of Harlem* and *The Cool World,* both about young blacks in New York; and *The Way We Live Now.* Miller published two more novels under the pseudonym Amanda Vail, and worked as literary editor of *The Nation.*

Miller was never paid anything for the *Return to Peyton Place* film rights, nor did he ever meet Grace Metalious. "If she'd met him," T.J. says, "it would have been another bloody mary down the shirt."

With both Warren Miller and Grace Metalious, Jerry Wald had done what Ben Hecht called the Hollywood producer's job: "turning good writers into movie hacks"—but only Grace Metalious' name appeared on the book. Only Grace Metalious suffered the reviewers' attacks when *Return to Peyton Place* appeared in November 1959.

"This sequel to *Peyton Place* has no interest as a novel, but is worth remark as a publishing phenomenon," wrote Edmund Fuller, who had liked *Peyton Place,* in the New York *Times*. He noticed Grace's dedication to Jacques Chambrun, "Who talked me into this book in the first place"—and wished "the plaintive note" in that dedication had been louder. In fact, Fuller said, Grace should have taken the advice Allison's agent gives: "The publication of an inferior work would do her more harm than good in the long run."

Fuller recounted the various plots of *Return*, criticizing the retelling of Selena's rape for being more sensational than the original. He praised the original novel as a competent example in the "*Kings Row* genre"—and concluded with a scolding for *Return:* "The whole book trade knows how the paperback tail wagged this hard-cover dog. It is foolish writing, cynical publishing and bad reading."

Phyllis Hogan, who had liked the "humor, heart, vigor" of *Peyton Place*, also had little good to say about *Return*. "There is a lot of through-the-keyhole activity and intrigue, recounted in language that is blunt if undistinguished," she wrote in the San Francisco *Chronicle*. "And there are no hard demands made upon even the adolescent reader."

The *Times Literary Supplement* reviewer liked the sexual scenes in *Return* ("among the livelier things in this novel"), but little else: characterization and construction fell flat. Rose Feld in the New York *Herald Tribune* tried to be tactful: "While Mrs. Metalious' preoccupation is still with sex, her language has lost some of its brash frankness and become more muted," but *Time* saw no value in *Return*, which "bears all the marks of a book whacked together on a long weekend. *Return* has little more scene-setting than a limerick, and the characterization is negligible."

The reviews humiliated Grace. Dell had arranged publicity appearances for her in Washington, D.C. and four other cities—but her drinking made the other four impossible. She did get to Washington—but she had already consumed some fifteen drinks, and the Dell publicity people could barely get her to bed.

Then she mustered her forces to fly to New York with T.J. They took a plush suite at the Hampshire House near Central Park and called in the media.

She never had "the slightest intention" of writing a sequel to *Peyton Place*, she told reporters. She'd looked at Jerry Wald's scenario and watched in amazement while he sold it to Messner's. She denounced his treatment of actresses and his refusal to give T.J. a part in the movie version of *Peyton Place*.

Mainly, however, she was appalled at what the *Return* reviews were doing to her reputation as a writer. "Am I going to live with this the rest of my days?" she wondered. "The book is just so much sludge . . . I wish that I had never let it happen . . . People are all saying I couldn't write a second novel. It's a Hollywood treatment. It was never intended to be anything else. It was a foul, rotten trick. They made a hell of a lot on *Peyton Place,* and they wanted to ride the gravy train . . . I've been played for a sucker all around."

Asked about Grace's denunciation, Jerry Wald said, "I am no Svengali, and she's no Trilby. It is to laugh."

The reviews sickened Grace—especially when everyone read the book. In *Return's* first three weeks, three million paperback copies were printed and distributed—which made it, according to Dell, "the fastest-selling paperback since *Peyton Place.*"

Return's major appeal came, obviously, from its connection with *Peyton Place*—not from its own merits, nor from Warren Miller's contributions. Miller's *The Way We Live Now,* published in 1958 and said to be autobiographical, has little in common with *Peyton Place* or *Return*. It belongs to a different literary world—of upper-class, melancholy intellectuals. But books for a mass market thrive on tragedy, comedy, passion, tears, and excitement, which *Peyton Place* delivers, but *Return to Peyton Place* does not.

Return continues the story of Allison MacKenzie, whose novel *Samuel's Castle* not only becomes a best seller, but makes Allison a celebrity. She goes to Hollywood; her stepfather, Mike Rossi, is fired as school principal in Peyton Place because of her scandalous book. Meanwhile, Selena Cross falls in love with a self-centered traveling actor, who mistreats her—and Betty Anderson, sent away to give birth to Rodney Harrington's child, is brought back to Peyton Place, because Leslie Harrington wants his grandson. Allison falls in love with her publisher, who is killed in an auto wreck while she is driving—but the sudden arrival of a movie star, Rita Moore, makes Allison think she has hope for the New Year after all.

Grace had little hope after the reviews of *Return to Peyton Place* appeared, a month before the New Year 1959–60, though *The Tight White Collar* was finally in production. When she had toured to promote *Peyton Place* three years before, Grace sometimes met people who criticized the book—and she'd turn to T.J. in her grand manner and command, "Give them their money back!" T.J. stood ready to produce $3.95, but there were never any takers—just people who enjoyed Grace's dramatic gesture.

With *Return to Peyton Place,* Grace made no such offers—lest she be taken up. Though the two books cost the same—$.50 in paperback and $3.95 in hardback—*Peyton Place* gave much more for the money, and even more pages: 372 to *Return's* 256. Only parts of *Return,* mostly the early pages, show remnants of the *Peyton Place* inspiration.

Return also begins with a description of the season in New England: wintertime. The old men who ruminate at Ephraim Tuttle's Grocery Store are still tart-tongued New Englanders, with an occasional flash of humor. The dialogue of New Englanders reads true—but Allison speaks clichés she would not have uttered in *Peyton Place:* Kitty Messner would have edited them away. In *Return,* for instance, Allison tells her publisher-lover: "You are young with me because you have love to give. A man is old only when he's exhausted his store of love." *Peyton Place's* Allison was far more original, and lived in a world with more love to go around.

Return to Peyton Place is populated by bitter women: deserted by men, misused by them—or simply evil, for no apparent reason. Ted Carter, Selena's childhood sweetheart, brings home a "rich bitch" Boston bride—and Jennifer Carter is contemptuous toward him and murderous toward his mother. She torments Ted psychologically and sexually, and *Return* illustrates the power of women over men—especially women who have no constructive outlets for their energies.

Selena, meanwhile, has taken to drink, because it "blunts the edges" (the same reason Grace gave for her drinking). Out of loneliness, Selena finally agrees to marry her lawyer, apparently forgetting what she said of him earlier in the book: "Peter is such a bore." But more likely the two writers and several editors who produced *Return to Peyton Place* so quickly never coordinated the end with the beginning.

Allison's story, which dominates *Return,* has somewhat more coherence, since it draws on Grace Metalious' life during and after *Peyton Place*. Allison's best seller, *Samuel's Castle*, contains "rape, incest, murder, suicide, and a dozen different kinds of screwing around"—and the publicity campaign for it brings out some familiar characters. The publicist has more than a touch of Alan "Bud" Brandt; he takes Allison to a hearty-looking columnist who behaves—and writes—like Hal Boyle. The Hollywood director who films *Samuel's Castle* resembles Jerry Wald, but his studio photographs make Allison look glamorous, and he listens closely to Allison's ideas. As with *Peyton Place,* Grace seems to be writing—and improving—the script for her own life.

But the view of women in *Return to Peyton Place* is far more pessimistic. Women's friendships are far less important, and Jennifer Carter is thoroughly evil. Rita Moore, the glamorous actress who comes to teach Allison that work and independence are all-important, has just taken her fifth husband (Rita is clearly based on Lana Turner). The illogical plot has little to do with women's dreams, or hopes: Unlike *Peyton Place,* it does not meet its author's emotional needs.

Ironically, the movie version of *Return to Peyton Place* junked much of the Metalious-Miller book. Jennifer Carter, the murderous rich bitch from Boston, is changed to an Italian siren; Selena's American actor-lover becomes a Scandinavian ski instructor; and Rita Moore does not appear at all. But before the film appeared in 1961, Grace had published *The Tight White Collar,* changed the man in her life, and set herself, finally, on the path toward self-destruction.

During the thirty days Grace spent writing *Return to Peyton Place,* the Thomas and Geraldine Makris libel suit was settled out of court. "It cost me a lot to learn you can't fight City Hall," Grace said gloomily. Meanwhile, the Italian film version of *Peyton Place* had record earnings: $1,241,000—but Grace had sold the film rights outright. None of the profits came to her.

Grace worried about money—and after the debacle with *Return to Peyton Place,* she worried more than ever about her public career, as a writer, and her private one, as a wife and mother.

George had always considered Grace's ideas about love unrealistic. She thought romance should last forever; he insisted that "love doesn't feed the body. It only feeds the soul." After *Return,* Grace desperately needed food for the soul—and she turned to her children.

"Our mother had to be told with the complete consistency of a flowing brook that echoes, 'I love you, I love you, I love you,'" Marsha wrote later. "We did love her strongly, but after awhile, 'I love you' became a ludicrous expression—worn to its nap like a rug traveled on day after day and night after night."

Grace's need to have love confirmed "was probably her worst fault," Marsha recalls. It was also one of her tests for loyalty—a quality she began to demand more and more as her romance with T.J. disintegrated. She could not turn to her mother for loyalty—especially after their auto accident on April 22, 1959.

With Laurette and Cindy, Grace had been driving home from the Winnisquam House Restaurant on Route 3 in Belmont when she lost control of her red Buick station wagon. The car flipped off the approach to an overpass, flew through the air, and plunged down a 50-foot embankment—where it somehow managed to land right side up.

Grace, at first knocked out, had a severe cut over her left eyebrow; Cindy, eight and a half, held her mother's hand while the hospital personnel sewed up Grace's eye. Cindy remembers Laurette's screaming that she'd broken her arm—but Laurette objected most to Grace's behavior.

As the car went off the approach, Grace had thrown her arm in front of Cindy, to protect her. Laurette, sitting by the other door, complained that Grace had done nothing to guard her own mother.

Five months later, after a summer recuperating at Grace's house in Gilmanton, Laurette sued her own daughter for carelessness and negligence causing the mother's "serious and permanent personal injuries" and making her "incapacitated to perform her usual labor." On the same day, September 22, 1959, her husband, Charles Kugel, sued for loss of his wife's "society and services" and the cost of medical care. They demanded $30,000.

Though many people believed Laurette's suit was an effort to get a quicker response from the insurance companies, Grace took it personally. Her own mother was suing her. If Grace had dreamed of a healing conversation with her mother, like Allison's with Connie, she found the opposite: that her success estranged them more than ever.

T.J. no longer got along well with Laurette. As Grace's manager, he considered Laurette's various investment schemes unworkable. He listened with increasing impatience to her criticisms of *Peyton Place:* The book hadn't been written properly; it could have been better; it could have made more money. Like George, T.J. became less and less sympathetic with Grace's unquestioning generosity toward her family.

When she had been drinking, Grace sometimes told T.J. that she considered herself a family disgrace: She'd made herself a notorious person; she'd written shocking books that embarrassed her relatives. Her Aunt Georgie in Manchester, for one, never read Grace's books—she heard they were improper and immodest. But Grace felt particular guilt toward her mother, whom she ordinarily called "Laurette," except when she had been drinking heavily. Then Grace cried about "my mother."

CHAPTER 18

Grace's daughters never felt close to Laurette, and Marsha often thought Laurette's behavior incongruous. Well-dressed, her white gloves with her, her gray hair in an elegant twist, Laurette would eat blueberries and cream, praising the combination as an aristocratic delicacy. But then she would follow her elegant dessert with beer drinking in front of the TV. One time, Marsha recalls, Laurette fell off the bed while watching wrestling (her favorite show), and wriggled on the floor, her legs forming a V in the air before she collapsed.

Suzy Roy, Bunny's daughter who lived in the Metalious household, remembers only Laurette's complaints about her menopause. Cindy, who once struck Laurette with a yellow sweater in a childish fit of anger, noticed that Laurette never displayed affection toward Grace.

Neither the children nor T.J. could accept the complicated ties linking Grace and her mother: guilt, envy, longing, anger—and similarity. Grace had Laurette's knack for dramatizing emotions on a large scale. She also had Laurette's interest in books, art, and music—and her ambition to "be somebody."

Yet they never came to the serene acceptance of each other that mothers and daughters usually achieve by the time the daughter reaches her mid-thirties—when both are adults, no longer competitors. Since Grace and Laurette never had the reconciliation that Constance and Allison achieved, the court proceedings in Laurette's lawsuit proved intensely painful for Grace. Even to get to Concord to testify, she had to be "liquidly fortified," George said.

When the lawsuit was settled on May 8, 1961, Laurette Kugel received $10,972 for her injuries in the accident; Charles Kugel was awarded $6,034.50. Not long afterward, Laurette moved to Florida, where she reportedly bought a condominium; Charles remained in New York and bought a farm on Long Island with money Grace gave him. Charles remained friends with Grace, but Laurette seems to have disappeared. No one heard from her at the time of Grace's funeral; no one in the Metalious circle even knows today whether she is dead or alive.

Bunny remained in Grace's orbit rather longer, occasionally as a party to quarrels with T.J. Bunny could be loyal: "What are you doing to my sister?" she would demand of T.J. When Grace and T.J. fought, Grace often called on others for support: Bernie Snierson, Bunny, sometimes even George. After one particularly fierce squabble, she called Jacques Chambrun for help.

Grace had frequently lavished money on Chambrun—flown him to Laconia in her chartered plane when she felt lonely, or in need —and he was quite willing to advise her about her love life.

"Chérie," Jacques began, in his Continental accent. There was something she had to understand, he said. Though she had money, fame, and success, she was most of all a *woman*—and T.J. was a *man*. Naturally, a man found it very difficult to be married to a woman richer, more famous, and successful than he. ("It doesn't work if the woman is the big name," Rita Moore tells Allison in *Return to Peyton Place*.) If Grace kept that difficulty in mind, Jacques suggested, she could learn to be patient—and her relationship with T.J. would surely improve.

In the conflict between creativity (assertion, a healthy selfishness) and femininity (self-sacrifice, nurturing others), Jacques came out for femininity—and the media, even in 1960, supported him. When the noted critic Marya Mannes published "Female Intelligence: Who Wants It?" in the New York *Times Magazine* (January 3, 1960), numerous readers wrote in to say they didn't. A relationship was the woman's responsibility, Jacques Chambrun and others believed: She must change to fit the situation. She would be blamed if the relationship failed, if the man and his ego did not receive her total support.

Yet Jacques needed Grace much more in her other role—the creative one. While she looked to him for fatherly guidance, she was still by far the most profitable writer in his "stable"—and until 1960 she managed to close her eyes to Chambrun's less savory dealings.

Depending on Chambrun, Grace ignored—or discounted—what she knew about his own relationships with women. She had publicly criticized Jerry Wald for treating actresses as a "flesh market," but Jacques Chambrun was also famous for the endless parade of tall, beautiful show girls he lured to continuous house parties at his home in Greenwich, Connecticut. Frank Taylor, his Connecticut neighbor, called the parties "astonishing," and what actually happened was a matter for intense wonder and speculation.

Taylor, the boss at Western Printing, and Knox Burger, then a paperback-book editor and later an agent, also wondered why Grace Metalious did not see through her agent. Taylor thought Jacques Chambrun's manners were syrupy and cloying; Burger thought Chambrun perfectly suitable "if you were casting an unctuous Levantine villain in a 1950 film *noir*." Helen Meyer of Dell thought Chambrun resembled a Mississippi gambler without the moustache, and she doubted his claim to be truly French. Though Chambrun had excellent taste in food, dress, and manners, Burger considered him a "feral character." Jacques was also using Grace Metalious as bait to attract other clients.

Chambrun had used one fish to attract others for years, and his biggest bait had been W. Somerset Maugham. When an author's name appeared in print, Chambrun sent a standard letter, offering to represent the author at a 10 percent commission, and pointing out that he served as Maugham's agent.

John Leggett, later the author of *Ross and Tom,* received such a solicitation when one of his stories appeared in *Ladies' Home Journal*. Ross Lockridge, one of Leggett's subjects, got one when his *Raintree County* appeared, and wrote friends that Somerset Maugham's literary agent had suddenly taken a great interest in him—and even wanted Lockridge's old high school stories to sell.

Knox Burger got a similar letter when his first story appeared in *Collier's* in 1945, and learned that Chambrun had a special assistant just to send such letters.

By 1959, the letters noted that Chambrun represented Grace Metalious, the well-known author of *Peyton Place;* meanwhile, Grace did not see anything amiss in Chambrun's work. When she signed her contract with him, she was unaware that few agents have contracts with their authors: most rely on a handshake. Grace still found Jacques charming, respected his loyalty—for he had taken her manuscript when no one else would—and depended on him as friend, mentor, and agent.

She did not know, yet, that Chambrun was stealing from her.

She did find his encouragement valuable as she dedicated herself to finishing *The Tight White Collar* through the summer of 1959. Kitty Messner had announced in December 1958 that the book would be ready, she hoped, for fall 1959 publication—and she was most eager to see Grace complete it. Jacques came to Gilmanton every week, to read what Grace had written and lend his support.

"I walk up and down in front of my typewriter and it jeers at me like a monster," Grace told Bernie Snierson—but from the Royal electric monster and its manual predecessor, over the years, she had produced many fragments that finally became parts of *The Tight White Collar*. The stories of David Strong, the homosexual music teacher, and Nate and Margery Cooper, the parents of the Down's syndrome child, came from the years at U.N.H. But Grace had also thrown in her trunk, together with the *Peyton Place* manuscript, a variety of other pieces, the only extant fragments showing how she actually composed a novel.

Grace said that she thought about *Peyton Place* for years before she wrote it, and the same is true of *The Tight White Collar*. Even before *Peyton Place* appeared, she had consulted the archeologist Solon Colby about Indian place names, to find out what they really meant. She thought of including them in *The Tight White Collar* for New Hampshire local color.

"I used to think that the Indians must have been a people totally lacking in imagination," she began one scrap—then showed how the white man was the unimaginative one, "who had trans-

lated Indian words to suit himself." In another scrap, Grace sati-
rizes a schoolteacher who explains Indian place names to suit herself rather than the facts.

Grace also wrote paragraphs about the Merrimack River, which
she had first seen on a trip with her father, and she wrote about
"Clinton," New Hampshire (clearly Gilmanton, including its
route numbers), in the story of an ancient quarrel between two
Gilmanton men. She tried several ways to begin a story about a
writer who was coming home to Clinton to die. She attempted the
first person, the writer as "I"; she tried calling him Alan Osborne
—and seemed more at ease with a male character described from
the outside. (Alan finally became Anthony Cooper of *The Tight
White Collar*—a writer who comes home to die but never gets
around to it.)

Apparently for practice, too, Grace wrote a paragraph about
New England mill towns; a description of old houses in the Gil-
manton/Laconia/Belmont area; and the beginning of a story
about a man who once ran a sawmill but decided to manufacture
skis instead. Most important, Grace created two characters to represent herself and George: George and Mary Steele (Mary for
"Marie," Grace's real first name, and "Steele" for "Metal," the
first part of Metalious).

In Grace's scraps, Mary and George Steele marry at seventeen,
have their first child while he is in the army, move to the "Clinton" area, and settle in "Tioga" (Belmont)—where, as outsiders,
they are distinctly unwelcome. George teaches and coaches, while
Mary plays Mrs. Schoolteacher—and they starve on his salary.

But the scraps show more than the basic facts of Grace and
George's lives—for Grace was attempting, somewhat clumsily, to
express her deepest and most tender feelings. She shows Mary
Steele's fear and anger when her daughter "Lolly" (Cindy) hurts
herself; and she has Mary explain to a neighbor why she married
at seventeen:

> "I loved him," she said.
>   She had a way of saying those words. She didn't say them
> offhandedly or simply. A deep note came into her voice so
> that you thought of her in bed with him.

Mary also has the sensitivity of her creator: "She would say things in a temper and be so sorry afterward that I have seen her lacerate herself for hours over a remark that most people forgot in five minutes."

Like Allison MacKenzie, Mary Steele is extremely vulnerable—but she is a grown woman, with adult concerns. Through Mary, Grace was developing herself as a more mature character—with, perhaps, a certain desire to justify her past and rework it (Mary plays "Mrs. Schoolteacher" rather better than Grace did). But the fragments show Mary only in relation to others—as wife and mother. Mary is not an independent woman, and not a writer—as if Grace rejected her own unconventional identity and decided to conform after all. (The Steele fragments, transformed, became part of Chris and Lisa Pappas' story in *The Tight White Collar*. Lisa, too, has no creative ambitions.)

Grace, in any case, was producing only scraps—not the novel she had been promising Kitty Messner and Jacques Chambrun for years. T.J. complained that her fragments were "as disjointed as if I tried to tape a three-hour radio show, a half-hour a month." Finally, because her fits and starts were not getting *The Tight White Collar* written, T.J. pushed her to make a schedule.

Grace had often proclaimed what she considered the best rule for writing: "Apply the seat of the pants to the seat of the chair." When she kept her schedule of hours at the typewriter, she got her writing done.

T.J. would read her pages back to her, but when the writing did not go well, she would become consumed with anxiety. "I can't do it. How can I ever top *Peyton Place?*"

Sometimes Grace would rebel against her schedule—with long stints in the bathroom, chores to do, and making drinks. She hated being reminded of her schedule—and if T.J. reminded her too often, she would explode: "Who the hell are you? Who appointed you my guiding light?"

She had—but their relationship was wearing very thin. Grace wanted support from T.J., and unquestioning loyalty—a demand she made of all her friends, perhaps because she'd never received it at home. She still kept Bernie Snierson as her lawyer, though Kitty Messner and others urged her to get a New York publishing attorney. She stayed with Jacques Chambrun, even after she had warning signals about his less-than-honest dealings. She kept T.J. as long as she could. She could accept business problems, even dishonesties, more than unkind words—and there were many words she did not want to hear.

When T.J. or Snierson talked about trust funds, or made other financial suggestions, Grace refused to listen—and accused them of ganging up on her. To T.J., she'd say, "Oh, you and Bernie—I hope you'll be very happy together"—and then refuse to discuss the matter anymore. Like Allison in *Return,* Grace resisted being a "corporate entity"; she wanted not to think about dollars and cents, just as "Allison had never thought of success in terms of money. To her, it had always been a vague, amorphous dream with success consisting, in equal parts, of fame and freedom."

Grace found that success did not mean freedom—for success had to be managed. She resented the need for management, by anyone—and drinking let her forget the pressures for a while.

Though Grace was treated at the Laconia Hospital for flu on April 8, 1959, she was generally in much better health that year (despite rumors that she had been treated for cirrhosis of the liver). Through much of 1959 Grace and T.J. both gave up drinking. Before that, their drinking used to lead to terrible arguments: she would throw things and he would slap her. But in 1959 they had, he remembers, a calm, non-alcoholic summer with the children, much of it in a rented house on the water at Hampton Beach. They drank iced tea, played Monopoly, and walked on the beach, and in August returned to Gilmanton.

But somehow the serene life was not what Grace wanted. Being a conventional wife and mother was not enough—nor had she ever fully become the pretty, feminine woman that T.J. wanted her to be. She gave him that message in a most dramatic way.

One August afternoon, T.J. recalls, Grace looked beautiful: slender, tanned, in her white shorts, green shirt, and white gardening gloves. She had been sober for nearly a year—and she was gorgeous.

"I'm going into town," she told him. "I need something for the garden."

"I'll get it for you," he said genially. "What do you need?"

"No, I'll go," and she took off in her Buick.

She was gone for two weeks—and that was the last time he saw her truly sober.

She went to New York and resumed drinking. Reuben's, where she went for sandwiches just across the street from the Plaza, called to make sure T.J. would pay her bills. The Plaza phoned, too: they doubted they could honor the checks Grace was signing.

T.J. managed the situation somehow—but Grace had permanently gone back to drinking.

PART IV

✿✿✿

Tempest at Home
and Abroad

CHAPTER 19

Grace found she could escape any unpleasant scene more easily than she'd thought. She didn't really need T.J. to summon limousines or planes. She could make her own travel arrangements. She disappeared from New Hampshire one New Year's Eve, then reappeared at the Plaza. Sometimes she left abruptly for Baltimore, to visit Bunny—but when she brought Bunny back, T.J. was responsible for chartering Bunny's flight home.

Grace still resisted taking her money seriously. Though T.J. and Bernie Snierson both pleaded with her to give Bunny a regular allowance, instead of handouts, Grace said angrily, "But she's my sister!"

Grace refused to consider the impersonal money arrangements that wealthy people make as a matter of course. Instead, she insisted on loyalty and personal ties. At times, too, Grace admired Bunny for being true to their working-class roots: preferring beer (which everyone said made her "mean") to Canadian Club, favoring Levi's (sometimes) over mink.

Unlike Grace, Bunny seemed to feel very little guilt. She led the irresponsible life Grace would have liked to lead: living for herself and leaving her children behind. Grace had the money, but Bunny had the nerve. Grace's disappearances were an assertion of nerve, of independence from her role as wife, mother—and famous author.

Her solo flights also took her to New York and escapades with her old friend Marc, always glad to see her. They devoured seafood together and gorged themselves on Reuben's liverwurst and onion on rye. Grace loved the snails she and Marc ordered at the Portofino Restaurant in Greenwich Village, and she feasted on Caesar salads—but her New York outings also had their tensions.

Grace fought with Marc's aunt, who made anti-Semitic remarks. Later the aunt claimed Grace left her alone on a park bench in Central Park, as punishment. On another occasion Grace called Marc from a lesbian bar, not quite sure how she'd gotten there—and he took a cab from Brooklyn and brought her home.

Marc found her adventures amusing; she sometimes thought so, afterward—but T.J. was not amused. They would separate, then fly to each other's side, swearing eternal love—and then separate again.

Mike, sent to prep school at Emerson, did not like the hazing, and called home for sympathy. Grace took him out of school, and that led to a bitter quarrel with T.J., who thought Mike should stay. Finally, Mike went to live with George and Marsha in Martha's Vineyard, where George had taken a job as high school guidance counselor in March 1960.

Grace and T.J. continued fighting, especially over money. Not believing he could love her for herself alone, Grace accused T.J. of wanting to leave because so much of her money was gone. He could not cope with her being so much more successful, she said later—and as Allison thinks in *Return to Peyton Place:* "Lovers can always find an excuse for the hurt they do to others."

They fought over behavior, especially her drinking (she was already having blackouts), and her style of entertaining. T.J., who'd introduced Grace to the Plaza, was offended by beer parties in the Gilmanton kitchen. He wanted gentility; she preferred funk. Grace wanted to put on her blue jeans again—and told T.J., "Take away your mink and your phony friends!"

As George Metalious describes it, their last quarrel concerned money. T.J. challenged Grace to prove that everything she had was his also—by transferring the Gilmanton house to him. "I threw him the hell out when I realized what he was doing," Grace said, in George's account.

But T.J. describes it differently. In his recollection, their last quarrel concerned behavior. Grace had been gone for a week and returned from New York with a strange assortment of "hippies" and "Village people." Disapproving of them, T.J. refused to come downstairs for a party, and Grace snarled at him: "Don't give me any of that. You either come down or get lost!"

One way or another, T.J. got lost.

He left the Gilmanton house in early 1960, driving his blue Buick convertible, the back seat filled with his clothes, leaving behind glamour—but taking debts with him. Since Grace had never incorporated, what he bought as her manager was his responsibility—and to pay the enormous bills on his signature, he had to declare bankruptcy.

Roxy Rothafel rehired T.J. at WLNH; Dr. Leonard Slovack advised him to go back to drinking—"You're a nervous wreck." On Armed Forces Day, May 17, 1960, T.J. managed to arrange a ride in a tank for the new woman in his life, Betty Haenschen, a copywriter at WLNH—and afterward he celebrated with a tom collins.

He wooed Betty, a recent Smith College graduate, off and on the air. Grace had said he was the only man who could make love to a woman all day over the radio—and he made love to Betty all day, even playing the same song he'd played for Grace: "My Funny Valentine."

On March 1, 1960, Grace had filed for divorce, charging T.J. with "treatment as seriously to injure health." She demanded that all real estate in his, her, or both names be legally hers, and announced that her name would again be Grace Metalious. The divorce was granted October 6, 1960, two weeks after *The Tight White Collar* appeared.

Grace always spoke of T.J. as "the love of my life."

Twenty years later, T.J. called Grace "a wonderful woman: romantic, very sexual, a lot of fun, with a great sense of humor." Most of all, he recalled, she had "tremendous love to give"—which, for a while, she'd shared with him.

"Even in its beginning there is always the overtone of the ending—the promise of betrayal and good-by," Ben Hecht wrote of a love affair in *A Child of the Century*. "I wrote in my youth, 'There is a cry that rises from all endings.' I have heard this cry often and sat with its mournful echo in my heart. And while it lasts there is nothing as painful in the world. It is a sound that drains life out of the day. The air darkens. Not only yesterday but tomorrow lies dead."

Grace wrote about the death of love in "Edna Brown and the Charming Prince," her only published short story, printed in *Glamour* in March 1960—the month she filed for divorce from T.J. Edna Brown has a lot of Grace Metalious in her; The Prince has elements of T.J.

Carey Moulton, The Prince's bodyguard, tells the story of The Prince—really Elmer Bloch from the Lower East Side, a racketeer with a hankering for WASP respectability. Smart, shrewd, The Prince is still handsome and young looking, "tall, slim-hipped and Florida tanned, with a head of thick dark hair"—T.J. in his last year with Grace. The Prince has T.J.'s conversational charm, too— "that way he has that makes anyone feel like the only person in the world."

The Prince's chance for respectability comes with Edna Brown, a nineteen-year-old innocent from New Hampshire. Within two weeks, he gets Edna to marry him; within a year, he's broken her heart—and Carey, who resembles George Metalious, picks up the pieces. But Carey knows he has only the shell of Edna; The Prince still has everything else.

Glamour billed "Edna Brown and the Charming Prince" as a story "in which the author of *Peyton Place* reveals a gift for irony and an unexpectedly romantic heart." The story does have irony, but little romance—for everyone's illusions get a shattering. Edna, especially, loses her "innate belief that everyone was good"—the childlike idealism Grace still possessed. Edna Brown, Carey says, still lived in a fairyland, "where the Charming Prince would come up dashing on his white horse to carry her away."

With a male narrator, Grace shows Edna's powerlessness from the outside—and, for the first time, gives no real insight into a major female character's mind. "Edna Brown . . ." has no well-rounded women characters, who learn and grow and change like Allison MacKenzie, Constance MacKenzie Rossi, or Selena Cross. Though her experience with T.J. might have soured Grace on men, "Edna Brown . . ." instead presents women more negatively than ever before. Grace seems to blame the victim—as she so often blamed herself. Edna chose the wrong man—and the portrait of Edna suggests self-hatred on Grace's part.

"Edna Brown . . ." has a cynical view of love—and especially of women, as either deluded or grasping. Edna is sent back to New Hampshire, just as Grace—the bubble burst after the glorious romance with T.J.—was sent back to herself. T.J. later moved into a wider world, with peregrinations to New Haven, Boston, the Virgin Islands, and Fort Lauderdale—but Grace stayed in New England, mostly in New Hampshire, and mostly in Gilmanton. There she brooded on her losses.

Apart from T.J.'s permanent absence, the year 1960 seemed, for Grace, not that much different from 1959. Though student sit-ins at segregated lunch counters in the South began in February 1960, they had no impact in New Hampshire, where few blacks lived. Grace did admire the volunteer work John Chandler, Bernie Snierson's law partner, did for the National Association for the Advancement of Colored People in New York, and she called Chandler "God's Angry Man."

Generally, however, Grace, who considered herself a Republican, paid little attention to national affairs. The Southern sit-ins were an early clue that the 1960s—the years of student demonstrations, Black Power, Vietnam, and women's liberation—would be different from the fifties. But Grace could hardly anticipate how the world would change in that special decade.

By 1960 Grace herself had become a notorious and celebrated figure—and, like Jerry Wald, the subject of a thinly disguised novel. "The book had laid bare the secrets of an entire town," read the front of Vin Packer's *The Girl on the Best-Seller List,* a Gold Medal original paperback published in 1960. "Now the town would take revenge on the woman who wrote it," the blurb continued—and the front cover included a sketch of a woman in jeans and checked shirt, seated at her typewriter. But the novelist in Packer's book met a grisly (or comic) fate: she was poisoned by an overdose of an aphrodisiac.

More seriously, *Peyton Place* had made a cultural impact by the early 1960s, an opening wedge in the fight for freedom of expression. Henry Miller's *Tropic of Cancer,* a quirky amoral novel about sex among bohemians, had first been published in Paris in

1934—and was finally permitted in the United States in 1961. *Lady Chatterley's Lover,* D. H. Lawrence's 1928 paean to guilt-free sex, had finally been admitted in 1957 (and Jerry Wald made it into a movie). In *The Tight White Collar,* released in September 1960, Grace could use the word "fuck"—but on May 28, 1960 (nineteen days after the Pill was first approved for sale in the United States) a Newport, Rhode Island, man was convicted for selling an obscene—and world-famous—book to a minor.

Harry B. Settle, fifty-one, a news dealer, had sold *Peyton Place* to a seventeen-year-old boy (whose name, like those of rape victims, did not appear in print). The Superior Court jury ruled that the book was "obscene in terms of its effect on youths under the age of 18." Settle's attorneys questioned how Settle could be convicted of such a crime—when *Peyton Place* had sold over 7.3 million copies. They said they would appeal.

Grace lived on royalties from those copies during the summer of 1960, while she waited for *The Tight White Collar* to appear. She took care of Bunny, who was pregnant again and very ill. The Metalious children and Suzy Roy stayed with Grace while George took summer courses at U.N.H.—and visited every weekend.

After Bunny gave birth to her son David, she moved out. Marsha, Mike, Cindy, and Suzy had their own lives, and Grace spent most of August sitting, staring, and drinking. August was hot and steamy, like the August five years before when she'd first sold *Peyton Place,* and she cooled off with her favorite drink, "C.C. and 7-Up," interspersed with an occasional rye highball. She always had a glass in her hand—sometimes held against her right temple, to cool off. She rarely ate, except for huge salads late at night. Her face grew bloated from drinking, and her eyes seemed to disappear in folds of flesh.

Could he stay for a few days, to study for his master's exams? George asked on one visit.

"Sure, sweetie, use the den," Grace said.

"I'm not one of your chic New York friends," George said harshly, "so don't call me sweetie. My name is George."

"Sure, sweetie," Grace said, making herself another drink.

But when George prepared to take the children back to Martha's Vineyard with him, he suggested Grace move to the Vineyard, too.

"But Gilmanton is my home!" she insisted—and she still touched the hearth every time she came back to the house she loved.

"Then come for a while," George suggested, and pointed out that she'd have to return to Gilmanton anyway for her divorce.

"But why should I come?" she asked.

"Because I love you."

At the Vineyard Grace rented a little cottage overlooking the sea, and lived there with the children. She took long walks on the beach and thought about her next novel—and when *The Tight White Collar* appeared in September, it had better reviews than *Return,* and encouraging early sales. (Grace did not know that Doris Flowers, sales director at Messner's, had had serious reservations about whether *The Tight White Collar* would sell at all well. She and Kitty ordered a reasonable first printing—35,000 copies—which sold out quickly, putting the book on the New York *Herald Tribune* best-seller list. But the sales were far behind those of *Peyton Place.*)

George's appearance at the Martha's Vineyard Regional High School had inspired great interest from the start. "No idle rumor— the author of *Peyton Place's* first husband is being talked about for our guidance counselor—wouldn't tongues wag?" Lydia Crowell Howes Drew wrote to her daughter Virginia Crowell Bardwell, a first-year student at St. Lawrence University.

Lydia Drew, a teacher in the Edgartown School, liked George immediately—as did his co-workers. George, who had a contract for $6,000 a year, had come with excellent references. According to *White Gull,* the student newspaper, Mr. Metalious would be counseling students on their aptitudes, courses of study, and career directions after high school. Though his job called for work as a full-time counselor, he also taught an advanced history class.

George came to Martha's Vineyard with Marsha (called "Marjorie" in the student paper), and Mike joined them soon. George told his colleagues, especially Charles A. Davis, the principal who recommended he be hired, that he hoped to reunite his family. Shirley W. Mayhew, another teacher, heard that George was well-liked, and Davis says there was a lot of admiration for George's family efforts.

Once Grace arrived, however, the atmosphere changed.

Though she fell into a pleasant domestic routine—cooking, playing games, joking with the children—rumors immediately circulated that she would be writing a novel about Martha's Vineyard people. Doris Flowers, who has a house on the Vineyard, remembers another set of rumors as well: that when Grace first arrived, she stayed in a hotel and "had no solid food for three days." Those rumors, too, persisted and followed Grace everywhere.

It did not help that she was still married to T.J. until October 6, when she returned to Laconia for her divorce. "Metalious Sheds 'Nagging' Husband," the New York *Daily News* headlined on October 8—but Grace had already given her side of the story in the Boston *American* of June 14, headlined, "Peyton Place Wife Raps Second Mate."

She said she'd filed for divorce because T.J. nagged and criticized her, wanting her to "conform to his image of a suburban housewife while still embodying the glamour of theatrical and literary life." He had left her, she said, after a violent argument when she brought her ailing sister to their home.

In divorcing T.J. and citing his objections to Bunny, Grace kept intact her ideal of family loyalty, and her image of herself—but the divorce left her deeply depressed. After the court hearing, she crawled into her favorite corner of the living room in Gilmanton— and found she had trouble breathing.

It couldn't be a cold, she told herself: She hadn't had one for ten years. But she became more and more anxious and feverish, and sat huddled in her corner, thinking she needed just another drink to cure the cold.

The next evening, Friday, George burst into the house, saw Grace's condition, and took her in his arms. She looked at him for a very long time, looked out the window, and finally said, "Yes, I'm ready to come home."

On October 12 the Associated Press reported that Grace Metalious, "the plumpish writer of novels with a strong sex theme," had remarried her first husband George. At the Harwyn Club in

New York, Grace and George held hands while they announced their second wedding and Grace's conversion to an accepted social role.

"I'm taking her home to be a mother mainly," George told reporters. "Being a writer is just incidental."

They said they had remarried in Elkton, Maryland, on October 8. In Gilmanton, Laurie Wilkens wondered—for Grace had often avowed that two marriages were quite enough, and that she never intended to marry again.

There is no record of a marriage in Elkton—but the announcement of one would, presumably, cast Grace in a better light in Martha's Vineyard.

Privately, George had told his colleagues the major problem he faced: "to help get Grace sober." In their pictures from the Harwyn Club, George looks handsome and happy—but Grace had lost the bright eyes, firm mouth, and girlish charm of the "Pandora in Blue Jeans" picture.

Instead, she resembles a relative's description of Lillian Roth, the singer who fought her way back from alcoholism and wrote about it in *I'll Cry Tomorrow,* a 1954 best seller: "Your hair was wispy and straggly; your face and body were bloated, but your arms and legs were thin as pipe-stems." At thirty-six, Grace looked closer to fifty.

She loved the long, sandy beach and the ocean breeze at Martha's Vineyard, where they lived in Edgartown, called (even by Islanders) one of the stuffier subdivisions. Most Vineyard towns are dry, but Oak Bluffs and Edgartown are "wet"—and Grace was often seen in the bar at the Harborview Hotel in Edgartown.

As in Gilmanton, townspeople disapproved of anyone who spent hours in a bar ("honest working folk don't have the time and money"). A woman, in particular, did not belong in a bar—and most of all, a schoolteacher's wife.

Meanwhile, "The Martha's Vineyard set had better batten down the hatches," a New York newspaper columnist reported on October 16. "Grace Metalious intends to base her next novel on their morals."

George began to receive nasty letters and threatening phone calls.

"I don't think it is a matter of Grace Metalious upsetting the complacency of the Island," Lydia Drew wrote her daughter Virginia. "It is just a question of how authentically Vineyardy she could make a book on such short acquaintance with the locale. It would just be a general theme on sex and dirt applicable anywhere, but like Cinderella's slipper—many people would wonder where the shoe fitted!"

And that seemed to be the problem: not the authenticity, but the fear that the shoe might fit. Lydia Drew wrote on October 20; four days later Harvey S. Ewing of the New Bedford *Standard-Times* published what amounted to Grace's defense: "AUTHOR SAYS VINEYARD 'WON'T' BE NOVEL LOCALE."

"I have never said nor given any indication that I would write about the Vineyard," she declared, and Ewing noted the "obvious traces of irritation in her voice."

She was "mulling over writing another book," she said as she curled up on the living room couch, but wouldn't yet say what it would be about. "At this stage of my thinking I change my ideas almost each day, and what I might tell you now as to the type of book I'm going to write would be totally different from the finished work." (She had written *Peyton Place* and *The Tight White Collar* that way: a long period of mulling, then a short, feverish period of writing. *No Adam in Eden,* the novel she was thinking about, had already been on her mind for several years.)

Besides "mulling," Grace busied herself with housekeeping. "I'm going bananas with the housework," she told Ewing, "but for the first time in three years I feel a measure of peace and security. My previous marriage was by no means all that it should have been. Now I sort of feel as if I had come home."

Also at home she had an offer to write a weekly, half-hour TV drama; away from home, she made radio, TV, and personal appearances to publicize *The Tight White Collar* in New York and Boston. As of October 1960 *Peyton Place*—then four years old—had sold more than eight and a half million copies in the United States and abroad. The film version of *Peyton Place* had earned fifteen million dollars (none of them going to Grace, who had sold the film rights outright for $250,000, including various bonuses).

Ewing's article presented Grace as a good woman—a proper

housewife and mother. In an accompanying photograph, the whole Metalious family clusters around Grace and George in the living room of their rented house in the Katama section of Edgartown. Cindy, Marsha, Suzy, and Mike are all reading *The Tight White Collar* over Grace and George's shoulders. "Not pictured is the family's pet poodle, Rififi," the caption reports. George, holding his pipe, seems to be reading aloud—the same pose he had in the original publicity photos for *Peyton Place*, when he "lost his job" because of the book.

Return's jacket showed "Pandora in Blue Jeans" again, but *The Tight White Collar* has a different picture: one of the glamorous photos taken during Grace's first publicity trip to New York in 1956. Her hair is carefully pulled back, and her eyes and face made up; she wears a crisp white blouse, and—though it can't be seen in the published version—her slip. It had been so hot that August day that she'd taken off most of her clothes.

Grace sits directly above that jacket picture in the *Standard-Times* photo—and the changes are evident. She has a double chin; her cheekbones and eyes are disappearing. George looks much as he did in his 1956 picture, but Grace has aged.

Ewing's article apparently had little immediate effect on Martha's Vineyard. Mike got into a fist fight with a schoolmate who considered "Metalious" a dirty name. George continued to get late-night phone calls from people who strongly suggested he and Grace "get off the island."

Shirley Mayhew, who did not know George, nevertheless felt he was being unfairly punished—and she went to the Metaliouses' house to apologize for the Islanders' actions. The house was all locked up, with the curtains drawn—and it was a very long time before George answered her knock.

On November 15 George abruptly resigned, citing "personal business"—which Principal Davis knew meant the harassment. Harvey S. Ewing's article, with its compassionate attempt to present Grace as a proper follower of the feminine mystique, had failed. Ewing himself also had his problems. Above the *Standard-Times* dispatch about George's resignation is a picture of Ewing's car—attacked by a flying bat on his way to work.

The Metaliouses returned to Gilmanton before Thanksgiving—

but "Possibly they should have remained to weather the brewing storm of the Vineyard," according to George's account, "because Gilmanton, as it turned out, was no longer the place for them. The explosiveness of the atmosphere there was like home brew that had been made with too much yeast, which was secretly stashed away in Gilmanton's cellars." Stripped of metaphors, George means they were clearly unwelcome at home, though he says they had a "good winter—and Grace seemed somewhat happier."

But she never stopped drinking.

CHAPTER 20

Drinking is "the writer's disease"—an occupational hazard for people who spend unstructured hours alone with their typewriters. When F. Scott Fitzgerald feared he'd been drinking too much, his friend Ernest Hemingway told him not to worry: that every writer who's any good is a heavy drinker.

As a Barnard senior in 1962, Erica Jong heard the same thing from a Distinguished Literary Critic: "Women can't be writers," he growled. After all, what could they write about? "They don't know blood and guts and puking in the streets and fucking whores and swaggering through Paris at 5 A.M." Not knowing "life in the raw," he said, they were unequipped to produce anything worth reading—and "life in the raw" required, as it had for Hemingway, Fitzgerald, Faulkner, etc., consuming prodigious amounts of alcohol.

Jong soon realized that the Writer-as-Beast was a myth, a way of keeping women down—and that no man who spent all his time drinking, fucking, puking, and swaggering could write much of anything. Aided by a feminist analysis, Jong could dismiss what the male voice of authority said—but Grace Metalious, in 1960, had no such feminist support.

Grace drank for the same reasons other writers drink: to escape from the prison of self, to overcome shyness and insecurity, to reward herself, to celebrate, to ease disappointments—to "take the edge off things," she said.

She kept bottles everywhere, as Lillian Roth did before Alcoholics Anonymous saved her from self-destruction. "I had to have liquor to stop my screaming nerves, my exploding brain," Roth said in *I'll Cry Tomorrow,* "to dull the knife-life certainty that I was going nowhere, doing nothing, living as a shadow in an empty world."

Roth grew shaky; she blacked out, unable to recall what had happened; she was "maudlin, gay and maniacal in turn"; she could not have a hangover because she was always drunk. She drank to assuage anger, resentment, bitterness. Grace Metalious, who read *I'll Cry Tomorrow* and Diana Barrymore's *Too Much Too Soon,* also lived the most painful parts of their stories.

Roth was no writer (in fact, her book was put together by Mike Connolly and Gerold Frank)—but she was an alcoholic woman, a breed apart from the swaggering he-man drunk. The man who drinks has a certain social cachet: he lives on the glamorous edge of self-destruction; he goes to the limit, if he's a writer, in the search for meaningful experience. If drink makes him feel sexually omnipotent, so much the better. Drinking is a thoroughly "masculine" endeavor: aggressive, hard-driving, creatively macho.

But a woman who drinks is not considered charming. While a man's social role encourages action, drama, and swaggering, a woman's requires control and serving as a moral guardian for others. Femininity means self-sacrifice in the service of others, clear limits on sexual expression, passivity. Though a few women writers—Dorothy Parker, Edna St. Vincent Millay—have been noted for alcoholic consumption, they were eventually considered more pitiful than clever. A male writer who drinks and loses control can seem "heroically doomed"; a woman who loses control is a "bad mother," if not a "slut."

Grace Metalious had never fit the feminine role—for she wanted more than husband, children, home. She had always been criticized as a bad mother, poor housekeeper, and (later) an immoral writer-woman. When she drank, she could forget—but her drinking opened her up to even more criticism. When she returned to Gilmanton from Martha's Vineyard, people were already dismissing her, as townsfolk had her character Irene in *The Tight White Collar,* with "the most final words of all: 'She drinks.'"

The year without alcohol, during her marriage to T.J., had enabled Grace to finish *The Tight White Collar*. Like *Peyton Place,*
the book had mostly good notices from big-city reviewers.

James Kelly, reviewing it in the New York *Times,* felt the book
had much to recommend it. He praised the social commentary in
both *Peyton Place* and *The Tight White Collar,* and observed that
plot mattered less than Grace's real interest: "the town's composite behavior and her opportunity to put together a nosegay of
biographical flashbacks which may help to explain it. Decently
written, supported by a good reportorial eye and ear, 'The Tight
White Collar' contrives a sensual saga for each of the leading
characters."

Kelly praised the novel's readability, and the fast pace of
Grace's collage technique. *The Tight White Collar* was less violent
than *Peyton Place,* he observed, and he ended on a positive note:
"Grace Metalious knows how to put flesh on a variety of skele-
tons, and skeptical observers of her work to date will be happily
surprised at the maturing insights and skills she has learned to
control and exploit with 'The Tight White Collar.'"

Kelly's praise must have heartened Grace, for the *Times* review
has the greatest influence on sales. Few other reviews were quite
so favorable, although John Fink in the Chicago *Sunday Tribune*
remarked that "Grace Metalious writes well, and she shows tenderness and pity as well as sophistication and scorn. But perhaps
for those very reasons it is hard to forgive her for giving us so little of value."

Fink objected to the book's cynicism; *Kirkus Reviews,* to its
lack of a central theme despite Grace's "narrative gift" and "sense
of pace." *Time* magazine attacked the book with *Time* cuteness:
The Tight White Collar "bears the same relation to her first two
books that a B-girl does to a prostitute: its implied promise is sex
in return for money, but what it delivers is merely a phony hotel
room key and a whiff of perfume." Knowing Grace's reputation,
Time obviously wanted her to deliver: but *The Tight White Collar*
"is pallid stuff compared with the rape, incest, flagellation and
other veneries of *Peyton Place* and *Return to Peyton Place.*"

Grace seemed damned if she didn't deliver sex—and damned if
the reviewer thought she did. According to the *Times Literary*

Supplement, The Tight White Collar contained "The defilement of the most intimate of human experiences by language worthy of an advertisement for underwear."

As expected, one of the harshest reviews appeared in the Laconia *Evening Citizen,* under the headline "New 'Peyton Place' Revisited." W. G. Rogers retold the book's plots unsympathetically, concluding with "and for a new thrill, a Mongolian idiot named Robin who, or which, nuzzles mama or the nurses." Like *Peyton Place,* Rogers said, the new book "has the same knack for reducing the bedroom to a stud-farm stable, and has the same Peeping Tom view.

"It is Metalious' attitude, and I'm sure an honest one," Rogers conceded for Grace's home-town audience. "But it gave me a creepy feeling: this is the sort of thing for which naughty boys used to get their mouths washed out with soap; and on almost every page I was scared to heck—the only four-letter word not in this author's vocabulary—that some one I know would look over my shoulder and catch me reading the stuff."

Rogers, like most other reviewers, judged Grace by her reputation rather than by what *The Tight White Collar* actually contains. It includes only one four-letter word of note ("fuck"); the other mildly vulgar words in it are no worse than "tits" and "arse."

Nor did Rogers really have to worry about someone's reading *The Tight White Collar* over his shoulder—for *Peyton Place* really has many more "good parts." Just as Grace fought against pigeonholing as a standard wife and mother, she refused to repeat *Peyton Place* in her later books, but reviewers persisted in expecting *Peyton Place*—and seeing it even when it was not there.

The Tight White Collar, Grace said, means "the high white collar of respectability you can hide behind. If you're not careful, it will choke you until you're not human any more." For the most part, characters in the novel say "white collar" to mean white-collar professions—but respectability and hypocrisy both appear in the book, as they did in *Peyton Place.*

Like *Peyton Place, The Tight White Collar* consists of interlocking plots, though with more flashbacks and fewer crises.

Grace seems more interested in the long view—how people become who they are—rather than in immediate dramas of sex and violence. She shows how Nate and Margery Cooper cope—and fail to cope—with having a Mongoloid child; how David Strong finally escapes the prison of his own homosexuality; how Chris and Lisa Pappas handle his firing from his small-town teaching job. As with *Peyton Place,* characters have parts of real-life people Grace knew—but with her own imaginative flourishes.

Grace always considered *The Tight White Collar* her favorite novel—and her first. Dr. Gordon Cameron is her first crusty doctor; Chris and Lisa Pappas' years at the state university were in Grace's mind as early as 1950—when she wrote her own feelings at U.N.H.: "trapped in a cage." Except for a half-dozen words, Chapter 1 (Anthony Cooper's homecoming) and Chapter 5 (the university years) are, according to George, the same as Grace wrote them in 1950. Racier parts, such as an Irish maid's affair with a rich man who has an unbelievable pornography collection—are later additions, written to settle old scores and (perhaps) to meet the expectations of readers and reviewers of *Peyton Place.*

When Grace appeared on Ben Hecht's talk show in late 1958, Hecht had asked her what modern men are after—instead of women. Grace told him: "Well, they turn to each other, for one thing; they turn to liquor; they go home to their mothers and they turn to their jobs." In *The Tight White Collar,* Grace examines men much more thoroughly than she did in *Peyton Place* and *Return to Peyton Place,* and finds them pursuing those four goals: jobs, their mothers, liquor—and each other.

Grace had several gay male friends, and once mentioned to her musical mentor Bob Athearn that two of her companions were "queerer than purple teeth."

"Grace had no prejudices in that direction at all, and couldn't have cared less what anyone's sexual preferences were," Bob Athearn said later. He remembered the "purple teeth" remark as an odd, colorful expression. But Grace does show some doubts in the story of David Strong, originally begun at U.N.H. She wavers about whether David is oppressed—or stereotypically "queer."

David at times acts out a stereotype: advising women about fashion, telling them, "But that neckline, darling. It's just not you." But Grace emphasizes more the prejudice against homosexuals through David's morbid fear of what others might say; through his socially conditioned disgust with his own desires; and through his awareness that even the loudest and crudest of heterosexuals have more rights than he does—to talk about sex, to show affection in public. Theirs is "the great gift of normalcy"—the ability to conform and blend in that Grace Metalious never had. Despairing of ever finding peace, David takes his own life—and even mocks his choice of methods: not the "masculine job" with a gun, but the woman's way, with pills.

Grace kills David off too quickly, Alfred D. Rosenblatt complained in his Laconia *Evening Citizen* review. In fact, she'd just begun to delineate the "semi-pervert" rather well, Rosenblatt wrote. Rosenblatt thoroughly missed Grace's point of view, the outsider perspective that once informed her portrayals of women. As a man who harms no one but himself, David is no "pervert"—except in the eyes of those with limited understanding, those choked by the tight white collar. David, unlike little Norman Page in *Peyton Place,* knows he has no escape.

Grace made David one of many characters troubled by loneliness, the major affliction in *The Tight White Collar*—even for those men pursuing their mothers, liquor, or jobs. Virtually every character is an only child; mothers and children show little warmth toward one another. One woman torments her daughter with impossibly aristocratic ideals; another gives birth out of wedlock and guiltlessly abandons her baby in a church. (The first mother suggests Laurette; the second is named Doris, probably out of malice—for Bunny, who frequently abandoned her children at Grace's, was christened Doris.)

Still another mother sacrifices years of her life to seeking an impossible cure for her Down's syndrome daughter—and rescues herself only when she finally admits that she hates her child. Moreover, Margery—the retarded child's mother—is the only female character who shows genuine warmth toward other women. Grace seems to say that motherhood—or at least all-sacrificing motherhood, as demanded by the feminine mystique—destroys a woman's self, and her ability to form connections with anyone else. Unlike Connie MacKenzie in *Peyton Place,* no woman in *The Tight*

White Collar comes close to "having it all." No reconciliations are possible with a daughter who can never learn to speak.

In *Peyton Place,* Grace had followed a theory of compensating values similar to Hollywood's: the good people were rewarded, for the most part, and the evil, punished. In *The Tight White Collar,* however, people win or lose randomly: money, class, age, vice, or virtue have little effect. As she grew older, Grace felt less and less optimistic—and presented people as more and more trapped.

Even Lisa Pappas, whose life as a Franco-American adolescent, student wife, and Mrs. Schoolteacher recapitulates much of Grace Metalious' past, lacks Grace's creative drive and will to transcend her environment. Lisa reads constantly, but has no desire to write her own books: Instead, Lisa has an affair with an alcoholic writer. Significantly, Grace transfers creativity to men—and makes her female character thoroughly dependent. Even Lisa's lover says she is "dumb."

Only Anthony, the writer, combines Grace's writing ability and her sensitivity to hurt and oppression, and in *The Tight White Collar,* men are generally the more perceptive characters. Anthony also drinks heavily, in Grace's style: "without any appearance of speed . . . continually and methodically." But Grace knew that drinking for a woman has a different social meaning than for a man.

A minor character, Marie, drinks for the reasons Grace did: "Just enough to blunt the edges of things and make life a little softer and pinker." Terribly condemned in town, especially by women, Marie points out that a woman who drinks gets a reputation for moral looseness as well—but she is no whore. Marie serves as Grace's self-defense and shows vestiges of Grace's compassion and understanding for women. But overall, neither sex has much opportunity to escape the tight white collar.

By the time *The Tight White Collar* appeared, Grace had few dreams left.

Lisa does return, in the end, to a contented if unglamorous life with her Greek-American husband, and *The Tight White Collar* can be read as praise for George Metalious—though Grace was, while she put it together, still married to T.J. When the book came out, Grace, George, and the children were living at Martha's

Vineyard, and Grace autographed a copy: "To George—for all the reasons he knows so well, [the words she used to dedicate *Peyton Place*] and for the many, many more with which I am even better acquainted—From his wife, Grace Metalious, 1960."

But the public dedication, printed in *The Tight White Collar*, reveals why Grace took so long to write the book—and why, perhaps, she had become far more cynical about the possibilities for human happiness. "There are many things that go into the making of a book besides whatever small talents the author may possess," she wrote. "Not the least of these is love and encouragement on the darkest days of creation and love, enthusiasm and criticism on the brighter days. For these reasons and many, many more, this book is dedicated to my husband T. J. Martin, in gratitude."

CHAPTER 21

Not long after *The Tight White Collar,* the Metaliouses returned to Gilmanton, and Grace had to confront another long-standing problem: her agent.

One day, George had come home to find Grace in a terrible depression. "All I have left is five hundred dollars," she declared, "and I'm going to drink myself to death."

George, the man of facts, went over their books, and found about $100,000 due that Grace had not received. George called Jacques Chambrun, who said he'd forgotten to send the check. The check came, but George was becoming more than a little suspicious.

Jacques had long since become a family friend. Though Grace at first giggled at his Continental accent and encouraged Laurie Wilkens to listen on the extension when she talked to him, she valued Jacques's advice, depended on him—and insisted on being loyal to him because he'd been loyal to her work from the start.

Jacques attended Joanne Wilkens' wedding to Charles Pugh in January 1961; he'd known Joanne and Laurie since the sale of *Peyton Place.* Grace came to the wedding late, wearing ski pants and sitting in the back, creating a stir. At the reception at the Wilkenses', everyone clustered around Grace, as usual—but Jacques, at least, did not forget the bride and groom.

Hearing that Joanne and Charles would be honeymooning in a friend's jalopy, Jacques insisted on getting them a respectable rent-a-car. As always, Jacques was lavishly generous. But Grace had come to suspect that he was being generous with her money.

Publishers rarely pay their authors directly. Usually they send checks to the author's agent, who deducts the agent's 10 percent fee and sends the rest to the author, on the agent's check. On original book contracts, the author must sign, but on sales of reprint rights, excerpts, translations, and other subsidiary rights, the publisher or agent may approve for the author. Hence, the author need not necessarily see the amount of the contract—an unscrupulous agent's bonanza.

Although publishers' accounting procedures are notoriously difficult to decipher, Grace began to wonder if she was getting everything she'd earned. How, out of the millions of copies sold, could she have only $500 left?

In past years, Grace had often told interviewers about meeting her favorite author, W. Somerset Maugham, in Chambrun's office. The encounter probably never took place—but not only because Grace enjoyed telling stories. If the meeting did occur, Maugham would have come to Chambrun's office not to say hello, but to demand back payments. Maugham had a long and not very pleasant association with Chambrun, dating back to the 1940s.

When Maugham first needed an American agent, he had considered Jacques Chambrun, and asked advice from Ken McCormick, Editor-in-Chief at Doubleday. "He's a hell of a salesman," McCormick told Maugham, "but he's a crook."

McCormick had gathered a fund of stories about Chambrun's typical—and questionable—operations. Confronted by authors who thought they had not received their due, Chambrun would blame a clerical error. If more discrepancies appeared and an author threatened legal action (as many did), Chambrun would say: "If you put me in jail, I can't earn any money, and I can't pay you back. If you don't sue me, I'll pay you back." Most authors, more interested in payment than revenge, agreed—and the scenario continued for other writers, among them Fulton Oursler.

Oursler, author of *The Greatest Story Ever Told,* a New Testament retelling that made him something of a guru in the late 1940s, discovered he was not being paid for translated editions. Friends reported seeing foreign printings that he knew nothing about—and when Oursler confronted Chambrun, he discovered that between $50,000 and $75,000 had apparently disappeared into his agent's pocket. Convinced that Chambrun would pay him back if he did not sue, Oursler went on to another agent—as did countless other writers.

Maugham stuck with Chambrun longer than most. Unlike Jerome Weidman, an author-accountant who ran from Chambrun, "Willie" Maugham saw Chambrun as a challenge, and tried to outwit him—even hiring a lawyer at 2½ percent to watch over his agent's 10 percent.

Nevertheless, Chambrun sold away world rights to Maugham's books without notifying Maugham (or paying him); how much he actually earned from Maugham's writings will never be known. But he finally agreed to pay Maugham back in installments, and was still making payments as late as 1963—with his percentages from Grace Metalious' earnings.

Meanwhile, Chambrun was also earning money from Jack Schaefer, the author of *Shane,* who at first trusted his agent implicitly—even naming his prize Angus bull "Jacques." But Schaefer finally realized that much of his money, especially for foreign rights, had not reached him—and he went to another agent.

For years afterward, Schaefer would meet other writers who'd say, "Did you go through the Chambrun wringer, too?" But Schaefer had a modest personal revenge: After all claims seemed settled, Schaefer wrote Chambrun—for the hell of it—claiming that Chambrun owed him for some items never reported. By return mail, Chambrun sent a check for $78.

The hope for that kind of success—outwitting a sharpie—kept most authors and editors from taking concrete action against Chambrun. When Ken McCormick tried to organize a "crusade" at an editors' lunch club, only two other editors would agree to spread warnings against Chambrun. The other dozen still thought they could beat him.

Don Fine once did—in Grace Metalious' presence. She, her children, and Jacques had come to Dell/Western to pick up a check, and Fine bet Chambrun a dime on some inconsequential matter.

"I won," Fine recalls, "but the important thing is, I made him pay me. I said, 'Come on, break precedent and pay me.' He laughed and paid up."

Few, if any, of Chambrun's clients ever sued—but some had other methods. On one occasion, he was bodily thrown out of the *Saturday Evening Post* offices. On another, a music critic for the New York *World Telegram* threatened to throw Chambrun out the window of the agent's twenty-second floor office. Chambrun paid.

As Ken McCormick describes it, Chambrun had a "floating bridge of money" that went from author to author: Metalious' earnings helped pay off Schaefer; Schaefer's money helped pay off Maugham, and so forth. But Grace Metalious was Chambrun's "last big swindle"—and one that played on her particular vulnerabilities.

Grace "seemed to love being exploited," Knox Burger says, and "Chambrun was her Diaghilev." From the beginning, Grace had sensed herself an outsider in publishing, with Jacques her ally against the world—as George had seemed in their early days, and T.J. for a while. Further, Jacques did make big book sales, though much of his own wealth came through not paying his clients.

Apparently Grace Metalious was Chambrun's only major female victim. Her particular susceptibility to charm, her admiration for French ways, and her need for male approval all kept her with Chambrun much longer than his male clients. When the break came, with sure signs of Jacques's disloyalty, the blow to Grace's psyche was as severe as any to the purse.

Kitty Messner had spotted Chambrun's dealings before Grace did. She began paying Chambrun his 10 percent in one check, with the rest to Grace separately. Kitty's friend Philip Wittenberg, an eminent publishing lawyer, advised Grace to withdraw from her contract with Chambrun. Finally, not long after she returned to George, Grace contacted Oliver Swan, the agent she'd visited in 1953 with her early manuscripts.

Swan remembered her vividly—her girlish appearance, so incongruous in New York; her agitation; her enthusiasm. He also recalled the day he'd been vacationing in Boothbay and read about *Peyton Place,* recognized Grace Metalious' name—and chastised himself for a badly missed opportunity.

Terminating the understanding with Chambrun became a long, difficult process for Grace—as she told Ollie Swan in many phone calls. She'd wanted Swan to come to Gilmanton (as Chambrun had, at her whim and her expense), but Swan hesitated.

The following day she called to say she'd tried to break from Chambrun, but he'd gotten her drunk and made her sign another contract.

A little later she phoned Swan again, to say that she and George were on their way to New York. She deputed Swan to get copies of her three book contracts from Chambrun.

Swan met with Chambrun, but Grace's first agent was so convincing, suave, and persuasive that Swan somehow departed without the contracts.

Then at the Plaza, Grace, George, Don Fine, several other book people, Chambrun, and Swan met. Chambrun announced that Grace had come back with him. George (who reportedly had some mild fisticuffs with Jacques in New Hampshire) called Chambrun a liar.

When peace was restored, Grace announced that Ollie Swan of the Paul Reynolds Literary Agency was now her agent.

On March 28, 1961, she notified Jacques Chambrun in writing that she was legally terminating all his power to act in her behalf, "For various reasons which seem to me not only good but necessary for the protection of my interests." She demanded that Chambrun return all contracts, send her a complete accounting, and pay her all that he owed by April 15—and added that "The exigencies of the situation you will understand, since they have in large part been created by you."

Apparently unable to attract any more fish to continue his "floating bridge of money," Chambrun soon gave up the agent business. He began publishing *16,* a very successful magazine for teenagers, with articles on rock music and show people. He outlived Grace Metalious by twelve years.

Chambrun's death certificate lists him as sixty years old, though those who knew him believed him much older. He died in 1976— ironically enough, on September 8.

It would have been Grace Metalious' fifty-second birthday.

With her financial affairs in honest hands by the spring of 1961, and her charming but treacherous agent out of the picture, Grace had fewer worries about money. But people around her still worried about her drinking.

Townspeople often talked about her in negative terms, while friends defended her. Esther Peters remembers giving a party where Grace fell asleep on Esther's bed.

"Grace has passed out!" one guest crowed as she came out of the bedroom. "I took a picture of her!"

Esther tore up the picture.

Rodney Crockett, then the Belknap County Sheriff, never saw Grace with anything stronger than a beer, and was surprised to learn the extent of her drinking problem.

Sometimes having alcohol—even beer—became an urgency for Grace. On one occasion she called Peter Karagianis, owner of the Laconia Spa, and wanted him to bring a case of beer to her house. "I need it NOW!" she insisted.

It was 1 A.M., and Karagianis protested. He had no one to mind the store; Grace's place was so hard to find in the dark that he'd probably never get back (a common complaint).

Grace hung up, disgusted, and arrived at the Spa half an hour later, in her characteristic red-plaid shirt, blue jeans, and loafers without socks. With a scornful look she bought her beer, hoisted the carton on her shoulder, and dumped it into her car. Then she backed into the parking meter, seemed not to notice, and drove off.

When she drank at home, Grace could become both dramatic and hysterical. Richard Stinson, who had graduated from Laconia High School and was trying to decide what to do with his life, often visited Grace—and her drinking frightened him. "She changed personalities when she drank," he remembers. She could be vicious, "evil." But the next day, she might be "so wonderful that you'd forget the bad times, and do anything for her."

Stinson did what he could for her. Sometimes he autographed books for her, when she was feeling lazy; he tried to keep exploiters away. One day at a local gas station, Grace came in needing a gas cap—and an attendant put on a very elaborate, expensive, chrome-plated, key-locked cap.

"What the hell do we need that kind for?" Stinson demanded.

"What do you care?" the attendant retorted. "It's not your money."

"Well, I do care," Stinson said.

Local gossips warned Stinson's parents that their son was spending time with a wicked person—to which the Stinsons responded, "Well, she never did him any harm."

He tried to help Grace with one of her biggest problems. During an excursion to the Plaza, he suddenly realized that the people around Grace were afraid of her—and, especially, afraid to criticize her drinking.

Grace had left the bar to go to the bathroom, and told her friends, "Order more drinks." As usual, they'd be put on her tab.

Stinson ordered drinks for everyone else, "and ginger ale for Grace."

The others, including Jacques and Bunny, were stunned at his nerve.

Grace seemed not to notice the difference, and her having ginger ale made a much better evening for everyone else.

"People are no damn good," Grace often said while she drank—and Hollywood people still rated high on her enemies list. She had hoped that writing *Return to Peyton Place* would end her flirtation with Hollywood—but then during the spring of 1961 she got a call from Twentieth Century-Fox's publicity department.

Would Grace be willing to tour five cities to promote the *Return to Peyton Place* film, just completed?

"Only on one condition," she said. "That you have the premiere here in Laconia."

The studio agreed, and promised that four stars would come: Carol Lynley (Allison); Eleanor Parker (Constance MacKenzie Rossi); Mary Astor (Roberta Carter, Ted's mother); and Jeff Chandler (Lewis Jackman, Allison's publisher and lover. As it turned out, Chandler died of blood poisoning a month before the film opened). The studio promised a gala event, after Grace finished her promotional travels.

The grand tour began inauspiciously. She and George took a Boston to Chicago flight on Sunday, April 16—but the Chicago airport was snowed in, and they had to land in Detroit. There they took the train to Chicago, arriving at 4 A.M. Monday—to begin three days of frantic interviewing, publicity, and rushing from one place to another.

Though they stayed at the plush Ambassador East, they saw Chicago only from fast-moving taxis. Asked her opinion of the *Return to Peyton Place* film, Grace told reporters, "I don't know if it's a good movie. I haven't seen it."

She saw a little more of St. Louis, where she admired the Mississippi River and the gaslight section. At the Park Plaza Hotel she met reporters, among them Olivia Skinner, who described her in the St. Louis *Post Dispatch:* Grace wore a gray silk tweed suit, "neatly tailored," and "an Alice-in-Wonderland band which slicked her straight dark hair back from her forehead. Her pretty legs, which she much prefers unencumbered, were encased in nylons, and she had on high-heeled shoes. These she wiggled every now and again in a surprised and uncomfortable way." Olivia Skinner liked Grace's voice:—"a soft, curiously appealing young girl's voice"—as Grace answered reporters' questions.

How did she feel about small town versus big city? "In a big city there are more interesting things to do than be overly concerned with your neighbor." People call New York cruel, she said, because you can live in the same place for twenty years and never know your next-door neighbor, but "Which is more cruel? Isolation, or the constant prying and lack of privacy you have in a small town, where people love digging into each other's closets?"

Given her views, why stay in Gilmanton? "I live there because I couldn't stand to live anywhere else," Grace said. "In Gilmanton I don't have to be part of the town. George shuts the door and I can be perfectly safe."

"You just have to watch out for bears," George muttered at that point. (Olivia Skinner called him "a quiet, humorous, pipe-smoking intellectual with views on life as decided as his wife's.")

And Grace's views about life? "There are a great deal many more ugly human beings than beautiful ones." The ugliest thing she'd ever seen was a child dying of spinal meningitis in the public ward of a hospital; the most beautiful was her daughter Cindy's leg when it came out of the cast. Despite breaks in three places, the leg had healed perfectly.

Of her children, only Marsha had read all her books—and

Grace hoped none of the children would become writers. She also hoped they would never forget what life had been like before fame and fortune. "You learn so much more if you remember how it feels to be poor," she said.

As for her adventures as a celebrity, she particularly praised Ben Hecht, "The most beautiful man I've ever known in my life. He must be over sixty, but he looks at the world through the eyes of a child of ten. He has a tremendous heart."

And Grace's heart? Pessimistic—and honest about herself. "I'm stuck with my view of human nature."

From St. Louis, she and George flew to Dallas, where they stayed in the Governors' Suite at the Statler Hotel. "It's so cosmopolitan and beautiful," Grace said of Dallas. She complained that she had only a winter wardrobe, though—and a few hours later a cotton outfit appeared, courtesy of a local dress manufacturer.

"It could only happen in Texas!" Grace said, delighted.

At a cocktail party she met Patricia Gallagher, whose first novel, *The Sons and the Daughters,* had just been published by Messner's. Pat Gallagher would be appearing with Grace in Dallas —and they had much in common. Gallagher was also a housewife, from San Antonio, with a teenage son—and a passion for writing. She had been writing all her life, struggling to type out stories on a small portable on the kitchen table, between household chores— much the way Grace had written *Peyton Place.*

Like Grace Metalious, Pat Gallagher wanted to write realistically and truthfully. *The Sons and the Daughters,* like *Peyton Place,* sketches an anatomy of a small town, including the doctor, the priest, the newspaper editor, the wealthy playboy, and the maiden lady who inspires a young girl to read. Jill Turner, that young girl, resembles Allison MacKenzie in growing up fatherless, yearning to write, feeling sexual tensions. Messner's promoted *The Sons and the Daughters* as "the *Peyton Place* of Texas—Does for Texas What *Peyton Place* Did for New England."

Grace Metalious and Pat Gallagher posed together with their books—though Grace, who said she hated the way she looked, had to be cajoled into posing. Grace autographed Pat's copy of *Peyton Place*—with a warning to be careful when she wrote about small towns. Grace and George talked wistfully about a monument to her fame in Laconia, the way Atlanta honored Margaret Mitchell for *Gone with the Wind*—but George was more than a sounding board for Grace, Pat Gallagher noticed. Grace kept rye whiskey in her luggage, and George's job—together with two Twentieth Century-Fox representatives—was to keep Grace from drinking.

Gallagher remembers Grace's flawless, peaches-and-cream complexion, her hair pulled back in a rubber band, her lack of makeup, her omnipresent blue jeans. Grace, who looked considerably older than thirty-six, confided to Pat Gallagher how much she hated publicity appearances. They sneaked off to the bathroom together—which also got Grace away from the studio men who wanted her not to drink—and Grace told Pat, "I hate this stuff I have to do. And if you think you'll like it, you won't. And when I get really nervous, that's when I hit the bottle."

She hit the bottle so badly that she missed their major publicity appearance in Dallas.

George and Grace had a turbulent flight from Dallas to Atlanta, and "I thought I was going to die on the blasted thing," Grace said later. "This is no life for me. I can't wait to get back home to Gilmanton and get back to my normal way of living." The thought of taking another plane—at 5 P.M., after a full day in Atlanta, to get to Washington, D.C.—made her shudder. She said she would give anything to spend an hour or two in a beauty shop.

It seemed an uncharacteristic longing for the woman who'd said, "I'm just fat and happy," and "These Fifth Avenue stores are strictly for jerks." But a beauty shop would have given her refuge—peace, quiet, anonymity.

In any case, she had no time, amid publicity obligations. At a club luncheon in Atlanta, an audience member complimented her on the descriptions of seasons in *Peyton Place*. That made Grace happy, as she felt particularly proud of those passages.

"I found her witty, charming, a good reporter," James K. O'Neill, Jr., wrote in his column in Washington, D.C. Grace Metalious, he said, was "in love with the rustic side of New England, that never-never land of little progress, deep convictions (however arbitrary or false), and folkways so curious that to report upon them to the world at large brings down the wrath of whole communities upon the heads of those who would dare utter such things, true or untrue."

From Washington, Grace returned to Gilmanton, gratefully touching the fireplace, glad to be home. She also looked forward to the elegant, well-appointed celebration the film makers had promised for the *Return to Peyton Place* premiere. Instead, a cheap mimeographed invitation had gone out to Grace's guest list. She felt considerably miffed, though she had high hopes for the occasion at the Colonial Theater in Laconia, on April 27, 1961. One friend, George Cantin, was particularly eager to be there.

Cantin, a long-time Lakes Region resident, had never met Grace until she became famous. He ran a dancing studio, teaching adults and children, but encountered Grace for the first time when she had a need he could fill: "I had a dime and she needed to pee."

"Cantin!" she'd said, her hand in T.J.'s. "Cantin! You're the best goddamned teacher around. I'm taking my kids to you. Do you have a dime?"

He did, and she sent her children to him. Like Laurie Wilkens' children, Cindy, Mike, and Marsha took social dancing from "Cantin." (Grace never called him "George.")

"We clicked immediately," Cantin remembers, and he had soon become part of Grace and T.J.'s party circle. He and Grace liked comparing notes about their French poodles. At parties, Grace and Cantin's mother would swap off-color French-Canadian jokes. Cantin and T.J. concocted elaborate scenarios, including a scheme to rent a plane for Thanksgiving and buzz people's houses, dropping turkeys down their unsuspecting chimneys.

Cantin sometimes took people to see Grace, but only in the afternoon, when he felt fairly sure she'd be sober. When she felt in the mood, she'd play tricks on his sophisticated New York friends. For a while she kept a dime-store reproduction of a painting over her fireplace, with a spotlight. She insisted to the New Yorkers that it was an "original"—and giggled at their admiration.

But Cantin saw the painful side, too. Sometimes Grace would leave her children at his studio, become immersed in drinking, and not return—so he would drive them home, sometimes at 10 or 11 at night, after he finished his day's lessons.

Grace had "no privacy whatsoever" at home, he noticed. Strangers barged in constantly—wanting autographs, time, or advice on how to write a best seller. Often she'd hold her glass to her forehead and intone, "Ugh—people are no goddamn good."

She looked awfully good for the *Return to Peyton Place* premiere, recalls Cantin. Grace wore her hair in a perfect French twist (the Wilkens children called it her "Duchess-do"); her dress was simple, black, Empire-style, adorned only with an orchid corsage.

To Esther Peters, Grace confided that the dress, with its plunging neckline, embarrassed her, especially when she leaned forward. She had no hankering for the kind of Hollywood party Ben Hecht describes in *A Child of the Century,* with "the under-forty wives bare to the coccyges and matching tits for an evening with all comers."

Grace looked so elegant that many people did not recognize her —or, as Laurie Wilkens reported in the Laconia *Evening Citizen,* "Laconia looked and gasped and saw what has always been there to see—that Grace Metalious is beautiful."

For that evening Grace reigned as queen—but few of the invited subjects attended. Though the studio promised *Return to Peyton Place* stars for the world premiere, only Ina Balin, star of *From the Terrace* and occasional performer at the Lakes Region playhouse, appeared. Gertrude Brooks, the Twentieth Century-Fox fashion expert, attended, as did a *Silver Screen* reporter, J. Scott Davis. Other Twentieth Century-Fox officials came, but no stars. Mayor Oliva Huot had wanted to give the stars the keys to the city, but gamely gave keys to the "guests of honor" instead.

Grace circulated at Bernard and Muriel Snierson's private cocktail party, then arranged for a beautifully prepared dinner at the Laconia Tavern—but was herself too nervous to eat. Though the film would not be shown until 8:30 P.M., lines began forming in front of the theater by 6 o'clock. Main Street was closed to traffic, and by 7:35 all tickets had been sold. The street was flooded with lights; Grace signed countless autographs.

"Grace came, as always, with all flags flying," Laurie wrote in the Laconia *Evening Citizen,* "her hand clasped in that of her

wise, kind George and her beloved children all around her, showing a beauty and a dignity with which the world at large is not
quite as familiar as those who knew her and love her well."

Grace's children made a fine impression, too, Laurie reported.
Marsha, seventeen, "looked very lovely and grown up, in a
bouffant black gown and pearls, with those big brown eyes shining
like stars." Cindy, ten, looked "sweet," with a small wrist corsage
and "her honey-blond hair as smooth as silk." Suzy Roy, thirteen,
had a new hair cut, and "showed the full charm of her French ancestry with her sparkling brown eyes and flashing smile." As for
Mike, thirteen: "he looked a really truly young man, and so he
comported himself, watching over his mother and sisters, and
making guests feel at home."

Grace watched the movie with George and their children;
Laurie and Bill Wilkens; their youngsters Wendy, John, and
Phyllis—all Grace's godchildren; Roger Roy, Suzy's father; and
Lynn Richards, a New York pianist, former accompanist for Ethel
Waters, and a special favorite of visitors to the Plaza.

Laurie called the premiere Grace's reconciliation with Laconia,
a healing of wounds. It had been a beautiful spring evening, "with
traces of snow crowning the rocky hills of the northern New
Hampshire she loves so well, when at long last Grace Metalious
came 'home.'" Laconians, Laurie wrote, gave Grace "every possible show of affection and pride that a welcoming community could
devise" and Grace and Laconia became "best friends forever and
ever." Or so Laurie hoped—for the constant criticism of Grace had
hurt her, too.

Despite the studio's broken promises, Grace had given Laconia,
Gilmanton, and Belmont something to be proud of: a world premiere, prettily done, with dignity, glamour, and family feeling.
The film, too, was well-received, Laurie wrote, "and official party
and theatergoers were almost universal in their opinion that it is
one of the moving pictures of the year." Grace herself gave no
opinion, saying she hadn't had time to digest what she'd seen.

Even in Laconia, *Return to Peyton Place* had been promoted
far more aggressively than the original *Peyton Place* film, which

sold itself. Ads for *Return* in the Laconia *Evening Citizen* proclaimed:

> Now only the truth could set them free . . . free from the town's false morality . . . free to live their own lives in love, honor and decency! . . . IT BEGINS WHERE 'PEYTON PLACE' LEFT OFF!

The *Evening Citizen* ads listed ticket prices for adults only. Ads in other cities made the strategy even more explicit: "Children's Tickets Will Not Be Sold During This Premier Engagement," and "Mr. Jerry Wald, Producer, Requests That We Refrain from Selling Children's Tickets During Premier Engagement."

The lure of the forbidden, especially forbidden to impressionable minds, drew crowds—who often came away disappointed. Reviewers termed the script, by Broadway playwright Ronald Alexander, "shallow and diffuse"; Carol Lynley, as Allison, looked "bored" and "petulant." The only performer praised by everyone was Mary Astor, grandly evil as Roberta Carter, Ted's hateful mother. Despite her small role in the book version of *Return to Peyton Place,* "Roberta Carter" easily stole the show in the film.

The film follows, for the most part, Allison's story in *Return.* Her best seller, *Samuel's Castle,* costs her stepfather Mike Rossi (Robert Sterling) his teaching job. Allison goes through the publicity mill, including a photograph at her typewriter, with blue jeans and ponytail. Allison appears on a talk-show with format and lighting exactly like Mike Wallace's "Night Beat"; she is interviewed by a columnist who calls her a "chick"—to which she responds with a snide look. Another talk show, whose unctuous host bears some resemblance to Jerry Wald, parodies inane "happy talk" interviews.

In the *Return* book, Allison's driving kills her publisher-lover—but in the film she simply sends him away. She would rather be a solitary writer than a married man's mistress. Both endings show Allison's choosing independence—but the film's closing has more moral overtones, to please the censor. Likewise, the film removes the sexual kinks and murderous contrivances of the book.

The film's ending suggests still another sequel for Allison—and still centered more on her romances than her writing. As he turns away, Lewis Jackman tells Allison: "You'll be a great writer someday. And an even greater woman." But another Allison would almost certainly be needed for *Peyton Place III*. Diane Varsi, Allison in the original *Peyton Place,* had fled Hollywood in 1959, horrified at its invasions of privacy (she returned in 1971). Lynley, a blond, sleek former model, simply did not look like Allison, supposed to be an awkward provincial among New York and Hollywood sharpies.

Return to Peyton Place's reviewers again took the opportunity to lambaste Grace Metalious. Screenwriter Ronald Alexander did "tidy up Miss Metalious' purple-passioned sequel to her novel about private lives in a small New Hampshire town," Jerry Vermilye reported in *Films in Review,* but added that Jerry Wald had commissioned the sequel, and "Miss Metalious claims the novel is a slick, studio-engineered rush-job far below her usual standard (*sic*)."

Similarly, *Time* called *Return to Peyton Place* "a recrawl of the New England gutters so noisomely celebrated by Author Grace Metalious in *Peyton Place.*" But Jerry Wald "had to wash that smut right out of his script. That means there just isn't anything left." *Time* said the plot obviously followed "the author's own frantic life," including George's firing, Grace's affair with another man—and "in real life, the author fell in love with a disc jockey, left her husband and two children" (*sic*).

Fortunately for Grace, she had little time to brood on the pleasure critics take in damning authors. On May 15 Grace and George departed for Europe, on a combination vacation and publicity jaunt, which they called a second honeymoon.

They left feeling very romantic, thoroughly in love—but hit an evil omen as their jet approached England. "A real big thunderstorm," Grace told reporters later. "Scared? You bet! No more jets or any other kinds of planes." Naturally, she kept no such vow—but regarded all forms of transportation warily.

In London she and George stayed at the May Fair, one of the best hotels. They toured the English countryside, where Grace admired the fields, farms, and tidy English cottages. They visited the standard tourist attractions: the changing of the guard at Buckingham Palace, the jewels at the Tower of London. "She drank in these and many other sights with relish and a gourmet's delight," George reports in his biography.

But on a campus tour at Oxford University, Grace began talking about some very old anxieties. Though she often agreed with her *Tight White Collar* characters who claim a college education doesn't teach useful skills ("It don't take no four years at no college to learn howta count money"), Grace told George she wished she'd actually gone to college. (Sometimes she told reporters she had.) She also talked about her longing for serious literary recognition.

The six days in Great Britain included visits with British publishers and representatives, but mostly Grace and George kept away from the pressures of fame. The Pan paperback edition of *Peyton Place* had sold over a million copies, and Grace received her "PAN," a gold-plated statue of the god Pan, with phallus, goat tail, and legs, inscribed for her.

Taking the overnight boat train to Paris, Grace and George arrived in the early morning, when Paris glistens with pink and blue light. Grace decided not to play the role of rich tourist, and chose the small Hotel St. Simon, on the rue Simon le France—where she could speak French with a quiet and friendly concierge.

She enjoyed her anonymity in Paris, where she and George strolled along the Seine, watched the lovers and artists, visited the Arc de Triomphe and the Eiffel Tower—all of which, George reports, she preferred to nightclubbing. She and George discussed the arch and the tower, he wrote later, "comparing them to our own lives. We studied the aesthetic qualities of these man-built structures and compared them with personalities. We thought about time and how much we had left, and we both thought then that a whole new beautiful road stretched out ahead of us.

"How wrong we were, but there were six heavenly days in Paris that spring."

Acutely aware of other people and her obligations, Grace found it hard to be cheerful for long. During the third week of their trip, on the train to Milan, Grace became extremely depressed. Their Milan visit would entail responsibilities: meetings with her Italian publishers, Longanesi, and their representative, Bruno Lacitra.

By the time Grace and George reached their lodgings at the magnificent Hotel Principe e Savoia, she was consumed with dread. And then, George says, "a minor incident occurred which sent Grace into mild hysterics."

When they arrived, George had left a small amount of money on the bureau—and it disappeared. A waiter must have taken it after delivering room service cocktails (Grace had needed a drink).

Grace took the theft as a provocation, and felt hostile toward all the people she met afterward in Italy. Not knowing Italian, she could not communicate—and became extremely sensitive to emotional currents. When she saw the spot where Mussolini was hanged, she was sickened, she later told Marc. "She felt ugliness surrounding her," George remembers—and she also had *turista*.

At her insistence they returned to London three days early, and then home—as George says, "She couldn't wait to reach Gilmanton and the sanctity of her sofa and private corner."

CHAPTER 22

Grace returned home to more financial problems. Philip Witten-berg, the Messner's lawyer, had notified European publishers that Jacques Chambrun had "unwarrantedly dealt with" Grace's prop-erty and "purported to make agreements which were not binding on her." Wittenberg's letters went to Frederick Muller, Ltd., in Great Britain, Hachette in France, and Longanesi in Italy. But neither he nor Oliver Swan knew that Chambrun had also sold *Return to Peyton Place* and *The Tight White Collar* to Kindler Verlag in Germany—and apparently pocketed the money. Swan told Grace that he would pursue the matter.

Her "crooked friend" had left her affairs "hopelessly tangled," Grace wrote Swan on June 22. Nevertheless, she was "sick of sit-ting on my fat can and procrastinating." She was considering an-other *Peyton Place* book, to finance a project for George (who had not had a regular job since he left Martha's Vineyard with her. Marc remembers chatting with Grace on a visit to Gilmanton —while George sat, silently puffing on his pipe, painting dog and horse pictures by the numbers). Grace also promised to send Swan a short story for Robert Atherton, a *Cosmopolitan* editor. But she had not begun anything.

Dealings with foreign publishers occupied much of her energy. The German money Chambrun had withheld was rediscovered—but the German contract might include a forgery of Grace's signa-ture, Swan told her. Italy banned *The Tight White Collar*—which, Grace wrote Swan, might make excellent publicity. The Dutch publishers who had bought *The Tight White Collar,* sight unseen, changed their minds when they saw it. They were "not happy with the book," Amsterdam literary attorney Robert Harben wrote Swan—who informed Grace that the Dutch decided not to publish it.

At home in Gilmanton, Grace was mulling, drinking, receiving people who'd call up, wanting to visit. "Come on over, sweetie," she'd say, "and bring a bottle." Some guests brought their own; others sneaked into the kitchen and took one of Grace's, telling themselves she had more money than they did, after all—and carried it out to her. "You brought a bottle!" she'd say, very pleased.

Sometimes, late, uninvited visitors would break into the house to drink. One night Marsha, frightened by an intrusion, locked the other children in the cedar closet and prepared to defend them with George's old sword. When the danger seemed past, she unlocked the others, took them to the car, and drove around until daylight, when she felt they'd be safe again.

Grace's youngsters had another defender in Rex, a German shepherd puppy George had bought from the housekeeper, Ella Virgin, and her husband. Rex, who grew up in the house, took over protecting the family, and the children learned to sic him on any unwelcome sightseers who stopped at the foot of the drive.

Rex was also good for banishing unwanted friends, such as George Jarvin, who with his wife, Evvie, ran Jarvin's Music Store on Main Street in Laconia. During the party years Grace and T.J. had sometimes stopped for drinks in the back room of Jarvin's Music Store. Marsha, Mike, and Cindy had hated the crowded, grimy, smoke-filled back room and the people in it—most of whom later gave up drinking entirely. (One insurance man even became a born-again Christian.)

Somewhat later, George Jarvin tried to be more than friendly with Grace, and Marsha found him shouting, "I don't want Evvie to know about this!" when she came home from school one day.

"You'd better get out of this house," Marsha warned George Jarvin, "or I'll call the police!"

As Jarvin paused, Rex took a large nip out of his posterior.

"You bitch!" Jarvin yelled at Grace as he departed to get medical attention for his wounds. Grace was amused by that, but not by Jarvin's subsequent fate.

Like many of Grace's friends, George Jarvin had a talent—composing music—that went unappreciated. He had much less talent for business, and the music store failed. Jarvin failed with it: imagining persecution, calling Laconia "Draconia," fearing Communist subversion. He wrote letters to the newspaper, called radio stations, became unshaven and unkempt—until one night he had too much to drink, and died. He literally drank himself to death, friends agreed.

After his death, Grace brought Evvie to live in her house for a while—and Esther Peters, among others, praised Grace's generosity. But her friendship with Evvie and her sympathy for George did not stop Grace from following Jarvin's path herself. For her, too, drinking was both a solace and a disease. During late-night depressions when she had to call someone for comfort, Grace often called Evvie.

By then Grace had also become a grandmother. On September 16, 1961, Marsha married Edward Paul Dupuis at the Gilmanton Corners Church. Marsha was even younger than Grace at her own wedding—not quite eighteen—and Grace wanted her to wait, to go to college first. But Marsha knew she wanted to marry Eddie, her childhood sweetheart, and Grace finally gave her consent.

In Marsha's wedding pictures, Grace looks much older than thirty-seven. Though she smiles a great deal, as if contented with the world, her face looks ruddy with broken blood vessels, a sign of heavy drinking; her body looks bloated and ungainly. Still, she is smiling in most of the pictures—and holding a cigarette and a drink. She wears her hair upswept, no longer in her trademark ponytail, though later she claimed she'd abandoned her ponytail because it was inappropriate for a grandmother.

Marsha's wedding did, for a while, take Grace away from brooding on her own unhappiness, the pressures of fame, and her inability to write another book.

After Don Fine wrote her on September 22 with suggestions for a third *Peyton Place* book, Grace sent a furious letter to Ollie Swan. "I never expected Don Fine of Dell to make like Jerry Wald of Twentieth Century-Fox," she wrote Swan on October 3.

Fine's ideas, she said, were not his at all but Wald's, from a "severe case of running-off-at-the-mouth-itis."

In June, Wald had leaked word to *Time* that *"Peyton Place* is going to be a grandfather. So successful was *P.P.'s* first sequel, *Return to Peyton Place,* that it will have a sequel of its own, *Peyton Place Revisited.* Like its predecessors, the new installment will first be written in novel form: Producer Wald has already packed author Grace Metalious back to New Hampshire to soak up local off-color."

Grace had been in Europe when Wald leaked the news—and the ideas Don Fine sent did not appeal to her at all. It seemed a little "wild" to her, she wrote Ollie Swan, to be contriving a plot about Allison's seventeen-year-old daughter, when "poor Allison" had never even been married yet.

Further, the Wald—or Fine—scheme set the story in a college town. ("Spring Riot in Peyton Place" was one proposed title.) But Peyton Place had never had a college. Since all the New Hampshire colleges were quite old, Grace said, she could hardly "stick one" in Peyton Place.

She found one bright spot, she wrote Swan: Don Fine had said, "This is only a notion." She wished him to be informed that if another *Peyton Place* book were in the works, "I'll do it my way or not at all."

She made a similar show of strength to Kitty Messner. "For the last several days we are having here what I call the 'Great Return to Normalcy,'" she wrote Kitty on October 3. "The kids are safely married, honeymooned, and settled down." Then Grace settled down to her future: what to write next. Though she had fulfilled her three-book contract with Messner's when she finished *The Tight White Collar,* Grace still expected to write future hardcover books for Kitty.

Kitty was "not very happy," Grace had heard, that Grace might do another *Peyton Place* book for Dell. Why not? Grace asked. She assumed Kitty wouldn't want another hardcover book in the "series": "I thought we were in agreement concerning *Peyton Place* and *Return* and that was that we were both heartily sick of the whole thing."

And so Grace thought a Dell paperback about Peyton Place

would be better than a Messner's hardcover—for "one little paper-back would pass unnoticed in the publishing business, while still selling quite a few copies in assorted drugstores and railroad stations. This does not mean that I wouldn't have done the best job I knew how, because I would. Dell has been very good to me, and I've never let them down."

Why did she want to do another "PP book"?

Grace was blunt: "I need the money." She and George had bought a motel on Lake Winnipesaukee and wanted to build a dining room and cocktail lounge for their guests, since "there's gold in them thar tourists, and they have to eat and drink."

Meanwhile, Grace assured Kitty that she was not "trying to be another Chambrun going behind your back and all that," and asked to hear from Kitty soon.

Grace thought the motel, to be run by George, would be a good investment—and to do it she'd invest her time in writing another "PP book." Writing for money, as she'd done with *Return to Peyton Place,* also seemed simpler—less fraught with self-doubt—than writing for self-expression, as she had with *The Tight White Collar.* Writing for money required less craft and less commitment—and was less apt to produce paralyzing writing blocks.

But Kitty Messner knew authors' excuses and self-justifications, and knew Grace. "I would be much happier if you would stick to your 'creative' writing," Kitty wrote on October 4, "the sooner to prove that 'Peyton Place' *wasn't* a flash in the pan. Also, but believe me, the first reason comes first, is the business reason, that a 'big' book by you would pay off better than a minor one."

Having answered Grace's need for money, Kitty added that after all, "no book by you will pass unnoticed." Whatever happened would probably not affect "the reception of a real winner when you finally write it." She wanted Messner's, in any case, to be the original publisher of anything Grace did.

"Sweetie, write what you feel you have to"—and Messner's would publish it and get her cash as soon as Dell would. "I guess in this world you just can't afford to sit still until you produce another masterpiece," Kitty concluded.

Grace was not quite sitting still. She was worrying, pouring Canadian Club and 7-Up, and sometimes seeing Mrs. Mudgett, the house ghost, late at night. Mrs. Mudgett, the wife of the gangster Mudgett who had murdered some thirty-six people in Chicago, would come in, clad in ghostly white, and stand at the foot of Grace and George's bed.

Suzy Roy never saw Mrs. Mudgett, but Cindy saw her twice—and believed the attic was haunted.

When *Peyton Place* first became a success, Grace vowed she'd never again get up early—and she kept that promise most of the time. She usually rose at noon, starting her day with iced coffee. She'd chat with the youngsters, and that was the best time of the day for them.

In the summer Mike, Suzy, and Cindy sometimes walked to Loon Pond, four miles each way, if no one was available to drive them; after Grace and George bought the motel, the three youngsters worked there, cleaning cabins and doing chores. At home, meals were irregular; Grace rarely ate, except for her enormous salads late at night. Though she liked cooking, she rarely did any housework.

Her poodle Rififi ate well, however: frozen round steaks fried in butter. A present from T.J., Rififi had come dressed in a leather outfit—and family photographs show Grace holding Rififi in a Madonna and Child pose. For a while, Rififi had a reputation as a finicky eater—until Richard Stinson discovered that little Joe Brouillette, Bunny's son, had been urinating into Rififi's food dish.

Eventually Rififi was run over near Grace's motel—but malicious local gossip held that Rififi perished of cirrhosis of the liver. (Rex, the German shepherd, was shot by a neighbor for poaching chickens.)

At home Grace was affectionate, hugged the children, missed Marsha; George played the disciplinarian. Ambivalent, as always, about whether to be "feminine," Grace claimed not to care about her appearance, but kept a walk-in closet full of clothes, and liked to have Suzy do her hair, which was still fine, limp, and difficult to work with. Suzy liked to dress up in Grace's clothes, especially the mink stole, and listen to Grace's condemnation of people who wore "big diamonds and raggy underwear."

Grace's own underwear was very fine—though her outerwear was sometimes deliberately peculiar. She enjoyed flouncing to the grocery store in slacks or a shapeless muumuu—over which she threw her mink stole, with the air of a *grande dame*.

Basically, though, Suzy remembers her Aunt Grace as an introvert: rarely outwardly angry, more apt to be hurt, to cry rather than fight back. When she needed to, Grace could put on a show of sobriety: For a tax man's announced visit, she cleared away all bottles, cleansed the house of any sign of degeneracy, and greeted him as a proper, clean, New England housewife. Suzy's father, Roger, a frequent Gilmanton visitor, watched with amusement.

Nevertheless, the end of 1961—the year Grandmère DeRepentigny died—brought Grace very bad tax news.

When *Peyton Place* first appeared in 1956, Bernard Snierson had devised a tax structure for Grace: She would live on $18,000 a year and invest the rest of her earnings in order to spread the tax burden. But in 1958, when Grace's taxes were audited, Snierson and her tax attorney, Burton Williams of Boston, discovered she had not abided by her agreement: She had drawn advances from Messner's. At that point, Snierson and Williams made their first negotiations and adjustments with Internal Revenue representatives.

But Grace, it turned out, owed back taxes for 1958—as announced in a December 19, 1961, ruling. According to Internal Revenue, Grace had reported only $3,567 taxable income for 1958—and should have reported $233,116. She had taken out a bank loan and used the money to buy United States Treasury notes, reporting the interest on the notes as income and the interest paid on the loan as a deduction. But such an arrangement, not uncommon for high tax bracket people, was not allowed in her case. The government said she owed $163,400, plus 6 percent interest, in additional taxes.

As 1961 ended, Grace had yet another problem: Jacques Chambrun still pestered her, though she had dismissed him in March. She had trouble saying no to Chambrun, and wrote Ollie Swan on December 11 to thank him for talking her out of "what could have been a rather chaotic situation for me. To my sorrow, Svengali does not give up as easily as all that. My telephone has given me the jitters to the point where I don't even answer it anymore."

She added that she'd "spent most of my time in bed since my return to New Hampshire"—apparently a case of depression.

Swan tried to handle Chambrun for her and get her ready for her next obligations. The Dell paperback edition of *The Tight White Collar* was scheduled for sale January 16, 1962, and Dell began making publicity arrangements: a six-minute appearance on "CBS Calendar"; three radio shows; at least one newspaper interview; the Mike Wallace show; and a "very short" autographing party at Woolworth's. (Grace especially dreaded autographing parties.)

Knowing Grace's feelings about public appearances, and aware of her tendency to escape or disappear, Swan wrote her on January 16, enclosing six copies of *The Tight White Collar* and asking her to contact Phyllis Bellows at Dell, "as she has gone to considerable pains to make various dates for you, and it would be very awkward if you did not turn up."

Grace wrote that she and George would be arriving January 21, and "We have to come down on Sunday, since I will not fly on the matchbox which Northeast Airlines camouflages as an airplane, and we will, therefore, be driving."

They stayed at the Plaza where, in the Edwardian Room, Don Fine sat with Grace. She had a case of nerves before a television appearance, and could not eat. George tried to get Grace upstairs to rest (and not drink). Grace told George to take himself upstairs and rest.

The publishers also had an unhappy dinner for Grace in the Edwardian Room. Some negative comments were made about *Peyton Place,* and Grace was both insulted and tearful. She drank but did not eat, and after a while felt too queasy to stay at the table. She seemed in rocky emotional shape, Don Fine thought— and he doubted she could do much more writing.

Still, Dell had reason for celebration. By January 19, three days after publication, the first paperback printing of *The Tight White Collar* (800,000 copies) had sold out. Dell went back to press for another 200,000. It was the fastest-selling paperback on the market, and Dell expected to sell two million copies. (Eventually they sold 2,152,343—but *Peyton Place* sold over nine million in paperback, and *Return to Peyton Place* nearly four and a half million.)

Though Grace was gratified by *The Tight White Collar* sales, she also had a sense of failure. Again, she hadn't topped *Peyton Place*—and doubted she ever could.

Still, would-be writers respected her achievements. They sent manuscripts they wanted her to evaluate, and offered stories they wanted to tell: about immigrant experiences in America, about a blind man who used to drive a taxi. They wrote Grace that they knew she could use their material better than they could.

Many writers consider such letters "nuisances," and toss them out—but Grace, herself a former struggling author who wrote for seventeen years with virtually no encouragement, felt dutybound to answer. She wrote a gracious response herself, or passed the letters along to Oliver Swan, asking him to be kind to the authors.

While in New York for *The Tight White Collar* appearances, Grace gave Swan two chapters for a new *Peyton Place* book, together with an outline. It would settle Allison's future, she said—and make her creator some much-needed money.

The two chapters begin with Grace's characteristic description of the season—in this case, November, "the most hateful month of all—frozen, naked and barren." Grace recapitulates the major events of *Peyton Place* and *Return to Peyton Place,* then shows Allison, still recovering from Lewis Jackman's death, hurrying along Elm Street, past the lounging men at Tuttle's Grocery Store.

"As an outline maker I am a good brick layer," Grace wrote Swan with her outline on January 25. "I am putting this down as if it were a letter to you.

"What I am going to try to do in this book is to tie up all the loose ends left hanging in RETURN. So here goes.

"1 & 2. You already have.

"3. Selena Cross is going to find herself at last in marriage with Peter Drake, the attorney who defended her at her trial in PP.

"4. In RETURN Jennifer Carter murdered her mother-in-law, Roberta. In this book she is going to get her comeuppance, but good. I think I'll have her go off her rocker, but in a sort of underplayed way. What I mean by that is that Ted, her husband, is going to contribute to her downfall, in a very nice, mean, quiet, vicious way and that in so doing, he will wreck himself.

"5. Here we are going to have Allison meet a big, fat heel by the name of Philip Eldershaw. That is not his real name. He is really a shanty Irishman from the wrong side of the Boston tracks by the name of Patrick O'Neill. Allison will meet this charming rat in New York and decide to fall madly in love with him. This takes a while.

"6. Joey Cross, Selena's brother, is now seventeen years old and in this chapter he is going to discover girls. Not that he didn't know about them already, but this time it is going to be one particular girl by the name of Eileen Ferguson. At first this will go over with Selena like a lead balloon, but everything turns out fine because—Selena and Peter have a baby. A son whom I shall call Michael Joseph Drake.

"8. Allison finally discovers that Philip is no good at all. This naturally will take some doing because it is going to be painful as hell.

"9. Allison goes to Europe, where she meets a slew of charming men who, fortunately, happen to be her foreign publishers. I think I'll keep this more or less clean because what I want Allison to have here is a sort of spiritual rebirth or something of that ilk.

"10. In RETURN Betty Anderson was left pretty much up in the air. Here we are going to tell about her life with her father-in-law and her son, Rodney, Jr.

"11. Ted Carter's father, Harmon Carter, was also left at a loose end. In this chapter I'll tell about his life as a widower.

"12. Meanwhile back in the big city, David Noyes, Allison's ever faithful friend, waits. Here I'll tell about what's he's been up to lately, and of his relationship with Allison when she returns from Europe.

"13. Betty Anderson is going to meet a fellow Swede by the name of Karl Gustafson, but she is going to decide that another involvement is not for her.

"14. Stephanie Wallace, Allison's best friend, who was also left nowhere in RETURN. In this chapter she is going to finally become a sort of middling success in NY television.

"15. Allison goes home to Peyton Place.

"16. And at long, long, long last Allison is finally going to settle down and marry the ever present David. AND THEY ALL LIVED HAPPILY EVER AFTER."

Right after this plot outline—which clearly left no room for another sequel, as if its author knew she could do no more—Grace added a note of self-doubt. "Ollie, I know it doesn't sound like much written out this way, but you'll just have to trust me. It's going to sound a lot better when it is complete. Also, please don't be misled by the above chapter numbers. For every heading I've given you, there will probably be two or more chapters. When the book is finished, I figure it will run to about 350 pages. As usual, Grace."

Grace never wrote a third *Peyton Place* book. Instead, she suddenly turned to her more "creative work": an entirely different novel called *No Adam in Eden*.

She had been "mulling" over *No Adam in Eden* for years. Long before *Peyton Place* she had told Marc about a novel that would start with a man who spent a long time dying. (*No Adam* begins: "It took Armand Bergeron a long, long time to die and even then there was no dignity to his dying.") In August 1957 Maurice Zolotow reported in *Cosmopolitan* that "Mrs. Metalious has already mentally sketched out her third novel. It revolves around three generations of frigid women." To other reporters, Grace said she planned a novel about French-Canadian women.

No Adam would cover the autobiographical material she had begun for *The Tight White Collar,* and finally rejected; it would make points Kitty Messner had eliminated from the original *Peyton Place* manuscript. In *No Adam,* put together after both her grandmothers had died, Grace would portray bits of their lives, her mother's, her sister's, and her own—and settle some very old scores.

Grace had attempted her family's story at least once before—but from an outsider's point of view. In the trunk with her *Peyton Place* manuscripts and the sketches leading up to *The Tight White Collar,* she left one page, numbered "5," at the top. It begins with the word "happiness," the last word of a sentence from the previous page. The rest of the page, which connects with no other remaining fragment, concerns fathers, family love, ethnicity, Manchester, and her own families—all the subjects of *No Adam in Eden.*

happiness. Everyone there seemed to love my father. He could imitate any dialect or accent. The huge, blond Poles used to howl with amusement when he spoke, and the small, dark-skinned Greeks would smile for him. The Canucks punched him gently in the stomach and swore at him lovingly, and there was an Irishman who offered him whiskey every payday. I remember so clearly the feeling of love which surrounded us, so that I felt we were all like a family, with everybody belonging to each other. Then, within six months, I met two families who did not belong in Manchester. The first was the family of a man named John Royer, and the second was the family of a Frenchman named Jean Jacques de Repentigny.

I must rely on a faulty memory, on old snapshots and on overheard, half remembered conversations to tell you about the Royers. If I had been older when I first knew them, I would have written down their story then, but I was young and all that remains now are fragments and the essence of what they were.

Only *No Adam in Eden* remains to capture the essence of the DeRepentigny and Royer families—and in 1980 Alfred DeRepentigny, Grace's father, called *No Adam* their family story.

No Adam progressed very swiftly in the beginning. By March 7, 1962, Ollie Swan had received the first 102 pages—not mentioned in any previous correspondence. Grace promised to have the entire book done by April 1. It would run close to 400 pages, she said, "unless I can do one hell of a lot of pruning and still feel a little bit satisfied with the end result."

After that, she planned to work on the third Peyton Place book. "Barring any unforeseen complications such as the house burning down or getting hit by a truck, I think I can promise you a new PP book by December 1 of this year."

She was writing *No Adam in Eden* to express herself about her family; she planned the Peyton Place book for money—a major concern, after George had gone through "the income tax bloodbath" the previous year. She had to have $65,000 for taxes and motel work by April 15, she told Swan, and "after that I need $12,000 a year to buy groceries and other doodads." She asked Swan to see what he could get from Kitty Messner.

On April 10 Swan passed along a royalty check for $13,625.06 from Messner's—while Kitty began actively seeking more profitable arrangements for Grace and herself. Kitty, an astute businesswoman, asked why Dell, paperback publishers of Grace's first three books, should necessarily put out *No Adam in Eden*—if someone else would pay more for the paperback rights.

Paperback money often greatly influences a book's fate. When a book is to appear in hardcover, the author gets an advance first, then royalties later if the book makes a profit (only about a quarter of books published even earn back their advances). If the book is sold to a paperback house, however, the author gets 50 percent of the sale price and the hardback publisher gets 50 percent—so Kitty Messner had considerable business incentive. In 1962, moreover, auctions for paperback rights were not at all common, but Kitty began an auction for *No Adam in Eden,* with Philip Wittenberg handling the bids.

Kitty knew business, but she also knew Grace and her insecurities. Hence, her response to Grace's new manuscript involved feelings first, business later.

"I'm afraid you don't love me any more," Kitty wrote Grace on March 15. "But I love you and Ollie Swan, and I think the writing in 'No Adam' is some of the best you've ever done. And you've got that magic story-telling touch. I *have* some questions about the organization of the story—I think the theme has to emerge early-on, a little more obviously, but as long as the Muse stays with you, I wouldn't interrupt now."

Geoffrey Piper, representing Frederick Muller, Ltd., Grace's British publisher, also had doubts about *No Adam*. He thought the manuscript needed tightening, and wanted an outline—which Swan told him he had not succeeded in getting. Swan also planned to speak with Grace's lawyer "about restraining her indiscretions" with finances.

Meanwhile, Grace's progress had slowed considerably. Her own April 1 deadline passed, and then May 1.

"I have very little time to make like a lady author," Grace wrote Swan on May 1, and cited domestic troubles: Marsha had been ill, so Marsha, Eddie, and their new baby, Billy (born April 3, 1962), were staying with Grace.

Moreover, Grace felt extremely discouraged by reactions to *No Adam*.

"Maybe I should junk the whole thing and start over," she wrote, "because Kitty, too, seems to be unable to wait to begin writing the thing over even before she has seen the completed work." It seemed everyone in New York disliked *No Adam,* she told Swan. "If this is the case, perhaps I've been in the wrong business all along and better just make up my mind to start making beds up at the motel."

On the same day, she sent even more of a cry for help to Henry Klinger, the Twentieth Century-Fox representative in New York. Klinger had wanted to see the new manuscript, and she told him that being a grandmother had preoccupied her. Further, "You must not take it personally that this letter lacks a certain warmth. I just feel mildly suicidal today."

Perhaps Jerry Wald heard from Klinger—for he suddenly wrote to Grace on May 2 and May 14. He said he hadn't come up with a way to adapt *The Tight White Collar* for the screen, but he still wanted to see her new book. He congratulated Grace on owning a motel and being a grandmother, sent love to her family, and mentioned in passing that he'd just had an operation on his spine.

Though Grace claimed to despise Wald, she felt very flattered by his letters—which, as it turned out, were the last she ever received from him.

"The world was a race to Sammy," Budd Schulberg had written in *What Makes Sammy Run?* Sammy, whose career closely resembled Jerry Wald's, "was running against time"—and Jerry Wald's time ran out on July 13, 1962. He had ulcers and a spinal growth, but had refused to slow down; he had been in ill health for a year, with several operations; and his third heart attack in three days killed him. He was forty-nine years old.

CHAPTER 23

Putting together *No Adam in Eden* took Grace much longer than she expected it would, although her writing went well over the summer of 1962. Richard Stinson, Marsha, Eddie, Mike, Suzy, Cindy, and George were all occupied at the motel, originally called The Little Cape Codders. They renovated the cabins that were the motel's special feature—and then Grace and George decided to add a unique gimmick. They renamed it "The Peyton Place Motel"— thereby scaring away virtually all family trade. But it took a while before that business gaffe became apparent.

During the summer Grace tried to ignore constant letters and calls from publishers' representatives and movie people. When a New York public relations firm wanted her to appear at an East Fifty-fifth Street nightclub called Peyton Place ("dark enough to recreate some of the scenes from Grace Metalious' memorable opus"), Grace declined the invitation. While Swan prepared documents for the Italian obscenity trial of *The Tight White Collar,* Grace spent her mornings writing.

"She used to glue her ass to the chair," remembers Richard Stinson, who often visited Grace that summer. Her drinking seemed under control; instead, she chain-smoked her recessed-filter Parliaments.

Stinson had painted the house once and done construction work, and now worked at The Peyton Place Motel, but he never felt contented in Laconia. Grace encouraged him to leave New Hampshire, and wrote a recommending letter to hotel owners she knew in Florida. (Later Stinson did go to Florida and then to New York City, where he opened his own business.)

That summer Grace shared much of her life with Stinson, just turned twenty-one. When important people called, she'd gesture to him to listen on the extension—and they'd both giggle as "the bigwigs came begging for favors," he remembers. He used to sit on the big green couch in the living room, Grace across from him, and they'd philosophize about "growing-up stuff." Grace had beautiful hands, gestured while she talked, and always seemed interested in what Stinson was saying. He considered her a "jazzy figure," and was delighted the day he could explain a poem to her.

Outside, on the lawn, Grace sometimes discussed the *No Adam in Eden* characters with Stinson. As with *Peyton Place,* she lived the book: preoccupied with the characters, involved with their lives and thoughts. In the evenings she had Stinson read her manuscript back to her, and she'd mark corrections and changes on the yellow sheets.

He did one thing that infuriated her: he constantly mispronounced "Etienne," the name of the character who represents Grace's father in *No Adam.* Enraged, she'd have Stinson repeat the passage until he got it right. "You're interrupting my concentration!" she'd holler.

Despite his companionship and encouragement, *No Adam* proceeded very slowly. Though Grace seemed to be drinking less, her health was not good—and she often kept a heating pad on her stomach. Seated on the couch, she'd sometimes sit up and breathe suddenly, as if in pain.

She did go to see Dr. Leonard Slovack—but for research purposes only, she said. ("Her typical roundabout way," he calls it.) She wanted to know about the symptoms of cirrhosis of the liver, and undetectable ways to do away with people, and whether a baby could bleed to death after circumcision—details she planned to work into *No Adam,* her most morbid book. (She abandoned the circumcision motif.)

Her persistent questions about cirrhosis made Slovack suspicious. "Why don't you just hop on the table and I'll examine you?" he suggested more than once, trying to appear as casual as possible. But Grace continually refused, saying she was only doing research. Her interest in cirrhosis was purely a novelist's.

Grace stayed in her own secluded world, rarely keeping track of current events. Astronaut John Glenn had orbited the earth in February; President John F. Kennedy talked, in March, about sending combat troops to Vietnam; and the Supreme Court, in June, banned public school prayers. Helen Gurley Brown's *Sex and the Single Girl* appeared in May, and Brown shocked readers with her suggestion that the single woman might have a full sex life—and probably ought to. Brown's book was compared to *Peyton Place*—which had paved the way for it—and *Sex and the Single Girl* became an instant best seller.

Grace did notice, on August 5, the death of Marilyn Monroe, the actress Mike had most wanted to meet on the Metalious/Martin jaunt to Hollywood. Monroe, breaking under the pressures of fame and the belief that her work would never be taken seriously, had committed suicide quickly—an overdose of sleeping pills.

Grace Metalious, as Bernie Snierson and others noticed, was committing suicide more slowly, with alcohol.

On August 9 she wrote Ollie Swan that the completed *No Adam in Eden* would be in his hands by October 1. Instead, she followed an erratic timetable: 269 pages on October 22; pages 270 through 314 on December 5, with apologies that "George has been sick as a dog with some kind of bug that has his stomach sounding like Mount Vesuvius." Then she began to send pieces:

January 23—pages 315 through 342
February 1—pages 343 through 374
February 19—pages 375 through 404
mid-March—pages 405–423
mid-April—pages 424–429

The ending still needed work, but for the first time Kitty Messner would not be doing the editing. Kitty had bowed out of the picture.

Though Kitty's contract with Grace had expired after *The Tight White Collar,* Kitty had always assured Grace that she would publish Grace's work. On February 15, 1963, however, Oliver Swan received a letter from Pocket Books: "We have bought from Kitty Messner the contract with Grace Metalious." Grace's next novel,

No Adam in Eden, would be published by Trident, a new Simon & Schuster imprint that included hardback and paperback books. (Pocket Books, Simon & Schuster's paperback arm, would control Trident.)

The actual reasons for the shift were never entirely clear. Grace did get more money. Oliver Swan sold *No Adam* to Pocket Books for $50,000 in the morning, then in the afternoon sold the film rights to Twentieth Century-Fox for $150,000 ($10,000 on signing, $70,000 on January 15, 1964, and a final $70,000 on January 15, 1965—which Grace did not live to receive). It was Swan's single most profitable day as an agent—but money was not the sole factor in the publishers' shift.

Patricia Gallagher, at work on another novel in Texas, heard that Kitty Messner actually rejected *No Adam in Eden*—that it did not meet her literary standards. (Perhaps, too, Kitty objected to its antifeminism.) Helen Meyer recalls that Dell also rejected the book, feeling it was not very good.

By the beginning of 1963 Grace was, in Stinson's words, "in and out of reality," with the paranoia that often accompanies alcoholism. Her drinking caused dissension and violence in the household, and only outsiders found it interesting—or even bearable—to watch.

Stinson once nursed her through what appeared to be D.T.'s—then caught her sneaking drinks two days later. Mike and Cindy poured her liquor down the sink—but she hid it in out-of-the-way places, including her box of sanitary napkins. George tried to restrict her to beer, and got her into a New York "drying-out" hospital—but she escaped with her Irish nurse, fled to the Plaza, and called Marc. He got them all tickets to see Brendan Behan's *The Hostage*—which Behan himself, a rambunctious alcoholic, would sometimes interrupt from the audience, making chaos of his own play. Then George came and took Grace home.

In New Hampshire, Bernard Snierson got Grace to go to a psychiatrist, but she went unwillingly, and for only a few sessions. After the last one, she told Snierson, "Boy, has that guy got problems."

At home Grace liked to listen to records as she slowly sipped drinks. "She had records no one else did," Laurie Wilkens remembers. Grace had party records and peculiar novelties, but also loved all kinds of music, especially Joan Sutherland and Judy Garland (who lived until 1969, but was long troubled by self-doubts, drugs, alcohol, and the demands of fame).

"Give me Judy! Judy! Judy!" Grace would call as she poured herself another drink or held her glass to her forehead. Then, over Judy Garland's voice, her half-joyous, half-miserable monologue would continue.

"Down, down, down, ah—relax, Judy, relax. Mix me another, sweetie, I need it. I love people, don't you. I love people. I trust them. Go, George, go out and bring the whole wide world in—make them our guests—welcome them—turn the record player on louder—let's be merry—let's live, live, live!"

The charming earthiness Wendy Wilkens and other young people loved was slipping away—replaced by a strange, prima donna air that frightened them.

"Shit! Who cares about the phone bill?" Grace would shout if George mentioned their expenses. "I made it, didn't I? I wanna call those nice kids in Texas, and up your ass if I don't. Shut up about the phone bill. So what the Christ is two hundred dollars? Haven't I got it? Don't buck me, by Jesus, or I'll call China or any other goddamned place in the world. How's my stuff doing in England, George? Oh, shit, anyhow, turn on my record while I get my cigarettes. Lemme hear Judy."

Grace also made strange, and often unwelcome, visits. One night at 11:30, she arrived at the home of John O'Shea, owner of O'Shea's Department Store—uninvited, with a "weird total stranger," O'Shea recalls. The stranger stuttered and stammered until Grace announced that he was her friend, who'd been drinking with her at the Tavern. She wanted a nightcap.

Not wanting her to awaken his children, O'Shea refused—but made coffee for Grace, while her strange friend immediately fell asleep. Finally, Grace's driver, whom she kept on call, came to get her and the stranger.

Without her driver, Grace still found people to take care of her needs. Red Blunden, a taxi driver, remembers being in a hotel room on his wedding night when Grace came knocking at the door, needing a ride home. Blunden complied—but his wife never forgave Grace.

Late at night, Grace's miseries would take over: loneliness, fears for the future, regrets for the past. Then she turned to the telephone.

When she wanted to be amused, she would call George Cantin. "I was her court jester," he recalls, and he'd ask her slyly, "Are you wearing your Bette Davis scuffies?" Grace would laugh, gratefully.

She also called T.J. while he still lived in Laconia, though he had married Betty Haenschen. Restaurants would tip him off if they had reservations for Grace—so T.J. could cancel his own reservations and avoid a scene. Still, Grace sometimes called late at night: "I'm sorry for everything . . . I wish you all the luck in the world . . . I'm going to send you a platinum Rolls Royce . . . come and help me . . ."

She even called T.J. in New Haven, where he had moved in 1962 to work at WAVZ. "He was a soft-spoken man," remembers Kelly Blakeslee Rogers, then a New Haven youngster. "He was very kind and tolerant of what I now realize was a shrill and awful trio of kids," she says of herself and her two friends who used to hound T.J. at promotional appearances: a drugstore auction; the grand opening of a drive-in with roller-skating waitresses.

Grace called—hounded—T.J. twice in New Haven, at 3 A.M. She said, "I always did love you . . . Is there anything I can do? . . . Do you need anything?"

T.J. said no, he was fine. He and Betty had one son and another child was on the way. Eventually, Grace hung up.

She also called Bob Athearn, who had, during the war, introduced her to Wanda Landowska's record of Bach's "Goldberg Variations." He had moved out to Seattle, and once Grace called him in the middle of the night (2:30 A.M. his time, 5:30, hers). He knew she was in "an obviously inebriated condition and very tearful"—with the Landowska "Goldberg Variations" playing in the background.

She wanted Bob to repeat what he'd said about the recording "in the old days"—something he could barely do, after nearly twenty years, and in his somnolent state. She sounded "very depressed," he remembers, "mad at the world, lonely, cursing, saying that all the money she had couldn't buy her the love she needed." She wanted him to move back to New Hampshire—but by the time he returned to the East, she was dead.

Through late 1962 and early 1963, Grace worked fitfully on *No Adam in Eden,* as her schedule shows—yet disliked admitting her lack of progress. When she wrote Richard Stinson in January (her letter dated "January something or other, 1963"), she said, "Yes, the frigin' book is done"—though she still had nearly a hundred pages to go.

Stinson had gone to Florida, and wrote frequently. Grace's letter, addressed to "Dear Boozin'-Buddy," began with an apology for not writing sooner, but "things have been rather nuttier than usual around Nutsville."

George Jarvin had died the week before Thanksgiving, she wrote, "and I had rather a time of it with Evvie. First there was all the mess with the County Coroner, the Gilford Gestapo" and Jarvin's family, the funeral, and Evvie's going into the hospital.

Grace, meanwhile, had gone to New York with her book, "and on the way home I stopped in Manchester where I discovered one of my big fat aunts (the one who took care of Mémère before Mémère died) was well on her way to the booby hatch. I found her sitting alone in her house with Mémère's picture in front of her, bawling her head off." She added a footnote: Mémère was "my grandmother in case you've forgotten."

Another "big fat aunt" came to take care of the first, but the rest of the holidays were punctuated with short visits, long quarrels, injuries, and auto accidents—"while George sat in the dining room and played chess with himself. You heard me. With himself."

"All in all," Grace told Stinson, "I was damned good and glad to see 1962 over and done with"—though the New Year did not begin so auspiciously. New Year's Day had passed quickly, "which is a hell of a lucky thing since I had a hangover on which you could have climbed Mt. Everest." Then another friend had a hysterectomy "and Goddamn near croaked"—after which the friend's child got pneumonia. "Oh, shit."

As for Grace herself, she hit a telephone pole on the way home from New York, "that pimple in the ass hole of progress." She also smashed her finger in the catch of her suitcase, and "the finger now has a lump in it and looks rather leprous." That would be her excuse for "this lousy typing," she said—but her typing, as usual, was quite accurate.

Stinson's bosses in Florida, the Ruttgers family, had known Grace when she was Mrs. Martin—and they apparently inquired about T.J., for Grace added a suggestion for Stinson: "If the Ruttgers are still looking for Shit-Head, why don't you squeal and tell them that he is in New Haven working for station WAVZ? Or was, at any rate."

Come for a visit, she told Stinson: "We all miss you. Love, Grace." Grace felt very comfortable with Stinson—but with fewer and fewer other people.

Meanwhile, *No Adam in Eden* still had to be finished. Herbert Alexander of Pocket Books had assigned the book to a top editor: Bucklin Moon, then fifty-two and a novelist himself.

Moon, a white Southerner very troubled by Southern racism, had published two non-fiction books about race: *Primer for White Folks* (1945) and *The High Cost of Prejudice* (1947); in 1943 he attacked racism in a novel, *The Darker Brother,* about a black youth who goes North to a series of disillusionments. But Moon won his greatest praise for *Without Magnolias* (1949), a novel about a Southern black college, its students, faculty, and neighbors, and the color barriers they all faced. *Without Magnolias* won the George Washington Carver Award for "contributions to Negro life."

No Adam in Eden involved ethnicity, a subject of obvious interest to Buck Moon; he was also no stranger to the kind of condemnation Grace Metalious had received. His writings against white racism brought him the hatred of white Southerners who considered him a traitor, and in 1953 he had also been an apparent victim of McCarthyism—fired from *Collier's* magazine after a circular letter to *Collier's* advertisers called him "subversive."

The letter charged Moon with Communist front activities, and pointed out that one of his novels had been favorably reviewed in *The Daily Worker,* the American Communist Party newspaper.

Moon denied the guilt by association, found another job, and remarked that "this is a terrifying business that can happen to anybody." That terrifying business, the harassment by association, was all part, he discovered, of Grace Metalious' life.

Buck Moon was fairly tall, with a ruddy complexion and perpetually unruly black hair. He was "no Chambrun" in his clothes, according to Ken McCormick of Doubleday—and that helped gain Grace's trust. Stinson thought him "well-bred," and his only problem as an editor was a severe stammer which sometimes made conversations difficult.

Like Kitty Messner, Moon found Grace a troublesome author, particularly with the ending for *No Adam in Eden.* Grace had been sending smaller and smaller pieces, the mid-March one only eighteen pages, and Ollie Swan sent her gently chiding notes.

Buck Moon had trekked to Gilmanton once before, on a getting-to-know-you trip. He'd planned to stay a week, but left after five days: he and Grace got along so well that she was getting no work done. He thought she might do better on her own.

Over the next weeks he and Grace did a lot of telephoning. She needed more money (a lien had been placed on her house in August 1962); he said he couldn't get her any unless she finished *No Adam.* "When I asked how it was coming," Moon recalls, "she went into a crying fit and told me she couldn't. She said I should come up and help her. I said I couldn't." Finally, Herbert Alexander, Moon's boss at Pocket Books, said he'd better go. Moon was dispatched to Gilmanton in mid-March.

Grace had had trouble completing *The Tight White Collar,* and Helen Meyer remembers a rumor that someone else actually finished it for her (accounting, perhaps, for the sudden happy ending to a very grim book). With *No Adam,* Stinson recalls that Grace wrote and destroyed three different endings—and finally completed the manuscript in a room in the Laconia Tavern Hotel. Buck Moon was there—and so was June O'Shea, wife of the owner of O'Shea's Department Store.

June had long wanted to write a book, and that spring, 1963, John O'Shea called Grace to ask if she would help. June and John had just returned from a New York buying trip, and they had three youngsters—John, Jr., Tom, and Sally—close in age to the Metalious children.

"Of course, anything I can do," Grace said. She never forgot John O'Shea's giving her credit during her years of terrible poverty, and she tried to return his loyalty whenever she could.

June, who had just spent several months in a hospital, wanted to write about her experiences. She thought Grace could criticize her work, and teach her about writing. Knowing that solitude is a writer's greatest need, Grace offered June one of the cabins ("Little Cape Codders") at the motel, and June accepted with gratitude.

By the time Bucklin Moon visited New Hampshire, June had been spending considerable time in the cabin assigned to her—and sometimes did not come home for two, three, even four days. Occasionally she visited Grace in Gilmanton, and recalls that when she wanted to—or felt she had to—Grace could write very fast. Inspiration came quickly, in bursts; she was not a structured writer.

Grace rarely talked about her own writing, although she sometimes mentioned some real people she might draw on for characters. Overall, she seemed to have few writing plans. Nor did she say much about June's writing beyond, "You're a great writer, sweetie—you've got it." But she seemed to say it more out of need for company than from a genuine feeling for June's work.

And June O'Shea's presence at the Little Cape Codders ultimately began to bother Grace. June was very attractive, tall, and fair; like Grace, she had only a high school education. When she married John O'Shea, a Dartmouth graduate, she worked very hard at being the proper wife of one of Laconia's most prosperous and respected businessmen. But the role of perfect wife and mother left her lonely and unhappy, though still beautiful.

Grace Metalious was also lonely and unhappy. Grace, who had felt insecure about T.J. and accused him of pursuing other women, began to suspect that George was attracted to someone else. Nevertheless, George was with Grace through the last stages of *No Adam in Eden*.

"After three or four days of trying anything and everything I was ready to give up," Bucklin Moon says of his second trip to Gilmanton. Grace had shared all her fears—including Jacques

Chambrun's threat (she said) that he would pay to have her killed by voodoo or vampires if she didn't hire him back. She also told Moon that Chambrun was calling her almost every night to tell her Moon was a terrible editor.

Moon's main problem, however, was getting Grace to finish *No Adam*. "Then one day she gave me the answer," he recalled in 1980. She told him that she dreamed the ending of *No Adam* every night—"And after she woke up it was still so clear she could recite it like poetry, though later when she tried to write it down she couldn't."

Did she know a good typist? Moon asked. Someone she could trust not to tell anyone what they were going to do?

Yes, Grace said.

"Then bring them with you to my hotel room at 9:30 tomorrow morning."

By noon the next day they had the ending—though Grace kept saying she could not go on, and taking another Canadian Club and 7-Up to keep her going.

June O'Shea had been the typist, and the ending—pages 424 through 429—is not typed on Grace's regular typewriter. The pages include punctuation and paragraphing mistakes Grace never made, and for years rumors circulated that Buck Moon himself had finished the book, probably with Grace's acquiescence. Herbert Alexander never asked the details of Moon's trip to Laconia— nor did Merle Miller, who interviewed Moon some months after Grace's death. Pat Gallagher heard that Grace had someone else finish her last book because she no longer cared. But Moon himself denies the rumors.

"The words are hers and not mine," Moon said in 1980. "I worked them over as any good editor would do, but that is all I did, and chiefly because I wanted them to sound written rather than spoken.

"There have been better endings, I am sure," he added—and in 1963 he felt the ending needed something. The day after Moon returned to New York, March 28, Oliver Swan wrote Grace that Trident would want "fleshing out of the ending." She did nothing with it, and a month later Swan wrote again that Moon still felt the ending needed work. "I told him last Thursday," Swan wrote on April 24, "I was afraid you had given up on this, although I sincerely hoped you'd come up with something."

The pages Buck Moon brought back to New York had ended the book very abruptly: Angelique's demand for an abortion; her giving birth to a baby boy who bleeds to death; a confrontation between Angelique and her daughter Alana, and then Alana's sister Lesley; and finally Lesley's happy life with her husband, Gino.

But the published version includes five more pages between the confrontation and the final happy scene (which still comes too swiftly, out of the chaos and cruelty of most of the book). The five pages sketch out more of Alana's character (clearly based on Grace's sister Bunny), describe Lesley (Grace's) last meeting with their father, soon killed in World War II; and show Alana's crying over her lost life and three failed marriages.

Whoever wrote the new five pages knew something of Bunny's life and Grace's. Lesley has the sparkling enthusiasm Laurie Wilkens and her children loved in Grace: looking into cream swirling in a glass of iced coffee, Lesley exclaims, "Isn't that the loveliest thing you ever saw in your whole life?" Alana (Bunny) considers her older sister Lesley a "nut," a "drag," and a "real pain in the ass"; Alana seems much wiser in the ways of the world, and exchanges foul-mouthed insults with their mother, Angelique (Laurette). In a peculiar reference to Bunny's history, Alana's husbands even have the same ethnic backgrounds: Bunny's Roy, Farrell, and Brouillette translate into Alana's Turcotte, O'Brien, and Paquin—French, Irish, French.

Though the added five pages make the ending slightly smoother, Geoffrey Piper was still unhappy with the conclusion. Piper, one of the directors at Frederick Muller, Ltd., oversaw the British editions of Grace's works, and sometimes made changes for British audiences. He wrote Swan on August 29, 1963—a month before the American edition of *No Adam* appeared—that the first part had some of Grace's best writing, but the denouement simply did not hang together. After Lesley's marriage to Gino (George), he noted, virtually nothing is said about Angelique, her mother. He wanted more about Angelique, and her justifiable disillusionment and bitterness.

No new ending was forthcoming from Grace—whose thorough lack of sympathy with Angelique contributes to making *No Adam* "a spite book directed against her family," in George's words. Bucklin Moon also felt Grace "had it in" for her mother and sister. Still, Grace's overwhelming guilt about Bunny and Laurette made finishing her spiteful portraits that much harder.

Once she'd brought forth the last pages of *No Adam,* Grace was desperately unhappy. Writers find finishing any book painful—much like postpartum depression—but Grace's dissatisfaction with the ending, George wrote later, "served as an excuse for another series of bouts with her favorite sparring partner—Canadian Club. But, by then, if she hadn't had that for an excuse, she would have found some other reason. The most feeble alibis and the wildest rationalizations for her drinking grew more and more frequent."

Grace and George's relationship continued to deteriorate, and Grace hesitated about the dedication in *No Adam in Eden.* What she sent on May 22 turned out to be, like all her dedications, somewhat ironic.

THIS BOOK IS FOR THE PEOPLE WHO HAVE GIVEN ME MORE
HAPPINESS THAN ANYONE ELSE IN THE WORLD:

My husband, *George Metalious*
and my children,
Marsha and Edward Dupuis
Christopher "Mike" Metalious
Cynthia "Cindy" Metalious
Suzanne "Suzy" Roy
and the frosting on the cake,
my grandson,
William Edward "Billy" Dupuis

She needed more money, Grace wrote to Ollie Swan when she sent the dedication, and offered to do publicity during a visit to Canada. She gave him her number at The Peyton Place Motel, where she'd be working most of the time—though the name had backfired. Families stayed away, and business never picked up.

The motel also attracted disasters—including a motorcyclist who crashed into a corner building, killing himself. George had to wash away the remains—and began to think about changing occupations.

The motel's precarious financial state made Grace and George even more cross with each other, and he could do nothing about her drinking. Early in the day she would talk, but by 5:30 had consumed so many highballs that she was "not there." By the evening she had reached a stupor; in bed she was "not there." George often asked himself—and Grace—"Who wants to fuck a drunk?"

Grace, meanwhile, was full of self-pity. Once at 8 A.M. she called the O'Sheas, telling them she desperately needed a bottle of "C.C." When they arrived, she had her sofa turned into the wall like a crib and was crying, "Help me—help me—don't leave me—I'm scared." A few drinks restored her spirits slightly, but she cried about Laurette and Bunny, that they'd never really communicated with each other. She also cried about George.

The motel failed as the marriage failed again. Over the summer, George decided to take a job as guidance counselor in Ludlow, Vermont.

By the time *No Adam in Eden* appeared—on September 24, 1963, exactly seven years after the publication of *Peyton Place*—George was living in Ludlow. Cindy and Mike still lived with Grace, although Mike soon moved in with Marsha, Eddie, and their baby. *No Adam's* jacket copy conforms to the feminine mystique, and is thoroughly false: Grace "still lives, simply and happily, in rural New Hampshire with her husband and her children."

Grace had few friends left to comfort her when the *No Adam in Eden* reviews appeared—the worst notices she'd ever received.

Editors obviously no longer considered Grace Metalious a major author. *Peyton Place, Return to Peyton Place,* and *The Tight White Collar* all had prominent reviews in the New York *Times Book Review,* the barometer of literary importance. *No Adam* was also reviewed in the Sunday *Times,* but back on page 40—in a compendium review by Martin Levin, with the title "A Reader's Report." Grace's novel got only a paragraph; the rest of the space went to four relatively unknown writers.

Levin found nothing to recommend in *No Adam in Eden,* a book that he said "begins in one bed and ends in another," and

shows that "Man lives not by bed alone." He summarized the plot
—several generations of transplanted French Canadians "who
have terrible trouble with their women"—and had no sympathy
even for Armand Bergeron, the father-figure whose impending
death gives the beginning of *No Adam in Eden* its aura of doom.

To Levin, Armand Bergeron seemed "a chuckle-headed baker
. . . pushed into an early cirrhosis by the banshee he has
lucklessly married." As for Lesley, the only woman who "escapes
the family taint," Levin was unimpressed by her success in "winding up happily in the arms of a kindly truck driver."

Levin did capture exactly the atmosphere of the book, revealed
in "nervous flashbacks," the Bergerons pouring out their "unedited sorrows at the top of their lungs." But these excitable characters, he concluded, "are too single-minded to stir even the uncrit-
ical reader."

Time and *Newsweek* dismissed *No Adam in Eden* with sar-
casm. "Grace Metalious has done it again! Yes, fans, the sensational author of 'Peyton Place' has run another one through her
typewriter, just the way you like it . . . But you'd better hurry.
The author's supply of talent is strictly limited" (*Newsweek*).
Time questioned Grace's motives in creating a cast of such evil
characters: "She traces the roots of their wretchedness to a neighborhood of Quebec that could have been invented only by a writer
eager to fix Canada's wagon for banning *Peyton Place*. Her point
seems to be that frigidity leads to murder and murder leads to
sloth, drunkenness and terrible profanity."

Two other reviewers, though, gave some attention to the
strengths of the book, and its author. *No Adam's* characters are
"one-dimensional. The men are lustful but weak, the women evil
and domineering," and the style cliché-ridden, Miriam Yivisaker
wrote in the *Library Journal*—but added that the psychological
motivations are credible, and Grace's "story moves well, with 'the
fascination of the abomination' from page one to end."

Female reviewers, like Yivisaker, had frequently been fairer to
Grace in the past, and sometimes more perceptive. But a male
reviewer got to the heart of what makes *No Adam in Eden* a painful book. "Does Metalious Hate Women?" was Allan Keller's

headline in the October 1 New York *World-Telegram*—and Keller considered *No Adam* a betrayal of Grace's talent.

He called it "a very bad novel" from a writer "capable of turning out much better fiction," but who had been "going downhill all the time." Keller, editor of the *World-Telegram*'s "The Bookshelf," said he had liked *Peyton Place:* the people had seemed "living, breathing inhabitants of a small New England town." But not so the *No Adam in Eden* characters, especially the women— "venomous and callous as the queen bee, which leaves the male drone dead after their nuptial flight."

The problem, he concluded, was Grace's attitude toward her own sex. "It would seem that the writer hates women, individually and en masse. If she had anything kind or understanding to say about them, I confess to having forgotten what it was, so weighted down are all the female characters under a load of sin, lechery, selfishness and cruelty."

Not knowing Grace's family history, Keller could not account for her writing a misogynist novel—but Grace had been leading up to it all her life, from her early rearing in an all-female household.

"Grace liked some women," George Metalious said in 1978, "but overall, less than men." She liked Evvie Jarvin, Laurie Wilkens, and Kitty Messner, "but felt women were less honest—even though men took her in, and did her in."

Unable to blame the men in her life—and a patriarchal society— for many of the limitations placed on a woman who wanted to be a serious writer, Grace blamed herself. She blamed Laurette and Bunny; in *No Adam,* she blamed her grandmothers; and eventually blamed women generally for what they, and men, had become.

Grace had claimed during the long writing of *The Tight White Collar* that it would be a story of "man's inhumanity to man"— and it is. But *No Adam in Eden* is a painful story of women's inhumanity to women—as if experience had taught Grace that warm friendships between women, the kind she showed in *Peyton Place,* were not really possible in an imperfect world.

While Grace worked on *No Adam in Eden,* Kitty Messner had been concerned about the possibility of libel; before publication, Ollie Swan finally wrote Geoffrey Piper not to worry about it.

Nevertheless, *No Adam* cannibalizes the lives of Grace's grand-mothers, mother, and sister—and even the names sometimes betray their origins, as in "de Montigny" for "DeRepentigny." But Grace was not simply transcribing her family history. She had some points to make.

No Adam in Eden gives a grim picture of oppression, in three generations of women. Monique (Grandmother Royer's equivalent, though some twenty years younger) grows up in a tenement and goes to work in the mills at fourteen. She marries an ex-soldier from Quebec who rapes her on their wedding night, then neglects her—and drinks himself to death. Their daughter, Angelique (representing Laurette), tries to assimilate in Livingstone, New Hampshire (Manchester), but is still considered "Canuck pussy." She marries another Franco-American who mistreats and rapes her repeatedly—then enlists secretly in the service, and is killed in the Pacific. Their younger daughter Alana has three unsuccessful marriages and drinks too much; the older daughter, Lesley, finds happiness only through downward mobility (marrying a truck driver), having three babies in three years, and living thoroughly for others, without a will of her own.

The story shows the horrors of mill work, as Grace's grand-mothers knew them in the spinning room—where the floors under Monique are always shaking, and she has to scream to be heard. Most French-Canadian workers are trapped forever in the mills, but Monique, both lucky and ambitious, escapes before the Depression closes the mills and destroys the economic base of Livingstone.

Her daughter Angelique's story shows the power of ethnic prejudice. Angelique, who speaks perfect English, grows up in the Manchester Grace knew: "Deer Park" (Derryfield Park), St. George Church, even the Pilgrim Ice Cream Parlor (the Puritan Restaurant, where George Metalious first asked "Slats" DeRepentigny for a date). Angelique meets her dates at Bridge and Ash streets, where Grace lived as a child.

But neither Angelique's going to public school, her intelligence, nor her good looks can overcome prejudice against French-Canadians—and her WASP boyfriend refuses even to introduce her to his parents. In her Franco-American husband, Angelique finds another man who cannot accept her as she is—and wants to change an imaginative girl into a conventional wife, mother, and domestic servant. Angelique turns to lovers who appreciate her more—though mostly for her body.

Grace might have created sympathy for Monique and Angelique, mistreated by their husbands, but instead she blames the victims. In *Peyton Place,* Grace showed Lucas Cross' beating of his wife as vicious; in *No Adam in Eden,* she presents wife abuse as if it is justified.

Grace portrays Monique's strengths as vices. Her drive to escape is presented as manipulation; her saving money for her independence, as stinginess; her love of cleanliness, as fanaticism. Similarly, Angelique's dreams of escape appear as schemes; her self-protection, as hostility; her desire not to be used, as frigidity. Though Angelique is the most vital character in the book, Grace directs the reader's sympathies away from her—and toward her father, Armand, and her daughter, Lesley.

If Monique and Angelique are blamed, Armand is idealized. (Grace never knew John Royer, his real-life counterpart.) No love is lost between Armand and Monique, his wife: after raping her on their first night together, he never again touches her. When she turns to housework as the only outlet for her energies, he torments her with his slovenly ways, and takes an equally slovenly mistress. Nevertheless, Monique's coldness is blamed for destroying Armand's loving nature and driving him to drink. He dies of cirrhosis when Angelique is twelve.

She, meanwhile, idolizes her father as her knight, her prince— the terms both Grace DeRepentigny and Allison MacKenzie used for their absent fathers. *No Adam's* Angelique, however, never gets over thinking of Armand as the central man in her life: even as her husband takes her virginity on their wedding night, she cries, "Papa!" The father-love that was rather wholesome—and finally abandoned—in *Peyton Place* becomes, in *No Adam,* an obsession bordering on incest.

Even when her baby boy bleeds to death because of a corrupt doctor and negligent nurse, Angelique scarcely cares. As early as grammar school, Grace had been writing about her imaginary brother, based on Laurette's baby boy who died. When she wrote

No Adam in Eden, Grace had decided who was at fault: the mother.

The portrait of women in *No Adam* is not thoroughly negative —or, at least, it is not intended to be. Alana, at first, is an ally and friend to her sister, Lesley—who is the only woman with love to give. Lesley, meanwhile, escapes the family taint—coldness (or independence, looked at negatively)—but her section of the book is the flattest, most hurried. It reads as if Grace wanted to show romantic love, but did not truly believe in its possibility.

Lesley de Montigny, a small, round-faced, dreamy child who resembles Grace DeRepentigny, has an indulgent grandmother in Monique (who, however, becomes senile). Lesley finds a loving husband in Gino—big, dark, handsome, protective. In their idyllic marriage, they disagree about only one thing: her refusal to deny anything to her mother and sister. Gino makes a perfect husband, fulfilling the fantasy of the perfect man even better than Tom Makris/Mike Rossi did in *Peyton Place.* Lesley makes the perfect wife and mother: they want "dozens of babies"; and they live the fifties dream—perfect kitchen, perfect house, perfect children.

Their life together strikes the most false note in the book. Lesley and Gino's lives lack room for conflict or growth—and their conversations seem pointless, even silly. The other characters' cries of rage and pain have much more vitality, and seem far more real: like Grace, they are rebelling against confinement.

But the feminist vision that informed *Peyton Place*—showing women's independence, creativity, and community—is gone. In *No Adam* Grace could have analyzed women's powerlessness: how their having to act only through men corrupts both sexes; how women's lack of power can lead to avarice, frigidity, and murder. She might have shown Monique and Angelique as mother and daughter allies, both victimized by prejudice and patriarchy, drawing together to nurture one another—as Allison, Selena, and Connie do in *Peyton Place.* Selena manages to transcend poverty, desertion, rape, and violence—with Connie and Allison's unfailing support.

Instead, in *No Adam in Eden* Grace created cruel, competitive women, as if rejecting any feminine "softness" or sensitivity in herself. What Grace most wants to escape in *No Adam* is womanhood, including her own. In fact, the character who best represents Grace is not really Lesley—but Armand.

Like Grace, Armand wants only beauty, but finds ugliness—and turns to the bottle. If he stops drinking, his liver will regenerate itself—but he cannot. Though Dr. Southworth—the last of Grace's crusty, kind-hearted doctors—tells him that his cirrhosis comes from too much liquor and too little food, Armand cannot cure himself. Meanwhile, his wife, Monique, tells her family that Armand has cancer—which she seems to think is less shameful. (In the last months of her life, Grace told her son, Mike, that she had incurable cancer.)

But Armand and Grace both suffer from cirrhosis, with the same symptoms: blue, snaky-looking veins on a swollen abdomen; a hobnailed liver, like an old boot. Externally, they share "little spiderlike veins" on the cheeks; a sudden sharp pain on the upper right side; a pounding heart; and extra weight, but "not the kind of fat that comes from overeating. It was soft, bloated . . ."

Like Grace, Armand will not let a doctor examine him—and in an eerie forecast of Grace's own death, he dies in February, his last words warnings: "Be careful!" and "Watch out!"

The bitter message that Grace Metalious had extracted from success and fame—and endless pressure to continue—was that there was no point in dreaming, especially for women. By the time *No Adam in Eden* was published, Grace's money was spent, her career woman editor and her charming French agent had both disappeared from her life, and her husband was irrevocably lost. Her ambitions for serious literary recognition were dead, too, beyond resurrection. In *No Adam in Eden* she suggests that women do not even deserve to dream—for what pleasure had her dreams, finally, given her?

CHAPTER 24

After *No Adam in Eden,* Grace had little money, many debts—and more troubles. She could still manage to pay O'Shea's bills, but took a Polaroid camera on credit from Achber's Photography Studio in Laconia and never paid for it. She dyed her hair a garish henna shade and, Cindy says, became indifferent to her children. Grace had once listened intently to what others said and remembered everything, Laurie Wilkens recalls—but she lost that ability.

She also confessed to reporters that she and George had separated. " 'Peyton Place' Wife Writes Off Husband," the Boston *Record* reported on October 7, 1963. Grace and George's "remarriage" had ended in separation five weeks before, the article said, and George had been hired as a counselor at Black River High School in Ludlow, Vermont. (No one questioned whether they had actually remarried.)

A "Peyton pace of her own," *Newsweek* called it on October 21: Grace's divorcing George, marrying T.J., divorcing him, remarrying George, and "now heading for a third divorce." *Newsweek* quoted Grace on the reason: "My husband told me he was in love with somebody else. Just that." She had also decided to give up writing, she said, and explained, "I don't have anything more to say."

Grace had surrendered her identity as a wife and as a writer. With her children grown and independent the way she'd raised them to be, she had nothing to look forward to. On October 9, Oliver Swan wrote that it was too late to stop stories she didn't want publicized, for both the *Post* and the *Daily News* in New York had carried them. According to the *Post,* Grace had said George "doesn't love me anymore. Three weeks ago my husband told me he was in love with somebody else. He said, 'Goodby, Baby.' . . . I told him I will never hang onto a man who doesn't want to be hung onto.

"If I had to do it over again," she added, "it would be easier to be poor . . . Before I was successful, I was as happy as anyone gets." According to Judy Michaelson in the *Post,* Grace's voice was almost inaudible—and it "might have been a sad scene from one of Grace Metalious' own novels. Explicit, bizarre, poignant."

Swan also reported to Grace what he'd learned from Bucklin Moon: 45,000 copies of *No Adam in Eden* were in bookstores, an increase of 10,000 since publication—but the book was selling "rather slowly." Trident planned some intensive radio spots to stimulate sales (but apparently planned no public appearances for Grace).

Grace had visited Concord, New Hampshire, around the time *No Adam* appeared, and answered questions about her writing. "Livingstone," she said, the name for Manchester in *No Adam,* came about because she wanted "a one-name city for a change." Angelique's name she intended to fit the character: ". . . so rotten. I wanted to give her a sweet name." As for her role: "I consider myself an entertainer, not a writer or author"—but she had decided to "get out of the book business" after *No Adam.* "I couldn't quite quit without doing it. When you've thrown up everything that's inside you, it's time to stop."

What would she do with her time?

"Stay home with the kids and vegetate."

But the world kept coming to her home.

Donald and Elizabeth Athearn, proprietors of the Apple Tree Book Shop on Warren Street in Concord, had been apprehensive about inviting Grace Metalious to an autograph party for *No Adam in Eden.* Though Don's brother Bob had been Grace's friend for more than twenty years, Don had never met Grace until the Sunday afternoon he and Liz drove up to Gilmanton to find out how Grace would handle a public appearance.

They had some trouble finding her house: asked for directions, townspeople said Grace wouldn't want to see anybody. Undaunted, the Athearns finally located Grace's enormous white house—on which, Liz noticed, the paint was peeling.

Grace invited them in, and sat at one end of her long living room—while her mother sat at the other. Laurette, whom Liz remembers as white-haired and rather "housewifely" in appearance, said very little—and all of it to Grace, in French. The Athearns had the impression that she did not speak English—but later thought she might just have preferred private conversation with Grace. The relationship between mother and daughter seemed antagonistic.

Grace made drinks for the Athearns and played them her favorite record, Allan Sherman's "Hello Muddah, Hello Fadduh"—a kid's comical letters home from camp. Grace found the record hilarious and played it over and over; everyone else grew very tired of it.

Don and Liz hadn't known that Grace had a drinking problem, but they did know she "swore like a trooper"—and that had made them hesitate about an autograph party in conservative Concord. At first they felt relieved at her quiet demeanor—until, annoyed by a blaring television set down the hall, Grace yelled to her children, "Shut the fuckin' door!"

Then Grace realized it was Bob Athearn's birthday, September 8, as well as her own (he was fifty, and she thirty-nine), and decided to call him. She marched over to the phone, picked it up, and ordered the operator, "Get me Bob Athearn in Seattle, Washington."

The operator complied somehow—despite Grace's not deigning to provide a number—and soon Bob, just back from playing the organ at church, was on the line. She insisted he come back East; he told her why he couldn't. That was their last conversation.

Then Grace talked about her troubles. She needed much more money to keep up her house, she said, and the responsibility weighed on her. She still had less-than-cordial relations with townspeople, and reported that not long after *Peyton Place* came out, her well had gone dry—and no one would sell her water.

She also thought aloud about her death: that she planned to

give her body to a medical school, and wanted no funeral. Grace seemed extremely lonely, the Athearns felt—and morbid.

Grace did agree to an autograph party for *No Adam,* which Liz and Don advertised in the Concord *Monitor:* "Angelique was small, blonde, passionate—and as capable of emotional love as a broad-hooded cobra. She learned sexual blackmail at her mother's knee. Before she was through she bit off more of the apple than any woman since Eve. $4.95." Though Liz and Don liked Grace as she was, with her lack of pretense, they still worried about her language. Would she keep it clean for the autograph party?

She came well-dressed, in a print jumper that made her look slimmer. In pictures from the party, she wears her hair pulled back, with her glasses perched atop her head; her face looks puffy. She autographed Liz and Don's *No Adam in Eden* first: "To Liz and Don Athearn—in fond memory of times gone by and in hope of better ones to come. Love, Grace Metalious."

"I can't say that I ever get invited into their homes," she told one book buyer who asked about her Gilmanton neighbors. "But then, I'm not sure I'd care to go." Asked about censorship, she called it "a leaky, horrible sore on the body of all America. I'm extremely interested in what must go on in the minds of those people who can set themselves up as censors. Where do they go to read the books they censor? What kinds of thoughts must they have?"

Grace said little more about her own thoughts, beyond her plan to stop writing. She was quiet and gracious—and afterward, with relief, Liz, Don, and Liz's mother took Grace out to dinner.

There they suddenly understood what made Grace so bitter about neighbors and censors.

After a relaxed Highway Hotel dinner (which Grace drank but did not eat), they all went into the lounge—and two different groups of college-age young people recognized Grace. Both groups began, spontaneously, a series of loud, obnoxious, and crude remarks.

Grace, Liz remembers, was "kind of far gone" and didn't seem to notice—but Liz, enraged, said a few choice things to Grace's critics. Then she bundled Grace out of the lounge, and she and Don drove Grace back to Gilmanton.

Grace visited the Apple Tree Book Shop a few times after that, once with her new companion—a big Britisher the Athearns later learned was John Rees. On another expedition Grace charged several books, including *Gone with the Wind*. After Grace left, Liz—preoccupied, but even more struck by Grace's loneliness—found in her own handwriting, on Grace's book list, "Lonely the Wind."

Grace never seemed happy or enthusiastic to Oliver Swan, either. As her agent, he grew used to her calls for money: advances of $50,000, or whatever he could negotiate. As far as he knew during the early winter of 1963, her main worries were about money. She wrote him on December 12 that The Peyton Place Motel had failed, leaving her with enormous debts. Despite deals with her creditors, she would have to find $26,967 by January 2 to satisfy them. She also worried about future income taxes, since she had not managed to sell the motel.

"My present estimate," she wrote Swan, "is that by July of 1964, I will be obtaining material for a novel on bankrupt authors!

"Rather than do this, I am willing to earn money! Would you suggest to me ways that this can be done. Despite everything, I could write another book, but as of December 12, 1963, I feel that a contract and all the worry that that involves would be impossible for me. Is there a magazine market which could be met from Gilmanton, is there a newspaper market for Gilmanton gossip? Ollie, this is with you. I've outlined the problem, now please make some magic and try and give me some advice that I will be able to follow!"

If they needed to discuss possibilities, she added, she wanted to do it quickly, before Christmas, and in New York. "I don't want to discuss this on the phone, as it could only worry the children."

Grace's desire for Ollie Swan to help her, with "magic," the request she'd made of so many men in her life, could not be satisfied. Swan wrote back that he would try to get money for her, but added, "I'm frankly dubious as to whether we could get any substantial money from a magazine or newspaper dealing with 'Gilmanton gossip,' nor do I honestly think you ought to get involved in such a project."

Grace's next letter, on December 21, showed her even more

worried. She was glad, she said, that Pocket Books and Trident might offer her a contract, as her creditors had "been fed promises for a long time." But for now, she said, "I must think of another way of organizing things—who knows what 1964 will bring?"

Her mental state shows in the letter's form. Normally an excellent speller and typist, she has three mistakes: "I'me," "Unfortunatly," and "Decmeber." The letter was typed by John Rees, the last man in her life, who often wrote "I'me"—but a more alert Grace would have corrected the errors.

Grace had two more letters from Swan and one from Henry Klinger; then, on December 28, she wrote Swan with bad news.

"You will remember that some time ago, in your office, I left a synopsis of the first hundred or so pages of a book you wanted to call 'Allison MacKenzie of Peyton Place.' (I still think with horror of seeing that title on the shelves of any bookseller.)"

In any case, she wrote, her house had been broken into while she was away. "Apart from liquor, books, etc., the only other material stolen appears to be this manuscript.

"What use this can be to anyone I do not know, however, I thought you should be told, perhaps someone is going to make a collection of my unpublished works!"

As usual, Grace put what concerned her most in a postscript: "Because I identify the writing as 'AMOPP' does not mean that I have changed my mind . . . I still think that I can do better."

The robbery had motivated her to hire guards—and when Frank Roberts, her insurance man, came from Manchester to investigate the claim, two six-foot bodyguards refused to let him in. Finally, he got into the house by mentioning his wife Barbara—the Barbara Roberts who'd directed Grace, Marc, and Jay in their little theater group more than twenty years before.

"Frank, why didn't you say who you were?" Grace said, greeting him as an old friend.

She had obviously been drinking all day, Frank Roberts noticed, but was "not fussy about what she did with the beer cans." She was gracious and delighted to see someone from the old days —though she could provide almost no information about the robbery, and apparently did not remember what she had kept in the house.

Oliver Swan wrote on December 31 that he was sorry Grace had been robbed—but puzzled by her mention of the last manuscript. He remembered receiving, in January 1962, the first two chapters of an untitled novel and an outline, both of which had gone to Kitty Messner. But "I have no recollection as to having seen the synopsis and/or approximately 100 pages of the manuscript tentatively entitled ALLISON MACKENZIE OF PEYTON PLACE. Are you sure that this material wasn't submitted to either Messner, Twentieth Century-Fox, or Chambrun?"

Grace may have been confused. In any case, Swan never saw ALLISON MACKENZIE OF PEYTON PLACE. His letter of puzzlement is his last in the Paul Reynolds Collection at Columbia University. Grace's letter of December 28, with her P.S. that "I still think I can do better," is her last.

Her life was changing rapidly, and Swan was one of many people unaware of those changes.

Once she and George separated again, Grace was alone with two children, and then one, in the big house in Gilmanton. Grace curled up in her little corner on the sofa by the fireplace, and few people came to see her. With her drinking, her pervasive depression, and her demands, she was no longer fun. Her needs were too great.

"Grace sat on a couch, legs drawn up, dark glasses pushed up to the top of her head, brown hair fixed in a ponytail," John Rees recalled a year later, in *Cosmopolitan*. "She wore a yellow muumuu, and without saying a word, she filled the room with the tension produced by tightly reined rage."

Rees went to see the author of *Peyton Place* on October 7 with Ernie Crowley, a Manchester television personality. Though Grace had become reclusive, she considered Ernie and his wife close and loyal friends. Whenever Grace published a new book, Ernie interviewed her; the Crowleys had attended Marsha's wedding; and Grace had invited them to the world premiere of *Return to Peyton Place* in Laconia.

Grace was furious about a British article on *No Adam in Eden* —and Crowley brought her the means to answer it. John Rees, a stocky, bearded journalist then living in Boston, wanted to do a profile on Grace for the Boston *Daily Mirror*. He'd already done a piece about her for a London newspaper and had worked for the Manchester *Free Press*—and he'd been trying since June to get an interview with the author of *Peyton Place*. John Rees had a lively wit, a good memory for details, and a British accent; he'd been in the United States less than a year.

John Rees and Ernie Crowley arrived in Gilmanton during Indian summer, and when they entered the house, "I did not see Grace at first," Rees wrote later. "What I did see was chaos. In a large paneled room there were hundreds of books, magazines, and newspapers, the remains of several meals, unwashed glasses and an unbelievable confusion of classical and popular records. The background music at that moment was *The Music Man*"—and Grace sat on the couch, enraged.

While Crowley fixed drinks, Grace showed Rees the offensive newspaper article—and then they talked about his interview. If he doubted anything, she would call relatives and friends to verify it. Crowley somehow left the scene, and Grace Metalious and John Rees "talked till dawn, with Grace as much interested in my background as I was in hers."

John Rees had an unusual career: an Englishman (born in South End, Essex, July 22, 1926), he was a graduate of the University of Bristol, where he studied economics. He'd been a news editor for the *Ghana Graphic* and a construction company administrator. He shared his past; Grace shared her desperate unhappiness.

That summer, after George left, she'd lost the will to work. "I felt that I had been fighting something or someone all my life," she told John. "This summer I just gave up. I had been beaten so many times that it seemed impossible that I could ever be happy again."

She said she felt "disenchanted with life."

John, who had been staying with a Massachusetts woman, began visiting Grace whenever he could, once or twice a week. To his admittedly untrained eye, she seemed in good health, "but excitable," and she drank more than she should. "A more knowledgeable person would have considered her an alcoholic," he said in 1980.

But in 1963, not knowing that alcoholism is a progressive disease, John thought that keeping Grace busy would stop her from drinking. When she used a heating pad on her stomach, she said she had menstrual cramps. It did not occur to Rees that she might have cirrhosis of the liver.

"I've never been so happy in my life," Grace told Laurie Wilkens. John soon became her lover; by December he was living in the Gilmanton house with her, and she'd made him her manager. George, she told John, had lacked a sense of humor and would not protect her—two things she needed in a man. Rees was, of course, the physical type she had always preferred—but not, in his own estimation, especially qualified to be a business manager.

"To expect me to manage monetary affairs is like getting a fool to manage a town's activities," he said in 1980, "but I tried." He settled court orders against her for non-payment of bills, including a Bergdorf Goodman bill dating back to the party years with T.J. He wrote business letters for her and tried to organize her finances, and "she seemed impressed by that." He tried to keep her from drinking, and protect her from the greedy people who constantly hovered around her. Even Grace, generous to a fault, told him that too many people were trying to get money from her.

Without anyone's management, however amateurish, she had fallen into some peculiar schemes before. She'd managed to resist a famous entertainer's sister who urged her to invest in fallout shelters—but another strange plan, based on her genuine hatred for racism, involved giving the old farm behind her house to the National Association for the Advancement of Colored People as a refuge for Southern blacks. (The plan was definitely not an NAACP idea.) Somehow this plan was to educate local residents —but Grace finally became convinced that there were other, more practical things she could do.

Not long before Rees entered her life, she had become involved in another impractical, murky scheme—this one involving illegal aliens working as house painters in Laconia. Charles Rothenberg, her New York attorney, had to fly to New Hampshire to extricate her from that situation. (Rothenberg also had a Regent Hospital bill for $391.21 which Grace never paid, despite many reminders from Oliver Swan.)

Because he kept others away from Grace, John Rees made enemies in the Gilmanton-Laconia area. Townspeople regarded his influence as sinister, in part because of his appearance: husky build; large, black-framed glasses; big black beard. When Grace went to see Dr. Slovack, not long after John moved into her house, John began to follow her into Slovack's private office. "No, you're not related," Slovack said, and sent Rees to the waiting room—where Rees glowered fiercely, Slovack recalls. Similarly, Norman Weeks, a local businessman, barely missed a car collision with John Rees—who treated him to a volley of less-than-polite language.

Rees's frequent telephone calls from the booth near the Gilmanton Corners grocery store led to many theories: that he checked in every day with the Mafia or the Cosa Nostra or both. (After Grace's death, there were speculations that Rees was calling his wife in England.)

"Naturally, I was phoning Radio Moscow to report on the doings in Gilmanton," he said in 1980, but his ironic sense of humor and his British accent did make natives suspicious. What was real, and what was a put-on? Like Grace, John Rees was a storyteller, but in 1980 he also confessed that the phone calls were probably to friends in Boston or Manchester, since the Metalious phone was often out of order.

When Marsha called Grace, John would usually answer. Often he'd say Grace was out, or resting—and Marsha was infuriated by his "interference." Cindy recalls that T.J. always included the children in outings with Grace; she was unhappy that John didn't. John quickly made the same enemies Grace had: people who thought she "held a mirror up to their lives" (in his words), and those he considered "drunkards and exploiters." For them, he said in 1980, "I exercised my sinister personality, and ran the sons-of-bitches off."

Grace's old friend Marc, who had not gotten along with T.J., easily made friends with John Rees. Rees had the "look of a country squire," Marc thought, with riding boots, corduroy jackets, and tweeds. What seemed sinister to Gilmantonians seemed to Marc, an adopted New Yorker, a more interesting, even poetic quality. Esther Peters thought John Rees articulate, with an attractive voice, distinguished-looking in a mysterious way—and charming.

Grace not only trusted John to manage her work, but liked having him as a sounding board for feelings about her family. She obviously did not like her mother, Rees remembers. She called Laurette, whom John had never met, an Anglophile, with an affected pseudo accent—much like Angelique's second stage of drinking in *No Adam in Eden:* "when she became very dignified and British . . . during that phase everybody, including Alana and Lesley, was inferior and beneath her contempt." In that stage, Angelique would become "a true princess in her own eyes, and totally unaware of the smiles and ridicule of her friends or the shame and embarrassment it brought her children."

Like Lesley in *No Adam,* Grace seemed—to John Rees—afraid of her own mother. Grace frequently sent Laurette money, as if paying her to stay away; any discussion of Laurette would send Grace into an "emotional crisis" (much like the crying jags T.J. remembers, when Grace talked about "my mother").

Grace talked little about her father; as for her sister, she complained about Bunny's children and demands. But Grace envied Bunny's freedom, John remembers: "her working-class attitudes toward life, her iconoclastic style." Bunny's relationships with men were simple, while in all relationships Grace was "always very conscious that everyone was looking at her with dollar signs in their eyes, a fountain pen in their hand, and her checkbook in hers."

Grace also evaluated—for the last time—other important people in her life. When she mentioned women, she talked lovingly about her grandmothers. She gave John a picture of Grandmother Royer, in which Mémère is smiling impishly and does not look at all like the murderous Monique of *No Adam in Eden.* Grace said Mémère had had a great impact on her—as had Kitty Messner, a strong and not entirely positive influence.

As for men, Grace called Jacques Chambrun a charming thief who cost her a lot of money, "but it was worth it." She had always wanted to go to the Plaza and have violinists summoned to her table to play for her—and Jacques had made it all possible.

She also had good things to say about T. J. Martin—who, she said, took her money but gave a lot in return. He had an effervescent personality, he amused her, "and above all she felt grateful to him," Rees recalls, for "rescuing her" from her marriage. She even laughed about the time T.J. wanted a tan and said he was flying to Florida—but instead went to "live it up" in New York for a few days. Just before returning, he thought he'd better have a tan, so he bought himself a sun lamp—and a bottle of scotch,

He promptly fell asleep under the lamp, woke up with ghastly burns—and called Grace plaintively, "Come and rescue me!" She did, laughing.

Grace seemed "happiest and most vivacious," John says, when they visited her relatives and friends in Manchester. Since she called most of them "aunts" and "uncles," John never really knew who was related and who was not—but Grace was particularly fond of Roger Roy. Roger, Bunny's first husband, also remembers how much Grace enjoyed John Rees's company. Though she'd been desperately depressed before, Grace had obviously found someone who made her very happy—and Roger was glad to see it.

Grace was less happy with her immediate family. Her grandson Billy delighted her, but she felt insecure about her own children. She liked seeing herself as the "benevolent provider" (John Rees's term), but could not always provide what they wanted or needed. As for George, she felt angry and betrayed.

Her insecurity seemed to John her greatest problem, and the root of her financial and emotional troubles. She was not, in his opinion, "a nincompoop who couldn't run her own life," but a sensitive, generous person, "bedeviled by very poor friends, and self-seeking advice."

Their relationship had its insecurities, too: though John thought about marriage, his drawn-out divorce proceedings in England had only begun. Grace never mentioned John's wife and children to Laurie Wilkens—and to John, she hedged about whether she was legally married to George. She still insisted, to

Laurie and others, that she would never marry again—but other people rarely saw her during the fall of 1963.

Grace was "very much the New Hampshire housewife" that fall, according to John. She seemed happier, and eagerly prepared holiday dinners. She reveled in the Indian summer that year, and gave John a description: "Indian summer in Gilmanton is more beautiful than anything else you've ever seen. The hills and woods are a blaze of color, the days are as hot as those in July, but the burning has gone out of the sun. The nights are a deep purple, not black, and they give way to days that are pale gold, not yellow; over everything is a softness of good things remembered."

That fall, as always, her housewifely interests excluded cleaning, for Grace kept her childhood reputation: "she only had to be in a room for five minutes to make it look like a pigsty." John praised her cooking: French-Canadian meals deliciously concocted from meat, potatoes, and onions; English roast beef and Yorkshire pudding; and rigatoni, after her friend Joseph Vinceguerra had taught her the rudiments of Italian cooking.

Nevertheless, Grace did very little writing.

Still an undisciplined author, she refused to fix the seat of her pants to the chair. The thought of never topping *Peyton Place* still frightened her; that fear increased her drinking. John Rees wanted to change that.

The Tight White Collar and *No Adam in Eden* had both come from materials stored up long before, and Grace still had a few unpublished writings. She showed John the first chapter of a book beginning with a character who looks out a window, and sees something in the house across the way. Gradually the watcher ("voyeur") is drawn into the action—after a scene, John recalls, in which the voyeur observes people dining by candlelight. Someone at the dinner turns argumentative, destroying the harmony—and then the voyeur is unable to prevent something terrible from happening. But Rees no longer remembers the details—and the "voyeur materials," one chapter and an outline of the rest, have disappeared.

John tried to encourage Grace in projects, including newspaper serials and short stories, because she seemed unwilling, or unable, to embark on an entire book. When she showed him around New Hampshire, introducing him to people she said were in *Peyton Place* and telling him their subsequent histories, he suggested a nonfiction book about them—but Ollie Swan did not think it a good idea.

Grace had to "be stimulated even to think in terms of a book," Rees recalls—and she resisted any nagging. He encouraged her to tell him stories, and her grandmother's memories seemed to him particularly worth writing. Grace talked about the working conditions and poverty of French-Canadian immigrants to Manchester, and the gradual transformation of some immigrants into middle-class people—who then, sometimes, exploited the workers themselves.

Grace was still very interested in ethnicity, and she and John talked about doing a book on immigrants to New Hampshire from Canada and Great Britain, alongside the growth of mill towns in the nineteenth century. They talked about how the book would be organized and who would do which parts; they also discussed possible television plays—but Grace still had writer's block.

The wet weather in late fall depressed her, and boredom encouraged her to drink—so John planned ventures to Boston, New York, Vermont, and other parts of New Hampshire. While they were away on one trip, Grace's house was broken into—the robbery Frank Roberts came to investigate. On a trip to Concord to renew a driver's license, John and Grace encountered Esther Peters.

They had a few drinks in the Highway Hotel lounge in Concord —where the teenagers had been so hateful after Grace's autograph party. Grace and Esther agreed they'd get together again soon.

That was the last time Esther Peters saw Grace.

John went with Grace to a Manchester autographing party, and pictures show him standing behind Grace, who is signing books. Later newspapers, picking up the sinister tag, wrote, "John Rees hovers over . . ."

Grace and John also toured Manchester. Seeing the mills troubled her, and she thought about her grandmothers. "When I look at the old mill buildings I get a scary feeling," she told Rees. "I look at all those black smoky bricks and every one of them represents a life lost to what we call progress. A life lost to beauty and ruined by ugly things." Then she complained bitterly about "grasping mill owners, corrupt attorneys, and penny-pinching bankers"—the villains in all her books, from *Peyton Place* through *No Adam in Eden*.

Grace and John also trekked to Rye Beach, where she and T.J. had often gone during the party years. During sadder times, she told John, she'd sometimes taken off, driven to Rye, and sat for hours, staring at the sea.

They walked along the beach that winter, with a gale blowing, pretending to dodge waves. They had picnics in the car or went to Lamies Hotel for steamed clams or baked stuffed lobster: Like Marc, John shared Grace's passion for seafood.

"I sometimes felt sorry for Lamies Hotel," Rees recalled later. "It was very smart, the guests were elegant and well behaved. Grace and I would be dressed for the beach (very old hunting shirts, slacks, and boots) and probably were as uncouth as we looked. Thinking back, this is why we were always able to get a hidden corner table . . . But it was next to the huge open fire, the service was good, and the staff tolerant of our idiotic behavior." And unlike T.J., John was tolerant of Grace's "unfeminine" clothes.

Like Allison in *Peyton Place,* Grace felt a particular excitement before Christmas, "when she had a special gift to give to someone, and she felt, too, the particular happiness that comes from sharing something precious with a dear friend."

Grace and John shared New Year's Eve 1963–64 in Gilmanton, and for a party Grace wore her "Batman outfit": toreador pants, black boots, black top, and a black cape covered with decorations. When she entered the party, he remembers, it seemed "as if an extra-terrestrial creature had suddenly reached the place."

In mid-February Grace and John planned a jaunt to Boston, and Grace jubilantly called Roger Roy in Manchester. They'd stop by on their way, she said—but they never appeared. That was Roger's last conversation with Grace.

Before the Boston trip, Marsha also came by to visit. She had not seen Grace for almost a year, and she struggled through a snowy driveway on a cold, gray, windy February morning.

She called upstairs and began to make coffee—while she noticed the liquor bottles, garbage, old newspapers, and dirty dishes piled high everywhere. But the sight of Grace shocked her much more, Marsha recalled in 1978.

Grace wore a tattered and dirty robe and scruffy slippers and walked slowly, shuffling her feet. Her face looked puffy and white; her hair was lank and dirty; and her eyes bloodshot and empty looking. To Marsha she appeared lumpy, bloated, disfigured.

How was the new book coming along? Marsha remembers asking.

Fine, Grace told her, but Marsha says they both knew that was a lie.

After a few minutes of small talk, Grace said Marsha would have to go—Grace would be leaving town for a few days. She helped Marsha with her coat, and hugged her tightly—and as Marsha drove away, she thought she saw tears on her mother's face.

That was the last time Marsha saw her mother.

During high school, Grace had gone to Boston for Gilbert and Sullivan operettas, but as a famous author she'd made New York a home base. Boston, like all large cities, both fascinated and scared her—though she and John had always enjoyed their jaunts there.

They wandered around the North End, and ate in Italian restaurants. On Atlantic Avenue they watched ships loading and unloading; they browsed the Harvard Square bookstores and ate sandwiches in the Wursthaus. Grace shopped in large department stores and sought bargains in the discount houses. Intensely curious, Grace joked about "my nose trouble."

When she visited Roxbury, the black ghetto of Boston, she returned to the Parker House in a rage—about the squalor in which black people were forced to live. She had "a great loathing for social injustice," Rees says. Grace could not understand white attitudes toward blacks—and undoubtedly recalled the millworkers' poverty in Manchester during the Depression.

She also wanted to go to Sunday Mass at St. Anthony's Shrine in Arch Street—where Grace "felt at peace," with "a great longing to return to the Church . . . She never failed to light a candle to St. Anthony, who by miracles could achieve the impossible."

John Rees did not know that Grace Metalious needed the impossible. He noticed that she was overweight (between 150 and 160 pounds), and that she depended on alcohol—but she seemed to be drinking less than when he first met her. He did not know about advanced alcoholism: that long-term drinkers need less to produce intoxication because of advanced degeneration in brain cells (where the alcohol acts) and in the liver (where the alcohol is metabolized). Cirrhosis, the hardening of the liver, prevents proper metabolism.

"We are both full of cold and virus," John wrote Cindy on February 20, 1964, enclosing ten dollars for her. They had promised to get Cindy, thirteen, a Beatle wig in Boston. But they had encountered a bad storm, John said: twelve inches of snow. "Give our love to Laurie and all," he wrote, for Cindy was staying with Laurie Wilkens.

"See you on Monday," Grace wrote on the back of John's note. "So be good, have fun, and I love you." At the bottom of the page she drew a round face with a smile and curly hair—a special face she liked to draw for Cindy.

The next day, Friday, February 21, Grace went shopping, but began feeling very ill. No better on Saturday, she stayed in bed, telling herself, "This is all in my head. I'll be all right tomorrow." She had a phobia about doctors and refused to call one. She and John, who had taken their Parker House suite under the names "Mr. and Mrs. John Metalious Rees," spent the day in the hotel.

By Sunday Grace was hemorrhaging, and John insisted she see the hotel physician—who ordered her to the hospital immediately. Since no ambulance was available, they traveled in the back of a Police Department paddy wagon—where the attendants decided not to use a siren, to avoid upsetting Grace. Even then, Rees recalled later, Grace joked with the attendants.

At Beth Israel Hospital, Grace was gravely ill. On Monday she said she wanted a lawyer, to change her will—something she'd discussed with Bernie Snierson in November, though she'd never signed any papers. John Cremens, a Beacon Hill lawyer who happened to be crossing the street to buy cigarettes, was summoned, told only that a hospital patient wanted a new will made. A hospital visitor, whose name was later variously reported as Herman Knapp or Knaup or Krupp, witnessed the will. He, too, had no idea who was making it. John Rees was out of the room at the time, he said later.

On Tuesday, February 25, Grace told John she was dying. He stayed by her hospital bed, talking very little—but she gave him some wisdom she'd learned from her grandmother: "Darling, be careful of what you want. You may get it"—a comment that applied, clearly, to her own life. She also gave John a prophecy: "Run for your life, sweetie, there's trouble coming!"

That morning at 10:30 A.M., Grace Metalious died.

"She's dead," a doctor told John Rees, very gently.

John, not an emotional person, stepped slowly out of the hospital room. He walked down the hall until he found an out-of-the-way fire exit where he could be alone. There he stood—and cried.

CHAPTER 25

Within hours the news that Grace Metalious, author of *Peyton Place,* had died of "chronic liver disease" flashed all over the world. Even the *Illustrated London News* printed her obituary (as it had the death of President John Fitzgerald Kennedy, three months before).

T. J. Martin, living with his wife, Betty, and their two sons in New Haven, heard about Grace's death on the television news. Betty took the boys out while T.J. called Bernie Snierson, who advised him not to come to the funeral.

Richard Stinson, drafted five months before, heard the news at Fort Dix. Grace had been trying to get him a medical discharge, because he'd had polio as a child, and John Rees later completed the arrangements.

George Metalious, on his way to a Rotary Club luncheon in Vermont with only $7.30 in his pocket, heard the news on the radio. He drove to Gilmanton immediately to be with his children —who learned about Grace's death from the television news.

On Tuesday afternoon, February 25, Grace's will was filed in Belknap County Probate Court in Laconia. The deathbed will she had dictated to John Cremens shocked everyone.

Grace had left her entire estate to John Rees.

"I have purposely omitted to make any provisions in this will for my children, Marsha Dupuis, Christopher Metalious, and Cynthia Metalious," the will said, "as I have full confidence that they will be provided for by John Rees, should the need arise."

She also willed her eyes to the eye bank in Boston, "for the use of some needy individual." She decreed that "no funeral services be held for me, and that my body be given to the Dartmouth School of Medicine for the purpose of experimentation, in the interest of medical science." If Dartmouth did not accept the body, a penned notation said, then it should go to Harvard Medical School.

Since the family claimed the body, it could not be sent to a medical school in time. George, as the presumed husband, gave permission for a post-mortem. But the provision about her children stunned George, and everyone else.

Marsha and George retained John Chandler, Bernie Snierson's law partner, to contest the will on behalf of the children. George, who first claimed a third of the estate as surviving spouse, later announced that he intended to "waive any interest in favor of the children."

Snierson told the Laconia *Evening Citizen* that during the previous November, Grace had reviewed her will, which set up a trust fund for the children until Cindy was twenty-five (which would be in 1975). The will gave George custody of the children. Though she and George were separated, Grace had made no changes when she reviewed the will.

"I could not believe," Snierson said, "that the author who above all had a passionate attachment to her children, particularly the youngest girl, Cindy, would knowingly within hours of her death disinherit her children in favor of a man she had known only a few months."

On Wednesday, February 26, the Metalious children formally contested the will. That evening John Rees held a press conference.

Rees, thirty-seven, wore a black mourning suit—and according to one reporter, "looked really frightened." He told reporters he had met Grace five months before, had acted as her business manager, and was collaborating with her on a novel. He said they were "very close friends," but that the relationship was platonic, with no marriage plans. (He feared that admitting they were lovers might create even more of a legal tangle, but her children claimed they'd heard him propose marriage at least twice.)

According to Rees, described as a "handsome, broad-shouldered Welshman" (his father was Welsh), Grace wrote a new will because she wanted to keep George from having anything to do with her estate. Meanwhile, Rees would be "morally bound," he said, to see that the children "never wanted anything."

What they wanted immediately, however, was a funeral service —and Rees opposed that, as contrary to Grace's will. Attorney John Holland of Manchester represented attorney Cremens of Boston, arguing that the will stipulated no funeral. Because of the litigation, both Harvard and Dartmouth Medical Schools had declined Grace's body, but her eyes did reach the eye bank in Boston.

Since Grace's wishes had not been carried out, the New Hampshire Supreme Court ruled on February 27 that a funeral could be held. The case, known as Holland versus Metalious, is still a legal precedent: that the rights to the body of the deceased belong to the family.

"My funeral would be turned into a sideshow," Grace had predicted, when she wrote that she did not want a funeral—and she was right. Newspaper reporters and photographers jostled each other for pictures of the family; Tom O'Shea, then sixteen, remembers being very upset by their behavior.

Grace's old friend Marc came from New York for the service, held at 2 o'clock on Thursday, February 27, in the Wilkinson-Beane Funeral Home in Laconia. With his beard, Marc was mistaken for John Rees (who did not attend), and one of the mourners berated him.

Some twenty-five people attended the funeral, including Grace's father, Alfred DeRepentigny—although the newspapers reported his name as "Charles." He told his sister, Grace's Aunt Georgie, that she needn't come: Because of the frozen ground in New England in February, Grace would not be buried until spring. Neither Bunny nor Laurette attended the funeral. June O'Shea, whose divorce from John O'Shea would become final in March, had moved to Vermont, and attended the funeral with George.

George, Marsha, Mike, and Cindy had stipulated no flowers, and the only ones were white, red, and pink carnations on the closed, brown oak casket. Reverend John Morrison of the Gilmanton Federated Churches read several psalms, led the group in prayers, and referred to the author only once: "May Grace rest in peace."

After the service, George and the children knelt by the casket, and for the first time in their lives, the children saw their father weep.

Grace's body was taken to a vault in Union Cemetery, to await burial in the spring at Smith Meeting House Cemetery in Gilmanton. Grace had always wanted to be buried there, though the family received about a dozen phone calls from people who did not want "that bitch" to be buried in Gilmanton.

After the funeral—before she went to live with Marsha—Cindy rescued her hutch and a few of Grace's books from the Gilmanton house, including a one-volume edition of Edgar Allan Poe stories. Everything else had to remain until the estate was settled—and most of it Cindy never saw again.

On February 26, three appraisers (Conrad Snow of Gilmanton and Stewart Lamprey and Edwin Chertok of Laconia) estimated Grace's real estate at $25,750 and the total personal estate at $101,622.03. Grace had had $41,174.51 in national banks and $3,366 worth of personal furniture, all itemized—and some of the listings infuriated Marsha.

A broken and unfixable lawn mower was appraised at $35; an unfixable Kelvinator refrigerator-freezer at $50. Of the two hundred books valued at $140, Marsha wrote in the margin of the inventory that many were George's, hers, or Cindy's. The books included the Encyclopaedia Britannica, The Book of Knowledge, the World Scope Encyclopedia, 120 volumes listed as "Digest Monogram Edition," and twenty-three volumes of "Collected Literary Works." A ship model bought for $1.98 and put together by a relative was appraised at $5—and that gave Marsha some bitter amusement. Grace's beloved mink stole, T.J.'s gift from the party years, was appraised at $150. Her Royal electric typewriter, on which she wrote *Return to Peyton Place, The Tight White Collar,* and *No Adam in Eden,* was evaluated at $125.

But the matter of who would be Grace's heir was not yet settled —and newspapers began checking into John Rees's background. The Boston *Record-American* unearthed his work record, including two enlistments in the Royal Air Force, and several reporting jobs in Sydney, Australia. His marital status was listed as "single." The day of Grace's funeral, the Boston *Globe* reported that Grace had never remarried George—but Reuters News Service announced that John Rees had a wife and five children in England.

According to the *Daily Mail,* Mrs. Anthea Rees was waiting for a phone call from her husband, heir to Grace Metalious' fortune, "to tell me all about it." He had left for the United States in February 1963, she said, to get a newspaper job. She knew that he had met Grace Metalious and worked on writing projects with her; John had written his wife nearly every day and phoned every two weeks, she said. They had been married fifteen years, with two girls and three boys ranging in age from four to fourteen.

"This has all been a bit of a shock and is very upsetting for myself and my five children," Mrs. Rees told Ed Corsetti and Al Blackman, two *Record-American* reporters who published her statement on February 29. "I never realized my husband and Mrs. Metalious were such good friends." Rees says, however, that the marriage had ended by mutual consent before he left for the United States.

Blackman and Corsetti also unearthed a run-in between John Rees and local police in Massachusetts, over Rees's driving a friend's car and carrying his international driver's license. John and the police reportedly engaged in an indignant shouting match.

More problematical was the case of Grace's car, her 1963 Buick LeSabre station wagon, left at the New Method Auto Body garage in Somerville. George Thurrott, the owner, knew John Rees and Grace Metalious, he told the *Record-American,* and remembered that his wife, a nurse, had thought Grace Metalious was "a sick woman, that her color was bad." (Though Grace's face was a puffy white the last time Marsha saw her, cirrhosis of the liver can also lead to jaundice, giving the skin a sickly yellow color.)

Rees, who had introduced Grace as my "fiancée," had taken the Buick to Thurrott, to have a dented fender fixed, sometime before Grace's death. Two nights after her death, the car was stolen, then recovered an hour later after it plowed into two parked cars in Somerville. Several teenagers were seen running from the scene.

No one knows what happened to the car after that.

Then, on March 1, John Rees said that he would renounce any claims to Grace Metalious' estate because of his concern for her children. "My only wish is to carry out Grace's feelings in the will," Rees told the Boston *Globe*. "I think the best interest of the children will be served by avoiding a legal fight."

Bernard Snierson added that Rees's action was entirely voluntary, "without any influence on my part. Under this new agreement, nothing will be paid to Rees."

In a document he gave his attorney, Charles Rothenberg, John Rees added directions that he said represented Grace's wishes. The Gilmanton house should not be sold, "but maintained as an available residence for her youngest daughter, Cynthia, as well as the other children should the occasion or necessity arise."

The Wedgwood china and silver should be preserved intact, Rees said; Grace's diamond ring and mink stole should go to Marsha; and her cars to Mike. Rees also promised to assign to the estate for Grace's children "one half of all my earnings in the future from writings relating to my friendship, inspiration, and collaboration with Grace as a testimonial of my respect and affection. This will comprehend any other money that I may earn by the sale of film rights, etc."

Meanwhile, the estate, originally estimated at $1 million, had been appraised at $220,000—but a record of debts was still being compiled.

After John Chandler, Snierson's partner, visited John Rees's apartment overlooking the Charles River in Boston, Rees sent Chandler another list of decisions he'd made, dated April 3. He wanted a "formal renunciation" from George Metalious to any part of the estate; in turn, the estate would make no claims against George or T. J. Martin for "debts, monies improperly spent, etc." Rees added his reasoning: "It is obvious that such claims could lead to a denigration of Grace."

For Mike and Cindy's custody, he wrote that it would be "contrary to Grace's wishes if a Mrs. June O'Shea should become their stepmother, with George Metalious as legal guardian." Rees suggested that alternatives be explored: boarding school, paternal grandmother, Laurie Wilkens. He also wanted to make sure that

Mike had "reasonable pocket money," that Cindy could keep her horse, and that the children would be protected from press publicity.

Rees wanted a formal agreement that he be "the sole person responsible for research for biographical material retained by the family." For publication of any early manuscripts by Grace, he suggested that Oliver Swan or Bucklin Moon be put in charge. He was considering a third *Peyton Place* novel, he added, "one on which Grace and I had done considerable work."

Finally, he apologized to Chandler for the "vexatious content" of his letter, but said he would be "obdurate in insisting that Grace's wishes be carried out."

His tone was rather more angry in a letter to Hugh Mulligan, who had published an Associated Press piece on Grace on April 12. Rees disliked being called the "bearded beneficiary," he said— and even more, "I am weary of the fornicating fortune hunter label which is again implied, more especially when it is implied that a fortune has been given up for base reasons."

Mulligan had quoted Rees's statement about Grace: that she was "the best friend I ever had," and that he was "enormously attracted to her, so much so that I would have given up everything for her, but she said she didn't want to be a three-time loser in matrimony."

However, "Grace Metalious knew that I was married," Rees wrote Mulligan after the article appeared. "She sent presents to my children, inscribed books to my wife, wrote and received letters to them." As for her reasons for leaving him the estate: "I may yet make these public, but my main interest is to make sure that her wishes are not frustrated."

Also in April, Rees tried to sell an article about Grace to George Newnes, Limited, in London. But the managing editor, Eric Grimshaw, wrote Oliver Swan, acting as Rees's agent, that the article did not live up to expectations. Grimshaw wanted more "meaty" content: the inside story of Rees's life with Grace, especially since he left a wife and children in England; a full discussion of Grace's reasons for leaving him her estate; and the true story of Rees's renouncing the estate. Rees refused to write such an article.

Then, when Manchester attorney John Holland, the executor, visited the Gilmanton house on April 20, he found it had been looted. Someone had jimmied open a patio window, said Belknap County Sheriff Rodney Crockett, and pushed in the screen. A silver tea set, valued at $950, was missing, along with silverware worth $500, a movie camera, two rifles, a shotgun, a bicycle, a chain saw, and a few smaller things. The house had been vacant since Grace's death, but after the looting Marsha and Eddie went to stay there.

Meanwhile, negotiations between the Metalious family and John Rees broke down when George refused a formal agreement that Rees have the sole rights to biographical materials concerning Grace. At the Probate Court hearing in Laconia, Dr. Herbert W. Saver testified to Grace's condition when she signed her last will: "clear, coherent, rational and oriented," at 8 P.M. the night of February 24, fourteen hours before she died.

On the morning of that day, however, he had found her condition "that of a dying woman. She was stuporous throughout the examination, and her case history showed profuse hemorrhaging for ten days prior to her death." Two hours after signing the will, she suffered a stomach hemorrhage, then died the next day. Saver added that her cirrhosis of the liver came from drinking a fifth of liquor a day for five years.

On June 30, Probate Court Judge Carroll W. Stafford ruled that the will was valid. John Rees was awarded the entire estate, then estimated at $127,732.

Grace's books were still selling well, although *Peyton Place* (8 million sold in paperback alone) and *Return to Peyton Place* (4 million paperback) far outsold *The Tight White Collar* (2 million) and *No Adam in Eden* (less than a million, though full returns weren't yet in). In New Zealand *No Adam* had been brought before the Indecent Publications Tribunal in Wellington—which ruled on July 17 that it was not indecent and could be circulated in New Zealand. Nevertheless, the Tribunal added the kind of comment that had always hurt Grace: *No Adam* was "a sordid and undistinguished work quite devoid of merit."

In July John Rees, Oliver Swan, and attorneys Cremens and

Holland were still trying to untangle Grace's financial affairs—and finding far more debts than assets. By the time an auction was announced in November 1964, Grace's estate had $211,153 in liabilities (mostly federal income taxes owed) and only $37,690 in assets.

There was no estate for anyone to inherit—although that September the *Peyton Place* television serial began. Grace's name appeared in the TV show's credits for five years, but her estate earned almost nothing. She had sold the television and movie rights outright, for $250,000, all of which she had spent. Twentieth Century-Fox owned "the property," and protests from Oliver Swan brought only another $5,000.

On February 20, 1965, Grace's house and The Peyton Place Motel were auctioned for $140,000 to pay the estate's debts, and on May 9 several hundred people jammed Leavitt Park in Lakeport, near Laconia, for the auctioning of furniture and personal belongings.

The auctioneer was Robert Zanes, from the same family interviewed by the newspapers nearly a decade before, during the media assault on Gilmanton—in pursuit of the author whose spicy novel had cost her husband his job. Gilmantonians bought up what Grace Metalious had left: an electric grandfather clock ($400), a grand piano ($80). As for the things contributing to her fame, Lawrence Luneau, who had already bought Grace's home and motel, paid $135 for her typewriter—with an affidavit that she had used it for her novels. Joseph Stanton of Pawtucket, Rhode Island, bought Grace's old typewriter (the *Peyton Place* one) and the kitchen table and chair she used while writing *Peyton Place,* all for a total of $75.

Only one person bid against Stanton for the prize: the *Peyton Place* manuscript, and pieces of *The Tight White Collar,* on the yellow typed pages stored in Grace's old trunk.

Stanton, his wife, Lorraine, and his brother Gerard had known Grace and Bunny in Manchester some twenty years before, when the Stantons ran the Brass Rail Restaurant on Central Street across from Merrimack Common. Grace used to come in, wearing a reindeer sweater, to have a few quiet beers. Bunny, whom the Stantons called "Boonie," was "the wild one—skinny and mean" and so different from Grace that the Stantons wondered if they were stepsisters.

Joseph Stanton had some ambitions as an entrepreneur: in 1948 he had bought Adolf Hitler's personal limousine and exhibited it around the United States for the next seven years. He hoped to exhibit Grace's possessions—furniture, records, books—at the New York World's Fair, and expected the manuscripts to be his star attraction.

He bought the *Peyton Place* manuscripts for $220—but never exhibited them.

The contents of Grace's Gilmanton house brought a total of $5,450, according to attorney John Holland, the court-appointed administrator of the estate. The money would all go to the Internal Revenue Service to meet taxes.

For more than a year after her death, newspapers and magazines were preoccupied with Grace's financial affairs, her larger-than-life (and self-destructive) doings, and the mysterious British journalist to whom she'd left her entire estate.

"I even shaved off my beard," John Rees told *Cosmopolitan,* "because I became tired of hearing people whisper, 'Hey, that's the guy who got Grace Metalious' money.' But I grew the beard again because I found it's the difference between being petulant or bad tempered. People think you're petulant without a beard; with a beard you're just bad tempered."

Cosmopolitan published Rees's memoirs, "Grace Metalious' Battle with the World" in September 1964—about his memories of Grace's last days. The article includes the "Pandora in Blue Jeans" picture, a shot of Grace's house, and another photo labeled, "High school sweethearts Grace and George"—showing Grace wearing a corsage and squinting into the sun, but the man with her is her high school friend Jay Boivin. Nevertheless, Rees gives a loving portrait of Grace's talents, eccentricities, and hatred of injustice. Though he praises her achievements as housewife and mother, he also presents her as a creative individual whose drive was not appreciated.

Rees himself soon dropped from sight to avoid publicity. He worked in a nursing home, did research on narcotics, and gathered material for a possible third *Peyton Place* book. He kept the rights to Grace's unpublished writings—the letters and scraps that show both her compulsion to write and, after a while, her inability to continue either as a writer or as a woman.

Meanwhile, Grace's other friends and family handled their grief as best they could.

Grace's drinking buddy and "court jester," George Cantin, had lost his driver's license, through various peccadilloes, just before Grace's death. The day she died, he made the rounds of local bars on foot, and "hoisted one" in each, honoring "Gracie" in his own way.

"No one in Gilmanton could believe that Grace had died," Laurie Wilkens wrote in the February 26 Laconia *Evening Citizen,* under the headline "Author's Friend Writes Gilmanton Tribute." People gathered silently around TV sets for the next newscast, Laurie reported; others home for lunch "listened in shocked amazement"—as did men emerging from the snowy woods, for confirmation of "incredible rumors."

Laurie recalled Grace and George's moving to the area, and living at the village home across from the Gilmanton Corners store. Hearing that Grace might have a New York publisher, Laurie had visited "the slender young girl with the flashing brown eyes," who was also "an extraordinary woman of brilliant intellect."

But the pressures of fame had descended upon Grace, "the gifted and sensitive woman for whom life was bigger than reality." Grace had refused to leave Gilmanton, or her house—"and the world did come to her door." In Gilmanton were the people who missed her most, and Laurie spoke for herself when she wrote:

"One would ask nothing more than that she should come in the door once more, electric with discovery, a book or a record clutched in her hand—to hear her say just once more, 'Oh, listen, LISTEN—just listen to this—' and then bring a printed page or a graven record to flaming life in the brilliance of her insight."

One other obituary expressed the sense of tragic waste, and it was written by Grace Metalious for Armand, the character whose slow death of cirrhosis fills the first part of *No Adam in Eden.* Like Armand, Grace died in February, her last words a warning against dangers soon to come.

In *Peyton Place* the female characters are the ones who weep; in Grace's later novels, the male characters are the sensitive ones who cry with the pain of living. In *No Adam in Eden,* Armand Bergeron tells the cynical Doctor Southworth—who resembles Grace's own Dr. Slovack—about his memories of Paris, and waking up beside a loving woman.

"She barely moves as you play with her and she breathes softly, gently against your skin and makes little sounds you can barely hear. But under your lips you can feel her heart beating until it must surely break away from her, and it is then that you know that your greatest pleasure comes not from your own joy spilling into her but in hers coming to you."

And then Armand muses: "Sometimes I wonder where they have all gone—the apple blossoms and the wild strawberries and the little, blue-lighted rooms of the world."

Armand's glass falls to the floor, but the crusty, critical doctor does not hear it break. Listening to his friend's lost dreams, Dr. Benjamin Southworth is quietly crying.

PART V

❀ ❀ ❀

Legacy

CHAPTER 26

Kitty Messner outlived Grace Metalious by only six months. She knew she had breast cancer, and had refused to have an operation. When Kitty died on August 4, 1964, *Time* recalled her greatest coup: in 1955 she "accepted a manuscript that five other publishers had rejected, spent a year editing and toning down its lurid, sex-studded account of small-town U. S. life" and "saw the gamble pay off as Grace Metalious' *Peyton Place*."

The publishing company Kitty founded did not survive her. Julian Messner, Inc. became a division of Simon & Schuster. Doris Flowers, once sales manager for *Peyton Place,* went to work for the Messner division—selling books for children.

Ben Hecht, whose *A Child of the Century* had meant so much to Grace, outlived her by less than two months, dying on April 18, 1964 at the age of seventy. Hal Boyle, who had published the story of the spicy novel that cost a school principal his job, lived until April 2, 1974, when he died of a heart attack at sixty-three. At his funeral Saul Pett, Associated Press special correspondent, called Boyle "the clown, the brooder, the sensitive, defenseless child"—descriptions that applied to Grace Metalious as well.

Even after Grace's death, fan mail came in to Oliver Swan's office. A man in Germany wrote that between World War II and March 1967 (when he was writing), no author "has ever written such a thrilling and overwhelming novel as *Peyton Place.* Your book is the best of the world." He asked for a photograph, and said he hoped to come to the United States some day, "to say personally that you are the greatest."

A man from North Carolina was inspired by Grace, he wrote in July, 1968. "I was trying to satisfy my sex desires by going to a nasty movie that must be a money-making pile of trash trying to catch a fast train to riches with *Peyton Place* as the engineer," he scrawled on motel stationery. Several pages later he explained that he'd seen *Return to Peyton Place* and been inspired to read Grace's books, because of "the beautiful person you have to be." It would take a while to read her novels, he conceded, "because I have never been interested in reading before. In fact I cannot remember reading a book cover to cover before." Nevertheless, he felt he might even want to write a book, and he concluded, "Bearing in mind that as years pass we all change, I hope you're still Allison MacKenzie."

John Rees worked for a while on the book he called *Peyton Place Third,* a sequel to *Return*. He expanded the outline Grace had sent Ollie Swan in January 1963, and included his own touches: more about Selena's marriage to her lawyer, Peter Drake; more about Betty Anderson's romantic involvement with a fellow Swede. For Jennifer Carter, the "rich bitch" who murdered her mother-in-law in *Return,* John Rees specified a particular comeuppance. Jennifer becomes a voyeur, spying on her husband, Ted (Selena's childhood sweetheart), who becomes involved with still another woman.

Ted and his other woman drive out onto a frozen pond, play the radio, drink, make love—and fall asleep. The heater melts the ice, drowning them both—and recapitulating the true story Grace had told Howard Goodkind and Bud Brandt in 1956 when they were first planning to make her famous as the author of *Peyton Place*. In *Peyton Place Third,* there is an inquest—after which Jennifer goes mad.

John Rees also reworks Allison's love life. Grace gave Allison an affair with a "no-good Irish heel"—but Rees makes the heel "of course, a disc jockey, working for a local radio station." In an obvious parallel with Grace and T.J., Allison and her disc jockey have their party years, going to New York and spending money "as if it had just been discovered."

Finally, Allison sees through her Irish rascal, and escapes to Europe—but without returning to the ever-faithful David Noyes, who pursued her through the first two books. Instead, Rees's Allison meets an Englishman, Harry Foxley. They haunt British pubs together; gorge themselves on frog's legs in France; and finally settle "happily ever after" in Allison's "native habitat"—Peyton Place.

For *Peyton Place Third* John Rees incorporated material Grace had been "mulling" for years—notably the illicit lovers who drown in the ice. But he also used his plot-making as Grace used hers in *Peyton Place,* her most optimistic book: as a way of improving upon life. In *Peyton Place Third* Allison and Harry take the trips John had not been able to take with Grace—because time ran out. Allison and Harry enjoy endless people-watching—something Grace and John delighted in doing.

Most of all, Allison never dies.

John Rees never completed *Peyton Place Third*—nor did he write the biography of Grace Metalious he considered doing: He felt too emotionally involved. T. J. Martin says he was offered $10,000 to do a book on Grace—but turned it down. Then, in November 1965, George Metalious and June O'Shea published their version of Grace's life, *The Girl from "Peyton Place."*

June O'Shea, who as a would-be writer had gone to Grace for help, put together *The Girl from "Peyton Place"* in three months, using newspaper and magazine clippings and George Metalious' memories. They signed a contract with Dell on April 14, 1965, for immediate delivery of the manuscript—which Don Fine of Dell farmed out for a quick once-over editing, including deletion of a chapter on John Rees as possibly libelous. George and June's advance was $3,000—twice what Grace had received for *Peyton Place.*

Like the *Peyton Place* paperback, *The Girl from "Peyton Place"* has a yellow-and-black cover, with the front copy in red: "The stark, revealing true story of Grace Metalious, whose private life was as startling as her world-famous novels." The "Pandora in

Blue Jeans" picture appears on the cover—and Pocket Books immediately sued.

In the settlement of Grace's and Kitty's estates, Pocket Books—the paperback arm of Simon & Schuster and new owners of Julian Messner, Inc.—took over rights to the *Peyton Place* books and *The Tight White Collar*. (As original publishers, they already had *No Adam in Eden*.) When the Metalious-O'Shea biography appeared, Pocket Books sued Dell, charging that the new book's cover deliberately confused buyers into thinking *The Girl from "Peyton Place"* was a sequel to *Peyton Place*.

Justice Owen McGivern, of the New York State Supreme Court, was unimpressed.

"This Court feels that there simply must be some limits to the claimed asininity of the paperback reading public," Justice McGivern commented, as reported in the New York *Times* (March 25, 1966). Experts had testified, he added, "that the paperback devotees are a gullible lot, they are 'lip-movers,' 'the lowest common denominators,' 'impulse purchasers,' and their inspection of a book does not extend beyond the cover; they do not even discern authorship.

"This Court does not agree," he concluded.

The Girl from "Peyton Place" sold well to booksellers, but not so well to the public. *Peyton Place's* return from booksellers was only 3.1 percent—a negligible amount that could come from pilferage or bookkeeping errors. *Return to Peyton Place's* was 10.2 percent and *The Tight White Collar's* 7.8 percent—but on the Metalious-O'Shea biography, Dell got back more than a third (38.5 percent) of books sent to stores. *The Girl from "Peyton Place"* did sell 292,568 copies—but that was far below the publisher's expectations.

"Every word in it is true," George Metalious said in 1979 about *The Girl from "Peyton Place"*—but like any biography, it presents an interpretation of the facts. Grace Metalious as pictured in *Girl* is vulnerable, insecure, the victim of a predatory mother and sister. Metalious and O'Shea do not view Grace through the prism of modern feminism: as the victim of a society with too little appreciation for women's ambitions. Metalious and

O'Shea talk a great deal about the pain Grace caused herself, and others—but say much less about her dreams.

The Girl from "Peyton Place" begins with Grace's death, in winter. "She must have died dispirited," Metalious-O'Shea write, "sick at the thought of grasping people who took but never gave . . . The stereotype of those same grasping people and that same realistic life surrounded her as she literally gave up her physical life . . . The evils in her books had by this time truly saturated her being and conquered her at the final ending." Grace, Metalious and O'Shea seem to imply, was killed by the evils in her books—an ending that would have pleased her enemies. But reality has more than two sides.

The Metalious-O'Shea biography does show both sides of Grace and George's early quarrels—with quotations from George's paper for Fred Jervis' "Case Studies" class, and excerpts from Grace's paper answering George's. *The Girl from "Peyton Place"* shows Grace's early love for nature, and her lifelong interest in making up stories. It also records, faithfully, Grace and George's marital ups and downs, and years at the University of New Hampshire—followed by *Peyton Place* and fame, the party years, and Grace's retreat to her home and her bottle.

But *The Girl from "Peyton Place,"* like most coverage of Grace Metalious, says little about her as a writer, except in nineteen pages at the end—mostly quotations from reviewers or the books themselves. According to Metalious-O'Shea, Grace "was abused as a celebrity (who had every right to be her individual self)"—but the book treats her as a celebrity instead of as an individual.

Further, *The Girl from "Peyton Place"* judges Grace as the "ax mouths" of Gilmanton did: as someone who did not fit a conventional woman's role. "She was feminine," Metalious-O'Shea write. "Why did she change her dress from the girlish dirndl to the lumberjack's red shirt?" (Unanswered question.) The authors criticize Grace's sloppiness, her swearing, her attracting male "buddies"; they find her "strident and ostentatious," and ask why, as a wife, "did she kick aside her matrimonial obligations so often?" (Also unanswered.)

Judging Grace as wife and mother, Metalious-O'Shea find her wanting, "a frightened little girl" whose husband, George, and children nevertheless loved her until the end. The biography portrays Grace almost entirely in relation to other people, not as a creative loner. It says little about Grace and George's final separation, and nothing about Grace's last will.

Most of all, *The Girl from "Peyton Place"* leaves out Grace's uniqueness: that despite ax mouths, alcoholism, poverty, exploitation, and constant criticism, she managed to produce four novels, including one of the best-selling books of the century. As Bud Brandt noticed as early as 1956, Grace Metalious had the strength to "hack her way" out of poverty into fame. She did violate conventional norms for women—but she did so because she had the "singular purpose" Jan Williams saw as early as the U.N.H. years.

Grace wanted to "have it all": fame, sexual pleasure, family happiness, creative recognition. She also had messages to convey: about power and powerlessness, sexuality and violence, women and men. But *The Girl from "Peyton Place"* recognizes neither her messages nor her yearnings nor her strength.

In any case, by 1965 *Peyton Place* was no longer known primarily as Grace Metalious' message to the world. *Peyton Place* had become a television property.

As of March 1964, the month after Grace's death, the first *Peyton Place* film had earned $11,000,000—enough reason for Twentieth Century-Fox to begin exercising what Grace had sold to them outright: "exclusive live television rights."

Before his death in 1962, Jerry Wald had "huddled" with Twentieth Century-Fox about a weekly "teleseries" based on *Peyton Place*. Grace would share in the profits, according to *Variety*, but since the series had to be "clean," both Wald and Fox said they doubted she would be doing scripts—because of her "tendency to be risqué." Instead, Fox turned the idea over to Paul Monash, who became executive producer for TV's "Peyton Place."

Monash, a wiry man in his mid-forties with a grin resembling Will Rogers', had published two novels himself some fifteen years before. But like Kitty Messner, who'd herself published a novel more than twenty years before meeting Grace Metalious, Paul Monash saw himself more as a midwife to other writers—or, in his words, an "organizer." He had organized—or created—several long-running shows in the past, including "The Untouchables."

Kitty Messner had loved *Peyton Place,* but Paul Monash loathed it. According to Ira Mothner in *Look* magazine, in fact, Monash had never even read the novel—though he had seen the movie. But Monash himself gave Cecil Smith, Los Angeles *Times* television columnist, another version: "I've read the book. I've seen the film, several times, and I got more from the film. It carried an underlying expression of tenderness and affection that wasn't in the book."

Paul Monash gave Leo E. Litwak a more detailed critique for the New York *Times: Peyton Place,* he said, is "a negativistic attack on the town, written by someone who knew the town well and hated it." To Cecil Smith, he added: "The book is a harsh, unloving document, and we intend to put our stories at a different emotional level."

Like most readers and reviewers of *Peyton Place,* Monash noticed the sex, violence, and pessimism—and ignored the idealism represented by Allison, Norman, and Selena. Still, the *Peyton Place* movies did come closer to what television needed: "an extremely recognizable property" (in Monash's words) that could highlight innocence triumphing over evil, and put characters through soul-searching and terrible traumas before rewarding the good and punishing the wicked. "The general feeling we have of the town," Monash said, "is of people evolving toward the light."

The creators of TV's "Peyton Place" often portrayed Grace Metalious as the dark side of things, her novel "grimly descriptive," according to Monash. His Peyton Place would be "a town of the mind," its streets and buildings white and clean to imitate Camden, Maine. Monash would make his show the first "television novel" (he winced at the term "soap opera"), with a new geography for "Peyton Place": bounded "on the north by Faith, the east by Hope, the west by Charity, and the south by Residuals."

Still, Monash's pilot stuck rather closely to Grace Metalious' work. During the planning stages, TV's "Peyton Place" had been known as "Eden Hill," as if to hide the novel's "prurient connotations," but eventually the name "Peyton Place" was restored, since "presold titles" are considered sound economics in TV. In the "Eden Hill/Peyton Place" hour-long pilot, completed late in 1963 (while Grace Metalious was still alive), most of the book's major characters were introduced.

Mia Farrow played "virginal Allison MacKenzie," who according to the program notes is eighteen, and "a romantic who believes in good and purity and is disturbed by anything contrary to that." Ryan O'Neal, fresh from a failure in a series called *Empire,* played Rodney Harrington, the playboy heir to a mill fortune. Dorothy Malone was Constance MacKenzie, Allison's overprotective mother. As a skeleton crew, they remained unchanged—but other characters underwent peculiar metamorphoses.

Michael Rossi (Grace's Tomas Makris) began as the virile high school principal, and Matthew Swain as the town doctor and conscience—but before "Peyton Place" reached viewers, Rossi had become a doctor and Swain a newspaper editor. (Still the town conscience, Swain intoned an introduction to each episode.) But the Cross family suffered even more from television's requirements.

In the pilot, Lucas Cross appears as a drunken janitor (his job in the movie; Grace created him as a skilled carpenter). Lucas in the pilot has a "sensuous stepdaughter," Selena, and two other children—one played by Stephanie Monash, Paul's daughter (an apparent change in sex, since Grace's Selena had two brothers). The pilot has no rape sequence, although the circumstances are available for later use. ABC grabbed the series immediately; enthusiastic sponsors signed up.

Then Paul Monash was told the Crosses had to go.

"The Crosses represent a jarring element," said Edgar J. Scherick, ABC's vice-president in charge of programming. "Lucas is an unsympathetic character. The Crosses are a detriment to our series. They are the chief representatives of the novel's unsavory aspects."

Paul Monash could hardly deny the unsavoriness of the Crosses, but insisted they were essential to "Peyton Place." "The two things that people remember about the book," he said, "are Allison's illegitimacy and that Lucas Cross raped his stepdaughter." Unconvinced, ABC hired Irna Phillips in April 1964 (two months after Grace's death) as "consultant"—script doctor—before the show went on the air.

Phillips, known as "The Queen of Soap Opera," had spent thirty years preparing story lines, formats, and dialogue for soap operas. She knew public taste, and she agreed with Paul Monash's opponents. "When I saw the sensational story of Selena Cross and her father," she said, "I told ABC I thought it should be shelved. I did not think that this was the kind of thing to give an American public—a father seducing his stepdaughter."

As Richard Warren Lewis described it in *TV Guide,* "The Battle of Peyton Place" was then joined—especially when Irna Phillips brought in her own proposal for an appealing television plot. The series had to have a doctor, of course: according to Scherick, "Doctors are a vital essence of dramatic storytelling"—and "Dr. Kildare" was then one of TV's top shows. But Irna Phillips' doctor, Richard Bailey, would be new to Peyton Place. Soon after coming to town, he would fall in love with Allison MacKenzie, and she with him—and viewers would see kissing, necking, and maybe even a little more. And thus Constance MacKenzie, who had given birth to Allison out of wedlock eighteen years before, would be given a moral dilemma.

Finally Connie would reveal her secret to Allison: not only was Allison illegitimate, but Richard Bailey was Allison's own half-brother. Having rejected borderline incest with the lower-class Crosses, Irna Phillips suggested real incest with an upper-class doctor—and Paul Monash was outraged.

"I utterly reject this tasteless and profitless story area," he protested. "It is meretricious, trite, and tawdry."

Nonsense, said Irna Phillips—it could be handled "delicately and in good taste." She also questioned Monash's judgment, telling reporters coolly, "It is difficult for one who isn't in any way familiar with the mechanics of a serial drama to grasp the fact that essentially a serial is a story about people, people whose lives touch."

Their touching should not be incestuous, insisted Monash—and eventually got his way.

The creators kicked around other plot possibilities, such as the death of an elderly doctor, whose funeral would be attractive but whose lingering illness, they finally decided, might put viewers off. They considered the return of Allison's father, to be quickly murdered by Constance MacKenzie in an effort to hide her secret. Planners debated whether Connie would kill her ex-lover, Elliot Carson, with a bloody fire poker or a pistol shot at point-blank range—but Monash questioned whether a murderess protecting her "secret" could be a credible continuing character. When Tim O'Connor, as Elliot Carson, caught on with viewers, that plot was scrapped.

"The most important decision we made," Scherick said later, "was to start the series with Betty Anderson pregnant." As in Grace's novel, the father would be Rodney Harrington, and Rodney and Betty would not be married. In fact, Dr. Michael Rossi would hide Betty, about to suffer a miscarriage after a violent auto accident, in his office. He would then run the risk of a malpractice suit.

Monash thought it too early in the series for a life-and-death plot—but agreed, once the violent accident was somewhat toned down. When "Peyton Place" went on the air September 15, 1964, Betty (Barbara Parkins) was pregnant. Jack Gould, who reviewed the show for the New York *Times,* was generally unimpressed.

"Seven frustrations with but a single thought," he called it—the seven being Allison, Connie, Betty, Mike Rossi, Rodney, Leslie Harrington, and his wife, Catherine (named Elizabeth in the book and dead before the book begins). The show would run twice weekly at 9:30, and it was a new invention: soap opera at night. But "Peyton Place" suffered, Gould said, from the problem of most soaps: a yo-yo effect, with the introduction of so many interlocking plots all at once.

Still, he praised the program for creating a "reckless mood of ominous restlessness." He considered Mia Farrow, playing the "hesitant girl on the threshold of womanhood," and Dorothy Malone, "the mother with her residue of unspent affection," particularly effective performers, and called the settings and camera work "first-class."

His problem—like most reviewers'—came from his memories of Grace Metalious' "sordidness," her "community that never knows that exhilaration of wholesome laughter." Like the reviewers of the *Peyton Place* and *Return to Peyton Place* movies, Gould felt called upon to take swipes at Grace Metalious' work—as if to separate himself from something noxious. Publishers, he said, bore the ultimate blame for what TV had now produced—for the publishing industry had first "unloosed the blight of *Peyton Place*." Though the TV version was a "sanitized derivation from the late Grace Metalious' novel," Gould suggested that something else might have been chosen to fill nighttime television.

What had been chosen was undoubtedly sanitized—and thoroughly middle class. Art director Jack Senter's set is Hollywood-New England: a town green, with a Colonial memento identified as the Peyton Place pillory, surrounded by essential buildings: bank, bus terminal, apothecary, jeweler. Constance MacKenzie, who ran the Thrifty Corner Apparel Shoppe in the book, now owns a bookstore instead, its façade copied from one in Camden, Maine. TV's Peyton Place also has a red-brick town hall, a newspaper office, a fire department, and an elaborate waterfront life, with seafood restaurants and lobster boats. (Grace's Peyton Place had been on the Connecticut River, the border between New Hampshire and Vermont—but even the other side of New Hampshire, where the television show ostensibly takes place, has only twenty miles of seacoast, mostly superhighways.)

TV's Peyton Place has one industry: Leslie Harrington's dying textile mills. It has no movie theaters, few stores (except a drugstore and a tavern), no schools—and no children, since they would have nothing to contribute to the life-love-and-death plots of the series. Grace's town had 3,675 people, of all ages; TV's sign says "Population 9,875"—but virtually all are between eighteen and fifty-five, and most between eighteen and thirty-nine (the ages of the target viewing audience). Nor does Peyton Place have any apparent government—prompting Otto Friedrich to ask in *Esquire:* "Is this the ultimate soap-opera town in which everything is governed by doctors?"

The doctor and other ruling-class people in Grace's book—notably Leslie Harrington and newspaper editor Seth Buswell—lived in the sanitized, prosperous part of town, but were aware of the rest. The shack dwellers, like the Crosses, lived not that far away from the center of town. But surrounding TV's Peyton Place, beyond the camera's eye, was Century City, an apartment development being constructed by the William Zeckendorf corporation. A wayward camera might take in rubble, cranes, and concrete. TV's Peyton Place was, in fact, a tidy New England village surrounded by the skyscrapers of Los Angeles—but nowhere near the shack dwellers of Los Angeles or anywhere else.

Though the producers of TV's "Peyton Place" said (just as Grace Metalious had) that they were interested in realism and "truth," in some ways the television show realized her worst nightmares. In October 1961 Grace had objected violently to the idea for a book called *Spring Riot in Peyton Place,* to take place at the town college—which, Grace pointed out, did not exist.

Since all the New Hampshire colleges were quite old, Grace had said she could hardly "stick one" in her fictional town—but TV's producers did exactly that. Rodney Harrington becomes something of a "golden boy" and letterman at Peyton College; Allison and Norman take classes there; and a new character, Paul Hanley, dispenses wisdom about English literature. Even Stella Chernak—a later addition with a working-class background—has worked her way through college. TV's "Peyton Place" has no genuine poor people.

Besides eliminating the Crosses, the "Peyton Place" TV creators upgraded the Andersons. The original family had been Swedish born millworkers, with Betty blonde, sexy, and eager to use her body to get ahead in the world. But on television Betty's parents are Julie Anderson, a housewife, and her husband, George —who wears a suit, since he is a salesman. Betty herself is dark-haired, to contrast more obviously with blonde Allison—and to use the visual association of innocence and blondeness, darkness and sexuality. Betty is still sexy, but no longer poor—so her difficulties with Rodney have nothing to do with class, money, or power.

In essence, the makers of television's "Peyton Place" eliminated Grace Metalious' anger.

They also eliminated her vivid portrayals of alcoholism; her depictions of violence; and even her time period. Grace's *Peyton Place* takes place before and during World War II; TV's "Peyton Place" is "contemporary" (but, in fact, innocent of the civil rights demonstrations, student rebellions, and Vietnam protests that gave the mid-1960s their unusual energy). Much like "The Waltons," "Peyton Place" on TV takes place in a timeless realm with small-town innocence. As Otto Friedrich pointed out in *Esquire,* Grace Metalious' realism becomes Paul Monash's fantasy—even in the character of Allison.

Allison remains an innocent—and without the sinful journey to New York, the best-selling book, or the sexual initiation by her lustful agent. "This series is about love," Paul Monash told Cecil Smith, "and the basic theme of the show is a quest for love. Allison MacKenzie is searching for love. She is afraid that love leads to sex, and wants it to be more than that." But Grace's Allison knew that love led to sex, and learned to separate the two. Her quest was not so much for love, but for an independent self—a female quest too radical, apparently, for prime-time television.

The other characters transferred from book to television were also transformed. Grace's Rodney Harrington had been heavy-lipped, with dark curly hair and a sensual air—but Ryan O'Neal is the blond, all-American boy. Constance MacKenzie remains blonde and beautiful—but instead of marrying Dr. Michael Rossi, she weds Elliot Carson, who fathered Allison eighteen years before and then went to prison for killing his wife (who, it gradually comes out, was actually murdered by Leslie Harrington's wife, Catherine). Carson soon takes over the Peyton Place *Clarion* from editor Matt Swain—apparently because actor Tim O'Connor became an audience favorite.

TV also kept Rodney Harrington alive. Grace's Rodney, the thoughtless playboy, got his father to buy off Betty Anderson when she became inconveniently pregnant, and Rodney himself died in a car-truck collision. But on television Rodney not only lives, but marries Betty—who is a changed woman. Since they get along poorly, Leslie Harrington finally does buy off Betty: If she'll agree to an annulment, he'll pay her father's medical bills (George Anderson has had a nervous breakdown). Betty agrees. Instead of the tough, me-first Betty Anderson of the book, TV's Betty thinks first of the men in her life.

Another character who becomes more clean cut and ordinary is Norman Page, who in the novel suffered from an overbearing mother who delighted in giving him enemas. Grace's Mrs. Page fussed over Norman with an almost incestuous air, encouraged him to be weak and sensitive, and generally ruined his life.

In TV's "Peyton Place," however, Norman Page becomes Norman Harrington, Rodney's younger brother. As played by Chris Connelly, Norman looks quite robust, even all-American. Instead of enemas and voyeurism, Norman Harrington's problem is adolescent confusion, which makes him overly studious (reading books is not generally favored on television). Norman's difficulty is largely resolved when he gets himself a girlfriend, Rita Jacks (Pat Morrow), a new character whose mother runs the only tavern in Peyton Place.

The most significant new character, however, is Stephen Cord (James Douglas), Rodney and Norman's illegitimate half-brother —whose parentage is not, of course, quite what everyone thinks it is. Cord, a lawyer, plays the dark young villain Rodney played in the book—while Rodney himself is the fair-haired innocent. Betty oscillates between the two: After she and Rodney end their marriage, she marries Stephen—then divorces him to remarry Rodney and inherit money from Martin Peyton, the family patriarch (a TV creation).

But Rodney also has an innocent (fair-haired) romance with Allison MacKenzie. They lie on the beach, drink Cokes, and talk about snowflakes and birds (much as Allison and Norman did in the book). Their growing attraction is one of many plots; another is the Cord-Harrington conflict; a third comes with the intrusion of the Chernaks, the only working-class people in "Peyton Place."

The Chernak household consists of an unemployed father, a factory worker who drinks too much; a beaten mother who cleans house for the Harringtons; and two children—Stella, a laboratory technician, and Joe, a street fighter. The parents and Joe suggest Grace's Cross family, in which the feisty brother was named Joey and the mother worked as a domestic, while the father drank too much—but Stella escapes her class background far more easily than Selena could. Ted Carter's parents scorned Selena as a shack dweller—but Stella easily becomes Dr. Rossi's love interest. Joe, however, is hopelessly lower class.

As a result, he gets into a fight with the Harringtons, after Norman Harrington has stolen his girlfriend. But the show's sympathies are all with the brawny, middle-class Harringtons against the uncouth intruder. When Grace's Selena and Joey fought back, they won—against their equally lower-class father. But "The television eye is the middle-class eye," Otto Friedrich noted about TV's "Peyton Place"—and TV's lower-class Joe must die. His sister Stella survives—but only working-class people who conform are allowed to stay in the series.

Whatever the changes, TV's "Peyton Place" was an instant smash hit. It ran for 514 episodes, from 1964 to 1969, and soon went from two to three nights a week. Watching it once or twice was, in Friedrich's words, like taking "a few modest shots of skag"—immediately addicting.

Some viewers found the same appeal as the book: "Everything that happens in 'Peyton Place' could happen in any small town," they wrote the network. Others thought the show sexier than it was: in Manchester, New Hampshire, students at St. George Grammar School were told not to watch it, even though a Manchester woman from their parish had written the book. Robert Perreault, then an eighth grader at St. George, was told "Peyton Place" was "for adults only"—and yearned to see the show. Rumors even spread that Grace had lived in a haunted-looking house at Walnut and Pearl streets, the home of nineteenth-century liquor dealers named Harrington. (Grace actually had no connection with the house—but St. George pupils watched the house longingly.)

At its height, "Peyton Place" held three of the top five slots on the Nielsen and A.R.B. television ratings—for the three nights it appeared. Some 60 million people—nearly one out of three Americans—watched it regularly, and kept eight Hollywood writers and three "plot navigators" in a constant state of frenzy.

Richard De Roy, executive story consultant for "Peyton Place," ran the "plotting board" in Hollywood: story lines mapped out horizontally, individual characters mapped vertically. Thirty-two major characters were listed on orange, blue, and yellow cards, according to age groups, and lines and boxes indicated when each of them had last met some other character. The show employed two directors who alternated—Walter Doniger and Ted Post—and within a year had gone through fifteen writers, half of them women, all but two paid better than $1,000 a week. The pace was killing, insomnia-inducing: De Roy told Leo E. Litwak of the New York *Times* about waking up at night with "the sense of Peyton Place being alive, its residents breathing in their own right"—the same feeling Grace Metalious had had about her characters.

Grace had created characters of all ages, but TV viewers overwhelmingly favored youth, and devoured information about the young stars. Fan magazines reported on Barbara Parkins, who played Betty Anderson, and emphasized Parkins' single life and her determination: "I can't fall back. I have to go ahead. In this business you have to watch out for yourself." Parkins' view of herself, in fact, resembled Betty Anderson's in *Return to Peyton Place:* Grace's Betty matures, discards romantic illusions, acquires a level-headed view of life.

Magazines also covered the friendship between Ryan O'Neal and Mia Farrow—who, it was written, often visited Ryan, his wife, Joanna Moore, and their daughter Tatum. Though fan magazines assured their readers that Ryan and Joanna's marriage was happy, the two were divorced during the "Peyton Place" series. O'Neal's second wife was a late addition to the show, actress Leigh Taylor-Young.

With the focus on "Peyton Place's" wholesome, youthful TV stars, Grace Metalious was rarely mentioned in fan magazine articles—but *Peyton Place People,* a special 1965 issue by Dell, informed its readers that "Grace Metalious was a small-town teacher's wife when she wrote her first book, *Peyton Place.* Success came quickly—followed by divorce, ill-health, and death." But Grace's story was only a vehicle for *Peyton Place People's* discussing the stars, "others who've been touched by sadness": Jeff Chandler, who died before the *Return to Peyton Place* film was released; Diane Varsi, the original Allison, who fled Hollywood; and Lana Turner, about to shed her fifth husband, Fred May. Other celebrities upstaged Grace—just as Grace's own celebrity life had upstaged her writing.

The selling of *Peyton Place*—book, in fact, had more than a little in common with the marketing of "Peyton Place"—TV. Grace's husband's "losing his job" had helped promote the novel—and the off-screen adventures of TV's stars often stole the show, particularly in Mia Farrow's case.

Wide-eyed, innocent-appearing, with long blond hair, Mia Farrow was just eighteen when "Peyton Place" began. She played Allison MacKenzie as vulnerable, shy—"something of a wallflower . . . the part of everyone that is frightened by a room filled with strangers," she said. Mia Farrow's father had died the year before the show began, and fan magazines said her ideal man was "someone more powerful than I am." She found that man, her father's age, in Frank Sinatra—and threw the "Peyton Place" producers into a panic.

During the summer of 1965 Mia Farrow abruptly left "Peyton Place" to go yachting off Cape Cod. Her companion on the *Southern Breeze* was Frank Sinatra, forty-nine. She, at nineteen, was known as "America's favorite teenager." In desperation, the scriptwriters put Allison MacKenzie in a coma, after a hit-and-run accident. For several weeks her grieving parents talked by her bedside (with a stand-in playing her inert body)—until Mia finally returned for further episodes, shot three months ahead of time.

But Mia's relationship with Sinatra did not run smoothly, and the results could not be hidden from "Peyton Place" viewers. Allison MacKenzie had always been characterized by her long blond hair—until one day, in a fit of pique over Sinatra, Mia ran to her dressing room and cut off most of her hair.

"It didn't look too bad," Paul Monash thought, trying to make the best of things. And then: "How am I going to use this?"

Anyone reading the newspapers knew what had happened—and rushed to see how television would explain Allison's new pixie cut. Monash provided the explanation: Allison had cut off her hair as a sudden teenage declaration of independence. Audiences giggled knowingly—and stayed tuned.

Meanwhile, the scriptwriters were slowly moving toward a marriage between Allison and Rodney, the all-American Girl and all-American Boy—the wholesome character types who did not exist in Grace Metalious' *Peyton Place*. But Mia again declared her independence: she decided to marry Sinatra and leave the show for good.

The producers considered using another Allison, since Lola

Albright had once filled in for Dorothy Malone when Malone was ill—but Monash decided that Mia Farrow, so closely identified with Allison's role, could not be replaced. Instead, Allison was last seen walking in the fog, along the highway to New York City.

Without Allison, *Peyton Place* was not the same. Lee Grant had won an Emmy as Stella Chernak, but she attributed the award to her being blacklisted during the McCarthy era—not to her own, or the show's, merits. By 1968, the show's ratings had fallen terribly —finally plummeting to eighty-fifth on the Nielsen lists.

Peyton Place, at least in the TV version, had become "irrelevant" by 1968—the year of assassinations, riots, the Tet offensive, student revolts, and women's liberation (including picketing at the Miss America Pageant). Twentieth Century-Fox quickly announced that in the new fall season "Peyton Place" would deal with "electrifying subjects: the war, the draft, riots, music, God, and godlessness."

In a first stab at being "relevant," the town of Peyton Place suddenly had its first black family. But Dr. and Mrs. Harry Miles, played by Percy Rodriguez and Ruby Dee, had little in common with the blacks appearing on television news all over America. Harry Miles was a neurosurgeon, and a Canadian—as if to avoid any imputation that he might not fit into the very middle-class world of "Peyton Place." Meanwhile, offstage, some new black cast members and old white ones had a few racial tensions of their own.

By early 1969 Rodney Harrington was paralyzed, Betty Anderson was going to Boston, and Dr. Rossi was about to be tried for murder—when, abruptly, "Peyton Place" died. After a brief announcement on the air that it was over, cast and crew had a last party. Only Chris Connelly (Norman Harrington) and Ed Nelson (Mike Rossi) had been with the series for all 514 episodes—and Grace Metalious would have appreciated what Ed Nelson said he'd learned from five years on the show: "I've found that the most important thing for an actor is honesty. And when you learn how to fake that, you're in."

Despite its sudden death, the show that *Variety* called "an amalgamation of adolescence, adultery, alcoholism, and amours" had earned lasting fame for the performers. When Mariette Hartley became known for Polaroid commercials with James Garner, publicists pointed out her original break-through: she'd played Dr. Clair Morton, a disenchanted doctor returned from Peru, on "Peyton Place." As late as 1978, Dorothy Malone, who had since starred in *Rich Man, Poor Man* and many other films, was still called "Peyton Place actress" in headlines in *The Star*.

Mia Farrow, meanwhile, never lost her identification with Allison MacKenzie. When she made the film *The Hurricane* in Bora Bora in 1978, her lover was played by Dayton Ka'Ne, a twenty-three-year-old Hawaiian who felt extraordinarily bashful about their love scenes. "I grew up watching 'Peyton Place,'" he confessed, "and, wow, she's Mia Farrow, and I couldn't believe I had to touch her."

The "Peyton Place" television series earned $62 million for ABC, and $2 million for Paul Monash—and nothing for the estate of Grace Metalious. Meanwhile, reruns and foreign sales made "Peyton Place" known all over the world. Though a spin-off based on Betty Anderson's life in New York—called *Girl from Peyton Place*—did not work out, the original "Peyton Place" was immediately sold to English and French television.

By the end of its first season, "Peyton Place" appeared on television in some thirty countries—including Thailand, Korea, and the United Arab Republic. As late as 1980, dubbed reruns were playing in Japan. When "Peyton Place" began showing in Yugoslavia in 1971, under the title "Gradic Peiton," restaurants closed as people stayed home to watch it. But Belgrade authorities announced in December 1972 that the show would no longer be shown after the spring. "Gradic Peiton," they said, fostered "petit-bourgeois values"—thus conflicting with Yugoslavian socialist ideals.

"Peyton Place" was, after all, television's "first situation orgy" —or so Jack Paar called it. He added to the chorus of publicity— but gave unusual prominence to Grace Metalious, who started it all. On February 21, 1965, when the "Peyton Place" television series was only five months old, "The Jack Paar Show" (NBC) included a twelve-minute segment about Gilmanton, New Hampshire.

Paar trekked there to interview local people about Grace and

Peyton Place, and found two willing to talk: Joseph Clairmont, operator of the local sawmill, and Sybil Bryant, a member of the school board and owner of a yarn shop, "The Ruggery." Paar, Clairmont, and Bryant chatted on camera about the book, movie, and television show—and Bryant said she resented the whole idea of *Peyton Place,* "but with a twinkle in her eye," Paar reported later. As for Clairmont, Paar said: "He thinks the whole idea is great."

Whether cowed or reticent, Gilmanton residents gave Jack Paar the distinct impression that "no one in Gilmanton is angry about *Peyton Place.*"

"Would you say the sexiest thing you could do in Gilmanton is listen to the telephone party line?" Paar asked Sybil Bryant.

"Could be," she said.

The "Peyton Place" television show itself had the same appeal as listening to a party line—and little more sexual excitement. Despite its reputation for "raw sex" (mostly because of its title), "Peyton Place" never actually showed more than a few kisses—as *MAD* magazine pointed out in a parody: "Passion Place," by Mort Drucker and Stan Hart.

MAD's Betty Anacin and Rodney Hairbrain are shown appealing to everyone's imagination, as the television show did—but by necking in his convertible in the middle of a traffic jam. Constance McFrenzie, the town widow who wears sexy clothes but doesn't trust men, tells narrator Matt Swine that her bookstore won't carry such "kids' books" as *Fanny Hill* and *Tropic of Cancer.* But she is only part of the steamy atmosphere of "Passion Place."

Swine, the newspaper publisher, finds Leslie Hairbrain in a passionate clinch with Julie Anacin (Betty's mother). Rodney teaches Allison McFrenzie, who brags about her naïveté, how to kiss—and then shows her the chart of "Passion Place" characters, including Doctor Michael Rusty and Norman Hairbrain. But the episode finally does have a plot: in the last panels, Rodney discovers a terrible truth.

Allison, Rodney learns, really has a normal, happily married mother and father. Rodney escapes in horror—for "going with a *normal girl* from a *normal family*" will ruin his reputation in "Passion Place" forever.

Even Grace Metalious' reputation as the most shocking novelist of her time was losing its power. A year after her death, the Manchester, New Hampshire, police chief banned Terry Southern and Mason Hoffenberg's *Candy,* calling the novel "the worst I've ever seen." According to Chief Francis P. McGranaghan, *Candy* would cause "impressionable fifteen- or sixteen-year-olds" to suffer "irreparable damage for life." And to clinch his point, he told reporters in Grace Metalious' birthplace: "This book makes *Peyton Place* look like a Sunday school text."

Peyton Place's reputation obviously needed shoring up—and Pocket Books tried to provide new shocks with nine new books: *Again Peyton Place, Carnival in Peyton Place, The Evils of Peyton Place, Hero in Peyton Place, Nice Girl from Peyton Place, Pleasures of Peyton Place, Secrets of Peyton Place, Temptations of Peyton Place,* and *Thrills of Peyton Place.* All were filled with sex and violence, often updating in lurid detail the lives of minor characters in Grace Metalious' books.

Carnival in Peyton Place, for instance, shows Kathy Ellsworth Welles twenty years later, married with three children, still trying to cope with having only one arm. She'd lost the other in Leslie Harrington's carnival machinery in *Peyton Place,* and Lew Welles —her fast-talking boyfriend—married her quickly, as if to show that her having only one arm did not matter.

But in *Carnival in Peyton Place,* Lew is having an affair with a woman in the church choir—whose major attraction is that she can hold him with both arms. Meanwhile, the Welles son deliberately tries out all kinds of vices, to make himself a more knowledgeable minister. One daughter, beautiful but not especially interested in the boys she dates, worries that she might be frigid; the other daughter, less popular, is the family's "brain."

Carnival in Peyton Place shows no particular insight into any Welles characters—nor any empathy with the women who would have been Grace Metalious' focus. Instead of sex as part of a woman's growing sense of herself, sex in the spin-off books (attributed to author "Roger Fuller") is both overheated and silly.

"There came the almost-forgotten, glorious, frantic, pulsating moment," begins *Thrills of Peyton Place* (1973), the last of the series, "when Miranda was seized by the slow-spiraling waves of sensation that swirled faster and faster, mounting higher and higher within her until she was seized by a consuming urgency. She was going to make it! 'Come on,' she gasped hoarsely in Gary's ear. 'Oh, come on, come on, come on!' Then, just as she teetered on the brink of delight, just as the frustrations would have exploded in a gushing release, just before she was flooded with pure bliss, the doorbell rang."

Though *Thrills of Peyton Place* later has a comical episode, in which a Mrs. Louella Philbrook travels to a dairy farm for an orgy with three Swedish farmers atop a haystack, the spin-off books generally try harder, but with far less inspiration, than anything Grace Metalious ever produced. Few of the spin-off books stayed in print for more than a year, and Otto Friedrich called them "pornographic sequels that a flock of scavengers had picked out of the debris of Mrs. Metalious' creation."

Friedrich also had his theory about the mysterious "Roger Fuller": that the pseudonymous author was a team of scavengers, consisting of a police reporter, a Barnard student with a heated imagination, and a schoolteacher with an overdue mortgage. But "Roger Fuller" was actually Don Tracy, a well-known historical novelist (author of *Roanoke Renegade, Chesapeake Cavalier,* and other books). Tracy, who died in 1976 at age seventy-one, wrote the *Peyton Place* spin-offs because he needed the money.

Grace Metalious had never written solely for money, although she had tried to with a third *Peyton Place* book. She had a vision to communicate—about women, about outsiders, about small-town hypocrisies. Possibly because hypocrisy springs eternal, *Peyton Place* has become a story for all seasons—and all political climates. Grace had written *Peyton Place* and *Return to Peyton Place* during the bland Eisenhower years. The books continued selling through John F. Kennedy's almost three years in office and Lyndon Johnson's five, while the TV show was running. Even before the Johnson years the name "Peyton Place" symbolized a small town with steamy adventures going on behind closed doors—

and songwriter Tom T. Hall used it that way for his 1968 song, "Harper Valley P.T.A."

Mrs. Johnson, the heroine of the song, is persecuted for being single and attractive—an outsider woman like Constance MacKenzie of *Peyton Place*. Mrs. Johnson raises her daughter permissively —and the P.T.A. violently disapproves. In the end, as recorded by Jeannie C. Riley (and later portrayed by Barbara Eden on film), Mrs. Johnson confronts her accusers with an account of their own sins: secret drinking, affairs, abrupt departures from town. Most devastating is her summary: that their town's a little Peyton Place —and they're the Harper Valley hypocrites.

Peyton Place rose again during the Nixon years—with "Return to Peyton Place" (NBC), a new daytime soap opera that ran from 1972 to 1974. A highly publicized nationwide search netted a new cast: Katherine Glass as Allison MacKenzie (with "the proper degree of fawnlike sensitivity," *Variety* reported); Lawrence Casey as Rodney Harrington; Bettye Ackerman as Constance MacKenzie Carson; Guy Stockwell as Dr. Michael Rossi; Stacy Harris as Leslie Harrington; and Ron Russell as Norman Harrington. Julie Parrish, as Betty Anderson, strongly resembled Barbara Parkins.

Though the show ran for two years, focusing on Allison's return from her three-year disappearance in New York and the (as usual) shaky marriage between Betty and Rodney, the new "Return to Peyton Place" never really caught on. More popular was another version, a two-hour NBC special called "Murder in Peyton Place." By the time it appeared in the fall of 1977, Jimmy Carter had succeeded Gerald Ford as President—the fifth new President since Grace Metalious had set her typewriter on her lap to write what she hoped would earn her a little money and a small place in the sun.

Billed as a reunion, "Murder in Peyton Place" brought back many of the original TV stars: Dorothy Malone as Constance MacKenzie, Ed Nelson as Dr. Michael Rossi, Tim O'Connor as Elliot Carson. Barbara Parkins did not want to return; Lee Grant and James Douglas had other commitments; and Ryan O'Neal and Mia Farrow had not been asked. "I didn't think they'd be interested," said producer Peter Katz.

Farrow and O'Neal appear in old clippings, and then die in an auto accident—the "Murder in Peyton Place" being the death of Allison and Rodney. Janet Margolin plays Betty Anderson Rorick (her fourth marriage) and Stella Stevens is Stella Chernak, the ultimate villainess of the piece. The script, by Richard De Roy—head script writer for the first "Peyton Place" series—includes mysterious hospital records, switched corpses, and a vicious attack by Doberman pinschers, all culminating in the triumph of good over evil, and middle class over working class.

But "Murder in Peyton Place" concludes with a nostalgic note: shots of Allison's and Rodney's graves, as mourned by Connie, Norman, and the rest of the cast—while the theme from *Peyton Place* (Franz Waxman's tune, from the original 1957 film) plays in the background. The last credits go to the two original creators: Grace Metalious and Paul Monash.

Not that *Peyton Place* died, however—for in 1979, fifteen years after Grace Metalious' death, Twentieth Century-Fox made still another attempt to resurrect their property.

"What goes on behind the closed doors of a small New England town?" asks the brochure for *Peyton Place '79,* a syndicated show offered for sale.

The answer: " 'Peyton Place,' Grace Metalious' novel, skyrocketed across the world, answering that question and leaving a trail of controversy." *Peyton Place '79,* the brochure promises, "has all the impact of the book, movie, and television series. Plus more."

The "more" consists of the next generation—for Allison, Rodney, Betty, Stephen Cord, and the others have spawned a new generation of teenagers named Spring, Tom, and Jamie. Moreover, the brochure insists, television is now in a new generation, with "today's mature themes . . . situations that their parents never dreamed of!"

"Is the public ready?" the brochure asks—then promises that "for the first time we are able to do justice to the searing central themes that could only be *suggested* before." But the come-on failed. *Peyton Place '79* became *Peyton Place '80*—and then went into limbo.

Still, Grace Metalious herself retains her influence: on the public, on other writers, on those who knew her—and, in a development that would have delighted her, on college campuses.

CHAPTER 27

No, Jacqueline Susann did not inspire him to write *Lonely Lady*, says Harold Robbins.

"The original idea came from Grace Metalious, with whom I was friendly," Robbins told Isobel Silden for an article in the November 1976 *Pageant*. "She was a much more fantastic woman than most people realized. And I saw what success did to her: the changes in her family and the society around her.

"I watched her deterioration psychologically and physiologically twelve years ago. At the time I was in partnership with the firm which published her last novel"—Pocket Books, whose editor, Bucklin Moon, worked on both Robbins' and Metalious' books.

"This was before the women's movement," Robbins added, and as he began research for *Lonely Lady*, "I saw many correlations between Grace's life and the movement." JeriLee Randall, Robbins' lonely lady, reflects Grace's background: a small town, away from the centers of "action" that Jacqueline Susann knew intimately. With Grace Metalious, Robbins said, "I saw firsthand what success can do to a woman."

Still, Robbins' angle of vision is not Grace Metalious'. JeriLee Randall, like Grace Metalious and Allison MacKenzie, wants to be a writer—but Robbins never shares her writing with his readers. Allison's stories and her love for words appear in *Peyton Place*, but JeriLee's teenage years mainly involve sex: a teenage boyfriend who crashes into a wall at the sight of her bouncing breasts;

several oversexed youths who try to force her into a sex "scene"; and JeriLee's own discovery of masturbation.

Both Allison and JeriLee go to New York to seek their fortunes, but JeriLee does not go as an independent woman. She marries a much older playwright, who is often impotent, and divorces him after six years. Meanwhile, she has won a Tony award for one of his Broadway plays—but again, her work is never shown. After her divorce, JeriLee goes through a mélange of sex (with both sexes), heavy drinking, and enormous quantities of drugs.

When JeriLee finally wins an Oscar for best screenplay, she uses her acceptance speech for a contempt gesture, telling her audience she had to "ball everybody on the picture except the prop man" to get it made—and that she got the award as a woman, not as a writer. Then she throws off her dress, showing the gold Oscar painted on her perfect figure.

The audience goes wild, thoroughly missing the point of her protest—and JeriLee ends the book looking out over the bright lights of Los Angeles and crying, just as Grace Metalious sat in the corner of her living room, drank her Canadian Club and 7-Up, and cried. *Lonely Lady* is true to the core of Grace Metalious' life: self-destruction; rejection of support from other women; misunderstanding by the media—who interpreted her and her characters' struggles for autonomy as struggles for sex. But JeriLee Randall is well-connected, not especially introspective, and extremely beautiful—not the sensitive outsider, like Allison MacKenzie, who wants love and independence on her own terms.

"The students took the book seriously once they got over giggling about its name," says the first professor who taught *Peyton Place* in a college course. Susan Koppelman put the book on her reading list at Bowling Green University in 1973—and students responded eagerly.

They admitted they hoped for a dirty book, with lots of "raw sex"—for the name *Peyton Place* still evokes great expectations. Instead, students found themselves seduced by the story—as Susan Koppelman had been in 1956, when she first read *Peyton Place* as a Cleveland Heights teenager.

She had listed Allison's traits in her journal: "Adventurous, imaginative, creative, contemplative, fully orgasmic, self-determining, triumphant—a female Horatio Alger, who wins through luck and pluck." Though her graduate school professors prevented her from writing a master's thesis on *Peyton Place* ("too trashy"), Koppelman remembered the book, and found her students reacted to it as warmly as she had.

They grieved when Allison's friends deserted her to be with their boyfriends; they laughed at the comical drunks; they took a grim satisfaction in Leslie Harrington's comeuppance; they enjoyed (of course) Mike Rossi and Constance MacKenzie's intimate midnight swim—and they cheered when Selena Cross fought back, and was vindicated. Though they'd been toddlers when *Peyton Place* first appeared, they found the book still had power to entertain and move them.

With the vision of the 1970s, they also saw the book's implicit feminism—and saw in Allison MacKenzie a role-model: the image of the woman they would like to be.

Grace Metalious would have been pleased that her book reached college syllabi—for she had always longed to be taken seriously as a writer. She would have liked knowing that two more Bowling Green professors—Christopher Geist and Jack Nachbar—have since taught *Peyton Place*. She might have been amused at the academic discussions: the literary conventions, parallel characters, similes and metaphors unearthed—and even *Peyton Place's* "Emersonian qualities." She wrote with less lofty aims—but students recognize in hindsight what a liberating cultural influence Grace Metalious was, as she paved the way for honest and realistic depictions of women and men, violence and sensuality—thus opening the door for the women's movement.

The women who created Women's Liberation in the late 1960s tended to be in their twenties and early thirties—the generation most influenced by *Peyton Place*. Betty Friedan's *Feminine Mystique* galvanized frustrated housewives, but the slightly younger women who began the demonstrations and consciousness-raising were the ones who remembered most clearly the examples of Allison MacKenzie, Constance MacKenzie, and Selena Cross. In their formative years, they had naturally gravitated toward the forbidden, "sexy" book, but they also absorbed its messages about women's movement issues: abortion, rape, women's friendships, battered women, sexual freedom, and independence. Without knowing it, they'd read—and loved—a feminist book.

Since its first publication in 1956, *Peyton Place* has never been out of print. Sold first for fifty cents, it sold for $1.95 in its seventeenth Pocket Books printing (1977); it is number ten on the list of best sellers between 1920 and 1980. Though Grace Metalious is far less known than her creation, her name still has the power to frighten. Ellen Golub, a frustrated graduate student in 1976, reported in *College English* that she threatened a librarian with renaming his area "the Grace Metalious Room"—and he blanched in horror.

Grace's name can still terrorize a town, Lea P. Longo suggested in the July 1978 *Writer's Digest:* "A woman should never tell her neighbors she's a writer. They will think she's becoming the new Grace Metalious. Should I say more?"

The name *Peyton Place* still suggests ill fame: Yvonne Peyton, co-owner of a hotel in the most Arctic reaches of Canada, insisted that it be named "Peyton Lodge"—despite her husband's favorite candidate for the name (reported in the December 2, 1979, New York *Times* Travel Section). A character in Fred Zackel's *Cinderella at Midnight* (1980) says Sacramento is "a little Peyton Place"; a character in Mordecai Richler's *Joshua Then and Now* (1980) calls Westmount a "classy cesspool" that "makes Peyton Place look like the Waltons." A group of gay companions in Andrew Halloran's *Dancer from the Dance* (1978) shout the opening lines from *Peyton Place* to each other: "Indian summer is like a woman!" and "Ripe, hotly passionate, but fickle!" But *Peyton Place* is most often regarded as a threat. Challenged to provide "examples of Good News" for a *New York* magazine competition (April 24, 1978), Paul E. Smith of Pittsburgh won a runner-up prize for his entry: "YOU ARE NOW LEAVING PEYTON PLACE."

Peyton Place can also be a code word for an endless soap opera, the television view.

"I mean," Harry laughed, "I feel like I'm in Peyton Place. I have Stephanie Olsen in here at least twice a week, crying to me about you . . ." (Marianne Wiggins' 1980 novel, *Went South*)

"Reduced to a bare-bones synopsis, the movie may sound like *Peyton Place*." (Stephen Farber's review of the film *A Simple Story* in *New West*, February 11, 1980)

Peyton Place—and its scandalous associations—have long provided material for Erma Bombeck, a supporter of women's rights and women writers. Valedictorian Enis Ertle seemed "absolutely out of it," Bombeck writes sympathetically, describing her high school reunion in *I Lost Everything in the Post-Natal Depression*. Erma's solution? "I told her I'd give her my copy of *Peyton Place* when I finished reading it."

In a 1980 column about "regional sin"—inspired by the TV success of "Dallas"—Bombeck suggests a Midwestern version: "Cleveland." Her friends remain unconvinced, despite her argument: "Look at history. *Peyton Place* already put New England on the map." But in *At Wit's End,* Bombeck promotes *Peyton Place* as a weapon: to combat television football.

"Here's the deal," she writes. "We get the network to bring on *Peyton Place* thirty minutes early and watch exciting shots from last week's show, followed by previews of this week's action. Then we have Betty Furness interview Old Man Peyton and his grandson just for a little flavor."

After the pre-show preliminaries, *Peyton Place* unrolls, National Football League style: "The camera will replay in slow motion all the scenes, then stop-action all the dirty parts and have an instant replay of all the violent parts. After that, we'd switch to another camera for another view of Betty Cord in her negligee."

Then, for the half-time break: "They'd show action from the first half followed by an interview with Ann Landers, who would chew over the first half and offer advice on how it should be played the second half."

Finally, when the show ended: "Dr. Joyce Brothers would tally up the marriages for each, the divorces, the surgery, and their standing in the league."

At least one Bombeck friend, in despair about Monday night

football, is impressed: "It's just got to work," she says. "I'm so desperate, I'm beginning to talk to my kids."

But *Peyton Place* (book version), is more than an antidote to despair. It still suggests erotic yearnings: a character in Beth Gutcheon's *The New Girls* (1979) longs for a lost love, dreaming of "her firm breasts pressing against him, the nipples erect and hard as diamonds beneath his wandering fingers. He was not entirely naïve. He *had* read *Peyton Place*." Indeed he had—for Mike Rossi/Tom Makris tells Constance MacKenzie, "I love this fire in you. I love it when you have to move"—and then: "Your nipples are as hard as diamonds."

"There's better stuff Thursday, when the State Police come in," a court official told me in June 1978, when I visited Bernard Snierson's courtroom in Laconia, New Hampshire. Snierson, a tall, white-haired district judge, was handling minor offenses: a few scruffy youngsters had been caught smoking marijuana; one youth who'd had too much to drink had been seen urinating against the side of a public building. To judge by the cases, there wasn't much to do in Laconia in the summer—not unlike the summer of 1955, when Grace Metalious first sold *Peyton Place* to Julian Messner, Inc.

He'd led a more exciting life then, Snierson told me: Grace's movie deals, her affair with T. J. Martin, her midnight calls for help—all kept him hopping. John Chandler, still Snierson's partner, also has a far more sedate practice now—no more midnight calls to handle the problems of a famous author.

John O'Shea, similarly, still runs O'Shea's Department Store—but no scandalous local writer calls him in the middle of the night to order a monogrammed mink stole, as Grace Metalious once did. O'Shea, whose ex-wife, June, lives with their daughter, Sally, in Montreal, has remarried; his and June's son, Tom, is heir apparent at the store—the fourth generation to run it.

"We need your autograph on a copy of *Peyton Place*," John O'Shea, Jr., told Laurie Wilkens several Halloweens ago. As part of a scavenger hunt, O'Shea, Jr.—who lives in the Gilmanton Corners house where Grace and George once stayed, across from the village store—had to get Gilmanton's most famous book and

have it signed by the author's best friend. Laurie Wilkens, a retired schoolteacher still living in the big farmhouse at "Shaky
Acres," where Grace Metalious loved to visit, obliged John
O'Shea, Jr.—but begs off when she's occasionally asked to help
other people write best sellers. Grace Metalious was unique, she
says—and *Peyton Place* was Grace's book.

George Metalious, to whom *Peyton Place* was dedicated "For
All The Reasons he knows so well—" still lives in New England; he
and his second wife have a daughter. Grace and George's children,
now in their thirties, are all married and—like Grace—choose to
stay in New England, the only place they consider home. George
Metalious has five grandsons, only one of whom—Billy, Marsha's
son—ever knew his famous grandmother. Suzanne Roy, the cousin
who grew up with Grace's children, also lives in New England
with her husband and children—and has not been in contact with
her mother, Grace's sister Bunny, in some fifteen years.

Other residents of New Hampshire still remember Grace Metalious—and not always fondly. In 1976 Barbara Walters tracked
down Laurie Wilkens for a New Hampshire segment on the
"Today Show"—and afterwards local people complained about
NBC's giving Grace Metalious such prominence.

Still, residents of New Hampshire continue to read *Peyton
Place*. In the Laconia Public Library, the two well-worn copies
are taken out at least once a month—but the library does not own
Return to Peyton Place, The Tight White Collar, or *No Adam in
Eden.* Librarians tell visitors that Grace Metalious "wasn't really
from here"—but they do keep an up-to-date clipping file about
her.

At Durham, where Grace struggled to put George through
school, the College Road barracks no longer exist—and the University of New Hampshire library stocks only *Peyton Place*. In
1980 an education professor at U.N.H., in the department where
George Metalious got his degree, declared that he never had read
Peyton Place because of its immorality—and never would.

Nevertheless, "New Hampshire Writers and the Small Town," a
film/lecture program developed for late 1980, includes Grace
Metalious with Robert Frost, William Dean Howells, and Sarah
Josepha Hale (editor of *Godey's Lady's Book* and composer of

"Mary Had a Little Lamb"). Grace Metalious' "appraisal of life in a small New Hampshire community sold more copies than any previous American novel," the program brochure notes—and then it adds a defense: "The sensational response to the book has obscured the fact that *Peyton Place* is one of the most important novels written about small-town life in the state."

Only a few of the people who knew Grace Metalious remain in New England. Laurie Wilkens' daughters Joanne and Wendy, both of whom adored Grace, live outside San Francisco; Grace's friends Richard Stinson and Bert ("Marc") Marcotte, live in different parts of New York City, where Oliver Swan is still a literary agent. Leona Nevler, who spotted *Peyton Place's* potential in manuscript, is vice-president and group publisher at Fawcett Publications; Howard Goodkind free lances in Connecticut. Alan "Bud" Brandt, who masterminded the "Pandora in Blue Jeans" promotion, now runs a New York art gallery—and still sometimes thinks about his idea for a musical, "The Year of Our Grace," based on the life of Grace Metalious.

Mike Wallace, of course, continues to be the kind of penetrating interviewer who both frightened and challenged the author of *Peyton Place*.

T. J. Martin still greets his listeners with "HELL-o, you . . ." in his morning show on WKAO, Boynton Beach, Florida—the same greeting he used on WLNH, Laconia, when Grace Metalious fell in love with the sound of his voice. His marriage to Betty Haenschen did not last; his fourth marriage, in the Virgin Islands, also ended in divorce. He has no contact with Grace Metalious' family—nor does John Rees, Grace's heir.

Grace's "bearded beneficiary" dropped out of sight to protect himself from media harassment—but was a working journalist again by 1968, when he covered the Columbia University student demonstrations. There he met Sheila O'Connor, whom he later married. Now an American citizen, Rees lives with Sheila in Baltimore, travels frequently to New York, and covers politics and foreign affairs for conservative periodicals, including *The Review of the News, Information Digest,* and *Western Goals.*

When Laurie Wilkens saw *The Rose,* the bittersweet Bette Midler movie based on Janis Joplin's life, she thought of Grace

Metalious—the talent, the self-destruction, the need for love, the ultimate loneliness. Grace's lonely grave at Smith Meeting House Cemetery is five miles down a winding dirt road from Laurie Wilkens' farmhouse. Indian paintbrush, Grace's favorite flower, grows nearby—and once a year, on Memorial Day, a bunch of lilacs appears, anonymously, on her grave (from, it's said, Carl Newman, the local farmhand who loved her before she became famous).

Grace's tombstone, a white stone alone in a four-person plot at the edge of the cemetery, reads only, "METALIOUS GRACE 1924–1964"—the famous name, the short life, no personal touch from the writer who'd willed her body to science (and whose will was thwarted).

During her first burst of fame, Grace had stayed at the Algonquin Hotel in New York, liking its association with writers—especially Dorothy Parker, the wittiest woman of the twenties. Parker, who lived far longer than she ever intended to—and had her own self-destructive, alcoholic streak long before her death in 1967—had more than once suggested her own epitaph: "If you can read this, you've come too close."

But Grace Metalious had no chance to propose words for her own tombstone. If she had, she might have given her laughing-but-indignant answer to her critics. "If I'm a lousy writer," she might have had carved in stone, "then a hell of a lot of people have got lousy taste."

AFTERWORD

As I worked on this book, many people implied—often not subtly—that what I was doing was not in the best of taste. "Why in hell do you want to write about Grace Metalious?" Dr. Leonard Slovack asked me in Laconia. Why such a "trashy book"? countless other people wondered—usually people who'd never read *Peyton Place,* but knew thoroughly its wicked reputation.

My explanations—that I admire Grace Metalious' portrayals of women, her (unconscious) feminism, her vitality, and energy made little impression. Surely I must have other, more lurid mo-

374

tives, people thought, for even mentioning *Peyton Place* in most circles still evokes a snicker or two.

But Grace Metalious interests me for much more than her notoriety. I wish she'd lived to see the rest of the 1960s and the 1970s because everyone who knew her feels the women's movement would have heartened her. I wish she'd known other women writers. I wish she'd had more support for her anger and her vision of community.

And I know that *Peyton Place* brightened my life. When I read it as a twelve-year-old, I learned there was more to life than the bland conformity of the Midwest in the fifties. Life, I learned, held the promise of violence and pain—but also passion, independence, and integrity, especially for a girl who wanted to grow up to be a writer.

For that discovery alone, I will always be grateful to Grace Metalious.

SOURCES AND BIBLIOGRAPHY

COMMUNICATIONS AND MAJOR INTERVIEWS

For Grace's high school years: Robert Athearn, Louis A. Freedman, Barbara Roberts.

For the University of New Hampshire years: William Ewert, Frederick Jervis, Betty Menge, Gladys E. Pease, Barbara Taylor, Barbara White, Janis Williams.

For Martha's Vineyard: Charles A. Davis, Virginia Crowell Jones, Shirley W. Mayhew.

For Grace's life in New Hampshire: Donald Athearn, Elizabeth Athearn, Jim Bonnette, George Cantin, John Chandler, Charles Hegarty, John O'Shea, Jr., John O'Shea, Sr., June O'Shea, Esther Peters, Joanne Wilkens Pugh, Barbara Rotundo, Arlene Rowe, Bernard Snierson, Richard Stinson, Paul Tracy, Laurose Wilkens, Wendy Wilkens.

For Grace's relations with the media and publishing: Allan Barnard, Burton Bernstein, Alan (Bud) Brandt, Knox Burger, Patricia Carbine, Don Fine, Doris Flowers, Patricia Gallagher, Howard Goodkind, Diana Haskell, Kenneth McCormick, Marikay Mead, Helen Meyer, Bucklin Moon, Leona Nevler, Al Ramrus, Marlene Sanders, Jack Schaefer, Robert A. Signer, Oliver Swan, Frank Taylor, Carl Tobey, Mike Wallace, Philip Wittenberg.

For general information: Gerard Brault, Suzanne Goulet, Bertrand Marcotte, T. J. Martin, Jack Mertes, Cynthia Metalious, George Metalious, Marsha Metalious, Robert B. Perreault, John Rees, Roger Roy, Richard Sorrell.

Readers who shared their memories of *Peyton Place:* Jan Ackerman, Max Van Deusen Badger, Michael Begnal, Fay Blake,

376

Steven Delibert, Pamela Ecker, Helen Eisen, Ronald Filipelli, Daniel Golden, Elizabeth Holder Harris, Walter Harrison, Susan Koppelman, Victoria Leonard, Charles Mann, Nancy McCall, Margaret McFadden, Zena Beth McGlashan, Kiki Skagen Munshi, Michael Radis, Thomas Schlunz, Sandra Stelts, Laura Van Warmer, Gary Vujnovich.

BIBLIOGRAPHY
Grace Metalious' Writings

Novels

Peyton Place. New York: Julian Messner, Inc., 1956.
Return to Peyton Place. New York: Julian Messner, Inc., 1959.
The Tight White Collar. New York: Julian Messner, Inc., 1960.
No Adam in Eden. New York: Trident Press, 1963.

Articles

"All About Me and *Peyton Place.*" Series published in the *American Weekly* (Sunday supplement) May 18, May 25, June 1, June 8, 1958.

Short Story

"Edna Brown and the Charming Prince," *Glamour* (March 1960), p. 124.

Manuscripts and Letters

The manuscript of *Peyton Place* and parts of *The Tight White Collar* are in Special Collections, Pattee Library, The Pennsylvania State University.

Parts of the *No Adam in Eden* manuscript and a collection of Metalious letters are in the Paul Reynolds Collection, Butler Library, Columbia University.

SECONDARY SOURCES

Biography
Metalious, George and O'Shea, June. *The Girl from "Peyton Place."* New York: Dell, 1965.

MAJOR ARTICLES ABOUT GRACE METALIOUS

Baker, Carlos. "Small Town Peep Show." (Review of *Peyton Place*), New York *Times Book Review,* September 23, 1956, Sec. VII, p. 4.

Boyle, Hal. "Grace Unfolds to Hal Boyle Hazard of Husband Losing Job/Calls Peyton Place a Tobacco Road with a Yankee Accent." Laconia *Evening Citizen,* August 29, 1956, p. 1. (Column syndicated throughout U.S.)

Brooks, John. *"Peyton Place:* From Novel to Television Serial." (Unpublished paper, delivered at the Midwest Modern Language Association convention in 1977.)

Carbine, Patricia. "Peyton Place." *Look,* March 18, 1958, p. 108.

Chartier, Armand B. "The Franco-American Literature of New England: A Brief Overview." In Zyla, Wolodymyr T. and Wendell M. Aycock, eds. *Ethnic Literatures Since 1776: The Many Voices of America.* Lubbock, Texas: Texas Tech Press, 1978, p. 193.

Ewing, Harvey. "Author Says Vineyard Won't Be Novel Locale," Laconia *Evening Citizen,* October 27, 1960, p. 1.

Friedrich, Otto. "Farewell to *Peyton Place,*" *Esquire,* December 1971, p. 160.

James, T. F. "Millionaire Class of Young Writers," *Cosmopolitan,* August 1958, p. 41.

Litwak, Leo E. "Visit to a Town of the Mind: Peyton Place," New York *Times Magazine,* April 4, 1965, p. 46.

Miller, Merle. "Tragedy of Grace Metalious and *Peyton Place,*" *Ladies' Home Journal,* June 1965, p. 58.

Miner, Madonne M. "Return to *Peyton Place.*" (Unpublished paper, delivered at the Popular Culture Association convention in 1981.)

Mothner, Ira. "TV's *Peyton Place:* Sweet Virtue's County Seat," *Look,* October 19, 1965, p. 78.

Mulligan, Hugh A. "The Short and Unhappy Life of Grace Metalious," Philadelphia *Sunday Bulletin,* April 12, 1964, p. 8 (also syndicated).

Perreault, Robert B. "In the Eyes of Her Father: a Portrait of Grace Metalious," *Historical New Hampshire,* Fall 1980, p. 318.

———. "Un portrait de Grace Metalious, à travers les yeux de son père," *Le FAROG FORUM,* November 1980, p. 4.

Rees, John. "Grace Metalious' Battle With the World," *Cosmopolitan,* September 1964, p. 50.

Saint, Irene. "A Million-Dollar Spree," Boston *Herald,* December 13, 1964. (From *Herald-American* library, no page given.)

Skinner, Olivia. "Pandora of Small-Town New England," St. Louis *Post-Dispatch,* April 21, 1961. (From *Post-Dispatch* library, no page given.)

Sorrell, Richard S. "A Novelist and Her Ethnicity: Grace Metalious as a Franco-American," *Historical New Hampshire,* Fall 1980, p. 284.

"Unpopular Best Seller," *Life,* November 12, 1956, p. 104.

Wilkens, Laurose. "Publishers Spotlight Gilmanton," Laconia *Evening Citizen,* July 17, 1956. (In Gale Memorial Library file, no page given.)

———. "Gilmanton, Under Siege of Reporters, Continues Chores and Book Dispute While Author Weeps for Lost Relative," Laconia *Evening Citizen,* September 1, 1956. (In Gale Memorial Library file, no page given.)

———. "Author's Friend Writes Gilmanton Tribute," Laconia *Evening Citizen,* February 26, 1964. (In Gale Memorial Library file, no page given.)

Zolotow, Maurice. "How a Best-Seller Happens," *Cosmopolitan,* August 1957, p. 36.

OTHER IMPORTANT SOURCES

Articles
File of Kitty Messner materials (Simon & Schuster, provided by Doris Flowers).

Arlen, M. J. "At Last! The Mighty Marvelous Waldmachine," *Esquire,* May 1962, p. 128.

Barber, Rowland. "The Mighty Sound Track in Bungalow Ten," *Show,* March 1962, p. 86.

Lewis, Richard Warren. "The Battle of *Peyton Place,*" *TV Guide,* January 16 and 22, 1965. (In New York Public Library file, Lincoln Center branch, no pages given.)

Monash, Paul and Smith, Cecil. "Notes on *Peyton Place,*" *Television Quarterly,* Fall 1964, p. 49.

"Peyton Place," *Screen Stories,* December 1957, p. 17.

Silden, Isobel. "America's Best-Selling Novelist Harold Robbins Talks About Lonely Ladies," *Pageant* 32, November 1976, p. 85.

Wolfson, Barbara. "Who's Taking Care of the Babysitter?" *Women: A Journal of Liberation,* 1979, pp. 18–19.

Transcript
Transcript of Ben Hecht-Grace Metalious interview. Provided by Mike Wallace.

Books
Bellamann, Henry. *Kings Row.* New York: Simon & Schuster, 1940.

Brownmiller, Susan. *Against Our Will: Men, Women and Rape.* New York: Simon & Schuster, 1975.

Delaney, Janice; Lupton, Mary Jane; and Toth, Emily. *The Curse: A Cultural History of Menstruation.* New York: Dutton, 1976.

Fleming, Karl and Fleming, Anne Taylor. *The First Time.* New York: Berkley Medallion, 1975.

Flexner, Eleanor. *Century of Struggle*. New York: Atheneum, 1968.

Friedan, Betty. *The Feminine Mystique*. New York: Dell, 1963.

Haskell, Molly. *From Reverence to Rape: The Treatment of Women in the Movies*. Baltimore: Penguin, 1974.

Hareven, Tamara K. and Langenbach, Randolph. *Amoskeag: Life and Work in an American Factory-City*. New York: Pantheon, 1978.

Hofmann, Frederick G. and Adele D. *A Handbook on Drug and Alcohol Abuse: The Biomedical Aspects*. New York: Oxford University Press, 1975.

Jones, Kenneth L.; Shainberg, Louis W.; and Byer, Curtis O. *Drugs and Alcohol*. New York: Harper & Row, 1969, 1973.

Kirby, William. *The Golden Dog (Le Chien d'Or)*. Montreal: Montreal News Co., 1876.

Miller, Douglas T. and Nowak, Marion. *The Fifties: The Way We Really Were*. New York: Doubleday, 1977.

Morella, Joe and Epstein, Edward Z. *Lana*. New York: Citadel Press, 1971.

Morgan, Ted. *Maugham*. New York: Simon & Schuster, 1980.

O'Neill, William L. *Everyone Was Brave*. Chicago: Quadrangle Books, 1969.

Perreault, Robert B. *Weston Observatory*. Manchester, N.H.: Weston Observatory Restoration Committee, 1978.

Rich, Adrienne. *Of Woman Born: Motherhood as Experience and Institution*. New York: Norton, 1976.

Roth, Lillian, with Connolly, Mike, and Frank, Gerold. *I'll Cry Tomorrow*. New York: Frederick Fell, 1954.

Sandmaier, Marian. *The Invisible Alcoholics: Women and Alcohol Abuse in America*. New York: McGraw-Hill, 1980.

Schulberg, Budd. *What Makes Sammy Run?* New York: Random House, 1941.

Sheehy, Gail. *Passages: Predictable Crises of Adult Life*. New York: Dutton, 1976.

Weibel, Kathryn. *Mirror, Mirror: Images of Women Reflected in Popular Culture*. New York: Anchor, 1977.

Weintraub, Stanley, ed. *Biography and Truth*. Indianapolis: Bobbs-Merrill, 1967.

INDEX

382